Mile High Stories

Mile High Stories

{ 25 YEARS OF OUR BEST WRITING }

FROM THE EDITORS OF

5280

BOWER HOUSE

DENVER

Design and Typeset by Margaret McCullough
Front Cover Design by Dave McKenna
Front Cover photography by Preston Utley

Library of Congress Control Number: 2018937023
ISBN 978-1-917895-06-4

10 9 8 7 6 5 4 3 2 1

CONTENTS

Preface

Twenty-five years ago, when I started *5280* in the second bedroom of my Denver apartment, I had a few obvious motivations. Sure, I wanted to make a buck. And there was the independence that supposedly comes from being your own boss (spoiler alert: you'll still have plenty of bosses; there's just a different org chart).

But as much as anything else, I was also chasing a feeling. As a young journalist, I'd spent long hours in used bookstores, searching for anthologies by the masters of narrative nonfiction. From John McPhee, Joan Didion, Truman Capote, Gay Talese, and many others, I discovered the thrill that comes from stories that take you far beyond your comfortable chair and bring a chaotic world into sharper focus. I marveled at how these writers raided the novelist's toolbox, using scenes, dialogue, and lyrical turns of phrase to liberate the dry reporting I had been taught in journalism school.

I used these stories as templates for my own work, but by the early 1990s, inspiration was becoming more difficult to find. The corporatization of American media had shifted into high gear. Publicly traded behemoths were gobbling up locally owned publishers and had begun the strangling of newsrooms that continues to this day. Longform journalism was falling out of favor.

So I decided to create my own pipeline. Like the country's best regionals (hat tip: *Texas Monthly, D, Philadelphia, Los Angeles*), the magazine I envisioned would combine smart reader service with great reporting and compelling storytelling. The numbers in my meticulously polished business plan charted a clear course, but the reality was anything but tidy. The difficulty of attracting readers was surpassed only by the challenge of convincing advertisers to take a chance on an unproven magazine. Which meant that in those early years, blockbuster stories were rare in the pages of *5280*. For all of our ambition, we lacked the cash it takes to sustain that kind of work.

Instead, we devoted ourselves to reader service. From a writer's perspective, these news-you-can-use packages (such as "25 Best Restaurants," "Top Of The Town," and "Top Doctors") aren't terribly glamorous, but they're beloved by readers—and they're not nearly as expensive and time-intensive to produce as 6,000-word feature narratives. Over time, we built a loyal audience, and as the magazine's financial statements shifted from red to black, we were finally able to start commissioning the meatier stuff more frequently. Today, one or more manuscripts cross my desk every month that give me that same rush I was chasing all those years ago.

Some of my favorites are collected in the book you're now holding. I must admit there's a satisfaction that comes from publishing an anthology that might someday be discovered by another aspiring journalist. But even more than that, I hope these 20 stories give you the same kind of thrill they've given me.

Daniel Brogan
Founder, CEO, and Editor-in-Chief
5280

Introduction

Narrative nonfiction. Creative nonfiction. The New Journalism. Longreads. #longform.

The names for deeply reported and artfully told journalism have changed over the years, but the craft itself has not. Even in 2018, when hot takes and tweets and news aggregation have become *de rigueur*, there is still a need, and demand, for in-depth, nuanced, sensitive, and complex storytelling. Thankfully, talented, determined magazine journalists the world over recognize their obligation to deliver such transformative pieces.

For more than two decades, the editors of *5280* have made it a priority to include this kind of storytelling in every issue, to make these compelling articles part of the eclectic mix we provide to our readers each month—not just because they're memorable but also because they're important. These pieces don't necessarily sell magazines—publishers of city and regional magazines depend on dining and travel coverage and best-of packages to move copies on the newsstand—but they do connect readers to the publication in meaningful ways. When it's well executed, narrative journalism transports the reader to unfamiliar settings, to other eras in history, and into the minds of peculiar, mysterious, or extraordinary people. As Pulitzer Prize– and National Book Award–winning author Tracy Kidder and his editor Richard Todd put it in their book, *Good Prose: The Art of Nonfiction*, "A story lives in its particulars, in the individuality of person, place, and time."

Being able to construct a story that "lives in its particulars" is significantly more difficult than it sounds. Writers, in the act of writing, often send me (as their editor) notes that say, essentially, "writing is really, *really* hard"—typically with a few choice modifiers thrown in. They're right; writing *is* hard. But the challenges of crafting a compelling nonfiction narrative begin well before a writer sits down at her Mac to type out the opening words of a first draft. Although *5280* likes to break news, our mission as a monthly publication skews toward providing clarity and context and—if we're doing our jobs well—telling stories that offer some sort of universal insight into what it means to be human. Fiction writing offers this wisdom through the settings and characters authors invent; nonfiction writing is, by definition, rooted in all the messiness and improbabilities of the real world. There are very few neat narrative arcs in life. Sometimes these stories raise more questions than they answer. Sometimes the plots take unexpected—and nonsensical—turns. Sometimes they don't have satisfying endings. Nevertheless, it's up to the writer to discover the fundamental facts of the story and organize them in a cohesive, comprehensible way—finding the through-line, or narrative thread—that compels the reader to keep turning the page.

This all starts with reporting. "Reporting" isn't a particularly sexy word—it conjures images of a rumpled, caffeine-addled journalist pressing play on a digital recorder, or a bespectacled research assistant rooting around in musty archives at the public library—but no good nonfiction story ever came into being without meticulous, dogged reporting. The very best nonfiction writers, of which there are many in this anthology, pride themselves on their reporting—even, perhaps, more so than their wordsmithing. They are relentless in uncovering details, in taking time to understand their subjects, and in witnessing scenes that lend the richness that is unique to this kind of journalistic storytelling.

Then comes the "really, *really* hard" process of writing, of discerning the structure of the piece, of deciding how it will be told, of figuring out which storytelling techniques to employ. Writers work in different ways: Some hammer out a couple thousand words in a day knowing full well there will be significant revising the next day (and probably the day after that, too). Others produce a couple hundred words in the same period of time, agonizing over every single syllable. All the while, an editor is there playing multiple roles: cheerleader, psychotherapist, sounding board, friend. If there's one thing most people don't know about editors' jobs, it's the fact that most of what we do isn't rearranging words and sentences and paragraphs. There's a lot of that, yes, but there's also a lot of encouraging, cajoling, and listening. I have a quote from *New Yorker* editor David Remnick on my corkboard to remind me daily of my responsibility as someone who helps bring these stories into the world. "A real editor is focused totally on the writer's work and helping the writer realize a vision of the piece or the book he's set out to do," Remnick once said. "Editing requires a certain selflessness that is hard to find."

I don't mean to be precious about the struggles writers and editors face in the process of putting these stories together. We're not performing life-saving surgeries or researching ways to ensure the citizens of underdeveloped countries have access to clean drinking water. But ours is a craft that requires a specific skill set, one that includes the ability to sympathize with others, to listen, to be open-minded, to be observant, to be persistent, and not least, to be talented in translating ideas into words on a page. Having all of these skills is a rarity. We at *5280* are lucky to have employed and worked with a group of writers who are quintessential examples of what journalists can and should be.

Each of the stories in this collection is its own work of art. Each stands alone as a superior example of narrative nonfiction, regardless of whether it's a lyrical personal essay, a serious investigation, or a poignant look at life in Denver or Colorado. It has been my great joy and privilege to have worked with many of these writers and to have been a part of a few of these narratives. I hope you'll enjoy reading them, because as difficult as they are to produce, these are the types of stories we are proud of, care about deeply, and believe truly matter.

Geoff Van Dyke
Editorial Director
5280

1.

Gone

by Lindsey B. Koehler

It hasn't snowed in days, but the chill and wind remain. Randy Hansen is in no hurry to leave the warmth of his car, but he feels compelled. He scans the desolate expanse outside his car window: a seemingly endless open field of frosted grass. Twenty minutes, he tells himself, it's worth being out in the cold for 20 minutes to be able to cross this one off the list. The detective shoulders open the door, pulls a black wool cap tight onto his bald head, and walks into the field, his winter overcoat flapping in the wind. A former college football player, Hansen is tall and still possesses the kind of trim, sculpted physique that many men in their 40s have let slip away. Hansen typically exudes a formidable presence, but now, in this field in nowhere Aurora, he looks anything but.

A layer of old snow crunches underfoot. His eyes begin to water. He would tell you it's the wind. He keeps looking, squinting, searching the ground in front of his feet. He's not sure what he's looking for, exactly, or even if he's looking in the right place. After all this time, the unmarked grave of a little girl isn't likely to look like much. Maybe a modest mound rising from the otherwise flat field, maybe a slight indentation in the dirt. He knows that walking around this field—just like all the other fields he's examined after receiving a tip, or like now, on nothing more than a whim—is probably a waste of time. But he doesn't know what else to do, and he has to do something.

For a moment, Hansen allows himself to think. He's alone, in a field, in the cold, trying to unearth the body of a child he thinks he has to find. The phrase "obsessive-compulsive lunatic" pops into his mind. But then *her* face flashes in front of him, and he remembers how he got here. How he chanced upon this mystery, and how it changed his life in so many ways. On that snowy night years ago, in 2005, when he first got the call, Hansen could not have imagined how intertwined his life and this case would become. He could not have guessed he would not be living in his Arvada home, or that he'd be divorced. He wouldn't have envisioned he'd be spending as much time as he does at an Old Chicago drinking IPAs and talking to cute bartenders about his lack of a love life. He could not have foreseen that all these years later he would be ferreting around a vacant field hoping to find Aaroné.

Monday, November 14, 2005, 7:45 p.m.
Across the room the TV was blaring, filling the basement of an Arvada home with the resonant voices of Al Michaels and John Madden as they broke down the Monday night game between the Cowboys and the Eagles. Hansen had a clear view of the flat-screen from his weight bench. Working out was a requirement for Hansen, and not just because his job demanded basic fitness. The repetition helped him rub out the details of long days spent working as a detective in the Aurora Police Department's Crimes Against Children (CAC) unit. The distraction of a good NFL game didn't hurt either.

Halfway into a set of leg presses his cell phone rang. The call wasn't unexpected: Hansen was on-call for the evening, which meant he'd be the guy the department would dial if a crime involving a child cropped up.

"This is Randy."

The lieutenant gave Hansen the details: A six-year-old female had been missing since approximately 1 p.m. Police were on the scene. The address was 16551 E. Kepner Place, Aurora.

Hansen hung up the phone, relieved. Missing children were rarely ever truly missing. They were often hiding in the attic; sometimes they were at a neighbor's house; often they'd "run away" and would come home on their own. But only a fraction of one percent of missing children ever ended up really vanishing into thin air. Chances were police would find the kid before Hansen even made it to Aurora. He pulled on street clothes and grabbed the keys to his Chevy Impala. On his way out the door he hollered to his wife, Carrie: "Got a call. It's just a missing kid. I'll be right back." It was a line she had heard her husband say so many times before.

November 14, 2005, 8:30 p.m.
Hansen pulled into the cul-de-sac in front of the beige-brick home in Aurora. It had been snowing off and on for the past half hour. He stepped from the car into the 30-degree chill and looked for his on-call colleague, detective Chris Fanning. The other half of the detective two-some emerged from a navy-blue sea of uniformed patrol officers, many of whom had been searching the house and neighborhood for more than six hours but had yet to find any real leads. An Amber Alert couldn't be issued because there was no description of a vehicle or a potential suspect. Although police were already inside, Hansen and Fanning knocked on the front door. Aaron Thompson answered the door. He told the men he was the missing girl's father and showed them into the living room, where Shely Lowe, Thompson's live-in girlfriend, and the couple's other seven children were gathered.

Hansen surveyed the scene in the cookie-cutter home. He was immediately struck by the silence. In his experience, when a child was missing the family had a hard time controlling the volume. Someone was yelling or crying. Friends and family spilled in and out of the house—talking, updating, consoling. But not here. There was hardly a noise. The television was on, but the sound hovered just above a static whisper. The kids, who looked like they ranged from early elementary- to middle-school age, sat glued to the couches near the TV. Not one of them was talking. No one was playing a game. Hansen didn't even catch one trying to provoke another. The only activity they seemed to be allowed to do was their chores. Every few minutes, one would get up to clear away a dirty food dish or wipe down the kitchen counter or empty the dishwasher. Which was maybe why, Hansen thought, the house was so damn tidy. In fact, he couldn't remember the last time he'd seen a house full of children that was so clean.

He pulled up a chair to talk with Thompson while Fanning lured Lowe into the kitchen. In *Law & Order* fashion, the detectives interviewed each parent individually and out of earshot from the other. After so many years on the force, Hansen had witnessed a hundred different ways people react to stress, but he was still surprised that neither parent seemed the least bit emotional. No chin quivering. No eyes red with tears and exhaustion. No faraway stares. Thompson and Lowe were calm and cooperative as they told the detectives the same story they'd told patrol officers earlier that day: Just before noon, Aaroné and her sister were at the kitchen table. Thompson had just finished feeding them a late breakfast when Aaroné asked to have another cookie beyond what her father had already given her. When Thompson said no, the six-year-old threw a temper tantrum and ran upstairs to the bedroom she shared with her three sisters. Fifteen minutes later, Thompson went to check on his daughter and couldn't find her. A search of the house turned up nothing. After a brief look around the neighborhood, Thompson called Aurora police.

Thompson's retelling of the story seemed devoid of sentiment to Hansen. Even if it was the 10th time he'd told it that day, Hansen thought the father's lackadaisical delivery was strange. The detectives peppered the family with more questions, but neither Lowe nor Thompson nor the children could supply the detectives with any helpful information about where they thought Aaroné might be or whom she might be with. The little girl's parents said that Aaroné had no friends, didn't play outside, didn't have any extended family in Colorado, and hadn't yet enrolled in school. Hansen shot Fanning a frustrated look.

Hansen changed direction and asked for two things: recent photos of Aaroné and a tour of the kids' bedrooms. Lowe had handed over a snapshot of Aaroné to patrol officers earlier in the day. Hansen had examined the photo, but the blurry photograph showed a too-skinny toddler in a blue and white checkered outfit. Aaroné could barely have been four when it was taken. The missing girl was just two weeks shy of her seventh birthday. When he told Lowe and Thompson he needed a more recent picture of their daughter they couldn't produce one.

With the night growing late and the temperature dropping outside, Hansen hurried to the second floor. Thompson followed sluggishly. The detective looked out the windows, opened hallway closets, and then examined the girls' room. There were two sets of bunk beds for four girls, but only three mattresses. Hansen asked about the discrepancy, and Thompson explained that when he and Lowe bought the beds, they only had seven kids; when the eighth one came along, Aaroné began sharing a bed with one of her sisters. Possible, Hansen thought, but pairing that with the lack of photographs and the family's underdeveloped sense of urgency—something wasn't right. Walking out of the bedroom, Hansen found the girl's father in the hallway, standing with his eyes closed. As Hansen passed by, Thompson cracked open an eye, looked at the detective, and said, "I'm kinda tired—I'm gonna go to bed."

Tuesday, November 15, 2005

It was nearing 3 a.m. as Hansen tiptoed into his dark house, trying not to wake his sleeping family. He slipped silently into the warm bed next to Carrie. He'd perfected the move over the years; coming in late was part of the job.

He'd been a cop for 15 years—first booking inmates into jail, then working patrol—but the past three years as a CAC detective had been the most intense. He'd taken the detective exam because he'd had his fill of society's riff-raff, the drunkards and drug addicts. The CAC unit wasn't exactly what he'd had in mind when he'd gone fishing for a promotion. With a 14-year-old daughter and an 18-year-old son of his own, listening to tales of child torture and sexual abuse turned his stomach. He'd had to learn not to blush when a nine-year-old used words like "cooter" or "hoohah" to describe where her uncle had touched her. It was impossible not to see his own kids in the faces of young victims. He hated the job for nearly a year before he found a reason to love it: The first time he got a guilty verdict and put an end to a child's suffering, he knew why he was where he was.

Which is why he hadn't minded being in Aurora for six hours that night. It was his job to find a missing little girl, to bring her back to her family—even if that meant hours away from his own. With little more to go on than an old photograph, Hansen was aware of what lay ahead for him. Phone calls. Leads. Dead ends. Hansen mentally prepared for what was shaping up to be a real missing-child case—his first one ever.

Only five hours after he slipped into bed with Carrie, Hansen was back in Aurora. Time is precious when a child has gone missing. According to studies, the first few hours are the most critical: Nearly three-quarters of abducted children who are murdered are dead within three hours of the abduction. Aaroné had been missing for 19 hours.

Hansen checked in with officers who'd been canvassing the block. Out of the nine houses on the street, not one resident knew the Thompsons well. The consensus, patrol officers told Hansen, was that the family was unfriendly and reclusive. The kids never played outside. The parents didn't return a neighborly wave.

Hansen had hoped to scrape together some details on where the kids played and how often the neighbors saw Aaroné outside. Without that information Hansen had to find another way to get a bead on Aaroné. He had officers ask Lowe and Thompson for something of the girl's— anything from which bloodhounds could draw a scent. The trail the dogs sniffed off a baby doll evaporated in a field near the house. Hansen also asked the Thompsons for some of Aaroné's clothing for DNA extraction. Lowe sent one of the kids to fetch a bundle of Aaroné's tops and bottoms. Hansen held up each item of clothing and lifted a skeptical eyebrow—not one piece looked large enough to fit a six-year-old child. If there was one thing Hansen had learned during his years on the job, it was that the simplest explanation was usually the correct one: Aaroné didn't just go missing over a cookie.

Wednesday, November 16, 2005

The case was everywhere. The investigation was the lead story on every news channel. The community, unwilling to accept that a six-year-old had simply disappeared, pulled together to find her for her family. Missing-child posters with the blurry photograph of Aaroné were taped up all over the city. Volunteer search groups fanned out across Aurora, looking in parks, wooded areas, and open fields for Aaroné. Hansen manned his desk at the Aurora Police Department, making calls, setting up interviews, checking e-mails, and following up with his team. Police work, grunt work. Tips had been streaming into the hotline the department had set up, and Hansen had his people checking out the most credible leads. Nothing crucial surfaced. Nothing, until a call came in from the Colorado Department of Corrections: An inmate at the Colorado Territorial Correctional Facility said he had information about little Aaroné.

Of the eight children living in the Kepner Place house, none was the biological offspring of both Thompson and Lowe. Lowe was pregnant with what would soon be the couple's first child together. Two of the other children were fathered by Eric Williams Sr., a former boyfriend of Lowe's. Williams had since become a ward of the state of Colorado, a drug addict who'd ditched a court-appointed stay at a halfway house. It was Williams' cellmate who called the hotline. He said Williams had told him things about Aaroné that Hansen would want to know. She's dead, said Williams's cellie. She's been dead for years; she died in the bathtub, and they buried her in a field somewhere.

The tip made sense to Hansen. That was why there were no photographs. That was why there were only seven mattresses. That was why Thompson and Lowe's behavior seemed so off—it would've been nearly impossible for them to get appropriately emotional about a little girl lost in the cold when she was already dead. And that, Hansen thought, was also probably why Lowe and Thompson had reported her "missing" when they did—if family was going to visit after the birth of the new baby, they'd want to know where Aaroné was. That she'd run away or been kidnapped was a better story than telling the grandparents she'd died and had been buried in a field. Hansen sent detectives to Cañon City to interview both Eric Williams Sr. and his chatty cellmate. He wanted to know exactly why Williams thought Aaroné was dead. It took a moment to sink in, but Hansen realized his missing-child case likely had just become a homicide investigation.

With Williams's plausible allegations in mind, Hansen headed back to the Kepner Place house to interview the other seven kids. Thompson and Lowe initially had been unwilling to allow the detective to interview the kids alone. But they had finally relented. When Hansen arrived, all seven children were clean, dressed, and waiting. Hansen took the kids, one at a time, into another room for questioning. The interviews were, for the most part, unremarkable. The kids seemed nervous and tongue-tied, their answers clipped and unhelpful, until Hansen sat down with the youngest boy, a soft-spoken, squirmy, eight-year-old son of Shely Lowe's. Sitting in a chair in the middle of the room, the child's legs dangled, his feet barely able to touch the floor. Most of the session followed the same pattern as the others—seemingly easy questions followed by useless answers. But as Hansen finished this particular interview, the detective asked the young man if *he* had any questions. "Yes," the boy said. "Don't you want to know about Aaroné's favorite food and her favorite color and what she was for Halloween?"

Surprised by the question, Hansen replied that he *would* like to know those things.

Pizza, orange, and a witch, said the eight-year-old, obviously proud that he'd been able to tell the policeman what he thought the cop wanted to hear.

"Who told you to tell me that?" asked Hansen.

"No one," he said.

Hansen studied the child. It was the way the boy had said it, scripted and rote. The detective's own kids, Justin and Cami, were teenagers now, and although he was often away on the job, Hansen had been around his kids enough to know they never would have asked that kind of question at that age. When his kids were little, Hansen had worked the night shift to make things easier on the family. While Carrie worked at the hair salon they owned together, he had stayed home in the afternoons to watch Justin and Cami. He knew eight-year-olds. He knew their tendencies, he knew how they acted, and he certainly knew when they weren't telling the truth.

Thursday, November 17, 2005

At 5 p.m., Hansen arrived at the Thompson residence. The bland suburban house looked changed to Hansen somehow. More sinister, more ominous. A little girl probably had died in there, and Hansen had to make sure that didn't happen again. As he got out of his car, his heart pounding, Hansen realized he hadn't even thought about what he was going to say to the parents. He couldn't compromise the investigation by giving them too much detail, yet he had to tell them something: He was, after all, there to take their children away.

Having his own kids made police work harder—and easier—for Hansen. His work hours increased when he made the jump from patrol to CAC in 2002, which meant he saw even less of Justin and Cami—and Carrie too. At the same time, being a father gave him that parental instinct, a sixth sense that made him that much more protective of every child. And so, forty-four and a half hours into the investigation, Hansen knew he had a critical decision to make. Seven children under the age of 16 were living in a home in which both parents were now suspects in the potential homicide of the kids' sibling.

Hansen had a sound argument for wanting to remove the Thompson children. But was there enough hard evidence? He wasn't sure; however, if there was ever a time to employ the better-safe-than-sorry motto, Hansen figured this was it. As a CAC detective, he understood the big picture: Each year in the United States about 800,000 children are victims of abuse and neglect—and nearly 1,800 die from it. Hansen had picked up the phone to call the Colorado Department of Human Services. He'd requested a court order to remove the kids.

The decision might have been more difficult if Hansen hadn't already listened to the taped interviews with Eric Williams Sr., the inmate whose cellie had said he had information about Aaroné's death. That interview had provided Hansen with a more convincing story line than Thompson's cookie anecdote. According to Williams, in January 2004 Lowe had told him that Aaroné died from an episode in the bathtub, and that she and Thompson buried the girl in a field. Lowe had also mentioned to Williams that the night the couple went to bury the girl they were stopped by police, but that nothing came of it. Hansen checked out Williams's story: Police in Greenwood Village had, in fact, stopped Thompson and Lowe in their Ford Expedition behind a grocery store—near the rows of Dumpsters—at 2:40 a.m. on January 21, 2003.

Both Thompson and Lowe were home when Hansen knocked on the door. The detective calmly explained that he had information that Aaroné had been dead for more than two years. He requested their co-operation. And then he broke the news that social services would be taking the children. Hansen watched for a reaction. Thompson didn't move or speak. His stunted response made Hansen wonder if the man was even listening. Lowe had definitely heard him.

"You bald-headed, redneck motherfucker!" she screamed. "You get the fuck out of my house!"

As much as Hansen would've loved to oblige—to leave this unpleasant scene and go home—he could not. Along with a court order to remove the children, he also had a search warrant that allowed him and his team to take possession of 16551 E. Kepner Place. If Eric Williams Sr.'s story was accurate, Aaroné hadn't been inside the home for at least two years. Hansen knew it was unlikely he'd find much evidence of a crime scene. Blood could be washed away, weapons disposed of, evidence tossed out. But over the course of the next several days, cadaver dogs would prowl through the home anyway, sniffing for old blood. The dogs showed interest in the girls' bedroom and in the upstairs bathroom, but the blood residue the crime scene investigators found came from other children in the house—not from Aaroné.

Police scoured every room, bagging anything they felt could be evidence. Hansen took every toddler-size girl's shirt in case the CSIs needed to pull more DNA later. Officers also tagged bags of Halloween candy (seven), pairs of kids' gloves (seven), and toothbrushes (seven), none of which popped positive for Aaroné's DNA. NecroSearch, a Colorado organization that specializes in finding clandestine grave-sites, set up in the Thompson's backyard. As media helicopters hovered above the Aurora home, a team of volunteer scientists used ground-penetrating radar to search the property for disturbed soil. They noted a handful of suspicious patches of earth, but after hours of digging nothing was found. Aaroné, as far as anyone could tell, had not been tossed into a makeshift grave on the Thompson property.

Friday, November 18, 2005
Taking the Thompson kids out of the home the night before had been emotionally draining, but not nearly as challenging as Hansen had imagined. Even with Lowe's insults ringing in his ears, Hansen had calmly helped the children toward the door. He asked the kids to get their coats, and, for the most part, they walked out of their home without so much as a whimper. Hansen wondered if they'd learned the stoicism from their father, or if they were simply terrified into speechlessness.

After bringing the children to the police station, Hansen and another detective decided to question the oldest child, a 15-year-old, who was actually Shely Lowe's younger brother. The teenager had been living with the family since August 2004. He was old enough, Hansen thought, that he might be able to put something—anything—into context.

Hansen had a gift for interviewing. Detective Chris Fanning, Hansen's coworker of two years, always said it was Hansen's talent for maintaining an even keel that made him a good CAC detective. Even talking to a child molester, Hansen could keep his cool. But that night, after four days of wading through murky waters with the Thompson family, Hansen lost his patience when the teenager became defensive and the kid punched the wall. "What am I supposed to think when I see a father falling asleep when his little girl is supposedly out in the cold and snow?" Hansen asked, his tone this side of angry. The boy didn't answer. Hansen could tell he wanted to protect his sister, but it was obvious he wasn't entirely sure what he was protecting her from.

The interview dragged on for five and a half hours, during which time something occurred to Hansen: If the boy moved into the Thompson house in August 2004 and Aaroné died sometime in 2003, he might not have known she ever existed. When Hansen pressed the boy on whether he had actually ever met six-year-old Aaroné, the boy hesitated, then relented. He'd never seen her, he said. Not once.

Some of the other kids were interviewed on Friday morning at SungateKids, a child-focused facility where the Aurora Police Department took the vast majority of its youngest victims for forensic interviews. Listening to the recorded conversations, Hansen could tell the children were terrified, but for reasons he hadn't anticipated.

At first, the kids wanted no part of the interviews. They said they didn't know anything. They repeated that the last time they'd seen Aaroné had been Monday morning before school. But as the interviewers trudged on, strategically pressuring the kids and refusing to let any inconsistencies pass, Hansen listened to a bizarre plot twist emerge: As each kid opened up, he or she said that, more than a year earlier, Lowe and "Big A," as the kids called Thompson, had told them that Aaroné had gone back to Michigan to live with her real mom. They'd said they sent her back because she was bad. On Monday morning, the day Aaroné "disappeared," Lowe and Thompson told the kids that Aaroné had come back from Michigan that morning and had then run away. They told the kids to tell the police they had seen her before they left for school.

The stories confirmed what Hansen already suspected: Their parents had coached them on what to say to the police. The kids, vaguely understanding their parents were in trouble, hadn't wanted to say the wrong thing—were terrified of saying the wrong thing—concerned they might be sent away, or worse. To prove his theory correct, Hansen had the interviewers ask each child the same questions their eight-year-old brother had asked him: What is Aaroné's favorite food, what's her favorite color, and what was she for Halloween? "Pizza," "orange," and "witch" spilled out of the children's mouths, followed closely by the admission that their parents had told them to say those exact things to the police if they were asked. But the children weren't completely forthcoming. They still weren't offering up all of the answers to Hansen's questions. Questions like: *What happened the last time you saw Aaroné?*

Thursday, December 1, 2005

For almost three weeks Hansen had been working seven days a week. He drove home mostly to shower, change clothes, and sleep. He hadn't seen his kids in days. He and Carrie were barely talking. Not that that was unusual. Carrie often told him he was emotionally unavailable and distant, especially when he became engrossed in a big case. That comment stung Hansen, probably because he knew it was true; he had always struggled with verbal affection. He'd always been shy and reserved. These were traits that helped make him a skilled interviewer—but maybe not a communicative husband. It was in his genes. His parents, who'd been married for more than four decades, never said "I love you" to each other in front of the kids. They never even said it aloud to Hansen or his older brother. There was love in the house, but it wasn't overt. When Hansen met Carrie Parks at Saugus High School in California, he fell in love with how comfortable she was saying "I love you." Yet it took him becoming a father for those words to float off his tongue more easily. Kids were easy to love. Which was why Hansen had such trouble understanding Aaron Thompson's indifference—and why he winced when Carrie pegged him as distant.

When he did see his wife, he didn't offer up much about the case. They never talked about his job. Well, they rarely talked about his job—and even when they did talk about it they didn't *really* talk about it. After all, a conversation about his days spent listening to a 13-year-old talk about how her stepfather touched her breasts or investigating who fractured the skull and broke the ribs of a six-month-old wasn't kitchen-table conversation. Hansen began to realize, though, that if he wasn't talking about his job, he wasn't talking much at all, especially with his wife.

And so the detective spent hours at the station, where he could discuss the strange details with other detectives, people who understood. For all the time he'd been putting in, though, Hansen stood at an impasse. Lowe and Thompson were refusing to speak to him. The kids seemed unwilling to help with specific details surrounding Aaroné. After days of executing the search warrant, the house wasn't revealing its secrets. The only concrete information he had that Aaroné was dead was from Eric Williams Sr., a convicted criminal. And there was nothing that pointed to her death, if it happened at all, as a homicide. More than once, Hansen thought that the case was simply impossible to solve. That the drudgery of doing interviews and following up on tips was not worth the effort and time spent away from his family. Even the interview he had lined up for that afternoon seemed like a waste of time, but he visited Tabitha Graves at her run-down home in Denver anyway.

Listed as one of the Thompson kids' in-case-of-emergency contacts at school, Graves said she and Lowe were old friends who'd had a falling out more than a year before. They hadn't talked since, she said, and she certainly didn't remember Lowe saying that anything had happened to Aaroné. For Hansen, it was just another frustrating dead end. Hansen threw down his card and asked Graves to call him if she thought of anything that might help. It was one of those perfunctory, cliché moves, almost never worth a damn.

But later that evening, Graves picked up the card and dialed his cell phone. "Detective Hansen," she said, her voice trembling—he thought maybe she was crying. "I'm sorry, but I lied to you earlier today. Shely told me back in the summer or fall of 2004 that Aaroné was dead. She said Aaron did something with the body."

The typically unflustered Hansen couldn't help but feel his pulse quicken. It was already past quitting time, and his family was probably wondering if he'd ever come home, but Graves was on her way to the police station. She told Hansen she'd been in Lowe's car when Lowe said Aaroné had died. Lowe explained that one morning Aaroné hadn't come down for breakfast. When Lowe checked on her, she was in bed but wasn't moving or breathing. Lowe called for Thompson, who went into the bedroom with Aaroné for about an hour, came out with the girl wrapped in a blanket, and left in the family's Ford Expedition.

This was the break Hansen had been waiting for. He convinced Graves to make recorded phone calls to Lowe. And for five long months, from early December 2005 to early May 2006, he worked the relation-ship between Graves and Lowe. Hansen had Graves call Lowe just to talk, to catch up—and to build trust. To build enough trust, Hansen hoped, that Lowe would reveal not only how Aaroné really died—*in the bathtub? in her bedroom?*—but where she was buried.

Through dozens of recorded phone calls and three wiretapped meetings, Lowe maintained a healthy skepticism of Graves. Her distrust meant that Lowe rarely let her guard down enough to divulge much more than she'd told Graves in 2004. But there were moments of enlightenment, details that gave Hansen insight. During the third face-to-face meeting, Graves asked Lowe if the two of them could go place flowers on Aaroné's grave. Lowe balked at first, but then acquiesced: "I'll have Aaron do it," she said, adding to Graves, "You ain't going nowhere." Graves added pressure, saying, "Aaroné needs to be acknowledged, Shely." To which Lowe replied, "Ain't nobody forgot that baby."

Friday, May 12, 2006, 4:30 a.m.
The morning was still dark when a call came into Aurora's emergency dispatch center.

"911, what is your emergency?"

Aaron Thompson's voice was thick with alarm: *My girlfriend isn't breathing.*

Paramedics rushed to 16551 E. Kepner Place to find Shely Lowe unconscious and unresponsive. With Thompson at her side, Lowe was taken by ambulance to the Medical Center of Aurora. Shely Lowe died, at 33 years old, from heart failure.

Minutes later, the phone on detective Hansen's bedside table rang.

"This is Randy."

Sergeant Joe Young, the supervisor of the CAC unit, broke the news to a still-groggy Hansen, who climbed out of bed, once again, leaving Carrie alone. His first thought was that he'd lost the only line of communication he'd had—the one from Lowe through Tabitha Graves. His next and most heart-sinking thought was that any attorney could now explain Aaroné's death in a way that could get Aaron off the hook: Shely did it.

Late May 2006
Although Hansen would've liked to arrest both Lowe and Thompson for the crimes he thought they'd committed, he was just as content to cuff Thompson alone. And after more than six months of police work, Hansen thought he had enough to do just that. Hansen believed that the phone recordings between Lowe and Graves were damning enough to get a warrant on their own. But in his back pocket he also carried

evidence that Thompson and Lowe did not buy seven mattresses as Thompson had said—a receipt from Bedroom Expressions showed they'd originally purchased eight. Hansen also had a witness, a Catholic nun no less, who was in the Thompson home the morning of November 14, 2005, for a Section 8 housing check—and she did not see Aaroné. Hansen itched to move on the arrest. He met with Sergeant Young and Aurora's chief of police, Daniel Oates, who both agreed that Hansen had gathered enough evidence to make the arrest.

But after a meeting with Arapahoe County District Attorney Carol Chambers the group changed its mind. Hansen had accumulated a mountain of circumstantial evidence, but his stack of evidentiary have-nots was considerable: no body, no murder weapon, no cause of death. Chambers suggested taking the case in front of the grand jury to make sure prosecutors had enough evidence to get a conviction. A grand jury isn't a criminal trial; no one gets sentenced to prison by a grand jury. But prosecutors love them—the power to subpoena witnesses and present evidence behind closed doors often proves to be a tremendously helpful investigative tool. The majority of grand juries hand down a "true bill," or an indictment, that gives prosecutors cause to go to trial.

The grand jury convened for the first time in the Thompson case in late spring 2006. Hansen attended two daylong hearings each month. He had to reinvestigate dozens of aspects of the case to present to the jury. It felt like overkill to Hansen. He was frustrated and tired. But he understood the process gave him a chance to see what his investigation might look like seen through the eyes of a jury. Still, the thought of going through the case for the grand jury and then having to do it again for a criminal jury felt overwhelming. The work hours involved were staggering—and Hansen simply didn't have the stamina to manage the case and deal with his home life.

September 2006

If the end of the Hansens' marriage hadn't come during the Thompson case, it would have fractured during the next, or the one after that. Hansen would tell you the couple had been a bad match from the start, and that the end of their marriage was no different than any other failed marriage in America. There was both fact and wishful fiction in that explanation. Divorce is always about something, and in police marriages it's almost always about something to do with the job. The divorce rate for cops is 60 to 70 percent higher than the national average. Not that being a statistic mattered to Hansen. That didn't make the end any easier. Carrie would have to declare bankruptcy. Hansen, who would learn that he made, as he would drolly put it, "too much money" as a police officer to declare bankruptcy himself, would have to pay child support and settle up the debt from their hair salon. And someone would have to move out.

Four months into the grand jury proceedings, Hansen moved into a one-bedroom unit in an Aurora apartment complex. He furnished it with a cheap kitchen table and a futon for the living room. It wasn't like he needed nice stuff; with the grand jury taking up his days and nights, he hardly spent any time at the apartment anyway. Instead of driving home to Arvada to slip silently into a warm bed after a long day of work, Hansen could make all the noise he wanted. He lived alone, sleeping in sheets that were always cold.

October 2006 to May 2007

It had been nearly a year since Hansen pulled the Thompson children out of their home and placed them in foster care. For 11 months, they were nearly silent when it came to what happened inside 16551 E. Kepner Place. In the middle of the grand jury hearings, however, the floodgates opened. Perhaps it was Lowe's death. Maybe it was the natural progression of mental healing. It could've been some unknown trigger that released the deluge. What mattered was the kids were talking, and they were all saying the same thing: They had been brutally physically abused.

The kids called the abuse getting a "whoopin." And they said that both Thompson and Lowe handed whoopins out with near equal force, ferocity, and frequency. Lowe, they said, took a kind of pleasure in punishing, while Thompson just did whatever Lowe told him to do. Either way, whoopins were everyday occurrences in the home, brought down swiftly for eating a bite of Lowe's breakfast cereal, for a bad grade at school, for not doing their chores, for not being ready on time, for a dirty room, for spilling food, for thumb-sucking, or for wetting the bed.

These punishments were not the average swat to the behind—the kind of reprimand strict grandmothers might've handed out for back-talking. For minor offenses, Thompson or Lowe would whack the children's hands with a leather belt until welts appeared. Sometimes the kids had to stand on the fireplace hearth, hold a telephone book, and face the wall for hours at a time. When a younger child made a mess in his pants, Thompson's punishment of choice was to place the excrement in the toilet and hold the child upside down by the ankles over the pot while screaming, "Poop goes here!"

For more serious infractions, the kids received beatings in the basement. Lowe and Thompson would make the children strip naked, tie them to a pole with a scarf, and cane them with whatever instrument struck their fancy: a baseball bat, a broomstick, a metal pole, a belt, an extension cord. The parents would often take turns, tag-teaming the beatings so that when one got tired the other would take over. When the abuse drew blood, which the kids said it often did, Lowe and Thompson would make the kids clean up their own blood with bleach. After every beating, the kids had to take a hot bath to stem the swelling.

None of the children was immune to the wrath—not even four-year-old Aaroné. According to the kids, when Aaroné wet herself or the bed, which was often, Thompson would whoop her on the bottom with a belt. He would then put Aaroné in the coat closet—her "punishment place"—often for the whole day, sometimes overnight. Her older sister remembered Aaroné spending hours in the dark closet and said she would lock fingers with Aaroné when the little girl would stick her tiny fingers out from underneath the closet door.

The information from the children brought clarity to the investigation that Hansen—and the sitting grand jury—had been searching for: This was not a murder case. This was a case of rampant child abuse. A case where one little girl was beaten to death, and in which seven others were barely surviving a living hell.

Every line in the 50-page indictment handed down by the grand jury on May 16, 2007, read like something out of a horror novel. But of the 60 counts laid out in graphic detail, count number one—child abuse resulting in death—was the most serious. The charge carried a maximum sentence of 48 years in prison. With the indictment in hand, Hansen could've legally arrested Aaron Thompson. But he didn't. Instead, he sent patrol officers to make the arrest—an arrest he had worked more than a year and a half to make happen. Hansen thought it'd be easier that way; that Thompson would put up less of a fight or talk more freely if he weren't there. Hansen simply didn't need the spotlight, didn't need the instant gratification—what he wanted, needed, was for a criminal jury to convict Aaroné's father.

Opening Statements, August 7, 2009

Hansen's face looked taut. Like the old football player he was, he rolled his shoulders and stretched his neck attempting to shake off the stress. Aaron Thompson wasn't the only one on trial in the courtroom that day. Hansen knew his police work, his investigation, the last four years of his life—it was all on trial, too. He wasn't allowed to speak during opening arguments; that was Chief Deputy District Attorney Bob Chappell's job. Hansen would only be able to watch as the counselor stitched together his case. After four years of work, he was no longer in control.

Aaron Thompson wasn't in control either. Not in control of his children. Not in control of his freedom. He'd been in jail awaiting trial for more than two years. In court he sat quietly at the far end of the defense table in a blue, collared shirt. He was noticeably thinner than when he was arrested in May 2007. He murmured a quick good morning to his attorneys. Beyond that, he didn't speak or move. He stared blankly ahead, his eyes vacant.

It had been more than two years since police handcuffed Thompson on the side of the road in Aurora, and nearly four years since Hansen first arrived at East Kepner Place. Finally, the now 45-year-old detective found himself sitting at the prosecution desk. The previous two years had been an epic roller coaster of hearings, motions, delays by the prosecution, delays by the defense, resignations by attorneys, trial preparation, and a change in judges. Dressed in a dark-blue suit, Hansen took his seat as the case's advisory witness in the Arapahoe County Justice Center.

At the behest of Judge Valeria Spencer, the gray-haired Chappell rolled out his opening argument. With a click of a remote, he called up on two white screens a picture of Aaroné Thompson. It was not the overused, blurry photograph that by now everyone knew. This was a baby photo—and the image had its desired effect: In an instant, the concept of innocence lost hung thickly in the air. Chappell let the photograph sear into the jurors' brains before he painted a ghastly picture of the neglect and abuse that befell not only this baby but seven others as well. Thompson and Lowe, he told the jury, built a house of horrors in their Aurora neighborhood—one that ended for them on November 14, 2005, but that would haunt their children forever.

For 22 days the prosecution laid out its case. Without a body, a cause of death, or much forensic evidence, the trial came down to the testimony of nearly 100 witnesses and 24 hours of taped video and audio recordings. The jurors listened as each police officer, detective, crime scene investigator, and forensic interviewer explained his or her role in the case and what the evidence they had found suggested. It was long, exhausting, tedious testimony. Tabitha Graves and Eric Williams Sr., two crucial witnesses for the prosecution's case, took the stand and relayed their stories. The jury also listened to phone recordings of Shely Lowe, her language often vulgar and inarticulate as she talked to Tabitha Graves. The prosecution called detective Hansen to testify on a half-dozen occasions.

The most compelling—and heart-wrenching—testimony came from the children. Almost four years had gone by, but the Thompson children had not forgotten. Sitting less than 15 feet away from Big A, they described their stories of abuse. Scarred kneecaps. The soles of their feet beaten with a baseball bat. Whacks on the arms and hands for any little misdeed. For Hansen, this was the most difficult part of the trial. He knew that Aaroné had suffered what was most likely a painful death—a vicious beating that he believed left her with fatal internal injuries. But listening to the kids again, he realized that her death may have been something of a blessing. For if she had lived, she and her seven siblings would have endured abuse for their entire childhoods. Without her death, Hansen could not have come to their rescue.

The children testified to the last time they saw their little sister. Their recollections were slightly different, and none of them could give a date, but two of them described a similar incident: Aaroné had wet herself again, and Big A was whoopin her for it. One of her brothers heard the little girl's screams emanating from the basement through the air vents into his bedroom. When Aaroné suddenly stopped screaming, he heard Big A say, "Shit." Another sibling, a stepsister, said the last time she saw Aaroné was in the upstairs bathroom. Aaroné's sister had been using the bathroom when Big A told her to go to her room. She watched as Thompson, who was furious that Aaroné had wet herself again, carried Aaroné into the bathroom and shut the door. She remembered that

Aaroné was not at breakfast the next morning. Aaroné's oldest step-sibling, 18 years old when he took the stand, also testified to noticing strange incidents during that time: a missing shovel, a foul odor in the basement, Lowe praying and joining a church, and the eighth mattress disappearing.

After weeks of agonizing testimony, the prosecution rested its case. It was now the defense attorneys' opportunity to refute what they could. Hansen was not surprised by their strategy—he'd known what it would be after the moment Shely Lowe died three years earlier. The defense asserted that Lowe, not Thompson, was the abusive monster, and that she killed Aaroné. They submitted that Aaron Thompson's only two criminal missteps were helping Lowe cover up the crime and lying to police about the girl's disappearance. The defense called fewer than 10 people to the stand and focused mainly on discrediting the prosecution's witnesses. Thompson declined to take the stand, and the defense rested after only one day of presentation. On September 15, 2009, the case— and the last four years of detective Hansen's life—went to the jury.

Monday, September 28, 2009

Nine days is a long time for a jury to deliberate. For Hansen, each day that passed was another sign the jurors did not feel confident in the work he and his team had done to give Aaroné Thompson some small piece of justice. The thought of a hung jury—or, worse, a not-guilty verdict—made it difficult for Hansen to breathe. The wait was painful, but something else began to bother him too: the nothingness. For four years, the Thompson case had been his life. It had occupied his attention. It had taken over his work. It had pulled him out of bed and away from his wife and kids. It had become a part of him. When he had started this journey he was married, owned a house, and had two teenagers to keep up with. Now he was divorced and paying off debt from his married days; he lived in a one-bedroom apartment that still didn't have pictures on the walls; and his kids were old enough to live on their own.

For Hansen, a guilty verdict would validate more than his instinct that Thompson had tortured his daughter to death; it would mean that for all that he'd lost, there was some point, some good, that came of it. A not-guilty verdict would mean—well, he couldn't allow himself to go there. Not yet.

The trial had not attracted huge audiences during the long days of testimony, but the courtroom overflowed for the verdict on September 28. Hansen was too nervous to notice that the media and the public only wanted to see the end result—a fitting end to a tragic story all wrapped up in an hourlong session. They didn't want to sweat the details of how Thompson had been brought to justice—or who had brought him there—they just wanted to know that it was done.

As the judge began to read the verdict, Hansen leaned forward in his chair, his shoulders upright and rigid. In his mind, a full slate of guilty verdicts would've been justice well served, but he only needed to hear one "guilty" so long as it came after the words "count number one."

The first verdict dropped onto the still room—"guilty." Hansen's shoulders slumped, he hung his head, and a sad smile tugged at the edges of his lips. As the guilty verdicts piled up, eventually coming to 31, Hansen's eyes welled up. He was slow to get to his feet after the judge dismissed the jury and bailiffs took Thompson away. He shook hands with Bob Chappell and the rest of the prosecution team. He quickly checked his phone—he already had text messages from family and friends. One in particular caught his eye. It was from Carrie. It was short and to the point, but that didn't matter. It was one word that conveyed so much more: *Congratulations.*

Monday, November 30, 2009
Until four years ago, November 30 meant nothing to Randy Hansen. Now, the last day of November will forever register as Aaroné's birthday. Today she would have been 11. Instead, she is gone.

Maybe she's in a field like Shely Lowe once said, or maybe she's in the Aurora landfill under 200 feet of garbage. Hansen doesn't like either setting as Aaroné's final resting place, which is why over the years he has wandered across more than one open field, hoping he might chance upon the missing little girl. The detective had hoped that at the sentencing on November 10, Aaron Thompson would give up the location of his daughter's burial place. But despite pleas from Aaroné's birth mother, Lynette Thompson, who begged Aaron to draw a map so she could give her daughter a proper burial, and despite an admonition from an impassioned Judge Spencer, who told Aaron that he had failed as a man and as a father, he sat silent. The judge sentenced him to 114 years in prison.

Two years between a death and an investigation leaves too much room for time to erase the trail. That Hansen has not found Aaroné's body is not a failure to anyone except him. He expected he would find Aaroné's body, something of her, somewhere, but he understands that he has to say good-bye to a little girl he never knew, who dramatically altered his life. Which is why he helped plan a candlelight memorial for Aaroné on her birthday.

The ceremony begins at 4:30 p.m. as the sun begins to drop over the Rocky Mountains. About 60 people are gathered on a playground in Aurora. Hansen stands off to the side with his daughter, Cami. As darkness descends, the mourners light their candles. Hansen lights his daughter's candle and throws an arm around her shoulders. It's cold out, and she has no coat, but the half-hug is more for Hansen than for his daughter. After all the time he's spent thinking about and searching for Aaroné, an hourlong ceremony hardly seems like an appropriate end. And for Hansen, it probably isn't the end. Aaron Thompson's legal team will appeal the verdict. Acquaintances will ask him about the case at cocktail parties for years to come. And every time someone finds the body of a little girl—in Colorado or anywhere else—Hansen will be the first to ask if it's *his* little girl. But tonight, Hansen is trying his best to say farewell. Seven speakers are lined up to talk to the small crowd, but Hansen is not one of them. He knows he'll just choke up.

— February 2010

2.

Lost

by Robert Sanchez

One night early this year, Randy Bilyeu was on the phone with his best friend. He wanted to share some good news: After more than two years of searching Colorado and New Mexico for a hidden treasure chest filled with gold and jewels, he thought he'd finally discovered its location. It wasn't too far from Santa Fe. Now he just needed to go get it.

Bilyeu was looking for the celebrated Fenn treasure—a 12th-century Romanesque chest hidden by an eccentric arts and antiquities collector that's said to be packed with 42 pounds of gold coins, rubies, diamonds, sapphires, ancient jade carvings, pre-Columbian bracelets, and gold nuggets. Between 2014 and 2015, Bilyeu made nearly a dozen trips from his Broomfield apartment to Santa Fe in search of the chest. During his hunts, Bilyeu, who was 54 years old and twice divorced, had sent photos to his two adult daughters and to a dwindling number of close confidants, most of whom worried about his safety during his excursions and had become skeptical of the fortune's existence.

Among them was Tom Martino, a longtime friend in Orlando, Florida, who talked to Bilyeu on January 4. The stash, Bilyeu said, was near the Rio Grande, in a place called Frijoles Canyon on Bandelier National Monument land between Santa Fe and Los Alamos. It would be difficult to get, though. In early January, temperatures, especially at night, would fall far below freezing. He'd been near the spot in the past month, and Bilyeu knew he would need a raft to move down the river and deliver him to a sandy patch from which he could begin his search. Further complicating matters was the fact that Bilyeu wanted to bring his traveling companion, Leo, a nine-year-old poodle-terrier mix. Bilyeu had never piloted a raft, and Leo was afraid of water. "It was the craziest thing I'd ever heard," Martino says of Bilyeu's plan. He told Bilyeu the search seemed risky. Bilyeu agreed: It was too cold and the weather was too dangerous to make a hasty search. Even still, he wanted to try.

In fact, he was already close. Bilyeu had driven the roughly 400 miles from Broomfield to Santa Fe with Leo, he explained to Martino. He was staying in a Motel 6 outside downtown. He'd purchased an $89 raft from a local sporting goods store, and he had waders, a wet suit, a backpack, maps, and his phone. Bilyeu sounded impatient. The Rio Grande was fewer than two dozen miles away. Bilyeu would drive there, inflate the raft, and begin his search despite his misgivings about the dangers he might face.

The next morning, a light dusting of snow covered the ground. Bilyeu backed his 2011 Nissan Murano into a space near a well field just off the Rio Grande. A thick cottonwood tree, its bare branches exposed to the elements, stood almost directly in front of him. The river was at least 50 yards wide and likely barely above freezing. Leo wore a miniature white sweater to protect him from the chill.

Bilyeu inflated his new blue-and-gray raft, then loaded the dog, two metal oars, and a manual air pump into it. His phone was turned off, perhaps to conserve battery power. Bilyeu finally lowered himself into the raft and shoved off. Within seconds, he and Leo began moving down the Rio Grande. A few minutes later, they disappeared into the canyon.

Since the beginning of recorded history, people have searched for treasure. From Egyptian grave robbers to Coronado exploring the Southwest for the seven cities of gold to modern-day crews probing ocean floors for sunken riches, the allure of the hunt has always evoked a romantic mysticism. Tales of hidden or buried valuables abound in popular literature and in movies. *The Treasure of the Sierra Madre* is a classic of American cinema. *The Goonies* frightened and delighted Gen Xers during their childhood years. And Steven Spielberg will soon release his fifth installment of the iconic Indiana Jones franchise.

In recent years, Bilyeu had become obsessed with the Fenn treasure, which was hidden by an 85-year-old Santa Fe resident named Forrest Fenn. The prize is reportedly valued at $1 million to $3 million today and is stashed somewhere in the Rocky Mountains between eight and one quarter miles north of Santa Fe and the United States–Canada border. After hiding the 10-by-10-by-five-inch chest, Fenn gave clues to its location in a six-stanza poem he included in his autobiography, *The Thrill of the Chase*, which he self-published in 2010. He's since followed up the poem with a series of additional clues (among them: the chest is at an elevation between 5,000 and 10,200 feet) and a map of the search area that encompasses four states. *Outside Magazine* has called it "America's last great treasure."

Since Fenn's autobiography was released, tens of thousands of seekers have entered the wilderness to hunt for the hidden wealth. Books have been written. Several websites are dedicated to the search. At least two documentary films are planned for release this year. In its most elemental form, the Fenn stash is the everyman's fantasy, an easily grasped extension of treasure-hunting mythology. With hiking boots, a map, and basic transportation, the chest could be one overturned log or steep hillside away.

Bilyeu made his first trip to New Mexico in 2014, from his then home near Atlanta, shortly after seeing the treasure featured on the *TODAY* show. "It captured his imagination," his sister, Kathy Leibold, told me this past spring. Bilyeu ordered Fenn's book and studied the poem. He took several trips to the outback near Santa Fe, sleeping in inexpensive motels and spending much of his free time poring over maps and the poem. In 2014, he quit his job as a retail salesman and moved to Colorado because of its proximity to the search area. Alone in his apartment just northwest of Denver, Bilyeu, six feet tall with gray stubble and a high arch of receding hair, would find himself imagining his future fortune.

The day Bilyeu and Leo shoved off, and for several days after, Martino left messages on Bilyeu's cell. "Randy always came back OK, which is stupid to assume now," Martino says. This time, Martino began to worry almost immediately. Nine days had passed since their last conversation, and there was no sign Bilyeu had returned from his adventure. Martino sent a Facebook message to Linda Bilyeu, Randy's first wife. He told her about Bilyeu's latest hunt and the trip to the river. Linda called the Santa Fe Police Department the next morning and filed a missing-person report. Based on information from Martino, search and rescue crews deployed to an area called Old Buckman Road. Within a few days, they found Bilyeu's Nissan: Inside the vehicle were a map, a bag of pretzels, and Bilyeu's hiking boots. A search helicopter flying over the river also discovered Bilyeu's raft on a small sandbar along the east bank, about seven miles from the launch point at Buckman. The raft was turned over and pulled toward a large shrub in a way that indicated careful consideration. Under the raft were the pump and both metal oars, one of which was snapped near its middle; the other was bent significantly. Just a few yards away stood Leo, in his now-dirty white sweater, emaciated and frightened, but alive. Snow and rising water had wiped out much of the beach, erasing whatever human traces might have existed a couple of weeks earlier. Nearby plants didn't appear to be disturbed. The Rio Grande wasn't particularly deep, but dive teams searched farther downriver, in deeper, muddier sections. A trail from the raft to the canyon rim led several hundred feet up a rock wall, a difficult climb for almost anyone, especially in wintry conditions.

"It's like he just vanished," Linda told me by phone from her home near Orlando. It was March, and about two months had passed since she reported her ex-husband missing. There still weren't any clues to his whereabouts. Linda had spent nearly every minute ruminating on the situation and helping to coordinate a cadre of volunteer searchers. "There's no way in hell I thought I'd be in the middle of something like this," she said, bewilderment in her voice. "I don't want to be in this place, but here I am."

Linda hoped Bilyeu would show up alive, perhaps in one of the caves in the national park, which had been home to Ancestral Puebloans nearly 1,000 years earlier. Police ruled out foul play in the disappearance, and there was no indication Bilyeu was suicidal. In one of her wilder theories, Linda wondered if her ex-husband found the riches and simply made himself disappear, perhaps to live a millionaire's life on some sunny beach in Mexico. "If we find him alive," she sometimes joked, "I'm going to kick his ass."

Regardless, she'd spent much of her winter marshaling more than 20 regular searchers who kept in contact with her. Some knew how to fly drones, some were experienced hikers, and some simply were familiar with the search area. Drone pilots regularly sent video to Linda for inspection, and she studied each frame. Discarded trash bags in the rough form of a body, a plastic laundry detergent bottle, and old clothes left in the wilderness had gotten her attention many times. "You start seeing shadows and think, 'Is that him there? What about there?'" She posted the videos on a private Facebook page dedicated to the search and asked for help.

That the ex-wife of a man who'd gone underprepared in search of a hidden chest of riches was now helping try to find him was not lost on anyone. "It seems kind of crazy," said Michelle Stoker, Bilyeu's 26-year-old daughter. "But Mom's naturally a take-charge person, so it was common sense that she'd be involved. She wants to do the right thing, and this is the right thing." Said Linda: "Randy might have done just about the stupidest thing imaginable, but we share children and grandchildren. If it weren't for them, I wouldn't be doing it."

Other theories abound, almost all of them involving the Rio Grande. Bilyeu slipped and fell into the river, where he hit his head, became unconscious, and drowned; Bilyeu walked into the river, his waders became flooded, he couldn't get back to land, and he drowned; Bilyeu unknowingly stepped into a fast-moving stretch of the river, was swept under, and drowned. The Rio Grande dumps into Cochiti Lake, inside the Cochiti Pueblo Reservation eight miles south of the raft's location, but tribal authorities hadn't found anything in their searches. Perhaps it was still too cold, searchers speculated. Bodies in frigid water tend to stay low, like rocks, and pop up when they warm. Several weeks passed. Newspaper stories were written about the search. Missing-person fliers were posted near the river. Spring came, and the irony was inescapable: Randy Bilyeu should have been beginning his search. Now, instead, everyone was looking for him.

Before Bilyeu's call to Martino in early January, there was little in Bilyeu's life to suggest he was prepared to join the ranks of Long John Silver and Jim Hawkins as a swashbuckling fortune hunter. A grandfather to two young girls, Bilyeu spent much of his life ensconced in the mundane trappings of a middle-class, middle-age existence. He enjoyed playing softball and coaching hockey. A former food-services manager—he met Linda when the two worked at Hofstra University's campus on Long Island; they married in 1984 and moved to Florida two years later—he had recently quit a job as a salesman in Broomfield. He dated in Colorado, but not seriously. He maintained relationships with his former wives. He visited his children in Florida.

But Bilyeu was bored. His savings were dwindling. At his age, he imagined the rest of his work life would be a series of low-paying, dead-end jobs. Searching for something potentially worth millions of dollars seemed as though it could be the perfect solution to his problems.

He was not a religious man, but communing with nature had given Bilyeu a sense of peace and belonging, a higher purpose. He'd moved from Florida to Georgia to care for his aging parents, and when his father died in 2012, Bilyeu came to miss the man's presence in his life—the phone calls, the simple conversations. "He talked a lot about Dad," Leibold, Bilyeu's sister, said. "He'd say to me, 'Can you believe it's been a year since he died? Can you believe it's been two years? When I'm 60, Dad would have been 100.' Randy would go into the mountains to clear his mind, and I think that helped him." On his searches, Bilyeu sent texts to his sister and his daughters, giving rough details of his locations. He shot photos of waterfalls, of distant mesas. His only companion was Leo, whom Bilyeu brought on his adventures after the two moved to Colorado. He featured the animal in his many photographs. There's Leo at Capulin Volcano National Monument in Northern New Mexico. There's Leo in Bilyeu's arms, the pair hoofing across yet another trail. In his pictures, Bilyeu—often in a blue shirt with his gray hair combed back—is almost always smiling. He had come to call himself WhiteBeard. Leo was SpongeDog, a play on SpongeBob SquarePants.

Bilyeu, like many of the other treasure hunters, revered Fenn. A former fighter pilot with a high school education who'd been shot down twice in Vietnam, Fenn had survived kidney cancer and—despite an initially limited knowledge of art—became one of the most prosperous art and artifacts dealers in the Southwest, befriending the likes of Ralph Lauren and Jacqueline Kennedy Onassis. In books, the native Texan wrote passionately about the outdoors and his relationship with his own father, a former school principal who died by suicide in 1987 after being diagnosed with pancreatic cancer. To Bilyeu, Fenn exuded masculinity: brains, brawn, and most of all, the courage to believe he could shoulder his way into any situation and succeed. Fenn's life story was intoxicating. Bilyeu read his autobiography several times. For someone so enamored with Fenn and his treasure, it's likely he'd memorized the poem:

As I have gone alone in there
And with my treasures bold,
I can keep my secret where,
And hint of riches new and old.

Begin it where warm waters halt
And take it in the canyon down,
not far, but too far to walk.
Put in below the home of Brown.

From there it's no place for the meek,
The end is ever drawing nigh;
There'll be no paddle up your creek,
Just heavy loads and water high.

If you've been wise and found the blaze,
Look quickly down, your quest to cease,
But tarry scant with marvel gaze,
Just take the chest and go in peace.

So why is it that I must go
And leave my trove for all to seek?
The answer I already know,
I've done it tired, and now I'm weak.

So hear me all and listen good,
Your effort will be worth the cold.
If you are brave and in the wood
I give you title to the gold.

At some point, Bilyeu sent Fenn an email explaining his "theory as a deep-thinking/logical treasure hunter," Bilyeu told Dal Neitzel, the curator of dalneitzel.com, a Fenn site that receives thousands of visitors

daily. Bilyeu never posted publicly because he was afraid he'd acciden-
tally give out a clue to his search area. Though Fenn never replied to
Bilyeu's email, the two met briefly at a September book signing in Santa
Fe, where the pair took a photo together and Fenn gave Leo a dog biscuit.

Bilyeu spent time getting to know other hunters, too. "He told me
he was a full-time searcher, that this was his life," Neitzel said several
months after Bilyeu's disappearance. "You could tell he'd done his research. He spoke in generalities, but we talked about the Rio Grande.
Randy really believed that's where the treasure was." Bilyeu didn't strike
Neitzel as someone who'd gotten carried away with the search. "People
have gone bankrupt over this," Neitzel said. "They've gotten divorced.
For some people, it becomes too much. They go out of control. Randy
was so nice, really mild-mannered. A smart guy. He had that cute dog.
Maybe Randy was getting gold fever."

Bilyeu sent the photo of him with Fenn to his sister. Months passed.
Maybe it was old age creeping in, maybe he was getting bolder. In talks
with his friend Martino, he began to pepper search stories with tales of
near misses—of both the treasure and safety varieties. He'd fallen too
many times to count. He'd injured his back. During a climb, he tripped
and sprained his knee. Yet he also felt closer than ever to solving the
poem's riddle.

By early fall 2015, Bilyeu's sister and daughters were getting fewer
messages regarding his whereabouts; they had no idea how many trips
he now was making. They worried about what the hunt was doing to him,
both physically and psychologically. "It's all Randy could talk about,"
Martino says. "It was treasure, treasure, treasure." During one search
in New Mexico, Bilyeu told his daughters, he'd experienced shortness
of breath. He'd gotten dizzy and light-headed. Still, he shrugged off
doubts about his health and chalked the episode up to dehydration. "It
got to the point where you worried whether he'd be coming back," his
daughter Stoker said. "He felt like he needed to be out there. It seemed
to be getting riskier and riskier."

Bilyeu spent some of his savings on his trips, on gear and maps. He
purchased a GPS device. He sometimes slept in his vehicle to save money, counting the hours before he could hunt again. He spent Christmas
Day 2015 in New Mexico with Leo atop a bluff in Bandelier. Below
him was the Rio Grande. He scouted the area—search teams now think

Bilyeu was trying to get to a waterfall near Frijoles Canyon—once he realized the river was his best access point. He called his sister and wished her a merry Christmas.

Bilyeu made notes in black marker on his Bandelier map. Each corresponded to a clue in Fenn's poem. The area near Pajarito Mountain—northwest of the Rio Grande—burned in a wildfire years ago and was marked "Fire 'Blaze.'??" Bilyeu wrote "Quest" above that. To the southwest of Frijoles he wrote the word "Sunsets" and drew an image that looked like the sun on New Mexico's state flag. Farther southeast, near the east bank of the Rio Grande, he drew four X's and a dotted line. He wrote the letter E and circled it. Next to that, he wrote the initials "H.O.B.": Home of Brown.

One cool, sunny morning in mid-April, I met Linda and Stoker at the Santa Fe Plaza. Bilyeu had been missing for 101 days, and it seemed as though he might never be found. Linda, who is petite, with curly black hair and broad features, was on the front page of the local newspaper that day. In the story, she declared that she didn't think Forrest Fenn's treasure existed.

The article was her chance, she said, to drum up interest in the search while also poking Fenn, whom she indirectly blamed for this situation. Initially the two had cordial conversations via email, but those quickly devolved. Linda attacked Fenn on her personal blog for not disclosing the cache's location—if it even existed—which she thought could help searchers. She also accused Fenn of putting the many hunters' lives at risk.

Fenn's supporters shot back online. They accused her of blackballing well-intentioned treasure hunters from the search for her ex-husband and of misunderstanding Fenn. Fenn's allies thought of Linda as an attention-hungry opportunist, a person overrun with emotion who could never understand the deeper meanings of the hunt. Linda thought Fenn's searchers were like a cult, and she cast Fenn as an aging charlatan desperate to create a legacy. "These people are disgusting," Linda told me. "Someone's missing out there, and all they can talk about is some stupid treasure that doesn't exist."

It was Linda's first time in New Mexico and she wanted to get a feel for the place her ex had been so connected to. She'd already seen the Motel 6 and the Big Five Sporting Goods where Bilyeu purchased his raft the day before he went missing. They visited Leo, who was living a quiet, happy existence with an adoptive family. Linda and Stoker planned to sleep at least one night at a casino resort outside the city where Bilyeu had once stayed.

A prolific blogger even before Bilyeu's disappearance, Linda was gathering scenes and other information for a book she planned to write and self-publish about the search for Bilyeu. It would be her second time detailing a life-altering event: Less than a year earlier, she had written about her second husband, Dave Ligler, and his seven-year battle with prostate cancer (he died in July 2015). She hadn't had much time to grieve her husband's death when she was thrown into another difficult situation. Like many writers, she found recording her experiences was the best way for her to make sense of her current life. She billed her visit to Santa Fe as a way to meet the searchers in person; it was also Linda and Stoker's opportunity to look beyond maps and drone video and understand the circumstances under which Bilyeu had gone missing.

After visiting the plaza, Linda and Stoker drove to a strip-mall cafe down the street from where Bilyeu spent his last night in Santa Fe. Searchers filed in, hugged their hellos, and sat around several tables where they offered their latest information to Linda. Because she didn't know the searchers by appearance, Linda gave each a name tag. Linda scribbled her name in black marker with a little sun drawn just below it. Stoker added a smiley face and "#TeamRandy" to hers.

Among those who'd grown close to Linda was Peter Dickson, a British physicist and former Cambridge professor who'd come to New Mexico 20 years earlier to take his dream job running a research group at Los Alamos National Laboratory. An avid hiker and a volunteer with New Mexico Search and Rescue, he often spent weekends hiking across the mountains and the desert. Nattily dressed in a tan blazer with his gray hair pushed forward, he injected a sense of calm, helpful for a search like this.

Dickson pulled out a small laptop computer and placed it on a wooden table so Linda and Stoker could see it. A couple of other searchers huddled around. It was an aerial view of the initial search site. The Rio Grande meanders through a reddish-brown canyon. Dickson explained that the deeper Bilyeu ventured along the Rio, the steeper the canyon walls became. In some places, he said, the river is 1,000 feet below the rim. He pulled up a series of photos to emphasize the point.

"See?" he said. "Higher and higher."

Linda shook her head.

"You're met with a wall of Mother Nature," another searcher said.

A photo taken from one of the drones included the beach where the raft had been found. Because the raft was too heavy to carry out of the steep canyon, Dickson moved it closer to the rock wall to keep it from getting swept downriver. The pump was still there. One of the searchers had inflated the raft a couple of weeks earlier to see if it still held air. It did. The oars were gone, taken by a treasure hunter from Colorado.

"That's it, right there," Dickson said and pointed to the raft, which appeared as a gray dot. Stoker leaned in. She managed only a small "Wow."

Canyon and sagebrush extended to the edges of Dickson's computer screen. He bit his lower lip. "Yeah, so . . ." he said, his words trailing off. He pulled away from the table and put his wrists up, in a helpless posture.

"That's a lot of land," Stoker said, staring at the photo.

"It's vast," Dickson said.

Stoker and Linda wanted to see it for themselves. The next morning, Bob Rodgers—the head of New Mexico Search and Rescue—and Alex Viechec, a private-plane pilot who'd become one of Linda's most trusted searchers, escorted the pair to an overlook above the Rio Grande where the women could see the imposing landscape. Viechec—tall and thin with thick-rimmed black glasses and a lopsided grin—thought it would be a helpful visualization tool, especially since Linda and Stoker refused to visit the boat launch off Old Buckman Road. No one pressed them.

The river was at least 500 feet below White Rock Overlook. In the distance, to the left and across the Rio Grande, Old Buckman Road appeared like a ribbon of brown leading to the water. The temperature was below 50 degrees at the overlook, but it felt much colder. Clouds were low and gray, and the river looked like glass. Green shrubs clustered atop the Bandelier outback, wild grass and large rocks protruding from nearly every square inch. Light snow fell on the Jemez Mountains in the distance. Viechec took a few photos with his camera and then said, "When Randy left that morning, the weather would have felt a little like this." Linda wrapped her arms around her waist. Stoker threw a red-and-blue scarf around her neck.

"Randy would have been four or five miles up from there," Rodgers said, pointing to the place where the Rio Grande curved and disappeared to their right. From below, the canyon rim would have looked massive to him. "Pull that canyon face up to the river, and that's what you'd be looking at," he said. "Very steep."

"I can't believe he even made it that far," Stoker said.

Linda eventually made her way to Rodgers' search-and-rescue vehicle. Rodgers loaded a digital map of the area on his computer that showed a series of blue blobs, small lakes of cell phone service that would have been available to Bilyeu, had he made it up to the canyon's rim. Through cell phone forensics, authorities had discovered that Bilyeu's phone made contact with several towers during his scouting trip atop the canyon in late December. The next time, however, there were no such locators. Even if Bilyeu managed to turn on his phone, cell coverage on the river would have been virtually nonexistent. Rodgers again pointed out the canyon walls. Linda exhaled deeply, then covered her face.

Stoker took some photos near the overlook and called her husband. She spent a few minutes on her phone and then hung up. She stared at the water. Wind blew her long hair into her mouth. Viechec watched with a puzzled look.

"What do you think?" he finally asked.

"It's overwhelming," Stoker said. She paused for a moment. "It makes me sad he was so anxious to search this land for something that only might be there. I don't get this treasure thing. I don't think I'll ever get it."

Linda and Stoker weren't the first from Bilyeu's family to visit New Mexico looking for answers. In late January, Kathy Leibold arrived from Texas with her son and his fiancée. She intended to speak to Santa Fe police and to Rodgers and then retrace some of her brother's last moments in town. She also hoped to meet Forrest Fenn.

Fenn arranged a meeting at Downtown Subscription, a cafe several blocks off the Santa Fe Plaza. Just the previous week, he'd chartered a helicopter to fly over the Rio Grande with a television crew and some treasure hunters. Leibold says she had mixed feelings: She thought Fenn's trip might actually help find her brother, but she also worried Fenn was using her brother's disappearance to add even more intrigue to his mythos.

The meeting lasted 90 minutes. "He started out by telling us how sorry he was that Randy was missing," Leibold says. "He explained a little bit how he and his treasure hunters were looking for Randy and that he'd taken the helicopter flight. At that point, we knew he was there to plead his case." Leibold expected that from Fenn, but she didn't expect what she says happened next. After describing the rugged terrain near where the raft was discovered, Fenn said he didn't want anyone to find Bilyeu's body. He didn't want to know how one of his treasure hunters died, didn't want to know if Bilyeu suffered—if he knew his end was coming. "It was so bizarre," Leibold said. "My mouth dropped." Fenn, apparently unaware he'd offended the missing man's sister, continued talking. "He said Randy's bones probably wouldn't be found for 100 years," Leibold remembers.

She composed herself. "We thought he needed to call off the search and just tell people where the treasure is and be done with it," she told me. "But I know people had invested a lot of time and energy." Leibold said Fenn seemed uninterested in confiding the location of his treasure to anyone. In fact, his wife didn't even know. The hunt, he said, would continue long after his own death—possibly for decades, or even centuries. How he reached that number, Leibold didn't care. She was beyond annoyed. "I told him we needed to bring Randy home," she recalls. "I told him that Randy is our treasure hunt. He's our treasure, and we want him home."

By then, Fenn seemed to be done with the conversation. He told the three they should head home because there was nothing they could do to help in Santa Fe. He gave each of them a hug. "We left that coffeeshop feeling even worse than when we walked in," Leibold says. On the drive back to Texas, she began writing notes from the meeting. She was trying to make sense of the conversation she'd just had. Leibold read her words, line by line, over and over again. "The more I read, the weirder it sounded," she says. "I was like, Who does this guy think he is?"

Forrest Fenn was waiting at his front door when I pulled up the driveway to his compound off the Old Santa Fe Trail. He was slightly hunched at the shoulders but otherwise looked trim and healthy. He had long, hawk-like features, and his eyes appeared to be in a permanent squint, as if he were staring into an eternal sunset. His thinning white hair was swept from left to right and covered the back part of his ears. He wore a blue checkered button-down shirt tucked into baggy blue jeans held up with a belt secured with a turquoise buckle. On his feet were off-white leather slippers.

His house was low-slung with lots of right angles, in the way of most everything else in Santa Fe. The brown adobe looked like freshly dried mud in the morning light. Fenn introduced himself and directed me to his office off the foyer.

The room was large but intimate, with a kiva fireplace and hewn logs that ran across the ceiling. Artifacts took up virtually every inch of the office. Ten headdresses hung over a couch. Hopi kachina dolls filled a table. On a far wall were three peace pipes, a leather belt, moccasins, necklaces, and hatchets. Several knives were stored in elaborately beaded sheaths. On Fenn's desk was a model of the Air Force F-100 jet he flew in Vietnam. Near that was a small treasure chest filled with 800 $1 coins.

The Bureau of Land Management raided Fenn's home in 2009 as part of a broad federal sting meant to track down illegally obtained Native American artifacts. After the raid, a U.S. attorney agreed to drop the case if Fenn returned a basket, a kachina dance mask, and a sun-dance skull. Fenn agreed not to sue the federal government for falsifying a warrant. (One rumor, which Fenn denies, is that he set up his treasure hunt as revenge to get people to dig up federal land.)

Despite all this, Fenn remains a local celebrity, an active member of the community who is known around town for his generosity and peculiarities. He has cast 30 bronze bells and hidden eight of them in the mountains and desert around Santa Fe. On one of them, he printed the legend, "If you should ever think of me, a thousand years from now, please ring my bell so I will know." His former gallery—he sold it in the late 1980s—maintains an almost mythic place in the lore of modern Santa Fe. Once a destination for the wealthy and well educated, Fenn's former shop included rare black African parrots and two alligators, which lived in a pool out back. After publishing *The Thrill of the Chase*, he gave all the copies to a local bookstore to sell and doesn't collect money on the proceeds.

Fenn has always been something of an agitator, a plays-by-his-own-rules rebel who says and does curious things. After being shot down in 1968 during a mission in Vietnam, Fenn briefly considered living off the land; instead, he alerted the Air Force and was rescued. Today, he brings underprivileged children to the many ancient Native American sites he owns, where he and archaeologists teach them to dig for artifacts. Dozens of pots and hundreds of shards and other spoils fill a small room off his garage.

It was this outlaw spirit that moved him, after his cancer diagnosis in 1988, to plan his great challenge. The idea, at first, was for then 58-year-old Fenn to march out into the Rockies somewhere, hide the treasure, and in true Old West fashion, die next to it. He bought the 12th-century chest for $25,000 and began to fill it. A prewritten poem would give hints to the site, where searchers also would find, presumably, Fenn's bleached bones.

Of course, he lived. Shortly after surgery to remove his affected right kidney, Fenn was declared cancer-free in 1993, and the idea of the treasure floated to the back of his mind. More than a decade passed before he revived the plan as a way, he says, to get people off their couches and into the wilderness with their families. He was 80 years old by then and would live to see the search—or at least its beginnings. He finished writing his poem. (He says he looked up each noun in the dictionary to make sure there wouldn't be confusion about the words' meanings.) He invited a friend to photograph the chest, filled with its booty, and then went off to hide it.

As he sat on his office couch on that morning, his elderly, overweight dachshund at his side, Fenn admitted the hunt always worried him. "I've wondered about the worst-case scenario," he said. "People are going to get lost, I know that." He says he never considered someone might die.

Since Bilyeu's disappearance earlier this year, Fenn has been bombarded with media requests to talk about the treasure. In the press, at least, he avoided discussing the nastier details of his fallout with Linda, though it was clear he was keenly aware of what she'd written about him. "Linda said on her blog that the family is devastated, but when Randy disappeared, she said he wasn't the sharpest tool in the shed," Fenn said, recalling a statement Linda once made. "Now, all of a sudden, she's heartbroken? There's a lot going on here that I don't understand. If I'm to blame because Randy was searching for the treasure and got lost, then who's to blame when a hunter gets lost in the woods?" he said, repeating an example he'd previously used with his supporters. "If someone drowns in a swimming pool, should we drain the pool? There's been a lot of PR about Randy missing, but I'm not even sure he's missing. You know, he's not missing if he knows where he is." Fenn laughed.

At the very least, Fenn seemed perturbed at the thought of Bilyeu and his dog going onto the Rio Grande in a sporting-goods-store raft with no training and in the dead of winter. "I've said that people should not search in the winter," Fenn said. In the past, he also said the treasure isn't in a dangerous place. He said he made two trips from his vehicle in one afternoon—the first to carry the chest, the second to deliver the contents. "I don't want anybody searching where an 80-year-old man couldn't have made two trips," he said. "Randy's raft was very far from his car. Randy was going to go down the river, somehow get back, and he was going to do that twice? The chest is 42 pounds. What was his exit plan?"

That, he said, is just the beginning of his disappointment with Bilyeu's strategy. "The treasure is in the Rocky Mountains, at least eight and a quarter miles north of the north city limits of Santa Fe," Fenn said. "Frijoles Canyon is not in the Rocky Mountains. Why was he looking in a place that wasn't in the designated search area?" To Fenn, Bilyeu's poorly organized plan, and the area he decided to search, "point to the fact that maybe he didn't care. Maybe he wanted to disappear."

Fenn continued: "In the back of my mind I tell myself that, two years from now, Randy's going to say, 'I'm not lost. What's the big deal? I decided I wanted to go to Cuernavaca with a girlfriend and sip tequila.' And what's wrong with that? I spent nine hours in a helicopter flying up and down where Randy theoretically put a boat in the Rio Grande. The water is pretty much shallow. You can walk across it nearly any place. There are two snags—logs and such—in there that would have caught him. We searched those. If Randy was in the water, we would have found him. The canyon where he thought the treasure was, we searched that at great length too."

There is, however, one clue Fenn can't solve: Leo. "The dog is the only mystery," Fenn said. Even the most outrageous theories on Bilyeu's disappearance cannot fathom why he'd leave his beloved dog to die in the wild. Fenn remembered Leo from the September book signing and sensed how much the animal meant to Bilyeu.

After Leo was found along the river in mid-January, he was taken to the Santa Fe Animal Shelter & Humane Society. Fenn heard about it and went over to see the dog. At the shelter's office, Fenn and Leo were reintroduced. "He must have lost 25 percent of his body weight," Fenn said. Fenn bent over to get a better look at the animal, perhaps the only creature to know Bilyeu's fate. He reached out a hand to scratch the dog. Leo snapped at him. "He wanted to kill me," Fenn says. "That dog wanted no part of me."

In late April, a few days after she returned home to Florida, Linda received an anonymous email with an attachment. It was a photo taken at Bandelier National Monument. On the far right was a waterfall that spilled on the rocks below. The photo was taken from a distance to show off the hillside that rose from right to left, at roughly a 45-degree angle. Within the gray rocks, there was a blue backpack. Linda immediately called Bob Rodgers.

A group of Bandelier National Monument rangers organized at the site—a stretch of dangerous backcountry off-limits to hikers that had previously gone unsearched. The backpack was retrieved (Santa Fe Police did not return several calls asking for comment), and whatever was inside sparked a daylong search. Over the course of several hours, nothing else was discovered.

Even as the new search was ongoing, Linda had become skeptical of the photograph. It was common knowledge by now that Bilyeu probably carried a backpack on his trip; the rest of the stuff—like maps and whatever else might have been inside it—could have easily been replicated to make it look like it belonged to her ex-husband. It wasn't just her, either. Other searchers—including treasure hunters—had come to believe the backpack was planted as a macabre joke. "He's not over there. I just know it," Linda said, referring to the waterfall photo. She still hadn't given up that her ex-husband might be alive, but she acknowledged the chance was remote.

She wrote an editorial in the *Santa Fe New Mexican* that was published on May 28. It was a week before Fennboree III, a gathering of Fenn treasure hunters who celebrate Fenn's life and those who go in search of his riches. "Will Randy be respected by his peers?" Linda wrote. "Or will his name be pushed aside? Surely Forrest Fenn didn't forget about Randy being missing, and his family and volunteer searchers are still looking for him five months later." Linda hoped the other treasure hunters would remember one of their own.

They did. On June 4, more than 100 treasure hunters met at Hyde Memorial State Park, 15 miles outside downtown Santa Fe. They gathered under a log shelter and laid cakes and cookies and chips on picnic tables. Someone lit a charcoal grill.

The group was older and split equally between men and women. There was the disabled former Army lieutenant from Kentucky who said Fenn's hunt got him active again. There was the woman from Albuquerque who called Fenn the day she was laid off from her job and declared she was now dedicating her life to the search. There was the retired farmer from Missouri who had everything but sold it all so he could move to New Mexico. "I've never been happier," he said. He produced a box of photos, a collection of the places he'd been since he'd taken up the search, and passed them around.

Sacha Johnston, a real estate agent and treasure hunter from Albuquerque, set up at a picnic table in front of a weathered brick fireplace along one edge of the shelter. As one of the coordinators of Fennboree III, she'd brought prizes: four special-edition maps of the four-state search area, coffee cups with the Fenn map, Fenn Frisbees, and small backpacks emblazoned with "Fennboree 2016." To win, hunters would have to correctly answer questions about Fenn's life, such as the name of his high school Spanish teacher (Mrs. Ford) or how many gold coins are in the chest (256).

The picnic table quickly turned into a Fenn shrine. Someone built a mini treasure chest adorned with figures that included a leprechaun, Snoopy, and a green plastic Army man. There were photos from Fenn's September book signing, a necklace made of bottle caps, and a birth announcement from an absent hunter declaring she'd named her newborn son Forrest.

Next to the announcement was a framed photograph of Bilyeu, glasses atop his head, smiling widely for the camera. Leo was tucked under one of his arms. People came by to look at the photo or drop a dollar into an adjacent box for donations to the Santa Fe animal shelter. Someone set a rock atop it that looked like a horseshoe.

"Randy's brought us all closer," said Neitzel, the website curator who'd met Bilyeu at the book signing. "His disappearance has gotten more people to think about safety and how they need a plan if things start to go wrong. He made everyone take a step back."

Fenn arrived an hour into the festivities. He chatted with the long line of people who came to shake his hand or to offer him a gift or to share an idea on where his valuables might be hidden. He smiled and patted a few of them on the back.

After the food was served, Johnston stood in front of the picnic table and asked for everyone's attention. The people here knew about Randy Bilyeu's disappearance, she began. He had been one of them, and they were a family. They should always remember him. The people stood by quietly; some nodded. Johnston asked for a moment, a reflection, a prayer, a positive thought thrown into the universe.

Fenn stood off to the side. His white cowboy hat atop his head, he placed his hands in his pockets. He bowed and stared at his shoes. Then, finally, he closed his eyes.

EPILOGUE

Six weeks after Fennboree III, in mid-July, a body was discovered along the banks of the Rio Grande, just south of where Bilyeu launched his raft with Leo. Linda's searchers had been in the area—a place noteworthy for its steep incline and heavy vegetation—several times before, but it was a work crew from the U.S. Army Corps of Engineers who came across the decomposing remains hidden amid a tangle of branches and leaves. Waders were on the body's feet. The crew also found keys to a Nissan Murano and a cell phone matching Bilyeu's nearby.

The New Mexico State Police were called, and the body was removed the next day and delivered to the state's Office of the Medical Investigator. Linda was notified and kept vigil as she waited for confirmation. Friends began posting encouraging messages on the Search For Randy Bilyeu Facebook page: *You're in our thoughts*, they told Linda. *Stay strong.* "This is harder than I thought it would be," she told me on July 21. "I'm trying to hold it together." Her voice cracked.

Forrest Fenn emailed me shortly after the body was discovered. "They are analyzing the bones to see if it's Randy," he wrote. "Hope not." Bilyeu's dental records finally arrived from Georgia. Kathy received the family's first call on July 26. She phoned Linda.

It's him.

Linda had been expecting the call for nearly two weeks, but she still had to catch herself. Her daughters were nearby and saw the pained look on their mother's face. Linda thanked her former sister-in-law and hung up. She reached for her daughters and granddaughters, and the five of them hugged. Then they prayed. They agreed they would move on with their lives, that they would support one another. Linda and the family went out for dinner, and Linda toasted her ex with a Budweiser.

She called Bob Rodgers, from search and rescue, and delivered the news. Then she emailed me, and I reached out to Fenn one final time. "I am deeply saddened that Randy did not make it out of the Rio Grande canyon," he wrote in an email. "My prayers are with his family and friends."

Befitting the past six months of strangeness, Linda and her children had spent the afternoon of July 26, the day the call came, scattering her second husband's cremated remains. As she was finally letting go of one man, another had come back into her life. And Bilyeu will hang on for a while longer. Santa Fe Police consider the investigation into Bilyeu's death open and are awaiting results from the medical investigator's office on the cause. A police spokesman said in late July that there's no timetable on when the case might be closed.

—August 2016

3.
Changing Nature
by Luc Hatlestad

They were too late; he could feel it. Three hours into the frantic search for his missing friend, 30-year-old Chris Klingelheber and a specialist from the Alpine Rescue Team were huffing up a mountain some 3,000 feet above the flickering lights in the town of Empire. As their head-lamp beams darted about in the winter storm on that March night in 2006, Klingelheber's stomach grew queasier with every passing moment, as he became more and more convinced of what they would find.

Klingelheber shouldn't have been there. Although he had survival training, he wasn't an EMT or rescue specialist, meaning he was a le-gal liability for Alpine. But down in the parking lot near the trailhead, he'd successfully lobbied the apprehensive authorities. He's obviously up there, Klingelheber argued, pointing to the abandoned car of his friend, J.T. I know the trail, I know how he thinks, and I know what I'm doing. As the snow blew in and the hour grew late, there was talk, undeniably sensible, of suspending the search until morning. But Klingelheber and J.T.'s famous father, who had rushed to the scene, insisted that the search continue, and the Alpine officials acquiesced.

The Alpine snowmobiles had sunk into the unpacked powder and were rendered useless, so Klingelheber and two Alpine professionals had set off on foot. One dropped out from fatigue, leaving Klingelheber and the remaining specialist as the "team" that forged into the stinging snow and numbing wind. They were wheezing more than breathing, trying to ignore the pounding in their chests. Klingelheber's intimate familiarity with the terrain made the trek slightly less arduous. Ironically, it was J.T. who'd shown him the way. Countless times, Klingelheber had followed his charismatic friend up this mountain. At the top they'd pause and grab a bite while drinking in the view, before buckling into their planks and shredding the slopes back to their cars. This place was their escape from parents and girlfriends and droning, post-college jobs, a refuge where they could ignore all that tedium and self-doubt. For J.T.—who'd skied and hiked all corners of Colorado along with many spectacular spots around the world—this was his favorite place of all.

Suddenly, Klingelheber stumbled over J.T.'s splayed-out skis. His backcountry experience told him they'd been haphazardly discarded, and his heart sank. He and the other rescuer scrambled the last 600 vertical feet to the spot—a runway of snow-blanketed rock that, during those joyful past excursions, seemed to shoot off into infinity and possibility. The spot, J.T.'s spot, was a picture of Colorado magnificence, as beautiful, perhaps, as any photograph ever shot by his father.

Klingelheber peered over the crest and saw his friend. Lying there in his ski gear, J.T. looked not so different than many times before, back when they were housemates, crashed out after a long day of skiing or a long night of drinking. Back then he could be nudged awake with a simple, "Dude, let's go." This time, though, Klingelheber could see that J.T. wouldn't be rubbing the night from his eyes. His friend's mouth and nose were rimed over with frost; a halo of blood soaked the snow around 26-year-old J.T. Fielder's corpse.

On an otherwise empty, beige wall of a corporate building, a dozen photographs, all about four feet by five feet, uniformly hang in queue. In one of the pictures is a mountaintop; in the foreground a serene lake bathes in a soft orange glow as pink clouds float overhead. Greenery sprouts along the edge of the water, and the lake's surface reflects a rust-colored, rocky expanse stretching to a snow-dusted peak. John Fielder waited for hours in the San Juan Mountains of southwestern Colorado to get that shot, his patience finally rewarded with Fielder's favorite moment of light: a magical orange-pink alpenglow that was a small miracle of convergence he hadn't seen before and hasn't seen since.

It's February 2009, and John Fielder, Colorado's best-known photographer and one of the state's most recognized name brands, is showing off his work inside the closest thing there is to a John Fielder museum: the 12-story, football-shaped headquarters of RE/MAX International Inc. at I-25 and Belleview, across a suburban parking lot from a Paradise Bakery. To those who think they know Fielder, a mega-Realtor's headquarters is an odd place for this collection. After all, for more than 30 years Fielder has photographed Colorado's outdoors, particularly the pure, undeveloped outdoors, forever preserving—at least on film—the rugged, natural Colorado, and thereby a Colorado spirit that it would be a crime to subdivide and sell.

To those who really know Fielder, the RE/MAX display makes absolute sense. For as much as Fielder is a photographer and an environmentalist, he's equal parts showman and capitalist, a modern-day Thoreau meets Warhol, with a camera. He scours business pages for news of firms relocating to the state or building new space. He writes to executives, pitching his photos to hang around the office. No deal is too big or too small—he recently bartered his photos in exchange for $30,000 worth of knee surgery. And, despite his progressive leanings, among his clients is San Diego-based General Atomics, run by Coloradan Neal Blue, maker of the Predator UAS series pilotless warplanes that, in Fielder's words, "spy on and kill human beings."

While most of Fielder's corporate clients may buy 10 or 15 prints, RE/MAX purchased more than 500 of them, and on this February morning Fielder has agreed to give me a tour. The self-promoter is self-conscious, apologizing for blotchy skin, the byproduct of a preventive skin cancer treatment. The cosmetic setback doesn't get in the way of his flirting with the three receptionists. "RE/MAX always puts the best-looking women up front," he says to them with a swagger. "Don't forget to keep buying my books, ladies." Although Fielder claims to be most comfortable alone, above the treetops, you'd never know it from his deft public persona.

The merger of art and commerce has served Fielder well. He published the best-selling book in state history, *Colorado 1870-2000*, and he's sold more than two million books overall, plus countless calendars and picture collections. Among his fans are Mexican billionaire Carlos Slim Helu— once the world's richest man—and the late publishing magnate Malcolm

Forbes. Political power brokers have used Fielder's work to promote environmental issues. His book *Colorado: Our Wilderness Future* launched his activist career and helped promote the Colorado Wilderness Act of 1993. When former U.S. Senator and now Secretary of the Interior Ken Salazar wants to remind himself what he's protecting, he can turn to the Fielder book he keeps in his office.

The photographer has become as famous as his photographs. In 2007, the Colorado Film Commission inducted Fielder into its hall of fame, one of innumerable awards and recognitions. Governor Bill Ritter presented the accolade, saying, "God made what we see in this beautiful state, but it takes artists like John Fielder to capture the magical images." Fielder's forthcoming book, *Ranches of Colorado*, due out in October, features photos of the state's working ranches and essays on their importance to our ecosystem. In his methodical way, Fielder spent almost three years on the project and will spend months more promoting it and the environmental concerns that course through the words and images. His books, once filled with platitudes about Colorado's beauty, have evolved into something more urgent: Here's the crisis, and here's how we can fix it.

"The more habitats we protect, the more biodiversity we nurture, the greater the chance we have to preserve them," he says with a nod toward the tidy row of scenes on the RE/MAX wall. Fielder stands 6 feet 3 inches; a bird's nest of fleecy white hair circles his balding crown. His bold, peaked brows hover over olive-colored eyes flecked with gold, eyes that have seen as much tragedy as they have natural wonder—humbling experiences that have not only changed Fielder's photographs but also profoundly altered the man himself.

Viewed individually, each of the RE/MAX photos is spectacular. The scenes of rushing streams, electrically contrasting autumnal colors, and stark, subtle winter hues; reflection shots, employing his savvy use of water—all harness an arresting power that once lured a young Fielder from North Carolina to Colorado. Yet taking in the photos one after another, as they hang on the wall, the pictures start to blur numbly together. Here's a photograph of the autumn sun glinting through a thicket of aspen trees. Next comes a shot of a regally purple columbine blooming from a crevice between lichen-covered rocks. And here's an army of leafy trees set against the backdrop of distant snowy peaks. Ansel Adams, one of Fielder's role models, famously said, "A photograph is usually looked at; seldom looked into." When one looks into Fielder's collection and sees so much remote nature and hollow isolation, it's hard not to wonder how he feels about people. "People?" he says with mock indignation. "I hate people."

In the winter of 2005, Fielder and three companions, including a childhood friend, his budding activist protégé Aron Ralston, and his son J.T., skied to the Goodwin-Greene Hut near Aspen Mountain, one of the more remote in Colorado, for a photo shoot. Fielder meticulously designs his trips, studying topographic maps to gauge how and when light might hit and triangulating where he must be. He avoids most overshot spots, preferring to schlep his 65-pound camera and packs of gear into areas less traveled, if ever traveled. With his young "Sherpas"—his homage to the hearty Nepalese people who assist Himalayan ascents—and a few llamas, he navigates trails, creeks, ponds, and peaks. He prefers his assistants young because, as he puts it, "they can carry a lot of weight, don't complain much, and are fun to be with." Though he's nearing 60, these youthful Sherpas likely have a tough time keeping up with him, not the other way around. Three months after having that partially bartered knee-replacement surgery, Fielder was back on the slopes, defying his doctor's orders.

He can describe most of his shots—some almost 30 years old—in striking detail. After hundreds of speeches and media appearances, pressing flesh and selling his work, Fielder says, he rarely remembers people but never forgets a place. "Once you're there, it's very sensuous, not just views but smells, tastes, touch, sounds," he says. "All that makes an impression, so when I pull out a photo from 30 years ago, I can remember how it affected all my senses in that moment."

His teams hike for miles, usually over unbroken trails, as his name gets him access to swaths of land not open to the public. While his assistants set up camp, he looks for distinctive bouquets of flowers or lichen on rocks, mentally planning for the following morning, when he'll be groping around in the darkness, waiting for the first light. Rising with one or two assistants to get into position, he sets up and waits patiently for the moment to be just right. If that moment never comes, he packs up and moves to another site. He shoots until midmorning, hikes with the group to the next camp, and shoots again around dusk.

Colorado 1870-2000 required Fielder's most grueling physical investment, and it brought him the greatest renown. He conceived it around 1997, when his promotional instincts suggested that "a 'millennium book' might attract a good deal of attention." He'd discovered William Henry Jackson, who'd photographed Colorado's landscape in the late 19th century. Fielder searched historical archives, weeding through Jackson's more than 20,000 shots to find 300 scenes for the book. Fielder had dived into environmental activism after the 1993 Colorado wilderness book—overcoming his reticence about public speaking and embracing the limelight—and he sought to replicate Jackson's shots exactly, a century later, to "reveal the gross transformation of the landscape for which we humans are responsible."

The book was the apotheosis of his growth as a naturalist, an evolution Fielder describes with poetic flourish in one of his frequent soliloquies about the Colorado wilderness. "As I touched more spots around the state, visited more remote, beautiful places, witnessed more unbelievable moments of light, smelled the sensuousness of decaying aspen leaves in the fall, drank pure water from snowmelt at 12,000 feet, like everybody else that gets invited into nature, I began to appreciate the miracle of creation and evolution," he says. "I realized that this place is special, unique, and may be the only one like it in the universe."

On that winter morning in 2005, however, as he and his group holed up at the Goodwin-Greene Hut, nature wasn't so inviting. The area is notorious avalanche territory, and Fielder had awakened before dawn planning to climb on skis two miles up a 35-degree grade to a 12,000-foot ridge to take sunrise pictures. But now he and his team confronted a thick blanket of fresh snow and whiteout conditions. Visibility was reduced to about a foot. Fielder concluded the shot wasn't worth it and led the group out, a treacherous task. He'd take 10 steps on his skis, stop, reorient himself with his compass, and take 10 more steps. He heard the distant cracking snow shelves, cannon-blast hints of an incipient avalanche. "I had to call upon a lifetime's worth of skiing and backcountry skills," Fielder says. "It was a deliberate process, but justifiably so. I had three people with me, including my only son."

It was 1975, the golden age of polyester, wide collars, and bell bottoms, and a young and awkward twentysomething named John Fielder joined the May-Daniels & Fisher department store chain in Denver. He came to Colorado with an accounting degree from Duke University to fulfill a childhood dream. In 1964, he'd taken a middle school class trip to the West from his North Carolina home; one look at the Rockies convinced him that this was where he wanted to spend his life. For a year, he'd tried his hand at real estate, as a broker for farms and ranches, but opted for a career in the department store business, like his father.

Fielder had the retail pedigree and went to work as a buyer. Back home, Fielder's dad had been an executive who oversaw the growth of one department store into a chain of 30, but old man Fielder played no role in getting his son the job with Denver's May-D&F. "I didn't want to work for him, and I had the business and aesthetic skills to break into it on my own," Fielder says. On his first day at May-D&F, Fielder peeked around a cubicle wall and saw Virginia Yonkers. "Gigi" was blonde and stunning, and he was a gangly guy sporting plastic glasses. She had a boyfriend, but Fielder waited out that fling.

Gigi liked to ski, so Fielder taught himself the basics at Winter Park. A week later he returned to the resort with her, smugly saying this skiing thing was no big deal. She suggested they try a mogul run. About 45 minutes later he reached the bottom, where Gigi was waiting and laughing hysterically. When she dared him to take a second mogul run, he ignored the sharp pain in his shin. After another balky 45-minute descent, Fielder confessed: Maybe this skiing thing wasn't so easy after all. Gigi was charmed by his determination to impress her—even more so when they found that he'd suffered a boot-top fracture during that first run. The courtship was under way.

Fielder also was becoming more serious about his other love. While he was earning $7,500 annually at the department store, he began dedicating time to his budding hobby. He read just two books about the technical aspects of photography, studied the work of Ansel Adams and Eliot Porter, and otherwise learned by doing. He discovered that nature photography is more about painstaking preparation than patience. He picked up little tricks and discovered that photography is like fishing—it's most productive early and late.

John and Gigi married in 1978. The couple had three children, Ashley, Katy, and their firstborn, J.T. Even with the pressures of supporting a family, Fielder decided to pursue his hobby as a full-time job. The need for a "backup plan" became a staple of the career advice he later gave his children, and Fielder's idea of this was to simultaneously found Westcliffe Publishers to make it easier to print his own work and others' if the opportunity arose. "But there's still something to be said for being a little bit crazy and jumping off the deep end," he says.

The new career often sent Fielder on the road, and Gigi ran the household supportively and in stark contrast to her husband's type-A intensity. Fielder was the archetypical father who pushed his kids, while Gigi was the one who'd lovingly give them a boost. Their parental yin and yang shone through on Fielder family camping trips: hikes of five miles or more to a campsite, sometimes in subzero temperatures or before dawn, with Fielder always leading. He carried Katy in a Snugli during her toddler years. Fielder would beseech them to plod forward while Gigi gently urged along her frustrated ducklings. "We were hiking to these extremely remote places at six years old," Ashley says. "Now I think we were lucky to do it, but [Dad] definitely pushed us while Mom was always the sweetest woman in the world about it." Fielder knows these trips were tough; to this city-slicker kid who'd willed himself to become an accomplished outdoorsman, that was the point. "I'd push them pretty hard," he says, "but Gigi would let me know when it was time to have a picnic or build a snowman on the trail."

Gigi especially connected with her son. Although J.T. inherited his father's rugged charisma and love for the outdoors, he routinely sought out Gigi's tenderness while his dad would make him hike just a little farther, in so many ways. "His dad was more macho, testosterone-driven, all business, a man's man who let his son do his own thing," J.T.'s friend Klingelheber recalls. "There was a sense that because the father had to do it on his own, so did the son."

Byron Jones, J.T.'s best friend from childhood, remembers the father-son interaction as a sort of "abrasive love," a tension Jones experienced firsthand when he was 14. J.T. took his first Sherpa trip at 10 years old, ultimately assisting on about 20 projects, but this time Jones and another friend were helping Fielder on a photo trip without the buffer zone normally provided by J.T., who was home recovering from a broken leg. The group ultimately hiked about 85 miles over nine days, and halfway through Jones and his friend realized that they were lagging when a stern Fielder took them aside. "He pointed into the distance," Jones recalls, "and said, 'There's a road up that way; if you can't keep up, you should go up there and hitchhike home.'"

By his mid-teens, J.T. Fielder was the kid everyone wanted to be. Strapping, tall, and charismatic, he was a superb skier and skilled hiker, the personification of the Rocky Mountain high life. He and his friends, including Jones and Klingelheber, called themselves the Front Range Powder Factory, a group of high-altitude thrill-seekers who skied year-round—except in September when there's little snow anywhere in Colorado and they had to make do skiing sand dunes.

In the late '90s, J.T. geared up for college and his sisters blossomed into their teens, while Fielder consistently churned out books—his fame growing as his perfectionism intensified—but something wasn't right with Gigi. She had grown oddly forgetful and apathetic. Her detachment became a full-on crisis in August 1998, when Fielder and she were visiting her family outside Chicago. Because he was flying home a few days early, she took him to O'Hare airport—a mere 25 minutes from her parents' house. Four hours later his plane landed and he called her cell phone to check in. Gigi was driving in circles around Chicago, frustrated and bewildered, unable to find her way home.

Colorado 1870–2000 was the signature volume for proud residents to display or give as a gift. In 2002, a young outdoorsman and envelope-pusher named Aron Ralston got the book from his parents, with the inscription: "To Aron, who shares my passion for all things natural and Colorado. John Fielder." Ralston's mother had gotten to know Fielder in the Cherry Creek PTA. After receiving the book, Ralston e-mailed Fielder for career advice, and the following summer Ralston accompanied Fielder on a photo trip.

Like Fielder, Ralston had a corporate background as a mechanical engineer, yet couldn't abide a life of cubicles; he yearned to make a living outside. Seeing himself in the young man, Fielder began to paternally evangelize to Ralston about transforming his love of the wilderness into something more philanthropic. "Being out in a storm, or in avalanche terrain, or in the craziest shit-hitting-the-fan experience you could put together, I understand those places and rarely feel threatened," Ralston says. "We're alike in that way, and he showed me how to use these trips to be more selfless."

In spring 2003, Ralston took a solo bike trip to the remotest part of Canyonlands National Park in Utah, a trip that would alter him in ways he couldn't imagine. He wore only a T-shirt and shorts and carried a small backpack with water and climbing gear and a video camera. As he lowered himself into a narrow rock crevasse, a boulder gave way, crushing his right hand and wrist and pinning him in a three-foot-wide passage dozens of feet below ground level. For days he waited, he chipped away at the rock with his knife, he rigged a pulley system to try to lift himself out of the canyon, and he prayed.

Initially, he rejected self-amputation because cutting his wrist so deeply could be suicidal. Later, he contemplated killing himself. If he was going to die anyway, he figured, why suffer? Instead, he persevered. On day six, the tissue in his right hand dead from lack of circulation, exhausted yet unwilling to let the wild devour him, Ralston realized amputation was his only way out. He recorded a farewell message to his family, twisted his arm to break his forearm bones, and then he used his blade to free himself.

Ralston's harrowing story made him a celebrity. He was besieged by requests for interviews and speaking engagements, and his mentor's media experience and friendship brought them even closer. "I vetted all these opportunities through John, and it gave me a much deeper appreciation of all the media work he's done," Ralston says. One highlight came in 2005, when Fielder accompanied the Ralston family and several others on a hut trip with Tom Brokaw and his daughter. They skied all day, and the two families and Fielder—there alone, there for Ralston—spent a raucous evening sharing stories and wine.

Barely two months after escaping the canyon, Ralston was rock climbing again, scuffing up his new $15,000 prosthetic arm. Soon he was scaling fourteeners and training for ultramarathons. He continued to Sherpa for Fielder. J.T. and some friends, several years younger than Ralston, occasionally joined. Among them was Chris Klingelheber, who noted to himself how close Ralston and Fielder had become, and wondered if J.T. noticed it, too. Whatever emotion it might have triggered in

J.T., he kept it to himself. "He could socialize and hang out with guys," Klingelheber says, "but on a deeper level he was much closer to girls." He was particularly close to a mother who, with every passing day, could no longer give her son what he needed.

The O'Hare incident prompted visits to multiple specialists, who discovered that Gigi had early-onset Alzheimer's disease. The pragmatic businessman in Fielder took over. He already had the publishing company; he'd make Gigi's caretaking his other enterprise. To the kids, he cast the challenge of caring for Gigi as a blunt but reassuring to-do list. "He has this way of disconnecting from emotional situations so he can do what needs to be done," Ashley says. "It would've been horrible for him to get emotional. We were already losing one parent, so it was good to still see him as a solid force that was taking care of everything."

Gigi's illness hit the family just when Fielder had never been busier. The then-ongoing *Colorado 1870-2000* project required several years of full-time attention. He took over Gigi's care-taking whenever possible and added Alzheimer's to his list of crusades, taking on speaking engagements and headlining fund-raisers. He felt he had been forced into Sophie's choice: He could either work less and not afford to give Gigi the best care, or he could work more and leave it to others, including his increasingly stressed daughters. J.T. was at school—first Colorado State, later CU-Boulder—and returned home when he could, which made witnessing Gigi's deteriorating condition that much more difficult. While the rest of the family was onsite seeing Gigi's condition change gradually, to J.T.'s eye she was markedly worse almost every time he saw her.

Gigi's seven-year spiral followed the prescribed downward track for Alzheimer's patients in all but one way. The saddest phase of the disease is when the patient knows she's sick but can't do anything about it, nor can she quite grasp why. She might ask anguished questions about what will happen to her or her kids, and she might lash out, even violently. The Fielder family prepared mentally for this but rarely saw it. Gigi remained tender even as she wasted away, dying at home in her own bed on September 11, 2005.

A few months after Gigi's death, the mother of one of J.T.'s friends read her obituary and called her son about it. Until recently, J.T. had been living in Washington Park with some of his Powder Factory friends, now out of college and navigating their 20s. Neither Klingelheber, who shared the basement apartment with J.T., nor most of their longtime friends, had any idea that Gigi had died. "It was like pulling teeth to get him to talk about it," Jones says. "He always carried himself like the alpha male, with no emotions on the outside. His dad was the same way, but it didn't seem to bother J.T. when he was younger, because he had the balance with his mom."

J.T. drifted between jobs and girlfriends like recent grads do. He occasionally talked about it with his friends, but no one thought much of his struggles because they all were going through the same thing. J.T. often shot videos of the Powder Factory's extreme sporting exploits and considered building a career out of his hobby. He knew better than to ask Dad for a job lead. For years Fielder bored into J.T. the need for a backup plan, urging his son to get the business experience that had helped him chart, finance, and execute his own successful career. "Dad [wanted J.T. to] go into the corporate world and learn about marketing and how to work with people before he pursued other things," Ashley says. "But J.T. was just so not like that. He didn't take well to the corporate environment."

In Fielder's eyes, his son hadn't quite accomplished enough to earn a nepotistic boost. "We had not gotten to the point where I would help him find a way in some particular industry related to the outdoors," he says. "I didn't really want it to be photography. The combination of skills is so unique, I couldn't imagine anyone else having that—even my own son—so I wasn't aggressively steering him toward taking over my own job. Maybe someday I'd hand over the reins to him, but my attitude has always been that I'd do this until the day I die."

The fatherly tough love and J.T.'s own twentysomething angst bubbled up when he drank. J.T. might go into an angry rant about his dad, or get into a bar fight, or try to break a bottle over someone's head. Once, the Wash Park housemates awakened to find one of their bathrooms destroyed. "J.T. didn't really talk about his dad, but sometimes when he'd have a few too many drinks, he could get pretty upset about him," Klingelheber says.

J.T. muddled along, getting promoted from a low-level desk job at AIG before moving on to Izze, the Boulder-based soft drink company.

He moved to Boulder and soon stopped returning calls and wanting to hang out as much with his old friends. Not long after Gigi died, he got laid off from Izze with about 20 others and quickly landed another job at an information technology company. The big news was that J.T. met a woman he liked. He started telling friends she was "the One."

Still, the setbacks kept coming. In late 2005 J.T. felt numbness in his chest and his left arm turned purple, symptoms of thoracic outlet syndrome, in which an overly muscled torso cuts off blood flow to the limbs. He had a rib surgically removed to restore circulation yet still had numbness weeks later. He was also on a prolonged dosage of blood thinners, which meant he'd miss most of the ski season: doing something as innocuous as cutting his arm while backcountry skiing could be fatal. J.T.'s rugged, muscular physique—he appeared outwardly to be the sort of outdoorsman who might be worthy of respect by, say, an Aron Ralston or John Fielder—was paradoxically hurting his heart and cutting him off from the outdoors.

His frustration was evident. On a Friday in March 2006, J.T. drank too much at a company party and got into a fight—with his boss. That Sunday, he skied A-Basin with friends and no one noticed anything out of the ordinary. The next day, however, he sent his company a resignation e-mail and he spent most of that evening on the phone with his sisters and other female friends, agonizing over the girl, the One. He wanted her to go somewhere with him, to leave Colorado, to escape for a while. She couldn't, or wouldn't.

On Tuesday, March 21, J.T. awakened in Boulder and went to a female friend's house. He picked up skis he'd left there and lied as he said good-bye, telling her he was going to Butler Gulch with a friend. He drove up alone, parked, and, knowing his phone wouldn't work until he got to the top, began the three-hour climb up the familiar trail to his favorite place on Earth. He sat atop the mountain, knowing that this time there would be no downhill bliss, perhaps believing he'd find a more enduring contentment, an escape. J.T. drank in the view, precisely the kind of view his father had spent so much time with and had devoted his life to trying to nurture and protect. And precisely as his father had done tens of thousands of times, J.T. waited until the moment was just right. He sent a text message to his beloved sisters—*I love you both, and I'll always be with you in spirit. Tell Dad I love him. J.T.*—and he took a blade to his wrists.

The girls went numb when they got the text. Katy was leaving a store near DU and called her father. "J.T. wouldn't send such a thing just to get people stirred up," she says. "It sounds bad, but I felt like I'd already lost him the second I got the text."

Klingelheber had been skiing A-Basin with a friend and turned on his cell phone during the drive back. There was a voice mail from Fielder. He'd gotten Klingelheber's number from a preservation organization with which Fielder had helped set up a job interview for Klingelheber. Fielder's message said J.T.'s sisters had received a suicidal text message, and they didn't know where J.T. was. Klingelheber figured the family was over-reacting, but he called one of J.T.'s female friends. She told him J.T. had been by for his skis that morning and said he was going to Butler Gulch with a friend—the very same friend that was sitting next to Klingelheber in the car. "I got chills because it was a real lie," Klingelheber says.

Fielder, in a wool sportcoat, slacks, and a tie, had just left a luncheon with mayor John Hickenlooper in Denver when he got Katy's call. He went to a police station and had them call the Clear Creek County sher-iff. He then drove to Butler Gulch and met the sheriff around 3:30 p.m. near J.T.'s car. While Klingelheber and the rescue specialist ascended the mountain, every so often Fielder wandered away from the officials and the handful of J.T.'s friends who'd arrived for support. Fielder want-ed to be alone, but one of the Alpine specialists was afraid he might do something rash and asked Fielder to stay near the group.

It was after 10 p.m. when the Alpine rescuer radioed the grim dis-covery down the hill. The rescue officials made Klingelheber leave so they could begin the work of pronouncing J.T. dead and removing his body. When Klingelheber got back to the parking area, he, Fielder, and J.T.'s friends shared a devastated embrace before Fielder left the group and made the long drive home alone.

At J.T.'s funeral, Fielder delivered a 10-minute eulogy that included slides and video of his son, all while revealing little emotion. Ralston and Klingelheber were among those in attendance who were amazed at Fielder's composure. "I think a lot of people were surprised, because most parents in that situation wouldn't be able to talk," Klingelheber says. "It was almost like he was giving a normal slide show up there."

A month after J.T.'s death, Fielder still seemed removed from the tragedy as he led a three-week rafting trip through the Grand Canyon—a trip that J.T. and his best friend, Byron Jones, had planned to attend. Even though such trips have years-long waiting lists, Jones couldn't bring himself to go. Citing the five boats full of expectant rafters, including Ralston, Fielder followed through.

Toward the end of the trip, Ralston and Fielder drifted downriver in the lead boat, rapt in conversation. Ralston was angry with J.T. He couldn't reconcile why he, Ralston, had chosen life while J.T. didn't. To Ralston, it felt like a slap in the face, though he came to see it as a gift, a revelation he shared with Fielder on the water. Ralston was of the mind that "wanting life to be easy is the wrong goal to have, because just trying to eliminate difficulties won't help you succeed or grow." And Fielder agreed. They had become so engrossed that they drifted far beyond the planned campsite and were forced to spend the night on a sandbar. In time, Ralston interpreted J.T.'s suicide differently: "We both had come to remote settings with the same tools, yet made polar opposite decisions. But it really was the same thing; it was to free himself. And that was how I came to peace with it."

Fielder is still sorting through what meaning there is in J.T.'s loss, and in so doing, he's sorting through the meaning of everything. He sought counseling for the first time, a humbling step for any self-made man. "One of the great things in life is figuring out solutions to your own problems, but this one was more than I could handle," he says. "Gigi's death was predictable, and you could emotionally plan for it, but J.T.'s was a shocker."

It's an only-in-Colorado summer day, with cloudless skies, and the 80-degree temperatures are melting the last remnants of snow atop the Gore Range. Fielder glances around the living room of his home, a gorgeously rustic and cozy retreat just outside Silverthorne, as he reflects on J.T.'s eulogy. Everything that's ever mattered to Fielder is right before his eyes: the distant mountains he's worked so hard to nurture and protect; the awards he's won for those labors, along with mementos of past trips, all papering the walls of his dream house. On one side of his living room, there is a sideboard cluttered with a few dozen personal photos of friends and family. The freeze-and-squeeze pictures are posed, stilted, and trite, unworthy of publication in a fancy coffee-table book. And yet the way they're arranged, so carefully placed in disjointed, almost messy, rows—a stark contrast to the spotless order of the rest of the house—leaves the impression that they're now among Fielder's most treasured possessions.

Fielder can discuss both nature and work with striking fluency. "Even when it's a regular conversation I sometimes get the feeling he's rehearsing his marketing speak for how he'll pitch things," Ralston says. "He's genuine and real, but he's working all the time." But sitting here now, Fielder's words are halting. "It wasn't eloquent," he says, referring to the eulogy, his throat growing hoarse. "I wanted to celebrate J.T.'s life, so I gave a brief history and showed some photos of family trips, father-son trips, whatever. I tried to be as stoic as I could. I don't get emotional. My dad was that way, too; we've never been big fans of burdening people with our problems."

His visits with the psychologist came just in time. "I got very close to the place J.T. probably was. I didn't consider taking my life because I couldn't leave two daughters alone in the world after everything they'd already lost. But maybe there was a reason for me getting to that place," he says with a glance toward the sideboard. Displayed prominently toward the front is a Fielder family portrait, taken in front of their Greenwood Village home. Gigi and the girls stand arm in arm and J.T. cradles the family cat, all smiling broadly; in the photo, John has placed himself stiffly to one side, on the outer edge of his family. As his gaze meets the picture, he lowers his head and begins to cry. "Maybe somebody wanted me to know where J.T. was."

Fielder doesn't believe in the stereotypical white-bearded God. Redemption, however, is another story. To his environmental and Alzheimer's crusades, he's now added suicide prevention. He's more engaging and less preoccupied with himself. Everyone around him claims to see the difference. Ralston's once stoic and guarded mentor now possesses an empathetic softness. Klingelheber now sees J.T.'s father, once so coolly detached, hugging people hello and good-bye. "Our relationship with him has changed completely," daughter Katy says. "He's become more emotional and sensitive to us, which has brought us closer together." Fielder ends conversations with "I love you," and is keenly interested in his daughters' emotional health.

Fielder's friends and colleagues have watched him vigorously dive back into his work and suspect *Ranches of Colorado* might be his best project ever. As always, it has the striking vistas and earnest text, but it finally includes pictures of homes, animals, and *people*—ranchers and cowboys riding, roping, and working, surviving and thriving with dignity and diligence, as crucial to their landscape as any snowcapped peak or bursting columbine. "I have a lot more compassion now for people and their problems," Fielder says. "I think a lot more about how I'm coming across to friends or acquaintances—knowing how deeply distressing life can be and that they may be experiencing something like I did. I think about how can I make their life a little bit better by mitigating that."

He's made his own life a little better with a new relationship. After Gigi died, Fielder dated, but he never got serious until he met a woman named Alena. She's blonde and stunning, and she captured Fielder much like Gigi did: with a love-at-first-sight thunderbolt. She also handles Fielder's public relations and lives with him in his hideaway. Alena is about the same age J.T. would have been, but Fielder deflects whatever tension that causes within the family by reminding his girls, as their mother once might have, that "there's no limit on love."

On each anniversary of J.T.'s suicide, the Fielder family visits the peak above Butler Gulch. (The Powder Factory also prints an annual ski calendar as a tribute to J.T., with the proceeds going to suicide prevention.) A new world view—spurred on by intense reading about cosmology and the origins of the universe—helps Fielder get beyond what he might have done differently. It's taught him, or rather is teaching him, to recognize the beauty, energy, and light Gigi and J.T. brought to every day of their tragically abbreviated lives. The memories are more small miracles of convergence—much like the pink-orange alpenglow from his favorite moment of light so many years ago—only now Fielder doesn't have to wait for them; they arrive every hour of every day.

The relentless, gritty adventurer gazes out his picture window toward the Gore Range. His reflection stares back at him, putting him into the frame, where he's finally comfortable inviting people to join him. "My life was always focused less on humanity and more on the natural world, and there really has to be a bit of both in everyone's life," he says. "I would hope that my children and their descendants figure out the value of humanitarianism more quickly than I did."

—September 2009

4.

The Precious Ordinary

by Chris Outcalt

Maggie Jones drove out to the McPherons' on a cold Saturday afternoon. Seventeen miles southeast of Holt. Beside the blacktop there were patches of snow in the fallow fields, drifts and scallops wind-hardened in the ditches. Black baldy cattle were spread out in the corn stubble, all pointed out of the wind with their heads down, eating steadily. When she turned off onto the gravel road small birds flew up from the roadside in gusts and blew away in the wind. Along the fenceline the snow was brilliant under the sun.

— PLAINSONG

Cathy Haruf returns from the snow-covered backyard of her Salida home carrying a small box of papers. It's late in the morning on Wednesday, February 25, the day after what would have been her late husband's 72nd birthday. She sits across from me in an old brown rocking chair in the corner of the living room and rests the box on her lap. The chair creaks as it sways, and Cathy settles into place. On the opposite side of the room, displayed on a cabinet, there is a framed picture of Kent.

After a quiet moment, Cathy begins to sort through the contents of the box. There are handwritten letters, a spiral-bound journal, and a stack of manila papers. The sheets make up the manuscript of her husband's final novel, *Our Souls at Night*, which he worked on until the day he died, November 30, 2014. The pages are filled mostly with single blocks of typed text, and there are pencil marks and crossed-out words and passages and notes in the margins. For months Cathy has been mailing boxes of these papers to the Huntington Library in San Marino, California, where they will be preserved and catalogued alongside work by the likes of Shakespeare, Galileo, Henry David Thoreau, and Jack London. This is one of the last boxes she will send.

Kent Haruf is widely considered Colorado's finest novelist and one of America's most important contemporary literary voices. Critics have written that his sentences "have the elegance of Hemingway's early work" and that he "may be the most muted master in American fiction." His books have been translated into more than a half-dozen languages. His third novel, *Plainsong*, was a best-seller and was nominated for a National Book Award in 1999, one of the highest honors in American letters. The Denver Center for the Performing Arts has adapted three of Kent's books for the stage, most recently his fifth novel, *Benediction*, which in many ways foreshadowed his own death. And an award-winning director has already expressed interest in purchasing the film rights to *Our Souls at Night*, published last month.

In the bright living room, Cathy hands me one of the manila sheets: page 16 of the first draft of Kent's last book. She then places the box on the floor in front of us, and we look through Kent's papers together. A few minutes later, Cathy asks if I'd like to see the shed behind the house where Kent wrote *Our Souls at Night* and his previous two novels, *Eventide* and *Benediction*. With a pencil, she scribbles a three-digit sequence, the code for the combination lock on the shed, on a scrap of paper. Instead of accompanying me outside, Cathy hands me the paper and suggests, without hesitation, that I go alone.

The structure is just beyond the fenceline: a small brown shed with a fresh blanket of snow clinging to the roof. It looks like the kind of thing you'd pick up at Home Depot. This was Kent's sanctuary, the place where he daydreamed into existence a world that showed in all its simplicity that life is anything but plain. I walk around to the front, dial the combination, remove the padlock, and open the door.

Even now there are not many trees here, although people in towns like Holt have full-grown trees that were planted by early residents sixty and seventy years ago in backyards and along the streets—elm and evergreen and cottonwood and ash, and every once in a while a stunted maple that somebody stuck in the ground with more hope for it than real experience of this area would ever have allowed.

—THE TIE THAT BINDS

The drive from Denver to Salida—from the busy city highways to the quiet small-town streets tucked between 14,000-foot peaks and near a calm stretch of the Arkansas River—takes three hours, winding, and climbing, and dipping through the mountains along U.S. 285. I made the trip multiple times last summer to speak with Kent, and on each occasion we visited for hours in his home.

When I first reached out to Kent, I didn't know he was working on a new book or that he had seen very few visitors during the previous months. I'd recently read *Plainsong* and was moved by the rhythm and soulfulness of the story and of his writing, the way one might feel a connection to a beautiful piece of music or the brushstrokes of a brilliant painter. I felt compelled to reach out to the man behind the novel. I wanted to talk with him—and to listen. A publicist at Random House connected Kent and me via email; we exchanged a few messages, and he agreed to meet with me at his house in Salida on June 23. Cathy later told me that she was a bit surprised when Kent said there was "a young man coming down from Denver to visit."

I arrived at the Harufs' home around 4:30 p.m. that afternoon in June. Kent answered the door. He looked more frail than in the pictures on his book jackets, and there were rubber tubes tucked behind his ears and up into his nostrils. The tubing trailed behind him several dozen feet back through the entryway and across the kitchen floor and into the living room, until they disappeared under a closet door. Kent invited me in. We sat in the living room. He was winded from walking to the front door and back to his chair, the old rocker. We spoke for a long time, and like Kent's prose, his voice was soft and measured.

On my drive through the mountains several hours earlier, I listened to an interview with *New Yorker* writer Peter Hessler, who has spent years reporting from China. In the interview, Hessler explained that one of his strategies had always been to leave the big cities and travel to small towns. "Everything is more obvious in a smaller place," Hessler said in the interview. "It stands out more." Hessler's comments made me think of Kent's novels.

All of Kent's books are set on Colorado's Eastern Plains in the fictional town of Holt, which he created and then painstakingly brought to life on the page. Beyond the occasional trip to Denver or the mountains, his characters—Edith Goodnough, Victoria Roubideaux, the McPheron brothers, Dad Lewis—rarely stray far from the edges of town. Kent spent much of his childhood on the High Plains. He was born in the steel-mill town of Pueblo in the winter of 1943. Kent's father was a Methodist preacher, and the family moved often—Kent was an infant when they packed up and left Pueblo and settled on the plains east of Denver. The Haruf family spent the next 12 years in Wray, Holyoke, and Yuma, little towns amid expansive country.

As a kid, Kent didn't think much about becoming a writer. In his early years, he remembers being "more or less a happy kid." He also says that during that time, he "learned to live completely inwardly," a sentiment owed to the fact that he was born with a cleft lip. Kent's parents were too poor to afford treatment alone, but local churches helped raise money so the Harufs could send their newborn to Children's Hospital in Denver. Kent remained at the hospital for about a month while doctors did what they could to repair his lip. The surgeon planned to do more work later, but when he died in a plane crash, Kent's parents viewed it as a sign from God to let it be.

For more than 15 years, from the time he was 12 until he neared 30, Kent felt an impulse to conceal his face behind his hand, to hide what he considered an embarrassing imperfection. But his thinking changed over time. Later in life, he came to believe the deformity was a gift that had taught him to be more aware of the world around him and of the feelings of others. "Which are good things," Kent has said, "if you are trying to learn to write fiction about characters you care about and love." In his 30s, Kent grew a mustache to cover his lip; he kept it for the rest of his life.

Listening to Hessler's interview on that summer day, I wondered if Kent felt about his fiction the way Hessler did about his journalism, that the quiet setting of the plains somehow amplified the emotions and interactions of his characters. "I feel that exactly," Kent told me. It worked just perfectly, he said, to set his novels on the stark landscape of the plains because there was so little to obfuscate the story. Later, he told me, "I love driving around through the plains at night, when you see those yard lights scattered around in the country. It's so beautiful to me. And yet so lonesome.... There's a kind of tension between those two feelings, and I love that."

> Just once they took another boy with them to the vacant house
> and the room where it had happened. They wanted to see it again
> themselves, to walk in it and feel what that would feel like and
> what it might be to show it to somebody else, and afterward they
> were sorry they had ever wanted to know or do any of that at all.

— PLAINSONG

On that June afternoon when Kent and I first met, he told me he'd spent part of the morning reading William Faulkner. Kent deeply admired Faulkner's work, including *The Sound and the Fury* and *As I Lay Dying*—but there was one story in particular he held above the others, a short novel titled *The Bear.* Though he'd read the book at least 10 times, Kent told me he'd once again returned to *The Bear* because it was one of the first books he fell in love with, and thus he felt a connection to the story and a sense of joy while reading it. "That short novel," he said, "was absolutely crucial for me in making up my mind for what I was going to do for the rest of my life."

Kent asked me if I'd read *The Bear.* I hadn't and confessed that I'd not read much Faulkner at all. The next day I ordered the book and read it as soon as it arrived. The story, which Faulkner wrote later in his career, is set primarily in Mississippi in the late 1800s. One of the novel's central storylines is based around a relationship between a young white boy and an old mixed-race mentor, who teaches the adolescent to respect the wilderness.

Reading *The Bear*, I was struck by the contrast between the sound of a Faulkner sentence and that of one written by Kent. Faulkner's sentences are long and dense, language layered on top of language, whereas Kent's are more often simple and precise. I thought it was interesting Kent had cited Faulkner as his favorite author. The longer I considered it, though, I thought perhaps I was focused on the wrong aspect of Faulkner's writing. Maybe the reason Kent felt drawn to Faulkner had less to do with the aesthetics of a sentence or paragraph and rather the connection forged in the way the writing made Kent feel. Perhaps his love of Faulkner grew more from the man's ability to convey emotion than the way he used commas and periods.

Many of Kent's thoughts and feelings about literature first began to develop during his time in college. Kent attended high school in Cañon City. After graduation, he enrolled at Nebraska Wesleyan University, a small Methodist school in Lincoln, Nebraska, which he chose partly because of his father's background as a minister. He intended to study biology, but after taking one science course, he reconsidered. He enrolled in a Masterpieces of Literature class and during the next two years fell in love with authors such as Faulkner and Ernest Hemingway.

The small English department at Nebraska Wesleyan was a perfect fit for Kent. The professors were passionate about stories and less concerned with literary theory. That sort of scholarly thinking about writing never suited Kent—he didn't want to figure out the symbolism; he wanted to think about how the story made him feel.

Many years after he first read Faulkner, Kent was on a book tour for his third novel, *Plainsong*, which had become something of an overnight success. Kent shared with me a story about the time he did a reading at Square Books, a famous bookstore in Oxford, Mississippi. Oxford also happens to be William Faulkner's hometown. That night, after the reading, Kent went out with friends and got a little drunk and decided to visit the author's grave. He lay down amid the earth and stone of the grave site, his body close to Faulkner's remains. Cathy took a picture of him lying there, and before Kent left that night he poured a bit of whiskey onto the tombstone.

They came up from the horse barn in the slanted light of early morning. The McPheron brothers, Harold and Raymond. Old men approaching an old house at the end of summer.

—EVENTIDE

Though Kent had learned to love and respect literature during his undergraduate days, he spent the next several years of his life struggling to learn how to write his own fiction. He graduated from Nebraska Wesleyan in 1965 and left campus feeling, as he told me, "absolutely unprepared to make a living, except if they were to pay me to read." It was around that time that he first attempted to compose short pieces of fiction. Those initial stories were complete failures, he told me, "pitiful, imitating, reductive little things." Kent volunteered for the Peace Corps, which at that time was only a few years old, and was sent to a village in Turkey. During the days, he taught English to middle school students, and in the evenings he wrote. "That was the first time I'd ever been out of the country," Kent said. "I had hardly ever been out of Colorado. It was a good experience for me but of little value to the Turks."

After two years overseas, Kent applied to graduate school at the University of Kansas. He was accepted, and he and his girlfriend, Virginia Koon, who would later become his first wife, moved to Lawrence, Kansas. Almost immediately Kent felt out of place. The English professors discussed literature in ways that didn't make sense to him—literary theory and symbols. It was the opposite of what had sparked his love of Faulkner and Hemingway during his undergraduate days. Kent quit in the middle of the second semester.

It was the spring of 1968, and the country was tangled in the Vietnam War. No longer eligible for a student deferment, Kent was drafted, though from the moment he received the notice he had no intention of going to war or killing anyone. "I remember Cassius Clay said, 'I ain't got nothing against them Cong,'" Kent told me. "That was about my feeling." He applied for—and was granted—status as a conscientious objector.

Instead of fighting, Kent spent the next two years caring for life: He worked as an orderly at Craig Rehabilitation Hospital near Denver and later at an orphanage in Helena, Montana, where he and Virginia lived in a single room and had their first child. He was still writing consistently and submitted short pieces of fiction to magazines such as Harper's and the Atlantic Monthly. They were all rejected.

Feeling desperate, Kent applied to the University of Iowa's prestigious writer's workshop. (Alums of the program include esteemed fiction writers John Irving and Ann Patchett.) The program had turned Kent down two years earlier. This time, without knowing if he'd been accepted, Kent moved his family hundreds of miles in the middle of winter to an old country farmhouse east of campus and found a job as a janitor. He stopped by the admissions office so they knew he was in town. That spring, Kent was accepted to the workshop.

He wrote a third of a novel while he was in Iowa and later finished the book. (For the first time, he set part of the story in Holt County.) Harper & Row considered publishing the novel but eventually passed. During the next several years, Kent began a career teaching English: first at a small high school on the Colorado plains, later at his alma mater, Nebraska Wesleyan, and finally at Southern Illinois University. Kent and Virginia had two more children; their marriage eventually ended in divorce.

While he was teaching, Kent started on another novel—the book that would finally earn him recognition. "When I finished that novel, I wrote John Irving to ask if he would connect me with his agent," Kent wrote in an essay published after his death. "He said he had sent 50 writers to his agent and he hadn't taken any of them, but maybe he'd take me. And he did: I got a telegram (there were still telegrams back then) and he said he was impressed by the book and wanted to represent it. That was a great day for me. The book was *The Tie That Binds*." The novel was published in the fall of 1984. Kent was 41 years old.

He continued to write and teach, and his second novel, *Where You Once Belonged*, about the rise and fall of a high school football star and his impact on Holt, was published six years later. The following year, in 1991, though he'd never considered going to one before, Kent attended his 30th high school reunion. The gathering was in the basement of a Cañon City restaurant. Kent walked down the stairs and one of the first people he saw was his old friend and high school classmate Cathy. Though they hadn't spoken in years, they hugged each other right away, and in that moment fell in love. "Cathy says there are no accidents," Kent told me. "I'm ready to accept her explanation."

Cathy moved to Illinois, where Kent was teaching writing and English, and they later married. Having both grown up in Colorado, Kent and Cathy dreamed of returning to the state. After *Plainsong* found success in 1999, they left their jobs and together purchased a few acres of land 10 miles west of Salida, halfway up Monarch Pass, with a view of Mt. Shavano. There is a little town there now called

Maysville, but back then Kent and Cathy were the only ones around. For two summers, they camped out in a tent, traveling back and forth from a nearby campground to collect water from a pump. They hiked often and fished and drove around exploring different places. Eventually, they had a cabin built on the land.

After 12 years of living simply in the hills above town, Kent and Cathy sold the land, moved to Salida, and settled into a small home a few minutes west of downtown on H Street.

> He sat and drank the beer and held his wife's hand sitting out on the front porch. So the truth was he was dying. That's what they were saying. He would be dead before the end of summer. By the beginning of September the dirt would be piled over what was left of him out at the cemetery three miles east of town. Someone would cut his name into the face of a tombstone and it would be as if he never was.

> — BENEDICTION

When he was writing a novel, Kent would sit at his desk each morning from about 9:30 to noon. He would begin by writing in his journal and reading a few pages of one of his favorite authors—Faulkner, Hemingway, or Anton Chekhov. He liked having the cadence of those sentences in his mind when he wrote. Then he would compose drafts on an old typewriter. (He tried writing on a computer once but didn't like it.) Cathy could hear the keystrokes from just outside the house: *click, click, click*. Kent would dedicate each morning to a single scene, and he would write the first draft of each scene blind, his eyes closed and a stocking cap pulled low so all that was visible were the backs of his eyelids, something of a window through which he viewed the town of Holt and its people.

One such scene is the opening of Kent's fifth novel, *Benediction*. In the first chapter, the main character, Dad Lewis, receives a grim medical diagnosis: There is cancer in his lungs. A *Washington Post* critic wrote, "*Benediction* seems designed to catch the sound of those fleeting good moments." *Benediction* is the story of a dying old man, and as the tale unfolds, Kent's prose gives life to the process of preparing for death.

Kent once described the book this way: "This story is not about suspense. We know from the beginning that Dad Lewis is going to die. The difficulty is trying to portray this man's death in a way that is not monotonous or tedious, and yet focuses on the meaning he has as he's closing in on death." *Benediction* was published in February 2013, nearly nine years after his last novel, *Eventide*. Almost exactly a year later, Kent received his own unexpected and startlingly similar diagnosis.

Kent told me about his medical condition that first day I met him in June. We'd spoken for more than an hour, and eventually the conversation veered in such a way that I asked him if he'd been working on anything new. He said that he had a few ideas, but that he hadn't done much with them because he'd been too sick.

A doctor had delivered the news four months earlier: Kent had an interstitial lung disease for which there was no cure. One day soon the scarring on the tissue around his lungs would cause his organs to malfunction for good and he would suffocate. The doctor did not know when that day would come. Tomorrow. Or the day after. Or many days after that. It was a death sentence without a date.

His doctor prescribed steroids to help improve his breathing. Nothing more could be done. The news was unexpected and frightening, a shock to both him and Cathy. Kent told me he was trying to prepare himself for death. He said he'd been meditating more and reading spiritual texts. He wanted to have what he thought of as a good death. To be conscious until the end, to be present; to be loving until the last moment, to be unafraid.

With whatever time he had, he said he wanted to take pleasure in anything he could. He wanted to find enjoyment in simple, everyday things: the progress of the tulips in the backyard garden. The way a glass of lemonade looks. Those things were more important now. He didn't want to be distracted or waste time. There wasn't any time to waste. He said that's the way you're supposed to live life all the time: to find enjoyment in what he described as the precious ordinary.

Before I left that day, Kent and I made plans to speak again soon. On my way out of town, I bought a six-pack of beer. Before driving out of the valley and winding back through the mountains to Denver, I pulled over at a lookout with a view of Mt. Princeton. I opened a beer, took a sip, and, with Kent's words still in my mind, watched the sky change colors as the sun set beyond the massive peak.

Aren't you afraid of death?

Not like I was. I've come to believe in some kind of afterlife. A return to our true selves, a spirit self. We're just in this physical body till we go back to spirit.

I don't know if I believe that, Addie said. Maybe you're right. I hope you are.

—OUR SOULS AT NIGHT

Last summer, Kent and I planned to go out to dinner one evening. When I arrived in Salida he apologized and said that he was not feeling well enough to leave the house, so Cathy prepared a small snack, and Kent and I talked for almost two hours.

He told me he'd spent the morning reading spiritual books with Cathy and meditating. "What I do think I know and believe—feel as much as believe, I guess—is that we return to some spiritual form," he said. "I so love the physical world; I love being in a physical realm . . . and being with Cathy, and knowing people, all this stuff . . . I'm not ready to leave those things, but it's going to happen. So I'm trying to get ready for that, without being maudlin or morose or depressed about it. That wouldn't serve any purpose."

Weeks later, Kent and I traded emails about getting together in late August or September, and when summer began to transition to fall I reached out to see how he was feeling. I asked if the scenery around Salida was particularly beautiful this time of year and told him that I hoped to soon drive through the mountains to see the changing leaves. I heard nothing for weeks. I began to worry. Then, almost two months later, at 6:01 p.m. on Sunday, November 23, an email from Kent arrived. Though I didn't know it then, it was the last time I would hear from him.

Dear Chris,

I'm very slow in responding to your message but you've been on my mind. . . .

Earlier that month, I'd mailed Kent a copy of a piece I had written—one we discussed during one of our conversations. He wrote that he'd read the story and enjoyed it. Then he went on to say that he had been working on a project of his own.

> *On a personal note, I can tell you that I have written a new novel this summer. A short one. I began writing about the 1st of May and by the 15th of June I had a complete first draft. Then I began to rework it and Cathy has printed it into the computer about five times. And now my editor at Knopf has edited it and I've returned it to him and will get a copyedit this week, and galleys in January .... Its title is:* Our Souls at Night. *I feel pretty good about it and I feel especially good about even being able to do it. In many ways it gave me an added reason to stay alive. Cathy and I had a great time with it but I hadn't told anybody because I didn't know if I could actually finish it.*
> *I hope this finds you well and in good spirits.*

Warmest best wishes,
Kent

Seven days later, Kent died peacefully in his sleep in the early hours of Sunday, November 30. I read the news in a short piece posted late that evening by the *Washington Post*, and I cried.

One step past the doorway of Kent Haruf's writing shed and everything feels close. The back wall is less than eight feet away, and I can almost reach out and touch the walls on either side of me. The interior walls are draped with mismatched bedsheets, which are tacked to the beams of the structure, concealing a thick layer of insulation. Some of the sheets are pale blue and others are the color of lima beans.

Just to the left of the entryway, there is a small bookcase overflowing with old books. Many of the book jackets have faded and the corners are worn and there are distinct creases along the spines. The top shelf is taken up almost entirely by stories written by Faulkner, and a third of the way down, I notice a short story collection that includes *The Bear*. Kent's desk spans most of the length of the back wall; it's a light wooden desk with three drawers. There is a lamp in the far corner, and a brown suede chair. A large bull skull hangs from a nail to the left of the desk. Cathy told me Kent had hung the skull in his workspace as a reminder to not write bullshit.

Though my time with Kent was brief, I believe it was a gift. When I first met him I was focused on learning about his writing, but I realize now he was speaking more about life—and that the line between the two is not much of a line at all. There were no mechanical tricks to what Kent accomplished in his books; his writing was rooted in less tangible things like feelings and emotions. And beyond that, it was simply hard work. It seemed to me the precision in Kent's novels in many ways reflected the mindful way he lived his life. Kent once told me, "What I'm trying to do…is to suggest the value and the preciousness of ordinary life. Most of us don't see it very clearly. Maybe we do better than I think, but I don't think we do. I think our life passes in front of us without us being cognizant of it—of the dearness of it."

Before walking back inside, I linger in Kent's shed for one final moment. The late-morning sun cuts through a small rectangular window above his desk on the back wall. A white V-neck undershirt hangs over the window; still, a bright light spills beyond the boundaries of the window frame and into the room. Then I close the door and snap the lock into place.

Cathy tells me her friends have asked her if it has been difficult to mail Kent's papers to a library hundreds of miles away, to let go of this piece of her husband. She said there have been times at night, when everything is quiet, that she feels an overwhelming sense of loss. But when it comes to these manuscripts, the culmination of her husband's life's work, she chooses to see things differently. She'd rather these artifacts be somewhere she knows they'll be taken care of; when they were left out in Kent's shed, sometimes one of the cats would sleep on them.

For five months, Cathy was the only person who knew about Kent's new novel. He told her he was going to write a book about the two of them—a couple of old people talking all the time. She said Kent would return from his shed each morning pleased. "His writing was always very satisfying on days when it went smoothly," Cathy said, "but he would never have said it was fun. He just had the best time with this one."

Sometime during the writing process, still not having told anyone else he was working on the book, Kent thought he would surprise his editor, Gary Fisketjon, with a draft. Fisketjon had been with Kent since *Plainsong* and had become a good friend. The day Kent was ready, Cathy drafted an email that read, "Gary, here's a little surprise for you." She attached the draft of the book and hit send.

Our Souls at Night is a love story. In the book's first chapter, an older woman who has lost her husband wanders over to her neighbor's home in Holt, a man who has lost his wife. Thus begins a relationship, and the characters, Addie Moore and Louis Waters, together find enjoyment in the little things—the precious ordinary. Cathy later told me Kent really loved the last line of the book. And I've thought about the significance of that: The last sentence Kent Haruf wrote was one that he loved. "Dear, is it cold there tonight?"

On the drive home after talking with Cathy, I stopped at the same Mt. Princeton lookout I visited the first time I met Kent. Pausing here on my way back from Salida had become a routine. On this day, the early afternoon sun was up in the sky, high above the mountain. As I sat on top of a picnic table, I watched the sun trace the ridgeline, revealing contours that moments earlier had been hidden in the shadows.

—June 2015

5.

The Canyon of Why

by Daliah Singer

Bright colors danced before Josi Stewart, a blurry kaleidoscope floating in the distance. She blinked her chocolate brown eyes and implored them to focus. Slowly, her vision sharpened. Hazy blobs became rectangles. Ambiguous hues turned to familiar blues and pinks and yellows.

Her brain was still sludgy from the medication doctors injected to revive her. Josi couldn't remember how she ended up in this hospital bed, with an IV piercing her arm and a machine breathing for her. She recalled feeling overwhelmed by the responsibilities of her two new jobs. She assumed she would slip up and be fired soon enough. That was the scenario doctors once outlined for her: She'd never be steadily employed, so she should settle for simply trying to keep up with her meds.

Over the previous few weeks, hopelessness dominated her thoughts and flushed every constructive feeling from her mind. Shame paralyzed her; it prevented her from asking anyone for help. She was exhausted from trying to compress her emotions into something manageable, and she chastised herself as she lay in the darkness: *What's wrong with you?* She couldn't think of anything good about her life. Her blackest thoughts took over and fostered an emotional anguish that hollowed her out until she couldn't imagine living with the pain for one more minute. She decided to swallow every pill she could find. In that moment, like several times before, she just wanted it to end.

When you have a brain that's functioning as it should, it's nearly impossible to empathize with those whose minds are not. People aren't generally aware of the tangles of neurons inside their heads; the brain has no pain receptors. People like Josi, though, know an unsettled mind—one besieged by feelings of worthlessness—can rebel without warning and trap itself in a desperate labyrinth, far from reality.

Society has long stigmatized the issue with the phrase "committed suicide," which implies a crime or a religious sin. This taboo silences and isolates people dealing with suicide ideation (the term used to convey thoughts about or a preoccupation with suicide); it breeds shame so deep it collapses their abilities to seek or accept help. What most don't understand is that nine out of 10 people who survive a suicide attempt won't go on to die by their own hands. On this January day in 2008, Josi was in the majority. She was alive.

Her co-workers and family took shifts so Josi would see a familiar face when—if—she awoke. Two of them were sitting with her as her vision cleared and the colorful shapes sharpened. For a split second, Josi thought she had died and was having an out-of-body experience. Gradually she began to comprehend what she was seeing: Dozens of cards—from colleagues and friends, some store-bought, others made lovingly by hand—were taped on the wall across from her hospital bed, hopeful notes crafted over the past three days while she lay unconscious. She settled her gaze. Right there was proof of the impact she'd had on others. For the first time in her 29 years, Josi finally realized that her life might actually mean something.

Josi's experience is not unique. More than 800,000 people worldwide, including about 40,000 Americans, die by suicide each year. Suicide is the 10th leading cause of death in the United States—roughly twice as many people take their own lives annually as die by homicide—and it affects all age groups, sexes, and races (though death by suicide in the United States is most prevalent among working-age, non-Hispanic white men). Males die of suicide about four times more often than females. Women, however, are three times more likely to make attempts than men.

In Colorado, suicide is the second leading cause of death for people ages 10 through 44, and its highest mortality numbers are among 45- to

54-year-olds. In 2014, 1,058 people died by suicide in the state, the most since at least 1940, eclipsing the previous high in 2012. Elevated suicide rates are particularly prevalent in the mountain states—so much so that researchers have dubbed our region "the suicide belt."

The Centennial State currently ranks seventh nationally for suicide deaths and regularly appears in the top 10. It could be the large swaths of rural land that encompass 77 percent of Colorado's geography, where access to health care and mental health services can be limited. It could be the culture of rugged individualism and self-reliance, high rates of gun ownership, or the large population of transplants who sometimes lack strong personal ties nearby. It certainly has something to do with the general dearth of funding for prevention efforts. Colorado's swelling veteran population is also a contributing factor, as veterans die by suicide 50 percent more often than civilians in similar demographics. It might even be the mountainous geography: Researchers are exploring whether high elevations exacerbate the effects of mood disorders.

Two days after she woke up, Josi moved to the psychiatric unit at Presbyterian/St. Luke's Medical Center, where she spent the next few weeks recovering. She still can't remember many details because her hospital stays blur together. The now 37-year-old has paced hallway after hallway in such facilities fairly regularly since her first mental illness diagnosis at age 14.

The world has long burdened Josi's barely five-foot-tall frame. She lived briefly in an orphanage in her native Peru after her birth mother threw her from a moving vehicle. A single Caucasian woman in Colorado adopted her when she was two years old. Josi was bullied in school and sexually assaulted at least three times. This past May, she was diagnosed with fibromyalgia, a chronic condition whose painful physical symptoms, Josi says, don't compare to what she's long endured internally. Over the years, she's been diagnosed with everything from bipolar disorder to Asperger's syndrome to PTSD to obsessive-compulsive disorder. (All but bipolar are part of her current diagnosis, which also includes anxiety and schizoaffective disorder.) In the few weeks leading up to her most recent attempt, in 2008, Josi became more and more despondent, lost in a tangled web the light could no longer reach. Her mind slowly and deliberately discarded every option and homed in on what she mistakenly believed was her only solution.

According to the National Alliance on Mental Illness, one in four U.S. adults experiences mental illness, and one in 17 lives with a serious mental health condition such as bipolar disorder or major depression. When it comes to people who die by suicide, up to 90 percent have a diagnosable mental illness. But not everyone with a mental health issue experiences suicide ideation, even though such thoughts are surprisingly common throughout society. In 2013, the Suicide Prevention Resource Center reported that 9.3 million adults in the United States had serious thoughts of suicide in the past year. Of those, 1.3 million made an attempt and approximately three percent of them died.

Yet suicide remains among the country's least publicized health issues. News reports and press releases about the nine-month-old Colorado Crisis System—part of Governor John Hickenlooper's $20 million mental health agenda—sidestep the word almost entirely. "You should be as comfortable talking about your mental health with your co-workers, with your family, as if you have a cold," the governor told me this past June. "And yet the truth is, we're a long way from there."

The key to preventing suicides is connecting with people *before* despair and isolation turn passing thoughts into unwavering resolve. That's why advocates are encouraging attempt survivors and those who have experienced suicide ideation to share their stories of recovery. Narratives like Josi's, they say, may be the most crucial piece to saving lives because they spread messages of resilience and hope and the idea that feeling suicidal isn't a permanent state. "It's not an unusual story," says Sally Spencer-Thomas, a clinical psychologist and founder and CEO of Denver's Carson J Spencer Foundation. "It's just that few people are telling it."

Sleep sometimes eludes me. The world is still, except for the incessant hum of the air conditioning, and I lie there staring into the darkness until the wee hours, willing myself to tire. When I was a child, I'd occasionally give up and sneak out of bed to find my dad. Sometimes he'd be lying in bed, my mom fast asleep beside him, watching John Wayne Westerns, and I'd nestle in between my parents. Other nights,

I'd find him in his garage workshop and help with whatever electronic device he was tinkering with. He'd catch me up—on the plot of the film or how a speaker's wiring worked—and after a while, he'd tell me it was time for bed. My busy mind, now satiated and calmed, would finally be ready to turn off. I'd snuggle under my pink comforter, stuffed animals piled around me, and fall right asleep.

Samuel Singer was exciting to be around. An entrepreneur and engineer, he ultimately had eight patents to his name. He spoke four languages. He was born in Russia and immigrated to Israel and then Canada, where I was born. He taught me to swim and to ski and to ride a bike. He helped me with my multiplication tables and introduced me to *Doctor Who*. He built a treehouse next to the swing set in our backyard and a go-kart my brothers and I would zip around in near our childhood home in Pennsylvania. He loved to dance to the Gipsy Kings and read science fiction and eat and laugh. My small fingers would get lost in his as he twirled me around the dance floor. Those solid, strong hands wrapped ponytails that stayed perfectly in place during my band recitals. They were the same hands that tenderly picked me up and carried me to the car after I broke my leg playing on our tree swing.

He loved to take photos, hundreds of them, and captured every family trip and moment, big or small. He was behind the camera on December 15, 2000, documenting my eighth-grade semiformal dance. I beamed in the purple dress and dangly earrings I'd picked out with my mom. My older brothers no longer lived at home; one was in college, and the other had already started his career. I slept at a friend's house that Friday night and was home for a short time the next morning before my dad headed out the door. When I reminded him about our plans to shop for holiday gifts that weekend, he shrugged me off. I didn't think much of it, but my mom would later note that it seemed like an unusual response. I don't remember if he hugged or kissed me goodbye. But sometime later that day, my handsome, brilliant, gregarious father picked up one of his guns and never came home.

There's no single reason people die by suicide. Depression and previous attempts are among the most common risk factors, and feelings of hopelessness and exposure to trauma are also widely cited. But it's almost always a combination of factors. "It's important for society to see suicide as a major, lethal outcome of a difficult, often tragic personal situation or mental health condition," says Eduardo Vega, a suicide attempt survivor based in San Francisco who leads several prominent suicide prevention organizations.

Scientific understanding of suicidal behavior and prevention is a young field, but in his illuminating 2005 book *Why People Die by Suicide*, clinical psychologist Thomas Joiner, who lost his father to suicide, argues that in addition to myriad recognized risk factors (including mental illness, substance abuse, and age), there are typically three concurrent circumstances that contribute to death by suicide: a perception of burdensomeness, feeling disconnected from others, and an acquired ability for self-injury. "People are not born with the developed capacity to seriously injure themselves," he writes, but they can cultivate it via painful events throughout their lives.

Taken alone, these aren't unusual states of being; in adventurous Colorado, the thirst for perilous escapades is perceived to be commonplace. As journalist Tony Dokoupil wrote, "Joiner's conditions of suicide are the conditions of everyday life." An overlapping of all three, though, is rare. When they merge like circles in a Venn diagram, it intensifies a falsehood in the suicidal mind that the person's death is worth more than his life.

Timothy Bishop can relate to that self-deception. He received a diagnosis of bipolar 1 disorder with psychotic features at age 19; he's experienced two major episodes of mania and countless more minor instances, as well as at least two serious bouts of depression. He speaks eloquently and thoughtfully about his illness and its effects, a combination of the wisdom that comes with time—he's now 50 years old—and the professional skills he's learned. Timothy is a peer support specialist at Rocky Mountain Crisis Partners (RMCP), which runs the new 24/7 statewide crisis hotline, and a certified professional coach specializing in mental health.

Timothy says he's contemplated suicide hundreds of times. He once sat on his bed as a 16-year-old, debating whether to grab a shotgun from the hall closet. Another time, he walked out to the barn at his home in Elizabeth to see how much rope there was. He made one serious attempt, the summer before his diagnosis, while on a manic upswing;

his friends forced him to throw up the pills he'd swallowed. Sometimes, his suicide ideation appears in fleeting notions—a desire to escape the psychological torture his illness has wrought—but at other times it develops into an obsession lasting weeks or months.

As Timothy tries to describe those despondent moments, he repeatedly lifts his right foot and places it back on the floor, as if he's trying to ground his thoughts. His blue eyes gaze through his black-framed glasses, and he takes a deep breath. "If you've lost somebody close to you, that's sadness and that's grief," he says slowly. "Depression is that sadness where the bottom falls out. Where, if you can see a color, it is the blackest of the black. You can't see out of it. There's a hopelessness that this is never going to end. It feels like you're dead—you're dead and you want to be more dead."

It's been said that "only" is the most dangerous word in a suicidal person's vocabulary. Again and again, Josi and Timothy became trapped in the tunnel vision that often accompanies suicide ideation. Asking if someone is suicidal can break that intense focus; the frankness creates a connection, opens communication, and can provide a sense of liberating respite. Once the mind finds clarity beyond the haze, it's able to comprehend that there are other ways to fight the anguish. "In the mind's eye of that person, suicide is perfectly sensible," says David Jobes, a clinical psychologist and professor of psychology at Catholic University in Washington, D.C. "But it's the most extreme response to usually relatively treatable issues."

Jobes believes research like his may lead to more effective treatments. Currently, only a handful of replicated therapies have proven to reduce suicide ideation and behaviors. Among them are Jobes' contribution, Collaborative Assessment and Management of Suicidality; cognitive therapy; and the most promising suicide prevention treatment to date, dialectical behavior therapy. Sadly, most of these methods still aren't widely practiced. Traditional interventions such as involuntary hospitalization, quick-fix medications, or forcing patients to sign contracts saying they won't take their own lives are often knee-jerk and can be needlessly coercive. (Hospitalization can be beneficial, but experts say it shouldn't be the only option.)

Suicide prevention advocates want to shift their efforts upstream, pre-crisis, but a dam is blocking their path: The majority of American mental health professionals lack adequate suicide prevention training. It's typically not part of medical school curriculum; most physicians and clinicians learn about it on the job. "We have clinicians who are inadequately trained and patients who are suffering with treatable issues," Jobes says. "It's an emperor-has-no-clothes situation."

Susan Marine is a retired sociologist and a board member for the Suicide Prevention Coalition of Colorado. She lost her children, Kevin and Alice, to suicide in the early 2000s; both were young adults living with bipolar disorder. She says her one regret is that she wasn't educated enough on depression and other risk factors for suicide. In 2013, she surveyed 479 Colorado mental health professionals about their suicide prevention training. Forty percent said they received 10 or fewer hours of suicide education, even though 43 percent indicated that they deal with the issue on a weekly basis and 72 percent said clinical training would be helpful.

The only medical profession with formally mandated suicide prevention training is psychiatry. Dr. Michael Allen—a researcher at the University of Colorado Depression Center and member of the Colorado Psychiatric Society's legislative committee—says more than 90 percent of American psychiatrists receive suicide risk assessment training (compared to 50 percent of psychologists and fewer than 25 percent of social workers). This supervised learning amounts to a mean of just 3.6 hours of formal seminars and lectures during their residencies. In 2012, Washington state passed the Matt Adler Suicide Assessment, Treatment and Management Act, the first of its kind, which dictates that certain mental health providers, including social workers, psychologists, and occupational therapists, must receive six hours of training every six years as part of their continuing education requirements. In 2014, the law was expanded to include a one-time six-hour training requirement for physicians and nurses.

Colorado state Senator Linda Newell, with help from Marine and other advocates, attempted to craft a similar bill in 2013, but it never made it to the Statehouse floor. A number of groups, including the Colorado Psychiatric Society and Colorado Psychological Association, expressed concerns about the state's structural readiness for such a law, and they evinced a general resistance to outsiders—that is, politicians—setting requirements. These groups argue that not every type of medical practitioner needs the same type of instruction. (Until this past spring, psychologists in Colorado didn't even have a general requirement for continuing professional development.) To date, the result has been little or no required suicide prevention training at all.

This means those at risk often aren't being identified even when they seek help. Allen supports focused training but understands the lack of support for Colorado's bill. "We at least want a workforce to be able to ask questions and identify suicide risk," he says. "[The proposed legislation] was just kind of premature because the continuing education framework wasn't there."

The problem extends to primary care providers (PCPs). According to the American Foundation for Suicide Prevention, 45 percent of people who die by suicide have seen a PCP within the previous month. Asking about depression or suicide risk often isn't part of a routine medical visit, and even if PCPs do inquire and get an affirmative answer, lack of training means they may not have many—or any—vetted referral options. (Screening tools have been developed and accepted for use in PCP settings.) Paul Quinnett, president and CEO of suicide prevention training provider QPR Institute, has been involved in public mental health for more than 30 years and says, "Sometimes a failure to ask is interpreted as permission to proceed."

In Colorado, longtime grassroots efforts finally helped create a statewide Office of Suicide Prevention (OSP) in 2000. The 24/7 National Suicide Prevention Lifeline launched in 2005 and is overseen locally by the Pueblo Suicide Prevention Center and RMCP. When Governor Hickenlooper took office in 2011, he named suicide one of the state's "10 winnable battles." In 2012, federal officials updated the National Strategy for Suicide Prevention (suicide prevention was first declared a national priority in 1998). And in 2014, Colorado legislators created the Suicide Prevention Commission, a 26-member advisory group charged with leading prevention and intervention efforts here. Improving training absent a legislative directive is just one of the group's myriad objectives. These efforts can't evolve quickly enough: The number of suicide deaths in Colorado rose higher than ever last year.

Although the statewide crisis system has experienced some implementation hiccups since it launched in December 2014, there already has been a noticeable uptick in the number of people seeking help. "We know Colorado hasn't been at the top of anything when it comes to behavioral health funding," says Cheri Skelding, a licensed clinical social worker and clinical director for RMCP's 24/7 statewide crisis hotline and 14-hour-a-day peer support line. "This is the starting point for Colorado's commitment toward behavioral health in the future."

Now that the big-picture crisis system is in place—beyond the crisis and support line, it includes walk-in clinics, crisis stabilization units, mobile crisis services, and respite and residential centers—Colorado activists want to create a comprehensive continuum of care. Currently, "suicide prevention is really suicide intervention," says Jarrod Hindman, violence and suicide prevention section manager at OSP. In other words, while the crisis system is important, we still aren't doing enough to stop people from reaching the precipice of suicide—or to help them after an attempt.

For example, even though the period after discharge is particularly dangerous for suicidal people, Colorado hasn't established standards for what information hospitals must give patients or their families following an attempt. In 2012, our Legislature passed HB 1140, which required OSP to provide materials about suicide warning signs, post-attempt treatment, and community resources to hospitals. But a follow-up assessment found that only 51 percent of hospitals that responded reported using the materials.

A new pilot project at four hospitals (two metro, two rural) takes a different approach by having a clinician from RMCP speak with patients or parents by phone before the patients are released and then follow up several times over the next few weeks. Hindman hopes this more focused effort, which requires identifying a point person at each venue, will help bring more hospitals on board. Broadening awareness and identification of those at risk as early as possible is key because even those closest to a suicidal person may not recognize or believe there's a problem.

Memories of my dad were everywhere. His laugh and his booming voice still echoed through the quiet that had overwhelmed our house—interrupted often by recollections of the doorbell's chime, the cop standing there, and my mother crying.

I needed to get out. Some close friends gathered at a neighbor's house a few days later. I tried to be normal and joke and eat the holiday cookies my friend's mom baked every December. Their lightheartedness seemed purposeful, as if they were determined to cheer me up. When someone asked me what I wanted for Hanukkah, I desperately wanted to maintain the levity and forget my horrible new reality, but the words tumbled out: "I just want my dad back."

I couldn't cry the night he died, even when I tried thinking of something sad to generate tears. I realize now I was in shock, but at the time I was appalled at myself, even as I recognized that I was probably just trying to protect my mother from seeing her own pain reflected back.

As a suddenly fatherless 13-year-old, I was furious—at my dad, at my mom, at the world. *How could he have left me? He couldn't have been thinking of me,* I decided, *or he wouldn't have done it.* I felt guilty. *Did he call out for help and I missed the signs?* I had no idea how to face a world in which I'd barely heard the word "suicide" uttered before.

For every suicide death, researchers believe an average of 115 people—family, friends, co-workers—are impacted. Those who have experienced the suicide of a close relative are up to six times more likely to attempt suicide themselves. Two of my father's siblings, my aunt and uncle, also died by suicide. (None of them were ever formally diagnosed with mental illnesses, but family anecdotes reveal some instances of depressive and manic behaviors.)

I don't want that to be the legacy my family—my father—leaves my brothers and me. I want his creativity, his drive, his charisma, and his kindness to be what we carry with us. For people bereaved by suicide loss, those gifts often are overshadowed internally by anger, guilt, confusion, and a sense of abandonment.

For a long time after his death, I was lost. I slowly resumed my routines (school, volleyball, movies with friends), but something was still missing. That void resulted in arguments with my mother—two people stuck together in a house that should have been more full. It made me more of a risk-taker at times; when I got older, I'd drink more than I should, or I'd carelessly cliff-jump off a 50-foot precipice. The danger didn't concern me—not because I was a daredevil, but because I thought, *What does it matter?*

I never felt I lacked a male role model. I have two inspiring older brothers to whom I've always turned for life and career advice—or more often, a laugh. My mom has continued to parent the way she and my dad did before, by always supporting me and by giving me the freedom to find my own way. I know I'm not alone. And yet, we each carry our grief in our own ways. It's something we can't share.

My father's absence has also made me strong, confident, and independent. But his death did leave me with what one attempt survivor calls a psychological "limp." I am, in a way, broken. Unexpected early morning or late-night phone calls still cause a tightening feeling in my chest. I have occasional nightmares in which someone I love is in an accident. I've given mental eulogies to people who are still alive. I rarely make it through a father-daughter wedding dance without breaking down. Without him, I'm more stubborn, more hotheaded, more sure that my way is the right way. Because I need to know that if I have to, I can do it all on my own.

But now I realize something else: In researching this story and meeting people who've been through similar situations, I can finally, as a 28-year-old, empathize with how my dad must have felt, even if I'll never fully comprehend his state of mind.

My heart will always bear a scar, but today the sadness I feel is much more for him. I'm pained that my dad's worldview must have seemed so bleak and that his heart bore such a burden. How awful it must have been to carry that every day. I wish he had known that he could have lost everything—his business, his money, the rest of his hair—and we would have never stopped loving him. He taught me to be strong and face adversity with courage. We would have carried the burdens he couldn't. I wish he had given us the chance. I wish I had realized how much he needed us.

My father has already missed so many important moments—my college graduation, my first byline, my brother's wedding—and he'll be absent for whatever lies ahead. The yearning for his presence never subsides. Grief is a constant companion. You grow around it, the way a tree matures around a foreign object, but you never forget it's there. It arises at predictable times—anniversaries or birthdays—but also in the most mundane and unexpected moments, like when you see "Dad" pop up on your friend's iPhone screen.

It's difficult to keep my father's memory alive. My friends, colleagues, and boyfriend never met him. They don't know the person he was in his soul, so there's a part of me they won't ever fully understand. I'll never know who I would be today if my father was still here, but I hope I've grown into someone he would recognize and respect. I can't remember his laugh anymore, or his voice. I forget what it was like to have a conversation with him. I feel guilty that I didn't hold on tighter to those memories, that I let growing up fill in the holes.

I hope I never forget how safe I felt when he hugged me. And how much he loved me and how proud he always was of even my smallest accomplishments. I think I remember his smile, which amplified the creases around his eyes. But maybe that's because of a picture sitting on my bookshelf, a framed, sepia-tone photo of him captured by my oldest brother, Seth. I look at it every day.

Suicide attempts are a complex mix of impulsivity and planning. Those who attempt typically have underlying risk factors and, like Josi, have been fighting a losing battle against overwhelming feelings of hopelessness—usually while dealing with a mental illness—for an extended period of time. The decision to act, though, often occurs in hours or minutes.

Firearms are the most common means of suicide fatalities, partly because they're so lethal—about 85 percent of attempts with firearms result in death—and in much of the country, so accessible. "You're not more likely to become suicidal if you're a gun owner, but if you become suicidal, you're more likely to use a gun in your attempt and therefore to die," says Catherine Barber of the Harvard Injury Control Research Center.

Gun ownership will always be a contentious issue in Colorado, where 76 percent of all firearm deaths between 2005 and 2012 were suicides. "We need to demand a harder conversation politically about how long we are going to put our heads in the sand and not talk about the access to firearms," says Senator Newell, who has sponsored two pieces of suicide prevention legislation in the past three years.

Barber and many others are pushing to change social norms around firearm safety—what she calls the "designated driver approach." Whether it's locking guns in a safe or storing ammunition separately, means restriction (the reduction of access to lethal methods) saves lives. In Colorado, a gun owner can legally transfer a firearm, even to an unregistered person, for up to 72 hours—longer if it's being given to a family member or if it's "necessary to protect themselves from imminent death or injury." Research shows that just interrupting the acute crisis often creates enough time for the person to find help, or at least to take a moment to manage his thoughts. For instance, installing suicide barriers on bridges deters people from jumping at those spots; suicides dropped from 24 in six years to one in five years after the city erected a barrier at D.C.'s Duke Ellington Bridge. In 2014, officials in California approved a $76 million project to install steel-cable nets 20 feet below the Golden Gate Bridge, where more than 1,600 people have leapt to their deaths.

This past year in Colorado, OSP and other prevention groups ran a means restriction education training pilot program at Children's Hospital Colorado. It involved a mental health service provider meeting with parents or guardians of suicidal children to discuss how to make their homes safer. The program was successful enough that Children's has officially adopted the protocol.

OSP is also reaching out to gun owners with a project in five Western Slope counties that mimics a successful one in New Hampshire. The premise is simple: Find a gun enthusiast in each community to approach gun shops as a peer and educate them about warning signs they or their customers might encounter. OSP intends to expand and improve both programs over the next year, and Senator Newell and OSP's Hindman have hinted that some federal organizations, including the National Action Alliance for Suicide Prevention, are considering Colorado as a pilot site for federal-state collaborations.

This would mean federal money could start flowing into the state, easing one of the biggest impediments to suicide prevention: funding. "The burden of suicide in Colorado is disproportionate to the available resources," reads OSP's annual prevention report for 2013-2014. OSP's yearly budget of approximately $465,000 confines Hindman's efforts to small projects around the state. The money issue is bleak even when you zoom out. The National Institutes of Health's suicide-related funding has dropped by $10 million since 2011.

Perhaps the only benefit of this small till is that it breeds creative thinking. The negative, beyond the obvious, is that inadequate funding gives weight to pervasive stigma surrounding the issue and supports the idea—at a governmental level—that suicide can't be prevented. Until convictions change, money won't follow. "One of the greatest misperceptions about suicide—and that drives funding—is that when someone dies by suicide, it's their fault," says Michelle Cornette, executive director of the American Association of Suicidology, who compares the sympathetic reaction someone with cancer receives to the you-made-your-bed response to a suicide. "There's a tendency with a suicidal individual to say, 'Well, that's their choice.' We know that to be not true. It's not a choice."

Millions of people have stories similar to mine, and until recently, they're the ones who largely carried the suicide prevention flag. We're all confronted with the question that haunts those left behind, what Sally Spencer-Thomas's mentor calls "the canyon of why."

Spencer-Thomas lost her younger brother, Carson, to suicide in 2004. A successful entrepreneur with a young family, he was living with bipolar and substance abuse disorders. Two weeks before his 35th birthday, Carson took his own life. Spencer-Thomas is unsure exactly what changed that summer and fall, but a downward spiral of loss may have launched Carson into his deepest depression, a pit of self-loathing he never managed to escape. It flipped his view of himself from a confident, charming man into someone who could barely get out of bed.

Anxiety, sorrow, and fear consumed Spencer-Thomas after her brother's death. The assistance of family, colleagues, her faith community, and a survivor support group helped her move through the initial year of acute pain. They lifted her up again eight years later when she battled her own severe depression. Now, seated behind the desk at the foundation that bears her brother's name, a photo behind her of the two of them dancing at her wedding, Spencer-Thomas says she's become certain of one thing. "I'm pretty sure that he would have figured it out," she says. "I believe he could have made it through if he knew on the other side he could have gotten his life back. I feel like that's the part he had lost hope on."

As with other types of unexpected loss, those bereaved by suicide face tsunamis of grief as they sort through not only the anguish of lives cut short, but also the trauma of what is usually a violent death, the isolation of community stigma, questions of blame, and many other unanswerable thoughts. When the survivor's world is upended, how does he or she move forward?

Clinical grief support can be difficult to find, but volunteer organizations such as HEARTBEAT can ease some of that bewilderment. LaRita Archibald founded the support group in Colorado Springs in 1980 for those bereaved by suicide; there are now chapters in 15 states and three countries. Her son Roger died by suicide in 1978 at age 24. "Stigma was just thick," she says of that time, her eyes bright and her hair now white. In the late 1970s, there were few organizations in the country addressing grief, so she started her own. "Everybody who goes through this is knocked to their knees," she says. "But we can take things that happen and make meaning from them. It takes a lot of courage to face society when someone in your family has crossed a taboo boundary."

Today there is an international movement loudly clamoring for a paradigm shift called Zero Suicide. Though most people realize we'll never truly get to zero—suicide has been part of the human narrative for millennia—the phrase signifies a foundational belief that the suicide deaths of individuals who access health care and behavioral health systems are preventable. It's about keeping people from falling through the most basic cracks, and it's a bold, outspoken stance on a topic that's been feared for far too long. "The big message is that a million people attempt suicide every year in the United States, and most of them go on to recover their lives and find meaning and purpose in life," Eduardo Vega says. "We are not the 'other.' We are not strangers or aliens. And we have messages of hope that can help others if we can be heard. Suicide is preventable. The real tragedy is that in most cases, if most people had better supports—the right kinds of supports—they wouldn't get to that point of finally pulling the trigger."

Josi thinks her last suicide attempt was her sixth; it's difficult to recall the exact number. It's been seven years since that wall of get-well cards inspired her to focus on living, inspiration drawn from friends and colleagues who made sure to tell her how much they loved and appreciated her—even though her doctors weren't sure she'd ever wake up. "In the past, I felt like no one would care if I died," she says, her fingers constantly fidgeting. "For the first time, I had people who said they'd miss me." Josi now works as a peer support specialist at RMCP, where she uses her own experiences to help others overcome challenges.

She's also the drop-in coordinator at CHARG Resource Center, a Capitol Hill nonprofit that aids adults with mental illnesses.

Josi knows her mental health will be a constant struggle. She still has serious bouts of depression. January, in particular, has always been difficult; she doesn't know why. She'll probably have to go to the hospital again—she calls it a "pit stop"—to reset. Remaining so diligent can be exhausting. But it's critical. "For me, recovery is a day-by-day, hour-by-hour, and sometimes minute-by-minute choice that I have to make," she says. The need to continually revive her most basic will to live is a sentiment Josi shares with other attempt survivors.

On good days Josi pauses, urging her brain to remember every ounce of the positive feelings she's experiencing, burning them into her memory so she can draw on that reservoir whenever bleakness seeps in. She educates herself on her illnesses. She attends therapy regularly. She keeps a gratitude journal, jotting down three or four positive things that happen every week. "Those good things don't come to you when you're depressed," she says. "When I'm depressed, it's like I'm walking through this world but I'm not really a person, not really alive." It also helps to be able to look up at that collage of cards from the hospital: They're framed on a wall in her apartment.

In my bedroom at my mom's house, there is a handwritten message from my father on a ruled pink sticky note. The paper has faded with time, but his words, and their meaning, are unchanged. The note is taped to a Popsicle-stick bridge we crafted together for a junior high class. It's dated December 6, 1999, and reads: "Always do things right, and always have confidence in your work—makes life fun! I love you more than anything in the world!"

The last sentence became the foundation of a drawing my brother David made me for my 14th birthday, seven months to the day after my dad died. Sketched in pencil, the words are accompanied by hand-drawn portraits of my father and me. The precious gift hangs by my bed at home. When I visit, it's usually the last thing I look at before I turn out the lights.

On the night my dad died, I fell asleep at some point on his side of my parents' bed, my head resting on the pillow that still held an indentation from the last time he lay there. I'm not sure when I closed my eyes or for how long I slept.

There's a flicker in time, a split second between sleep and consciousness, when your brain hasn't fully rebooted and you float in an ethereal space as the light of morning hovers in a hazy golden kaleidoscope before your closed eyelids. In that moment I seemed to exist in some sort of in-between, a place of calm and peace where yesterday's reality had not yet resurfaced. The comforter swathed me in its warmth. As the sun streamed through the blinds onto my face, I slowly blinked awake into the unmistakable glow of the new day.

—September 2015

6.

Final Post

by Kasey Cordell

Room 143 sits approximately 60 steps from the front doors of the Denver Veterans Affairs Community Living Center. You know because you can count Julian Scadden's every step—change jingling in one pocket, a set of keys jangling in the other—as the 67-year-old passes through two sets of double doors, past the nurses station, down the hallway to the third door on the right. He knocks before he enters. He always knocks, even if the men lying in the beds can't answer.

The maple trees outside Room 143 have just begun to blossom, but the lieutenant, separated from them by just a few feet and less than an inch of glass, can't see the tiny buds and leaves unfurling. His eyes are open but clouded. "I haven't left you, partner," Julian says, approaching the bed. He carries a cool washcloth and gently pats the lieutenant's forehead. "I'm right here."

There's a peculiar odor in the room, the scent of strong coffee (Julian's: black, no sugar) and antiseptics blending with the sickly-sweet smell of sweat and soiled linens. Julian doesn't notice. That's in part because of his own bouquet; he's been here since yesterday. He came—as he always does—when the nurses called and said the lieutenant was close. No matter that it was evening. No matter that Julian had worked all day at the VA hospital next door, cleaning floors and toilets and emptying rooms of the ugliness that comes with illness. When the call came, he showered and drove the seven miles from his Aurora home back to the Community Living Center. All through the night he sat with the lieutenant, watching him seize, watching him fight to breathe, watching him struggle and win, and then watching him do it all again. Julian took a nap in his truck at 3 a.m. At 4:30 he said goodbye and went to work. Eight hours later, he's back in Room 143. He's shaken out his ponytail so his wavy gray hair flows down over his Home of the Brave T-shirt. He wants fresh clothes and a shower to wash off the smell of the day. He can't stand feeling grimy.

But he'll go without another night because the lieutenant needs him. Because this is what Julian does: He sits at the doorway to death, ushering his brothers through whatever portal separates us from the world we know and the uncertainty that comes next. No matter what time or what day, he's here. Patting, soothing, cooing. No, the smell doesn't bother Julian. He's breathed it in some 200 times before.

The Community Living Center has several names. The small, one-story building, connected to the VA hospital by a series of underground hallways, is also known as Building 38. Until a decade ago, it was called "the nursing home." Some volunteers and staffers still refer to it that way instead of by the modern moniker—the CLC—which is really just a sanitized way of saying "where soldiers go to die."

The name cards outside the 27 rooms at the CLC come in many colors: Green and purple represent short stays (rehab and geriatric rehab); orange stands for respite; brown equates to long-term care; and blue means palliative or hospice care. Most of the time, almost all of the cards are blue.

The patients on this floor come from all eras—World War II, Korea, Vietnam, peacetime, the Gulf War, and current conflicts. They are men and women, officers and enlisted personnel, pilots, sailors, soldiers, and Marines. Some have family and friends who visit. Many don't. Some play solitaire to while away the hours between meals and meds. Others simply sit and stare—at the TV, out the window, at each other. They come to the CLC from different places and different backgrounds and with different ailments, but they all share one thing: They know they will probably never leave.

Julian knows this, too. He's been a housekeeper at the VA for 10 years, and while his work during the day keeps him confined to the hospital's upper floors, he's often down here after hours. He watches to see which patients have visitors, which ones don't, and who's nearing the end. When they get close, he introduces himself. He makes friends. And then he sits with them until the end. He calls himself the 11th Hour.

Julian started his volunteer work eight years ago as part of the Denver VA's Compassion Corps. Established by the VA's volunteer coordinators and hospice care workers about 10 years ago, the program trained civilians and former military personnel in the art of being present for death. The CLC has many volunteers—the harp player who comes in on Mondays, the therapy dog that visits each Friday—but Compassion Corps was, and is, unique. Palliative care nurses oversaw the training, which included 16 hours of reading, videos, and role-playing. The videos weren't just of the afterschool-special variety, simply detailing how to talk to someone nearing death (although there were some of those, too). They were of raw, gritty, often gruesome war footage. Of men killing. Of men dying. Of pieces of what were formerly men. "They wanted you to see what the vets saw," Julian says, "so you'd understand." But Julian already knew something about this: He'd enlisted in the Army in 1967 at the age of 17.

You'll find Adams City High School where East 72nd Avenue ends and the plains begin. This is the place where storm clouds start to gather and turn Denver's blue skies the color of the plentiful concrete underneath. Apart from the school, there's little more than power lines and pavement and—across Quebec Parkway—a couple of pawn shops and quickie marts. There was even less when Julian was a student here.

Julian moved to the Denver area from Trinidad when he was in kindergarten. His parents had separated when he was two, and his mother was following the first of what would be four husbands. Julian and his eight siblings spent the next few years settling and re-settling into various homes and neighborhoods along I-76 between Denver and Fort Lupton. In 1960, they landed in Commerce City. Much like it does today, the area held a large Hispanic population, and by the mid-'60s, tensions between Hispanics and whites were high. They spilled over into the yellowed grass of Adams City High in the first semester of Julian's freshman year.

One day, as the five-foot-four-inch wrestler—"Tiny," to those close to him—waited in line with his friend at a store across the street from the school, two white boys dumped soda on Julian's shoe. They exchanged words, and later in the day when Julian saw the boys on school grounds, the argument escalated to blows. They fell, tussling on the hard, dry earth. One of the students ended up on top of Julian, hammering the teenager with punches. Julian's friend kicked the teen, hard, to get him off. The white boys ran home and called the cops. Shortly after, police officers showed up at Julian's home and took him in for questioning. They wanted him to identify his friend. He wouldn't. The boy had recently been released from a juvenile detention facility, and Julian knew fighting would get him sent back. The police were adamant, but so was Julian. He spent the next couple of days in jail—until his friend turned himself in.

Because the fight had occurred on school grounds, Julian would not be allowed back at Adams City High until he and his mother met with the principal. Julian's relationship with his mother was complicated: He was protective of the small-framed woman despite her occasional cruelty. When Julian refused to call his stepfathers "Dad," his mother would fly into a rage, telling him he was stupid, that he wouldn't amount to anything. Still, Julian was her "hijo," her son, and she loved him. So she went with him to the principal's office and, according to Julian, endured a torrent of insults about her lifestyle, her many boyfriends. "Are you done?" she asked the principal as Julian sat, twitching at her side. He nodded. "Sic him, Julian." The teenager leapt across the desk and punched the principal; office staff had to pull him off. Julian was expelled from Adams City High and kicked out of the school district.

He had few options, so at 15, Julian began working. He removed radiators at service stations and did yard work and other odd jobs. And so it went for the next year: Julian working during the day, sometimes fighting at night, occasionally getting picked up by the police. After an evening of pitching nickels with friends, police stopped Julian on his way home. It was close to curfew, 10 p.m. for minors. When the police discovered the change in his pockets—his winnings—they took

Julian to the station for questioning about a rash of thefts from soda machines, eventually releasing him after a few hours. But Julian was fed up. Not long after the incident, he and his friend Jim Vigil walked into the Marine recruiting office, determined to get out of town.

Julian's reputation followed him, though. At that stage, still relatively early in the Vietnam War, the Marines typically didn't accept teens with histories of fighting. But the Army did. "Jim and me went down to MEPS [the Military Entrance Processing Station] that day and took our tests," Julian says. "That night they had us on a plane to Fort Bliss."

The IV drips quietly as Julian leans over the lieutenant, a tiny sponge in one hand, a washcloth in the other. There's a small amount of pain medication in the IV, enough to keep the lieutenant, who's dying of lung cancer, somewhat comfortable, but that's it. He still seizes and strains against the disease. With his left hand, Julian presses the sponge to the lieutenant's lips, wetting them and giving him a sip of water. With his right, Julian places the cloth on the lieutenant's head, then gently rubs a thumb across his brow. "When I rub their foreheads, it's like when mama would rub your head when you were sick. That's how I let him know I'm still here," Julian says. "I learned it when I was watching my dad."

Julian was 36 when his father died. He'd gone to the doctor with a cold he couldn't shake. An X-ray revealed a spot on his lung. They did surgery right away, but when they got inside, they could see it was too late. They closed him back up. Six months, they said. He lasted three. He wanted to die at home, so hospice nurses came to the house and helped prepare Julian and his siblings. They explained that their father would slowly regress; he'd lose his memory, himself. He would need constant care, someone always at his side. "I told them, 'I can't do this. I'm too weak,'" Julian says. "But in the end, I did. I sat with him. I watched him. It was my first experience with death."

When he talks about his father, Julian almost always tears up. He was a good man, he'll tell you. He taught him manners. How to love. How not to judge. These are lessons Julian brings to the CLC every day, because while many of the patients are heroes, few of them are saints. Like most of us, they've made good decisions and bad ones. Some choices have cost them jobs, friends, families, and homes, and so some find themselves alone—or almost alone. "You can see some good and some bad in all of them," Julian says. "Once they come through that door, though, it doesn't make any difference who they are, what they are, or where they've been. Once you come in that door, you're mine."

Julian sometimes worries about making a connection with his patients. But he keeps coming back. Because if he doesn't, who will? Some of them, the ones still in denial about death, push him away. They can be grumpy—"ornery," Julian calls them, even mean. Others are easier. "Like him," Julian says, nodding toward the lieutenant. He's still holding his hand. "Just that little bit of time we spent together talking about things...I keep thinking, *We could have been friends*."

And they could have been. They're close in age, though illness has aged the lieutenant decades beyond those he's actually lived. Or maybe it was the stress of sending soldiers to their deaths in Vietnam. The lieutenant spent three years in the Army, one of them as part of an armored division in Quang Tri. The place sounds familiar to Julian, as it should to all of us: Nearly 1,000 American soldiers died in Quang Tri during the Tet Offensive. By the time he came home from Vietnam, the lieutenant had collected a Purple Heart, a Bronze Star, a Silver Star, and—to hear Julian tell it—invisible scars. Julian's war, though, was different.

Julian spent the first night of his deployment sleeping on a cot in the aisle of the barracks. It was June 1967, and the base on Okinawa didn't have room for him and all of the other newly arrived soldiers. At 1 a.m., the barracks door burst open. "Get up!" the first sergeant yelled. "Outside! Now! Form up!" Bewildered soldiers stumbled into the warm rain and fell into formation. They stayed there for the next few hours "practicing" slitting their wrists lengthwise, along the vein, instead of horizontally, because a private had tried—and failed—to kill himself that way earlier in the day.

Julian knew only five of the soldiers he stood next to. The rest of the men from his military occupational specialty had already been sent to Vietnam. Like Julian, those five soldiers were only 17, generally considered too young for combat. After basic training, Julian became a fix-it generalist—a jack-of-all-trades, master of none, as he's fond of saying. But when he arrived in Okinawa, his superiors signed him up for the missile crew. His job was to make sure the firing pins stayed in working order in the event Okinawa ever came under attack.

The island was a kind of in-between place for American troops. Young men on their ways to and from Vietnam would come through; battle-weary soldiers were sent to the island for a few days or weeks of R and R. "They were messed up," Julian says. "They'd act really strange." He remembers one soldier tossing his mattress on the ground outside the barracks and spending every hour, every day jumping onto it from the roof. He was practicing for a parachute, he told Julian. For the most part, Julian stayed away from these GIs. He instead spent his spare time near the Suicide Cliffs.

Tucked along Okinawa's idyllic southern shore, the Suicide Cliffs today are home to Peace Memorial Park, a remembrance of the more than 150,000 people who died on the island in World War II. During the 82-day Battle of Okinawa, thousands of Japanese citizens and soldiers leapt from these cliffs, opting to die by their own hands rather than face the Americans. (The Japanese army's propaganda depicted the Americans as demons and convinced many members of the local population that to be captured by them was a fate worse than death.)

When Julian was there, though, there was no park. There was no memorial. In fact, the rocky bluffs were largely off-limits to American military personnel. The Army warned troops not to venture to the area because the locals couldn't be trusted and many of them still might believe the old stories about Americans and try to harm them. Julian ignored the advice.

The cliffs were just a mile from where he worked, so he'd often wander down to them and the little store nearby. He'd buy two small bottles of sake: one for him and one for the locals. Although they couldn't really communicate, Julian still sat with the men and sometimes their wives and families. "Somewhere out there, there are a bunch of photos of me holding little Japanese babies," Julian says. They'd smile at one another, appreciate the landscape and the warm glow of the sake. Here, Julian felt most comfortable. He spent less time at the cliffs as his tour went on, though: When he had an altercation with a sergeant he never liked, he put in for a transfer to be a dog handler with the military police. The Army acquiesced, and Julian spent the rest of his time in Okinawa accompanied by his dog, Hettle. But the new job meant he wasn't always close to the cliffs—and his friends—on the southern shore.

Julian returned to the States in 1968 and was sent to Fort Sill, Oklahoma. His high school buddy Jim Vigil had come home before him, a Purple Heart recipient, but one who lived. Julian felt somehow lesser in the company of such men, the ones who had experienced combat. Outraged American protesters made no such distinction. "They called me baby killer, all of it," Julian says of his return. His mother and step-father even asked him not to come to a prayer group because they were embarrassed by his service. The experience was scarring. Julian served out the rest of his enlistment behind a curtain of shame: guilt for never fighting, for having lived, and for having been a part of something his fellow Americans hated, even when the choice really wasn't his. Hurt, angry, and confused, Julian did not re-enlist. On January 23, 1970, he walked out of Fort Sill and away from the Army. He did not take his uniforms—not a shirt, not a jacket. All he took was a hat. He was done.

Between episodes of *Everybody Loves Raymond* and nature shows, Julian and the lieutenant would talk about life. About cigars and women. About the war they were both a part of. How they hated it. Julian for the emptiness not fighting left in him, and the lieutenant for sending soldiers—boys—like Julian to die. "He told me I was lucky," Julian says. "That he understood I had regrets, but that I was lucky."

He pauses. The lieutenant's breathing has become labored. Atrophied chest muscles strain against the light blue cotton gown. "I'm here for you, brother," Julian says, his fingers around the lieutenant's, his thumb caressing a warm hand wrapped in tissue-paper skin. The lieutenant's cloudy eyes track toward Julian. One first, the other a heartbeat behind. He exhales. In the silence between breaths, it's easy to mark time; the clock's second hand is the loudest sound in the room. It ticks past 30 before the next inhale. Is it the last? How many more can the body fight for?

Those less familiar with death lean in, not wanting to miss the last inhale or movement, a final involuntary twitch. Julian doesn't. He's been here before. He's seen this. He knows watching for it won't change it. And so he reads. He watches television. He holds hands and when the pain comes, he grips tighter and whispers. But he doesn't give in to the threat of death. He doesn't squinch up his face and peer close, looking for the final marker. He simply waits.

You don't end up on Julian's street in Aurora's Expo Park neighborhood by accident. It's a direct route to nowhere for everyone except the people who live along the rainbow-shaped stretch of '70s architecture. The ranch-style homes on this working-class block come with big garages, tall trees, and large yards maintained to varying degrees. Julian's front lawn is tidy; the driveway is free of weeds. A flagstone footpath through the grass invites visitors from the sidewalk straight to the front door.

It's only about a 15-minute drive from the house, which Julian shares with his daughter and three great-grandchildren, to the CLC, but sometimes even that's too long. Sometimes by the time he gets there, his patients are gone. "Once I've left, if I come home, my family knows I've lost one," Julian says. The house is Julian's 18th residence in Aurora. He bought a rambling split-level here in 1976 with enough room for his then wife, Francis, and their two children, Angela and Julian Jr. A year later Francis was diagnosed with multiple sclerosis, and according to Julian, after that she changed. "She didn't want me anymore," he says. The two had married shortly after Julian returned from Fort Sill. He'd known Francis, a devout Catholic, since junior high, when he was close with her brother Jim, the friend with whom he'd joined the Army. "She was the best thing for me," Julian says.

After Francis' diagnosis, Julian's life began a familiar slide: He started drinking too much and fighting. After one particularly hard-drinking night, Julian ended up talking back to some police officers, which landed him first in jail, and then in a recovery center for those who have substance-abuse problems.

Julian and Francis divorced in 1986. He cut back on alcohol, but anger simmered just beneath his omnipresent grin. It took very little to set him off, particularly if he felt slighted by those in positions of authority, like his bosses. As a result, Julian floated between a series of jobs through the '80s and '90s, working at restaurants and apartment complexes and eventually for the City of Aurora. One of those jobs was at Mile High Frozen Foods, where his children also worked. The company would provide food to the families of returning troops at welcome home ceremonies, and in 2007 Julian went to one with his daughter. They waited on the tarmac with the families, who held banners and flowers as the planes came in.

"They landed so close you could see the faces of the men and women in the windows of the plane as they were coming down," his daughter, Angela, says. "This was the first time their feet were hitting American soil. There's hot food. It's a thank-you for your service. I remember his face when he saw the reception these young men and women had coming back. He was silent for a long time."

In 2006, Julian got a job at the VA, where his old high school buddy and former brother-in-law Ralph Vigil (Jim's brother), was also employed. Ralph, too, had served in the military. The Marine had gone to Vietnam a year ahead of Julian, and he came home with a Purple Heart. It was Ralph who recruited Julian into the VA's Compassion Corps. He'd joined the program in 2007. Growing up in Commerce City, he'd seen that Julian was always willing when the Vigil family—or any of his friends—needed help. Julian was the kind of guy who'd help you move a washing machine up three flights of stairs. He'd tip a waiter $10 on just a glass of iced tea. "You need something? Julian's right there," Ralph says. "And if he says he's going to do it, he'll do it." Ralph pestered Julian for roughly a year to join him. Julian deflected his requests, until one day he finally gave in. After his first training session, he could see the head nurse wasn't too impressed with him, but Julian had given his word to Ralph that he'd try—even if it were just to shut him up. "I wouldn't quit, and she wouldn't throw me out," Julian says. "So I was stuck."

As soon as Julian hit the CLC, though, something changed. In the presence of patients there was no latent fury, no anti-authoritarian anger—only a gentle spirit, wearing a smile, who seemed to always find the right words, even in the moments when there were no words. "Some of them want to tell you their life story. Some of them want to tell you about their kids. Some of them just wanna bullshit ya. I listen," Julian says. "Sometimes I'll ask a question if I get the feeling they want me to. Sometimes they want you to ask so they can tell."

Julian shares their stories, too. He has favorites, like the one about a grumpy patient who always had some kind of tall tale. He'd often say to his roommate and to Julian that when death came, he was going to outrun it. They all would laugh. One morning, after arriving before his shift to check on his patients, Julian asked a nurse about his storyteller. "That's funny," she said, "I haven't heard him bitching yet." Together they went to his room and found the man on the floor. As the pair picked him up, the nurse holding his lower body, Julian lifting his upper, a whoosh of air escaped. "I smelled it," Julian says. "The smell of death. 'He's gone,' I said." The roommate nodded: "He said, 'Here it comes. It ain't gonna get me.' And he took a step out of bed and went down."

Julian smiles a little when he tells that story. It's sad, but it's also kind of funny. And if you can't laugh at death a little, he'll say, well, you can't really live. He's learned other lessons along the way: Don't enter a room without being invited, don't interrupt, don't leave without saying when you'll be back, and make damn sure you keep that promise. "Because a lot of time all they have is you. They have nothing else," Julian says. "These people, they're watching for when you come and when you go. They're marking time by you."

The lieutenant doesn't have many visitors. The nurses and doctors, of course; a couple of friends from Nebraska; and the occasional volunteer. He has a sister in the Midwest, but she's ill herself and can't make it. When the lieutenant still could speak, the nurses called her so the pair might have a last moment together, if even just by phone.

But really, his only regular guest is Julian. He watches *Everybody Loves Raymond* on his own now, usually to keep himself awake. During the daylight hours he plays a CLC recording. A soothing female voice says over gentle nature sounds: *Follow the birds to a beautiful shore.* He watches the shadows slide across the bed and listens to the rhythm of the CLC outside Room 143—the crackle of the intercom, the swish of doctors' coats, a passing gurney's rattle and squeak.

Sometimes the squeak signifies death. It's often the sign of a funeral procession or, as they call them here, a Freedom Procession. In the CLC, there's usually about one a week. A couple of patients in wheelchairs often lead the procession, followed by family members and friends carrying tiny flags. Then comes the gurney, always creaking. A homemade flag drapes the body. Someone carries a boom box that plays "Taps." As the gurney passes each room, its resident, if he's able, falls in behind. They follow the gurney past the nurses station, past where the CLC's faux wood floor turns into linoleum tiles. Beneath fluorescent lights, shoed and slippered feet shuffle through a labyrinth of beige hallways, walking, limping, rolling all the way to the morgue. Here, they stop.

They remove their caps. They salute. They might say a few words, and then the gurney rolls through the final threshold. A nurse pulls the doors tight.

"It's a nice thing," Julian says. "A nice way to say goodbye to them." They are often nameless, at least to Julian. He's terrible with names; he's constantly forgetting. But maybe it's easier not remembering or ever even knowing. In life they're simply brother, buddy, partner, friend. For women, it's honey or dear. In death they become their stories. The man who survived the Bataan Death March. The soldier who had to call in fire on his own troops. The woman from the Women's Army Air Corps who blew Julian a kiss just before she died. The soldier whose family sat with him for an hour after he passed, not realizing he was dead. The man whose wife visited him every single day for months—and kept coming back to his room for a week after he was gone. The feisty officer who insisted he'd live to his 75th birthday. He did. Julian was there. A few minutes before midnight, Julian ran down the hallway to get a cupcake out of the vending machine to celebrate. The officer died the next afternoon.

And there was Julian's very first patient. "He wasn't religious," Julian says. "He didn't want last rites or anything. But before he died, he did tell me to thank my higher power for him." Julian rarely uses the word "God" with his patients. He'll pray with those who believe, and he can recite the rosary, but he doesn't impose his viewpoint on the dying. His perspective isn't easily classified anyway. A one-time Catholic, Julian stopped going to church years ago when he found himself unmoved and unable to focus. But he still believes in something bigger; he's spiritual but not selective about the spirit. He often wears a dream catcher earring. He prays. He meditates. It just depends on what he needs. "When you pray, you're asking for strength and forgiveness from the Lord," Julian says. "When you're meditating, you're looking for understanding—you're finding strength from the inside."

Julian's bedroom is six steps down from his living room. It's more than his bedroom—it's his sanctuary. "The kids, they know when the gate [at the top of the stairs] is closed, you don't go down there," his daughter, Angela, says. There's a couch and a TV and in front of the

TV an array of certificates, ribbons, and other memorabilia spelling out his grandkids' and great-grandkids' accolades in colorful card stock. A towel from Colorado State University, where his grandson is a student, hangs on one side of the TV stand; a carving from his best friend rests on the other. And in the middle, in a place where he can see it every day, sits his 2015 Irving Hale Veterans Organization of the Year award from VFW Post 1. Post 1 has given the award out for the past eight years to recognize organizations that have made significant impacts on the veteran community.

Julian accepted his award in front of more than 400 people—Medal of Honor recipients and former POWs among them—who packed into the Brown Palace's Grand Ballroom this past December at Post 1's Founders Banquet. They were quiet and attentive as Julian started his acceptance speech. "I'm not a veteran of foreign wars," he said. "I guess my heavenly father decided to put me in a different place so I could come back to do the volunteer work that I do. It comes from your heart, my teacher told me. And the way I've been honored tonight—all you people have shown me your heart—me and my brothers who went to war." He cited Jim Doyle, a Pearl Harbor survivor who photographed the horror of that day and who was seated at his table. He choked up. Recovered. Continued. "I usually don't get a chance to talk to them that way—usually it's on the bedside," Julian said. By the end of the short speech there wasn't an able body in a chair, only a handful of dry eyes, and as Julian left the stage, he cried.

If you weren't at that dinner, if you hadn't been in Julian's room, you wouldn't know just how much the acknowledgement means to him. In fact, you probably wouldn't know he was doing the work at all. You wouldn't know he's logged close to 2,000 hours at bedsides. That he's been present for at least 200 deaths. He doesn't tell people about it. His best friend didn't know for more than a year. He doesn't even really talk to his family about it, especially not about the dying. "But we know," Angela says. "When it's been a hard one, he comes home almost hyperemotional. He's sometimes overly happy—dancing and singing—to make up, I think, for the sadness." She knows he's hurting on these days, and that's difficult. But she also knows being there helps him heal whatever rawness is left from his military service. He says he feels like he's paying something back for not going to Vietnam. "It's liberating for him, even if it's emotionally hard," Angela says. "And we just have to be OK with not knowing."

There are other compromises, too: the hours Julian is away from home, the family dinners he has missed. His family not only understands his work, though; they also encourage it. His granddaughter, who earned an academic scholarship to St. Mary's Academy in Cherry Hills Village, graduated this past May. Her commencement was on a Saturday, and she had planned a big party for the following day. That same Sunday, though, the VA held its twice-yearly memorial service for all the patients who had died in the previous six months. It's a stirring ceremony complete with candles and bell-ringing and poem-reading and eulogies—a communal, solemn celebration of life and also of death. Julian hasn't missed one since he began volunteering. But this one, he would, of course, for his granddaughter, who was bound for the University of Missouri. *No,* his granddaughter told him. *The important part is the graduation, not the party. You be there for that. Then go be with your friends.* So he went to see his brothers recognized instead. "My grandkids, as they've gotten older, try to understand why I could sit with people and watch them die," Julian says. "I tell them it's because they don't have anybody. They don't have families, and they need someone beside them."

Perhaps that's why the patients without family are the toughest for Julian. That's when he prays. He asks for the strength to see through whatever wrongs they have done, to find a connection, to see their humanity. "In these times I wonder, *What kind of man could he have been if he had family to stand by him?*" he says. In their absence, Julian fills in. He wants to. He has to. While several VAs around the country have end-of-life volunteer programs—Denver Health has one, too—Compassion Corps has shrunk. When Julian started, the Denver VA's Compassion Corps had close to 20 volunteers. Slowly, that number dwindled, drawn down as volunteers departed, having seen too much, smelled too much, grieved too much. Today, there is one. There is only Julian.

On Thursday, the lieutenant stops breathing for a full minute. Julian waits and waits, and when the next inhale finally comes, he sighs, and then he cries. He doesn't do that often. But the lieutenant is different. He's special. Some of them, a few of them, are. It hurts his friend Mercy

Tekle—Julian's favorite CLC nurse—to see this. "I tell him, 'You can't go to the ground with them,'" she says. And usually Julian doesn't.

When he recovers, Julian says he gives the lieutenant another day, maybe two. The lieutenant's fishing buddy shows up a little while later. He's driven eight hours to see his old friend, and he's clearly shaken by the state he finds him in. The friend inquires about the people in the room, a little confused. "He doesn't have any family here..." he says, trailing off, eyes on the nurses, on Julian. Quietly, expertly, Julian excuses himself from the room. Outside the tears come again.

In the military, and in war, soldiers learn and live by this solemn oath: No man left behind. And to Julian, that goes for the dying, too. "We promised them," Julian says. "No man dies alone." With the lieutenant's friend now sitting with him in Room 143, Julian knows he can leave. He retires for the day. He promises the lieutenant he'll be back tomorrow, and he is. He's there before his shift in the morning and returns on his break at lunch. The lieutenant's friend has stayed by his side. As Julian leaves the room, the friend is joined by his wife. Ten minutes after Julian departs, the lieutenant dies. "It happens that way a lot," Julian says. "It's like they're waiting for someone to arrive, or leave, so they can go." He thinks the lieutenant was waiting for his friend's wife. Of course, it's just as likely the lieutenant was waiting for Julian to go. But there's no point in wondering. The why behind when people die is something those still on this side of the portal can never know.

It takes about an hour to prepare the body for the trip from Room 143 to the morgue. There will be no Freedom Procession for the lieutenant. He didn't request it. There was no family to ask for it. Instead, there's a small parade of nurses who cared for him, who liked him, and Julian. There is still, at least, the homemade flag. The walk to the morgue is quiet: no "Taps," no conversation, just rubber-soled shuffling feet. At the entrance to the morgue, they pause. They fold the flag. Julian salutes. The doors close.

It's a hard walk back. Julian moves slowly at the rear, jingling, jangling, fighting tears. He stops when he comes to a T. To the left is Room 143. To the right, the front doors, sunshine, and spring. He goes right. Outside, in the shade of a cherry tree, Julian continues to cry intermittently. What will he do now that his workday is done and the lieutenant is gone? "Oh, I'll probably just go home," he says. His truck is parked right nearby. It's Friday. He's got a weekend of family ahead; grandkids, great-grandkids, a lot of love. "I'll take a shower," he says. "Put on my brave face." But once he's alone, Julian stays in the shade of that tree. He stands there for a long time. Minutes—five, maybe 10. He looks up at the sky and down at the ground. He swats at tears. And then, once they have dried, he sets his shoulders and smooths his hair. He takes a step toward his truck, pauses, turns, and walks back inside.

—November 2016

7.

Walking Scar(r)ed

by Natasha Gardner

The birth of my first child, as is often the case, wasn't routine. On a Sunday night in October 2012, my husband Chris and I checked into the hospital to induce labor. We quickly learned that the jokes I'd been making about the size of my husband's rather large head being passed on to my baby weren't so funny: Our son was wedged sunny-side up. The Pitocin forced my body into contractions, but I wasn't dilating fast enough. My son rocked back and forth with the spasms—bruising and cutting his head—and I clutched Chris's hand when each movement slowed our baby's heartbeat. Many times, I thought I was too exhausted to continue. Finally, thirty-three hours after we'd arrived, my doctor made a six-inch horizontal incision across my abdomen, cut another slit into my uterus, and pulled Oliver into our world.

The anesthesia rendered my arms useless, so Chris held our new baby to my chest and we all stared at one another with the amazed reactions that are unique to seeing your child born. Time slowed, as if to remind me to capture the moment like I would a fact in one of my reporting notebooks. I mentally tucked it away, laughing while tears of joy and exhaustion rolled down my cheeks onto Oliver's wrinkly skin and Chris's cradling hands.

It would be minutes before feeling returned to my fingers, weeks before I could walk without wincing at any movement involving my stomach, and three months before I returned to work. Every day, I'd examine my new scar, a bubbling, wavy pink line that stretches across my abdomen. I was amazed it was healing so quickly and that my son was already so strong.

But I couldn't help but wonder why I was still so tired.

As a journalist, I frequently dig into the darker corners of life in an effort to extract not just facts, but also truths. At work, I'm meticulously—and among my colleagues, comically and notoriously—organized with spreadsheets, binders of notes, and boxes of documents. I tend to leave this orderliness at the office, so when it came time to have my first child, I never made a birth plan. I didn't read books. I hadn't even researched what could go wrong during labor. I figured women had been doing this for millennia, I had a good medical team, and my son and I shared a mutual interest in our mutual survival.

I'd soon learn how many varied and unexpected types of survival there can be. Shortly after my maternity leave ended, I leaned over to hoist Oliver out of his crib for a 2 a.m. feeding. His owlish brown eyes stared as I tried again and again to lift him, but my thumbs and forefingers wouldn't grasp his body. Eventually, I bent over farther, nudged him into the crook of my arm, and swung him onto the bed to nurse. Despite the warnings I'd heard about co-sleeping with your infant, I didn't have the energy and strength to move him back to his crib. Chris threw his arms around both of us, and Oliver dangled a pudgy leg over my arm, kicking gently at my C-section scar while we all dozed until the next feeding.

In the morning my fingers were moving again, but it felt like I'd sprained every joint in both hands. A quick Google search suggested it was probably a case of carpal tunnel syndrome caused by nursing. The more I researched, the more I realized nursing can cause any number of odd health problems. *That must explain my fatigue.* I concluded the lingering pain was just another humbling body change all new moms must face. I was even a little proud of it: *Look how much I've sacrificed for my son.*

Just when I'd learned to ignore and endure these minor physical hints, my body began sending me major warnings. On March 13, 2013, as I was about to walk across 17th Avenue after a family dinner, I turned my head to the right. Like all the routine gestures I made that day, and every day, the moment should have flitted past unnoticed. Instead, what I saw froze me.

Rather than the normal three lanes of traffic streaming toward me on 17th, I saw six. My right leg paused midstep. I blinked, then jerked my glasses out of the way. I stared and stared until Chris, startled, shouted at me to get out of the street. As we situated Oliver in the car and clicked our own seat belts into place, I kept looking right. I couldn't get the images in my eyes to merge. I explained everything to Chris—and again attributed it to nursing and just needing some sleep. I didn't need 20/20 vision to see the concern spreading across his face.

It's been Chris *and* Tasha longer than it ever was Chris *or* Tasha. We met in 1994 at an after-school meeting for the high school Student Congress team. He was a junior and wearing a letterman jacket, which was all I, a ninth-grader, needed to know. It took me a little longer to realize that this soft-spoken boy with sea green eyes had the gentlest soul I'd ever encounter. He was a rapt observer who could detect the tiniest shifts in my moods. And I, more than anyone, could make him laugh, constantly and with abandon.

The ability to turn on someone's smile is a simple foundation for a relationship, and it was all we needed during those awkward high school years when "dates" involved studying at the library or lo mein takeout while watching Tommy Boy. And maybe it's all anyone needs. Chris and I have survived seven years of long-distance dating as one or both of us went off to college and graduate school and semesters abroad. We've held each other steady through family crises. We've endured two decades of transformations that have changed us—emotionally and physically—into different people.

Last spring, Chris wasn't smiling much. Always practical and measured, he urged me to call my doctor; I preferred to do more research online. But he was unusually insistent, and I finally agreed. The doctors, it turned out, were worried, too. They told me to eat only protein—I have a history of low blood sugar—and to call them if my vision didn't improve.

Two days and a half-dozen fried eggs later, my eyesight was worse. After blood tests and a visit to the eye doctor, I learned about the right sixth nerve, which controls eye movement. Something deep inside my head was causing this nerve to malfunction, and an MRI might reveal what it was.

When we arrived at the appointment, Chris held my arm, guided me into the room, and helped me onto a gurney. He held my hand, stroked my hair, and watched as the skittish tech poked an IV into my arm. As the tech tucked a blanket around me and wedged my head into a rest so it couldn't move, he explained the 45-minute process. I had to remain perfectly still so I wouldn't blur the images like some Victorian-era photograph. Halfway through, they'd run contrast dye through the IV to see how the fluid moved to my brain and identify any depressions where it might pool. My primary concern was whether the dye would prevent me from feeding Oliver later that day. *He's with his grandparents. I have enough frozen breast milk for him, but I'd like to feed him when I get home. It'll make us both feel better.*

In that moment, Oliver's feeding schedule may have seemed trivial, but pondering it was the only way I could keep the voice in my mind to stop from screaming, *What if this is something serious?* The tech assured me I'd be able to breastfeed and quickly went back to his script: MRI machines bang, clang, and chime, he said, and he gave me earplugs with the caveat that they probably wouldn't make much difference. As the machine started hammering, Chris watched me lie on the gurney, my arms crossed protectively over my C-section scar. The noise helped drown out my internal warnings. I was so exhausted I fell asleep.

I have a mostly typical collection of scars. There's one on my forehead from the obligatory coffee table run-in as a toddler. A long one runs from the back of my knee to my ankle, a souvenir of my tangle with a barbed wire fence. Another has lined the side of my foot ever since I stepped on a rusty metal shard in a creek bed. And, as the MRI revealed, I have four more scars buried deep inside my brain.

When Chris arrived home on the day I received my MRI results, I was waiting outside. I didn't cry when a stranger called with the news of the abnormal activity in my brain. I didn't cry when I picked up Oliver and leaned in to smell his hair and hold him close. I didn't cry when I handed him to Chris's visiting parents to watch him while I spoke to Chris. I remained dry-eyed as I stood sentinel at the edge of our driveway. But when my husband climbed out of the car, unsmiling, as if he already knew—had always known—I fell into his arms. He held me up so my knees wouldn't sink to the ground. That's when the tears came.

"They think it's multiple sclerosis."

We paced our block as I recited—between heaving sobs that threatened my balance—everything I'd learned while researching MS in the past hour. *I'm not going to die from this. Most likely, I'll die from something else. Probably cancer. My dad had cancer. Maybe heart disease. As many as 350,000 people in the United States have MS. You know that only about a third of them end up in a wheelchair? I could get used to using a cane. I'm going to be walking at Oliver's high school graduation. I might go blind. I may not be able to walk. I will be crippled.*

After a few minutes of this, Chris stopped. He hugged me so firmly and so close I could not only hear his heart beating, I could feel it. "We got this. We got this. We got this," he softly repeated, until I stopped gulping air and could look him in the eyes. That's when I realized it wasn't just me who had been diagnosed. We had been diagnosed. And we—Chris *and* Tasha—had no idea what that meant.

When life is uncertain, it often helps to return to your most elemental self, so Chris and I did what we used to do in high school: We studied together. He researched the medications. I obsessively collected stories of people's battles with MS. We'd compare notes, talking in hushed tones after Oliver fell asleep.

We learned the abnormal spots in my brain were lesions where my immune system had attacked my brain cells and eroded the myelin coating that protects them. We heard that MS has a high incidence rate in Colorado, which might have something to do with the altitude—or not.

Researchers still don't know what causes MS or how to definitively diagnose it, let alone how to cure it. It's definitely a neurological problem and probably an autoimmune issue.

Stress, heat, and conditions such as postnatal hormone drops can cause exacerbations or symptomatic flare-ups, which is what happened in March 2013. It would be almost two months before my eyesight returned to normal. Recovery from that episode took about a year, and I moved through it knowing my vision might not improve and that the scar pressing against my sixth nerve might not recede. I also had no idea when I'd have another exacerbation.

Faced with so many unanswerable questions, all we could do was wait. Being me, I couldn't. I went right back to work. I even took a yoga class in an overzealous attempt to prove I was getting better. I rolled out my mat, breathed through some *oms*, and stood to start a tree pose. The instructor talked us through the routine: *Ground through your feet into the earth. Find your core strength. Now lift one leg...*

As I tried to concentrate on her instructions, I was panicking inside. I couldn't really feel my feet and my left knee was off, too, as if it were full of jelly instead of bone and tendons. Tingling numbness rippled through my arms. My head felt too heavy for my neck, like it might crush my vertebrae and collapse onto my torso. I was in shock for the rest of the class, barely moving as the other students flowed through their poses. Toward the end, as we all lay flat on our mats in "corpse" pose, I sobbed.

The disease didn't stop there. My left foot began to drag, which made me stumble or fall so violently that twice my big toenail ripped away from the nail bed. I'd have occasional bursts of pain in my head, never in the same spot, that felt like someone was pounding a nail *out* of my skull. I couldn't edit stories—one of my primary duties at work—because the pain of reading would have me in tears. Holding a thought long enough to string together a sentence became so difficult I finally took a three-week sick leave.

I was going emotionally numb, too. The way some people reacted to the news of my diagnosis presented more unwelcome challenges. They'd stare at me, stammer something about Oliver, and either start crying or, worse, try to laugh it off. Despite their best intentions, it's difficult for many people to hear news like this and not instinctively think, *Thank God it isn't me.* I could see the thought flash across their faces, and it was like being told I had MS all over again. To avoid that moment, I started sending emails, and even posted a Facebook announcement, so people could sort through their feelings before sharing them with me.

After spending my career covering newsmakers, now I was the news, and it brought unexpected consequences. Since my diagnosis, I've severed ties with friends who were coldly dismissive of my situation—or who just chose not to deal with it, or with me. Other people treated me with unexpected kindness, such as the legion of co-workers who started delivering daily meals to my doorstep, the most considerate get-well gifts I've ever received.

I needed those positive thoughts because I was angrier than I'd ever been. *New moms shouldn't feel this exhausted. I shouldn't have to stop breast-feeding because of medication. I should be worrying that Oliver might spit up, not that I might fall while he's in my arms.* I was furious that I couldn't read. Or walk. Or see. I was incensed that this disease was attacking my brain, the most important part of my body, the very core of who I am.

I spent hours lying on my couch, staring up. I pondered all the things I couldn't do and wondered what I'd still be able to do. I wanted to keep hiking and running, but right then, I couldn't even walk without feeling my way along a wall. I expected Chris to be my caregiver when I was 83, not 33. I couldn't fathom losing my eyesight. Would I miss seeing my son grow up, would I miss seeing him take his first steps, because my world was going dark?

There were things I thought about myself—or, more accurately, things I thought I knew about myself—that I now realize were false. They weren't so much lies or half-truths as they were smudges of fact, gray areas that existed between what I knew then and what I know now.

One of those moments happened during the summer of 1993. Back then I wasn't worried about much more than watching *Days of Our Lives*, prepping for eighth grade, and keeping my starting spot on my softball team in Dickinson, North Dakota. On practice days, my teammates and I would lean into the prairie winds while our ponytails flapped like pendants behind us. Our T-shirts clung to our bodies, and the infield dirt clogged our noses and throats. I coughed a lot that season, but I napped even more. I was perpetually tired, which I attributed to hard practices and the long summer days you only get that far north.

On the morning of July 8, the air seemed warmer than usual. My bike ride to the field was more tiring. And I was a little loopy. For years, that was my only explanation for what happened next: While we were warming up, the pitcher threw me the ball—and I did nothing. My brain performed the nanosecond calculations that told my hand to meet the ball, but my arm didn't budge from my side. The ball smacked my nose so hard the impact split open my nostril. My coach drove me home, although she made me ride with my head sticking out of the window so my streaming blood wouldn't ruin her seats.

At the doctor's office, the talk was all about whether or not I'd have a visible scar. No one was very surprised that my hand-eye coordination was off. Once a tomboy, by then I'd become a major klutz. Puberty didn't help. My penchant for acquiring minor nicks and scrapes was so well-established, my parents coined a phrase for it: "mind-tripping," because my thoughts always seemed to race ahead of my body.

I repeated this story so many times over the years it became part of my personal lore, but if ever there was an early warning that my brain was at odds with my body, that would have been it. MS is rarely diagnosed in children, and the incident may have had nothing to do with my brain's deterioration. Or it could have had everything to do with it. A year afterward, a doctor noted in my medical file: *History of falling and hurting her back. Gave mom the option of physical therapy referral to [get] strengthening exercises for her back.*

I'd have two more similar episodes. When I was a sophomore at Smith College in Massachusetts, a friend and I planned a spring break road trip to Florida. We'd close out midterms, hop in her hatchback, and cruise down the coast, splitting driving duties during the 18-hour trek so we could be on the beach by the weekend. I was concluding my hardest academic semester yet with midterms and papers that sapped all the words from my body. Two people very dear to me—including my dad—were battling cancer. Before my friend stuck the key into the ignition, I was spent. I slept through most of the Eastern seaboard and never took over driving responsibilities. By the time we hit Daytona, our friendship was in worse shape than her car—and it's never recovered. After a lot of sleep, though, I did.

Then in 2005, I was working in book publishing in New York City and newly married to Chris when I started having shooting pains in my head whenever I moved my left eye. When it didn't improve, I called my OB-GYN because I didn't have a general practitioner. As I sat on her examining table and explained the pain, I also gushed about getting married and an upcoming vacation, and how I probably just needed a new eyeglass prescription. As I jabbered, her look grew increasingly vacant, until she told me she had to leave the room and collect herself.

When she returned, she relayed her suspicions while fighting tears: This was optic neuritis, which can be the first symptom of multiple sclerosis. *Multiple what?* I asked, stunned and immediately picturing a wheelchair. If it was MS, she continued, because I was so young it might be a more aggressive form, and she ordered an MRI.

For about two weeks, Chris and I lived under the assumption that I had the disease. The research we did—about daily injections, loss of mobility, depression—scared the hell out of us. But the MRI came and went, and although it showed a few questionable areas, it was inconclusive for MS. Meanwhile, an eye doctor confirmed what we wanted to hear: I had an extremely rare instance of a strained eye muscle.

The MRI soon faded into memory. I forgot about MS, too—after all, I'd passed the test. I learned to treat my eye with the same care an athlete gives a sprained ankle: It would probably never be as strong as it once was, so when it started hurting, I knew I needed to slow down and try to relax.

Although I hadn't fully honed my investigative mind—journalism school was still about a year away—these tidy explanations should have made me dubious. My rosy outlook about my new life and new marriage obscured and buried the truth. I convinced myself I was perfectly healthy. I could still go to graduate school in Colorado. Take on a high-stress career. Hike 13 miles in the high country. Go without sleep. I was strong, young, and driven.

Now I wonder: If I had ferreted out these facts earlier, would it have changed my life path? College. Master's degree. Journalism. Would I still have done any of those things? What about all the stories I wouldn't have written, or the people I wouldn't have met? When I hold my sleeping son at night, I ask myself if I still would have been brave enough to bring him into this world, knowing how difficult it might become for me to give him everything a son should be able to expect from his mom. But when I think about our family disappearing—or even changing—I only feel hollow.

If there was ever a good time to be diagnosed with MS, it was 2013. While I was sick, the U.S. Food and Drug Administration approved an oral drug called Tecfidera. Developed from a material that was used to prevent sofa cushions from rotting, it has been prescribed for decades to treat psoriasis. MS researchers don't know exactly why Tecfidera works, but it may suppress the immune system in a way that helps prevent or limit exacerbations. It has downsides, of course, including intense stomach cramps and extreme flushing. It can lower white blood cell count, which can, in turn, compromise the immune system. Perhaps most troubling: It costs $55,000 a year, or about $75 per twice-daily pill. (Biogen Idec, which produces the drug, has seen its stock price double since last year.) Fortunately, having health insurance means I pay just $10 per month for it. That will probably change, as insurance plans tend to do. Coupled with ancillary costs—lost wages, babysitters, transportation—MS could become an economic hardship as well as a physical and emotional one.

The Affordable Care Act (ACA) has been a boon to people like me. It ensures I, and others with pre-existing conditions, can switch health carriers without worrying about my application being denied or a new plan being too expensive. The ACA also means people won't be bound to their current employers over the fear of losing their health insurance. Because of these two changes, much of the current literature about MS care and treatment is already outdated. Not only can I continue to work, but I'll also have more control over what "work" and "insurance" might look like in two years, or 20. The new medication means that instead of carrying around syringes, I can tuck my daily dose into my jeans pocket. The diagnosis process has also changed: twenty years ago, I would have been dismissed as an exhausted new parent who was overwhelmed by the unfamiliar demands of motherhood. *Maybe* they would have sent me to a shrink and prescribed antidepressants—while my immune system continued to attack my brain.

I can't shake that image: that little invaders in my head are chewing away at the myelin in my nervous system. And ironically, as I have been demyelinating, Oliver has been myelinating. Each day, his evolving nervous system adds more myelin around his cells to smooth and speed the transmission of neural messages through his body. As Oliver was learning to roll, trying to sit up, and thinking about crawling, I was slowly losing some of those rudimentary abilities.

During my pregnancy, Oliver was constantly moving inside me. That restlessness continued after he was born, and Chris and I worried about me being alone with him, especially as he started becoming more mobile. Simply rising from the couch to use the bathroom could knock me out for a few hours. I couldn't pick him up, and regular naps were even more essential for me than for my five-month-old baby. We agonized over schedules, getting live-in care, and whether Chris needed to take a leave from work, too.

Oliver made the decision for us. During my first week of sick leave, which my own fractured memory can barely recall, I remember one recurring scene with exquisite clarity. Whenever I napped, curled into the fetal position, I'd prop Oliver against my stomach and leave some toys within his reach. My Oliver, the baby who couldn't stay still, would sit quietly, never crying, never fussing. Whenever my eyelids fluttered open, he'd smile at me, then lean his head back and close his sweet brown eyes as if to tell me, *Go back to sleep, Mommy.*

Sometimes I imagine what my wheelchair might look like. Maybe it'll be a custom build, like people do for bikes. We'd have to redo our front entrance, bathroom, and hallway. We'd move our bedroom to the main floor. My home life would shrink to a very small footprint. But it's all doable.

Doable. To a writer, it's an ugly, boring, corporate word. It's too short, with too many vowels, and when you say it, it sounds like a wet cloth hitting the floor with a *splat*. But doable now dictates every day for me—because every day what's doable for me changes.

The trouble with Tecfidera is that although it helps prevent future outbreaks, it doesn't repair existing damage. At times, my eyes still hurt, my left leg is wonky, and my fatigue level can be debilitating. Factors such as heat, stress, and lack of sleep can make these old symptoms flare up until I feel like I'm experiencing an attack. A nurse once explained MS to me as being like a construction site. It creates a pothole, and our brains respond by throwing up roadblocks and finding detours, new pathways for neurons to navigate. Over time, more roadblocks arise, which stresses the infrastructure of the brain. Sometimes the roadblocks become too much to overcome—and the body permanently loses that functionality.

Every Friday morning, I take an individual Pilates session to help me determine what's doable. Some days I'm too weak on my left side to stand on one leg. Other weeks, I'm strong enough to actually work up a sweat. Regardless, the sessions give me 60 minutes to play peacemaker between what my brain says and what my body does.

My struggles aren't obvious to others, and although you probably wouldn't realize it by looking at me, I'm disabled. I find it difficult to go out socially. Play dates can become excruciating exercises in chatting with other parents and minding Oliver, all while straining to remain upright through my fatigue. I rarely have more than one drink in public because my symptoms—slurring, lilting—can make me seem drunk when I'm not. I schedule mostly one-on-one get-togethers because I can make it through dinner if I'm focusing on one person; mingling with a group often means I'll spend the rest of the night on the couch.

Sometimes at work I feel the numbness creeping up my hands and feet. Once, during an editorial staff meeting I was leading, I nearly passed out from the pain in my head. I'm fortunate to work from home a few days a week because without those respites—from the harsh overhead lights, meetings, and noisy distractions—I doubt I could work full time. Disability insurance is an option, but then I couldn't get paid to write or publish that book I keep dreaming about. I'm simply not ready to stop working because without journalism, I'd lose an essential part of myself that hobbies could never fill.

On long days, I can actually feel and see my body getting worse. When I start to tire, my left index and ring fingers get heavy, and I mistype my C's, D's, and S's. My left leg starts to drag. I slur my words. I start to shield my eyes from light.

But in the midst of this disability, all these things are still doable. The hard part is facing all of it just when I'm also learning how to be a mom. Getting Oliver into his car seat is sometimes so tiring that I buckle him in, slump in the seat next to him, and close my eyes for five minutes. The old Tasha—the person who didn't know she had MS—would have scoffed at slowing down like that. Now, I see these pauses as a cruel blessing. My disease forces me to halt or rest, but that also means I can sit in the backseat and listen to Oliver singing—*mmmm, mmmm, mmmum, mmom! Mom!*—as he learns to put sounds together into words. I'm more present now because I'm acutely aware that in five minutes, I may no longer be able to run or jump with him.

Those moments also make me worry that I won't be there for him and Chris in the future—for hikes and bike rides and graduations—and that my disease will debilitate me so much that I become a burden. As I write that, I can already see Chris denying it. He'd remind me that this is what he signed up for nearly two decades ago, and I know he believes it. That doesn't mean I have to feel good about it. It doesn't stop me from worrying about whether we'll have another child (if I'd even have enough energy to be a mom to two children), or when I'll get sick again—because there's no *if* about it. I obsess over when and how we'll explain to Oliver what's wrong with Mommy. I ask myself a very difficult question over and over: My family is everything I ever dreamed it would be, but will I be enough for them?

This past February, I had a follow-up MRI to see how my medication was working. I was battling a cold, and my depleted immune system was exacerbating my symptoms. My step had a weight to it you normally see in people twice my age. I slid into the machine, and as the noise started, I thought about what had changed since I'd last been in this sleek, sterile tube.

After we put Oliver to bed, Chris and I have a new ritual while we make dinner. I'll lay out what hurts, what feels better, what's numb. We sort through each one, trying to draw conclusions between symptoms, talking through ways to keep me healthy, and forcing ourselves to stay upbeat. We know MS won't kill me. I have a good treatment plan. I'm figuring out the elusive life-work balance earlier than most. I'd rather not be sick, of course, but I can't help but think MS has made me feel luckier, more grateful. I'm also learning how to be selfish and make choices with my heart. To spend genuine, quality time laughing with my family. To focus on the people and the things that make me happier and stronger. To say goodbye to the things—and people—that don't.

I can finally get Chris laughing again. And Oliver is my best possible audience. He has an almost constant giggle that explodes into shoulder-shaking guffaws at the slightest provocation. In those moments—when my guys are laughing—it's nearly impossible to think I'm sick. If anything, I feel downright invincible.

I used to run, and now I walk. Someday I may walk with a cane. That won't change who I am or what I can do—it may just change the way I do it. I'm constantly reminded of that as I watch Oliver learn to walk and jump and run. Those movements are something we all needed to learn at one time. Now, as my son is learning, I'm *re*learning.

I contemplated all this in February as the MRI logged image after image of my brain and, thankfully, found nothing new. The old lesions—the scars—remain, but my medication seems to be working. After we got the results, we were out for a family walk and once again sorting through the facts about my health. As we talked, Oliver insisted on abandoning his stroller, preferring to make his way on his own two feet. With a bag of Goldfish snacks in hand, he careened down the sidewalk with both hands in the air and his belly button peeking out from beneath the hem of his shirt like a real-life Pooh Bear. I pointed out a dip in the sidewalk to him, to make sure he didn't trip. It's the type of thing Chris usually does for me. That's when Oliver's hand shot up. For the first time, he was seeking mine for support.

Time slowed once again, and it gave me a chance to glance over at Chris. We were on the same block he and I had paced on the day of my diagnosis. Then, Chris had to hold me up. Now, I was holding our son steady. I could feel the Goldfish crumbs on his sweaty little palms. I could see Chris's smile. I could feel my toes. And I realized, having those three simple things—or any of them—made me feel strong again. Which meant *we* were strong again.

—May 2014

8.

Still Life

by Chris Outcalt

The Limon Correctional Facility sits atop the lonesome and expansive High Plains of eastern Colorado, halfway between Denver and the Kansas state line. Just south of the small town for which it's named, the location is a fitting place for a prison. There isn't much around; the surrounding fields, populated by cattle and crops, appear to go on forever. The only interruptions are the gas stations, budget motels, and fast-food joints off the occasional highway exit. On a cool late-summer morning last year, I drove the 100 miles from Denver to Limon to meet a 35-year-old man named Giselle Gutierrez-Ruiz, who is serving a life sentence for murder.

The fog was so thick I couldn't see the guard towers or barbed-wire fences of the prison until just before I pulled into the parking lot. After checking in with the guard at the front desk, I walked through a metal detector and passed through a series of mechanized gates, encased in razor-sharp wire, which beeped until they locked into place. I crossed a courtyard the length of a football field, and a second guard directed me through a short hallway and into the visiting room; the space resembled a high school cafeteria. Giselle arrived several minutes later. He wore a green prison jumpsuit and sported a neatly trimmed beard and buzz cut and a pair of thick, black-rimmed glasses.

Giselle and I sat across a folding table from each other and talked for nearly three hours. He spoke in a measured tone and was almost philosophical about his time in prison. He had already been incarcerated for almost 20 years. When Giselle was a teenager, an Adams County judge sentenced him to mandatory life without parole—a punishment the U.S. Supreme Court ruled unconstitutional in 2012. Giselle told me he tries not to spend too much time thinking about all that. As for what took place on the highway that night in 1997: "I never hurt nobody," Giselle says. "I just got trapped in the moment."

Mike Riebau's phone rang on the evening of Wednesday, October 22, 1997. Riebau was an Immigration and Naturalization Service (INS) senior special agent stationed in Colorado; he'd moved to Denver in 1982 and was later selected for a special multiagency drug task force run by the Offices of the United States Attorneys. Riebau spent most of his 33-year career working major drug-trafficking cases, which required him to develop confidential informants in the field. One of those sources, Raul Gutierrez-Ruiz, was on the other end of the line.

During the previous year, Riebau says, he and Raul had developed an arrangement: Riebau made sure law enforcement looked the other way on Raul's undocumented status so long as Raul fed him solid information he could use to crack big cases. On this particular night, Raul had details about a drive-by shooting that had occurred a couple of days earlier. From a pay phone, Raul explained that he knew the shooter only by his nickname, Guero. Guero had been in Denver less than a month. Raul said he sounded anxious and was talking about skipping town and heading back to California. Complicating matters was the fact that Guero had been in Raul's car that night, and Raul's younger brother, Giselle Gutierrez-Ruiz, had been driving.

Riebau told Raul to stick close to his pager; he'd get back to him shortly. In the meantime, he cross-checked the information with a detective friend who worked homicide in Adams County. Sure enough, five days earlier, there'd been two shootings in less than an hour on the highway near the interchange of I-25 and I-76—and the second resulted in the death of a man named Rumaldo Castillo-Hernandez. Two men found him hunched over in his car at the bottom of a highway embankment; the vehicle had sliced through a chain-link fence and landed in a thick patch of trees. What at first must have seemed like a car accident quickly became something else. One of the men found blood under Castillo's left arm, and it appeared to be coming from what looked like a bullet hole.

Police struggled to understand what exactly had happened. The Adams County Sheriff's Department investigated whether Castillo-Hernandez's death and the earlier shooting were related. The two drivers who were targeted didn't appear to be connected, and there was no apparent motive. A sheriff's department spokesman told a Rocky Mountain News reporter, "It could be anything at this point." Based on multiple eyewitness accounts, police did have a description of the shooter's vehicle, a maroon Buick sedan. Raul owned a maroon Buick. It was a solid lead on a days-old case that had turned up very few of those, and Riebau and the Adams County detective decided to make a move that night.

Riebau paged Raul and walked him through the plan: Raul would tell his younger brother to bring Guero and meet him in about an hour at Sheridan Billiards, a pool hall in southwest Denver. Once Guero showed up, Raul would lure him out of the car and a tactical team would move in and arrest him. At the arranged time, Raul's teenage brother, Giselle, who had no idea he was part of a setup, pulled into the Sheridan Billiards parking lot. Guero was riding shotgun—and there was a MAC-11 semi-automatic pistol under his seat.

Riebau watched the scene unfold through a pair of binoculars from across the street. Giselle and his nephew, who was in the back seat, climbed out immediately. Guero stayed put. After a few tense moments, Raul finally convinced Guero to get out of the car. Riebau gave the go-ahead, and the tactical team burst out of an unmarked van. They arrested Guero without incident. The team confiscated the handgun. They also handcuffed and arrested Giselle.

Five days earlier, hours before Castillo-Hernandez had been found dead, Giselle borrowed a friend's car and drove about 20 miles west on I-70 to the Buffalo Herd Nature Preserve in Genesee Park. Giselle discovered the buffalo preserve soon after arriving in Colorado less than two years earlier, and he'd been back at least 10 times. Giselle had always loved animals, but his fondness for this place was about more than wildlife.

Breathing the air up there, he felt a sense of freedom, and the landscape reminded him of home.

Giselle was born in Rancho Ruices, a tiny village in the rugged hills of Northern Mexico. Only a few dozen people live in Rancho Ruices; there are no stoplights, there's no mail service, and the dirt roads double as goat paths. The youngest of 11, Giselle was known throughout town as a good artist. One of his teachers remembers that the other students always wanted to be in Giselle's group. If there was ever a fight or a disagreement among his classmates, Giselle was quick to intervene. "He was a happy kid," his sister Lorena Gutierrez-Ruiz says, "always looking out for others."

For fun, Giselle swam in the nearby river or played on the dusty hills behind his family's house. He liked sports; basketball was his favorite. He found an old rim, attached it to a long board, and hung the contraption in a tree so he could shoot hoops. Giselle's uncle raised chickens and roosters, and he let Giselle keep one of the roosters as a pet. Giselle named the bird Hero, and, for a long time, he carried Hero with him everywhere he went.

As the youngest in the family, Giselle was especially close to his mother, Estela Ruiz de Gutierrez. "She was a beautiful mother," Giselle says. Everyone in town knew Estela well. She acted as the local census taker and briefly served as the police commissioner; she was also a skilled cook. Estela went out of her way to help those who were less fortunate. When a local child lost one of his eyes in a farming accident, Estela made sure he received treatment. The boy had no family, and when he returned to town, Estela took him in and cared for him.

Giselle never really knew his father, who left Rancho Ruices and moved to the United States when Giselle was an infant. (Several of Giselle's older siblings also left Mexico and settled in Colorado.) Giselle occasionally wondered about his father. Once, he was playing outside and noticed a strange man riding a horse; his stomach knotted into a ball of nervous excitement thinking it might be his dad. He longed for the man to stop and talk to him, but he never did. Giselle gazed at the man's back as he rode away.

When Giselle was 15, his mother developed a serious form of heart disease. The family drove her an hour to the closest hospital, where doctors treated Estela. She returned home—but she never recovered.

Before she died, Estela leaned in and whispered one last thing to her youngest son: She told Giselle to take care of his little nephew, Ruliz, as if he were his brother. Unbeknownst to Giselle, Estela had told Ruliz the same thing.

Several of Giselle's siblings returned to Rancho Ruices for their mother's funeral. The entire town, and many from surrounding communities, attended the ceremony. It was around that time the family decided there was nothing left for Giselle in Mexico, that he should live in the United States with his brothers and sisters. Giselle was too saddened by his mother's death to think about anything else. "I tried being strong, but in my loneliness I did not want to accept the loss," he says. "Everything was happening so fast." Not long after the funeral, one of Giselle's older sisters led him and his nephew on a journey to the United States. They left so quickly they did not say goodbye to anyone.

On his way out of Rancho Ruices, the only place he'd ever known, Giselle passed the cemetery where his mother was buried. One last time, he looked toward her grave. The tombstone was covered with flowers and pink ribbons. "It was only a glance," he says. "But I could see it."

When Giselle arrived in Denver, everything was different. There was no one like his mother to take care of him, and the 15-year-old bounced around, living at various apartments and duplexes with his brothers and sisters. Giselle attended West High School but dropped out in part because he didn't speak English. Giselle's brother Raul would occasionally bring Giselle along to help on jobs installing Sheetrock. Raul was always the brother Giselle most looked up to.

Not long after coming to Colorado, Giselle found comfort in the mountains. In his free time, he'd drive to Boulder and sit by the creek in the shadow of the Flatirons, dipping his toes into the rushing water. Eventually, he discovered the buffalo preserve in the hills west of Denver. From up there, the city looked small, like it was manageable. After spending part of his morning at the preserve that Friday in October 1997, Giselle drove back down the hill. That night, he went out to a dance club in Thornton called La Fantasia. Giselle liked to dance, and he often went to the club with his brothers and people they knew. According to court documents, Giselle left La Fantasia that night around 10:30 p.m. with a man named Guero.

The night of the bust at the pool hall, Adams County detectives wanted to question Giselle about the shootings, and he agreed to speak with them at a Denver police station. Since he was not yet 18, police contacted Giselle's father—a man Giselle hardly knew—to sit in on the interview. Raul was also present. Following protocol, the detectives had Giselle and his father sign a juvenile advisement waiver, which indicated Giselle agreed to speak with police voluntarily and that he agreed to do so without an attorney present.

Police questioned Giselle through a Denver Police Department translator until 3:30 a.m. the following morning. Giselle's father and brother encouraged Giselle to tell the police the truth. They thought that because Giselle was a minor and didn't actually shoot anyone, he wouldn't be in trouble. Giselle says he felt like he was doing the right thing when he detailed everything he knew about that night: how he was driving his brother's car on the highway and that Guero twice shot at other vehicles from the passenger's seat but that he was scared and didn't know anyone had been injured. Giselle says his family gave him the impression that after he spoke to the detectives he would be able to go home.

Instead, he unknowingly incriminated himself by confirming that Guero was responsible for both shootings and explaining what took place in between: After the first shooting, Giselle said Guero told him to drive to a girl's house near the intersection of 26th Avenue and Sheridan Boulevard. Giselle said they were "there for a while," he wasn't sure how long, and that they eventually returned to the club.

As police concluded their questioning, Raul asked what was going to happen to his younger brother. One of the detectives explained Giselle would be held in jail and might face a weapons charge but that the final decision would be up to the Adams County district attorney. Raul tried to reassure his brother that everything would be OK. After the arrest, one of Giselle's sisters, Kelly Gutierrez-Ruiz, got a call in Mexico from Raul; she says Raul cried into the phone as he explained what had happened. Giselle was in jail.

Four days later, Adams County District Attorney Bob Grant charged Giselle with first-degree murder and first-degree assault. Even though Giselle was 17 years old, legally a juvenile, Grant filed the charges in adult court. Because of the way Colorado sentencing laws were written at the time, that decision meant that if a jury found Giselle guilty, he faced a steep mandatory prison sentence: life without the possibility of parole.

The trial opened in an Adams County courtroom on the morning of July 7, 1998. Giselle had spent the previous nine months locked up in county jail. Initially, he was placed in solitary confinement. Later, he was moved to a cell with two others who spoke Spanish. Most teenage boys spend their 18th birthdays with their friends at the movies or at a party sneaking drinks from the liquor cabinet; Giselle's came and went with little fanfare in a cold jail cell. One of Giselle's cellmates remembers Giselle was "quiet and did not want to talk." On one of the rare occasions he did speak up, the cellmate recalls Giselle crying and saying he was in for a drive-by shooting but that it wasn't his fault.

Giselle was tried for murder under Colorado's complicity statute. The law states that a defendant can be punished for a crime someone else committed if, "with the intent to promote or facilitate the commission of the offense, he or she aids, abets, advises, or encourages the other person in planning or committing the offense." According to the law, if Giselle was in on the shooting—if he knew what Guero was planning to do or helped him pull it off—he was guilty of murder, even if he never pulled the trigger.

After Giselle's arrest, the family pooled enough money to hire attorney Wesley Miller. They turned to Miller because he'd previously represented two of Giselle's older brothers on drug charges. Miller, however, had made a career out of cutting deals on drug cases. He was also battling emphysema. During Giselle's trial, Miller passed many of the responsibilities to his co-counsel, Bruce Heilbrunn, who'd worked criminal cases before, but never a murder trial.

The prosecution team consisted of Brian McCoy and David Juarez, both deputy district attorneys. In his opening statement, Juarez laid out a straightforward argument. He told the jury that on the night in question, there'd been two shootings in locations close to each other on the highway and that the second shooting resulted in the death of Rumaldo Castillo-Hernandez. Police recovered shell casings from both scenes that were similar to the bullets found in the victims' cars. Juarez cited a statement from the victim of the first shooting, who told police,

"This guy in a maroon Buick comes up and he starts shooting at the back of my truck, speeds up, goes past me continuing to shoot."

Juarez then explained that the defendant, Giselle Gutierrez-Ruiz, was the driver; he said Giselle acknowledged that detail in an interview with police. There was one more thing, he said, that showed Giselle acted with intent to aid Guero: One of Giselle's cellmates, a man named Carlos Perez, relayed to an investigator that Giselle said, "When this thing was happening, the guy was veering really close, changing lanes, crossing lanes. I handed the gun to Guero, and Guero shot him."

Heilbrunn addressed the jury next. Giselle sat there silent, looking withdrawn. Heilbrunn used the word "chauffeuring" to describe his client's actions. It was as simple as that, he said; Giselle had only known Guero for about a month and was "surprised" when he opened fire "out of the blue" around 10:45 p.m. The second shooting took place about 30 minutes later. "And again," Heilbrunn said, "Mr. Gutierrez is scared. He's got a madman in his car."

Heilbrunn also argued that the statement from Giselle's cellmate simply wasn't true—Giselle's fingerprints hadn't been found on the weapon. He suggested Perez had only told police that to cut a deal on reduced jail time. "Giselle Gutierrez," Heilbrunn said, "did not aid, encourage, or even know that the passenger in his car was going to shoot. At the end of this case, I will remind you that mere presence is not enough, and I will ask you to return a verdict of not guilty."

During the next two and a half days, the prosecution presented a methodical and thorough case, calling 35 witnesses—detectives, forensic experts, highway witnesses, medical professionals, Giselle's cellmate, and even Giselle's brother, Raul. Heilbrunn's defense lasted 30 minutes. Heilbrunn called two witnesses, both aimed at discrediting the statement by Giselle's cellmate, Perez, about Giselle handing Guero the gun. One was Perez himself, who was combative and refused to answer questions directly. The other was veteran investigator Jimmy Spence, who had interviewed Perez in jail. One of the jurors, David Thomas, says, "I don't think anyone believed [Perez]."

Spence, who'd been hired by Miller and Heilbrunn and was the only member of the team who spoke Spanish, says they tried to get Giselle to testify, told him to just get on the stand and tell his story. But Spence says Giselle backed out at the last minute. "I think he was just afraid," Spence says. "He didn't know what the heck to do." And so Heilbrunn rested his case. The jurors spent more time at lunch that day than they did listening to Heilbrunn defend his client.

The jury returned a guilty verdict the following afternoon. After the trial, Spence spoke with some of the jurors about the verdict. One juror, he says, justified the decision by saying, "They'll just give him a slap on the wrist." In Colorado, except in death penalty cases, attorneys are not allowed to discuss a defendant's possible punishment. (That information can be considered prejudicial or irrelevant under the Colorado Rules of Evidence because sentencing is a function of the court, not the jury.) When Spence explained that Giselle's conviction carried a mandatory life sentence, the juror, he said, was shocked.

Indeed, Giselle's sentencing hearing, which took place five days after the trial, was merely a formality. Typically, the defense has an opportunity to present evidence about its client's character or the circumstances of his or her life, anything that might persuade a judge to deliver a more lenient sentence. In Giselle's case, because of the mandatory sentence, no such evidence was allowed—it wouldn't have mattered. Due to the nature of Giselle's defense at trial and the structure of the state's sentencing laws, neither the jurors nor the judge ever heard Giselle's story—who he was and where he came from. They'd been tasked with deciding the fate of a teenager whom they knew nothing about.

Before the judge imposed the mandatory life sentence, Giselle addressed the court. Through a translator, he said, "I'm very sad for everything that's happening. I don't know what's going to happen or anything. That is all." Giselle, a bewildered 18-year-old, left the Adams County courtroom that day in the custody of the Colorado Department of Corrections. It would take the American legal system another 14 years to catch up with the gravity of the circumstances that led to Giselle being sent to prison for life.

For someone who has spent the past decade as a defense attorney, Ashley Ratliff, who is 37 and the mother of two young children, has an uncharacteristically bubbly disposition. She often expresses her thoughts on a case by drawing a colorful diagram or picture, though she's quick to admit she's not much of an artist. She readies herself for stressful court appearances and face-to-face visits with imprisoned clients by blaring upbeat music in her car, everything from Taylor Swift to the Beastie Boys.

Ratliff specializes in juvenile defense and runs her own practice out of a small single-story building on Bannock Street in the Golden Triangle neighborhood. A large corkboard hangs on the wall behind her desk, cluttered with her children's artwork, letters from clients, and work-related memos and reminders. One handwritten note occupies a prominent spot, a piece of white paper that references a 2010 U.S. Supreme Court decision, Graham v. Florida: For a juvenile offender who did not commit homicide the Eighth Amendment forbids the sentence of life w/o parole.

Giselle had already been incarcerated for 13 years by the time Ratliff found her way to his case. She'd taken it on at a pivotal moment in her life: Ratliff and her husband had recently had their first child, and she'd left her job with the Colorado Office of the State Public Defender to spend more time with her family. She also wanted to focus more on juvenile defense. Her last day as a public defender was a Friday; the following week, she met with the executive director of the Colorado Juvenile Defender Center (CJDC), a nonprofit that advocates for excellence in juvenile justice. Ratliff was interested in taking on a couple of cases part time, and CJDC needed the help.

The previous year, in May 2010, the U.S. Supreme Court had issued an important decision on juvenile justice. In Graham v. Florida, the court ruled that sentencing a juvenile convicted of a nonhomicide crime to life without the possibility of parole violated the U.S. Constitution—specifically, the Eighth Amendment ban on cruel and unusual punishment. In the wake of the Graham decision, CJDC was tracking Colorado cases that could benefit from the ruling. That day, Ratliff agreed to take three or four folders from a stack labeled "high priority." Giselle's was one of them.

Ratliff felt strongly that sentencing a juvenile to life in prison was inherently unfair. As she examined Giselle's case, she thought the Graham ruling should apply to her client. Although Giselle had been convicted of first-degree murder, it was as a complicitor—he didn't actually kill anyone. And after meeting with Giselle, Ratliff believed he didn't know Guero was going to shoot anyone or that anyone had been injured.

Ratliff also learned that at the shooter's trial, the jury hadn't convicted Guero of first-degree murder after deliberation; instead, they found the 22-year-old guilty of extreme indifference murder, meaning they believed Guero acted with "extreme indifference to the value of human life" but that he did not act "with intent" or "after deliberation." If a jury found that Guero didn't plan to shoot anyone, Ratliff thought, how was Giselle supposed to have known? What's more, Guero—the man who pulled the trigger—had received the same sentence as Giselle: life without parole. "Giselle's not proud or happy about being in the car with someone who was doing those things," Ratliff says. "He's said, 'I deserve to be punished for what I did, but I didn't hurt anyone; I've done my time.' And I really believe that."

As Ratliff crafted Giselle's appeal under the Graham ruling, the U.S. Supreme Court released another landmark decision regarding juveniles. In a June 2012 case, Miller v. Alabama, the court took the Graham ruling a step further and stated that sentencing a juvenile to mandatory life without parole—even in homicide cases—was unconstitutional. "Under these schemes," the opinion reads, "every juvenile will receive the same sentence as every other—the 17-year-old and the 14-year-old, the shooter and the accomplice, the child from a stable household and the child from a chaotic and abusive one." Miller v. Alabama did not go so far as to outright ban life without parole for juveniles; rather, the court ruled it could not be the only option at sentencing, that juveniles had a right to individualized sentences that considered their "youth and attendant characteristics"—precisely the type of sentence Giselle hadn't received 14 years earlier.

In the months and years following the Miller ruling, the question became whether the decision should apply retroactively. When the opinion was released, there were about 2,100 people in the country serving mandatory life sentences for crimes they'd committed as juveniles, including 50 in Colorado who received mandatory life without parole for crimes committed between 1990 and 2006. (One has since been released on an unrelated matter, and another died by suicide.) From 1985 to 1990, juveniles convicted of first-degree murder in adult court received life with the possibility of parole after 40 years; before 1985, the sentence was even more lenient. In 2006, the Colorado Legislature returned to the sentence of 40 to life for new cases. The only ones left in question are those 48 inmates.

During the past three years in Colorado, the retroactivity debate has played out in the state Legislature. In 2015, Representative Daniel Kagan proposed a bill that would have given each of the 48 inmates (including Giselle) a resentencing hearing and provided a judge with the option of either life with possible parole at 20 years or a reduced sentence of 24 to 48 years. The opposition was fierce, and Kagan withdrew the bill. District attorneys and victim advocates have argued since the Miller decision was released that it is unfair—and, indeed, cruel and unusual—to ask those who lost loved ones to these crimes to relive the events years later by holding new hearings.

Even if the Legislature did grant 48 resentencing hearings, says Denver District Attorney Mitch Morrissey, whose district contains the highest number of these cases, most of the crimes are so heinous that he believes a judge might send the bulk of the inmates right back to prison for life. "These are the worst of the worst during that period of time," says Morrissey, referring to the cases in his district. Those who advocate on behalf of the juvenile lifers, as they are often called, see things differently. "I think it's very simple," says Mary Ellen Johnson, executive director of the Pendulum Foundation, a juvenile advocacy group. "Do we believe in redemption, or do we believe in retribution?"

After three years without a resolution on the retroactivity question from the state Legislature, the Colorado Supreme Court ruled on the matter this past June. In an opinion that consolidated the cases of three of the juvenile lifers (Michael Tate, Tenarro Banks, and Erik Jensen), the state's highest court said the Miller decision only applied to cases that were still on their initial appeal. That amounted to two of the 48. (A third case might also apply under the ruling.) Sometime this year, they will be resentenced at separate hearings, during which a judge will determine whether they should be parole-eligible at 40 years or continue to serve life without parole. For the others, including Giselle, the state court ruling provided no relief.

As the 2016 legislative session opens this month, Representative Kagan is again considering sponsoring a bill that would require a judge to resentence the juvenile lifers; he's also considering other options. "I think the [state] Supreme Court decision in Tate, Banks, and Jensen was stunning," Kagan says. "I think it was just wrong."

Twelve states and the U.S. government agree with Kagan: Wyoming, Nebraska, Iowa, Illinois, Texas, Arkansas, Mississippi, Florida, New Hampshire, Massachusetts, Connecticut, South Carolina, and the U.S. Department of Justice have all taken the position that the Miller decision applies retroactively. Colorado, Montana, Minnesota, Michigan, Louisiana, Pennsylvania, and Alabama have said that it does not.

The U.S. Supreme Court may finally end the debate later this year. In October, the court heard oral arguments in the case Montgomery v. Louisiana, in which it could determine whether the Miller decision applies retroactively. The nation's highest court is expected to release a decision by June.

Over the past five years, while the country sorted through the Graham and Miller decisions, Giselle's attorney Ashley Ratliff became an expert on the topic. She now chairs a Miller and Graham litigation committee set up by the CJDC, and earlier this year she spoke at national conferences on juvenile defense in Utah and Washington, D.C.

And Ratliff continues to fight Giselle's case. Initially, the Colorado Court of Appeals granted Giselle a resentencing hearing. While preparing his case, she drew a picture of what Giselle's life was like to help herself further empathize with her client. She even hired a videographer and traveled to Mexico to interview Giselle's family and friends. But for the time being, Giselle's case, which was sent back to the Colorado Court of Appeals, exists in legal limbo. Unless the Legislature acts or the U.S. Supreme Court rules that Miller must be applied retroactively, Ratliff may not get to tell Giselle's story and share what she sees as the injustices her 36-year-old client has endured. "From the moment I touched his case," Ratliff says, "I've wondered why his attorneys did things the way they did."

There had been so many new developments in Giselle's case that Ratliff felt it was time to call a meeting. One morning this past October, five members of Ratliff's legal team gathered in her office on Bannock; they sat on couches and chairs huddled around a small coffee table. Ratliff looked tired. She'd pulled her hair into a loose ponytail and cradled a mug of coffee with both hands, as if attempting to warm herself from the outside in.

Ratliff said she'd recently connected with one of the jurors from Giselle's trial, a man named David Thomas. After all these years, Thomas still thought about the trial; he wanted to know more about Giselle and talk about his case. Ratliff shared details Thomas said he'd never heard in the courtroom, like how Giselle says he didn't know anyone had been injured that night until he was arrested several days later. By the end of their conversation, Thomas says he thought the additional information might have made a difference to the jury.

The more Ratliff learned, the more she believed Giselle's defense lawyers hadn't done their due diligence in investigating his case. Miller and Heilbrunn, she says, never drove to the crime scene; never reviewed the tapes of Giselle's interview with police; and never contacted a number of witnesses. As for those claims, Heilbrunn says he wasn't the lead attorney on the case and that those types of decisions would have been up to Miller, who died in 2007. "If Mr. Miller didn't do something, that's on him," Heilbrunn says. "I didn't accept a retainer or anything from the client; in terms of everything but the trial itself, the decisions were Mr. Miller's."

Ratliff also learned that Heilbrunn, who did end up handling the bulk of the responsibilities at Giselle's trial, had been temporarily suspended from practicing law seven years before he represented Giselle. According to a report from the Colorado Supreme Court's Grievance Committee, Heilbrunn had exhibited a "consistent pattern of professional misconduct" in at least 17 separate instances spanning two years. The report said Heilbrunn would take on clients and then fail to work their cases or return their phone calls; he'd eventually "abandon the client and the case, causing actual or potential damage." The report indicated that much of the misconduct stemmed from Heilbrunn having "suffered from severe and chronic depression leading to drug and alcohol abuse."

According to the report, Heilbrunn had made an effort to "rectify the consequences of his misconduct" and also voluntarily agreed to remain on depression medication and submit semiannual psychotherapy reports to the grievance committee. Lastly, Heilbrunn agreed that when he was reinstated he would only practice law under the supervision of another attorney.

A few days after that morning staff meeting, Ratliff filled in one of the investigative gaps she felt Heilbrunn and Miller had missed. She tucked her two children into bed, drove north to the site of the old dance club in Thornton, and retraced Giselle's route on the highway. Witness statements and police evidence indicated that about 30 to 40 minutes separated the two shootings, which both occurred near the interchange of I-25 and I-76. In his statement to police, Giselle said in between the shootings Guero told him to go to a girl's house near the intersection of 26th Avenue and Sheridan Boulevard. It took Ratliff approximately 25 minutes to drive their route, one way.

Ratliff connected the dots in her mind. She wasn't sure where Giselle and Guero had gone that night, but she was pretty convinced it wasn't a house near 26th and Sheridan. Ratliff's legal team also interviewed one of the girls Giselle and Guero had reportedly visited; according to Ratliff, the woman said she did not see Guero that evening. Ratliff wasn't sure why Giselle had told those things to police, but at the very least, she says, she would have brought up the question of timing at trial. At least one juror said what happened in between the shootings weighed heavily in the decision to convict Giselle.

All of this new information, Ratliff says, would make for a claim of ineffective assistance of counsel, and she says she's considering that option. Ratliff is also waiting on the U.S. Supreme Court to decide whether the Miller decision is retroactive. "I just want him to go home," Ratliff says. "And I think he should go home. There are a lot of people—more than on an average case, and not just the defense—who say enough is enough."

When I contacted many of the lawyers and investigators who were involved with Giselle's case in the late '90s, every one of them remembered it, and two of the people who were involved in putting Giselle in prison told me they didn't think he should be there.

The first is former Deputy District Attorney David Juarez, one of the two lawyers who prosecuted Giselle. He told me that he had resigned his position with the Adams County District Attorney Office a few months after Giselle's trial in part because of how that case was handled. In particular, Juarez referred to the negotiations of a plea agreement.

Digital records didn't exist in 1997; everything was filed on paper by hand and then later transferred to microfilm. According to the Adams County DA's office, there is no official record of the plea deal in the case file; that record either never existed or was lost. Juarez recalls that the deal was an offer for Giselle to plead guilty to second-degree murder, which would have been accompanied by a sentencing range of 12 to 48 years.

Juarez believed the deal was too punitive for someone whose family cooperated with police and helped track down the actual shooter. He said they might have offered the same agreement to a complicitor who didn't have either of those things to his credit. "It didn't seem fair," Juarez says. "I did not feel great about giving the family nothing for their help and cooperation." Juarez believed they should have offered a class-three felony, which he says carried a prison range of 10 to 32 years when a deadly weapon was involved. Inmates who earn credit for good behavior are often released in two-thirds the time of their sentences.

The former DA, Bob Grant, who is retired, also remembers offering Giselle second-degree murder. Grant said that, given the evidence, he believes the offer was "appropriate and generous." I asked Grant whether it was fair that Giselle was serving the same sentence as the man who actually killed Rumaldo Castillo-Hernandez. Grant again pointed to what he thought was a fair plea agreement and said he was disappointed the defense had not taken it. "We tried to make it as fair as we could," Grant told me. "What was fair was he was given an opportunity to plead to a lesser charge. That's a decision he and his lawyers made. The question of fairness is for them to answer now. You don't roll the dice and get the dice back again."

When I contacted Heilbrunn to talk about the case, he remembered Giselle's name right away. He also recalled there being an offer for a plea deal. Heilbrunn didn't remember whether it was for second-degree murder but did say the deal was for a specific number: 30 years. One of the first things Heilbrunn told me was that he regrets not having pushed Giselle harder to take the deal. "It's hard to tell a juvenile, 'You have to accept 30 years,'?" Heilbrunn says, "so we went to trial."

Heilbrunn said he thought they would prevail because Giselle wasn't the shooter. He also said he and Miller believed they had filed a strong motion to suppress Giselle's statement to police, but the judge ruled against them. Ultimately, Heilbrunn said, that statement, in which

Giselle described the time between the two shootings, was what hurt him the most. "We might have prevailed if the two shootings took place immediately one after the other because the driver couldn't do anything about it," Heilbrunn says.

The second person involved in sending Giselle to prison who told me he doesn't think Giselle should be there anymore is Mike Riebau, the special agent who helped arrange the undercover bust in which Giselle was arrested. Riebau told me he often thinks about how Giselle got wrapped up in all this and was so severely punished. "I'm not an advocate, I want to make that perfectly clear," Riebau says. "I'm the guy who put him in jail. I'm not getting out my handkerchief and crying over this kid. But I did feel bad when he got hammered." The father of two sons and two daughters, Riebau says Giselle's case reminded him of one of his boys, who was hanging out with the wrong crowd when he was about 17. Giselle's case made Riebau think back to that time in his son's life. "I'm thinking to myself, Man, that could happen to any kid," he says.

Riebau told me that when he retired, he considered writing a letter to the governor on Giselle's behalf, something that explained what had happened and expressed how he felt Giselle didn't deserve to spend the rest of his life in prison. But as so often happens, life got in the way, and Riebau never got around to penning the letter. He told me that if he had the chance today at a resentencing hearing, he would testify on Giselle's behalf: "What I'm saying is, I don't think justice was served by this kid getting the same sentence as the shooter."

Before I went to visit Giselle at the Limon Correctional Facility, Ratliff told me a few things about him. One was that he had taught himself to speak English in prison. Another was that he'd become a talented painter. Giselle drew pictures as a kid, but within the confines of Limon, his artistic skills flourished. According to a Department of Corrections Progress Assessment Summary, Giselle struggled during his early years in prison, accumulating multiple code violations. In 2010, however, he began a record of good behavior, and in 2011 he was admitted to Limon's Incentive Program. Inmates in the program are "held to a higher standard and are afforded the opportunity to earn extra privileges." For

Giselle, that meant access to art supplies: canvases, paint, and brushes. Painting became a way for Giselle to express himself, to experience a sense of freedom that he cannot physically access.

The day we spoke in the Limon visiting room, Giselle seemed thoughtful and at ease given his circumstances. He spoke about energy—good and bad—and how he feels it swirling around the prison. He spoke about fate and how it is almost as if being locked up has allowed him to become the person he is now. He told me he's proud of the man he's become and that even though he's serving a life sentence, he is at peace. "I think I came here to be me," Giselle told me. "In the streets I would have never been a painter."

Ratliff updates Giselle regularly on his case, but he doesn't focus on that. Instead, he thinks about his artwork. This past summer, Ratliff arranged for some of Giselle's work to be shown at a gallery in the Santa Fe art district. His work generated almost $2,500 in sales, and Giselle donated the money to Children's Hospital Colorado. Recently, he was asked to paint a large mural on the barren walls of the prison's educational building. The mural spans the length of an entire hallway. Giselle painted the outside world: images of stars and the galaxy, snow-covered mountains and skiers, and deep-sea divers and marine life.

Eighteen years after the fact, Giselle says he doesn't remember many of the details of that night. Ratliff speculates they are either gone completely or too painful to recall. She once asked Giselle to review the transcript of his interview with police; Giselle told her he couldn't bear to read the words—his words—that in many ways led to his lifelong imprisonment. "They only believed the parts that sent me to life in prison," Giselle says. I asked Giselle whether he still speaks to his brother, Raul, the sibling he most looked up to and who involved him in the bust to arrest Guero. (Raul declined to be interviewed for this story.) Giselle said he doesn't talk to his brother and no longer respects him. But he says he would take a bullet for Raul. "I would still give my life for him, but not because of him," Giselle says, "but because of what I inherited from my mother, my blood."

If Giselle were ever to leave prison, he says he would go back to Mexico. The home Giselle grew up in still stands in Rancho Ruices, and his sister Kelly goes by every few weeks and cleans up just in case Giselle is one day able to return. Giselle thinks of painting in the dry fields behind his house, the very place he was reminded of the morning of the shootings, up at the buffalo preserve. "I would like to take my paints and paint," he says. "I want to start a life over."

Recently, Giselle finished a new piece called "Sacrifice." Giselle's feelings and emotions are embedded in each of his paintings, but this one is particularly meaningful. A few months earlier, Giselle received a letter from Ratliff with important news: She and her team had contacted the widow of Rumaldo Castillo-Hernandez, the man Guero shot and killed. In her letter, Ratliff explained that this woman, who has since remarried, had agreed to meet with them. During the meeting, Ratliff said, Castillo-Hernandez's widow expressed no resentment toward Giselle; she said that she believes Giselle's childhood was taken from him and she hopes he is given a second chance—she said, given the opportunity, she would "not stand in his way."

Upon learning that this woman was even willing to meet with Ratliff and her team, Giselle turned to his paintbrush. He closed his eyes and painted the picture he saw in his mind. The colorful painting's dominant image is of an eye; a teardrop drips from the eye and forms the outline of a person, who is positioned in a way that resembles Christ on the cross. In the bottom left quadrant of the painting there is a small man rendered in black ink, and a butterfly drifts into the open space above the man's head. "I painted it with a good feeling," Giselle says. "It's a healing painting; I want to help her to heal if I can." Ratliff later presented the painting to Castillo-Hernandez's widow, and she accepted it; the painting is in her home.

Giselle has always felt a connection to nature. Many of his paintings contain animals, and he's known around prison as an animal lover. That day at Limon, Giselle told me a story about a butterfly, much like the one in "Sacrifice." He said he'd recently been out in the prison yard with a few friends. They were all seated on a bench talking when one of the guys noticed a large butterfly in the distance. The man excitedly pointed out the creature to Giselle, knowing he'd like to see it. Giselle responded by holding his hand up in the air. The butterfly began to travel toward Giselle's palm. It came so close, it seemed as if it might land on Giselle's hand. Just before it did, Giselle pulled his arm away, and the butterfly flapped its wings and glided into the boundless space beyond the prison walls.

Giselle Gutierrez-Ruiz was released in November 2016 after spending nearly 20 years in prison. This story played a significant role in the court's decision to free Gutierrez-Ruiz.

—January 2016

9.
Homegrown Terror
by Garrett Graff

Special agent John Scata, part of a Denver international terrorism squad, had barely slept since getting the call the previous day. Intelligence officials had intercepted several email messages from a Denver man to suspected terrorists in rural Pakistan. The man was using what appeared to be code words—*marriage, wedding, recipe*—that hinted at a plot.

At 5 a.m. on Tuesday, September 8, 2009, Scata gathered his team in the parking lot of a P.F. Chang's one mile from the Vistas at Saddle Rock apartment complex on East Smoky Hill Road, where Najibullah Zazi—a 24-year-old shuttle bus driver who worked at Denver International Airport—lived with his family in a third-floor unit. They had to get eyes on Zazi. Scata had a simple message for his agents: "This isn't the usual drill."

Shortly after dawn, Zazi emerged from his apartment building, climbed into his car, and drove away. Several FBI vehicles followed him as he went about his day. By midafternoon, Scata was back in the Denver field office, briefing his supervisors—including Jim Davis, the Denver FBI special agent in charge, and Steve Olson, the assistant special agent in charge—and getting updates.

Counterterrorism work is all about chasing ghosts. On an average day, the United States government fields some 3,000 terrorism leads. Virtually none pan out, because the bureau's routine record searches quickly eliminate most leads. "We had expected the next piece of information that comes in would wash him out," Olson says. But in the first hours of the investigation, every trap, every records check, every step pointed to one thing: This was no ghost. "People don't understand how close he was to being successful," Olson says. "Another 24 hours and he would have gotten in his car without us knowing who he was."

That evening, surveillance teams followed Zazi and his father, Mohammed Wali Zazi, as they rented a red Chevrolet sedan. The bureau began to play out scenarios. They still didn't know who Zazi's co-conspirators might be or what their plot was. And they couldn't figure out why someone like Zazi—who presumably could have used one of the vans he drove every day—would need to rent a car.

The FBI has been involved in combating terrorism for most of its 100-plus-year history, but it wasn't until 9/11 that counterterrorism became the bureau's overriding priority. On the morning after those attacks, President George W. Bush delivered to Attorney General John Ashcroft and FBI Director Robert Mueller a clear message: "Don't let this happen again." Thousands of agents and analysts were hired, and others were reassigned from criminal matters to counterterrorism investigations. They were dispatched to Afghanistan, Iraq, Pakistan, and scores of other countries to pursue terrorism links, with a new emphasis: "Prevent. Disrupt. Mitigate."

Since 2001, the bureau—often helped along by informants—has been instrumental in stopping at least 40 known terrorist plots, most of them smaller, "lone-wolf" schemes. Although it has faced some criticism for its activities and investigative techniques, the bureau's post-9/11 record is remarkable, with no subsequent Al Qaeda attacks on U.S. soil. The person who came closest to breaking that streak, according to federal prosecutors, is Najibullah Zazi.

Wednesday, September 9, 2009
For the second straight morning, Zazi left his house at dawn and placed what looked like a laptop computer in his trunk. It seemed like his normal routine until he turned toward I-70. The shuttle driver was known among his co-workers as a diligent employee, putting in long hours, scrambling to find riders, and chatting up potential customers. Yet as the FBI surveillance team accelerated onto the interstate,

following a healthy distance behind Zazi's rented Chevy, it became clear he wasn't going to work. The suspect's car quickly shrank on the horizon, the V6 engine accelerating to speeds of more than 100 miles per hour. It was a struggle to follow without attracting suspicion. There weren't many cars on the road at that hour, and those that were weren't hitting triple-digit speeds.

The Joint Terrorism Task Force (JTTF) called the Colorado State Patrol and asked one of its troopers to stop Zazi as if on a routine speed trap. Colorado trooper Cpl. Chris Lamb pulled behind the Chevy and flipped on his cruiser's lights. Zazi stopped. The driver seemed nervous, Lamb noticed, but Zazi explained his edginess by saying he was hurrying to New York because his coffee cart business in Manhattan was having some problems.

Najibullah Zazi was born on August 10, 1985, in a northwest frontier Pakistani province that borders Afghanistan. (Although published reports have said Zazi was from Afghanistan, his family only claimed to be from there on its immigration forms because that made it easier to gain entry to the United States.) His father, Mohammed, left the family in the early 1990s to immigrate to Queens, New York, where he began driving a cab. He earned enough to pay for his family to join him a few years later.

Zazi seemingly adjusted well to life in Queens. He played basketball and attended high school in Flushing. But he was a poor student and eventually dropped out, and he later ran a doughnut and coffee-vending cart in Lower Manhattan that sported a "God Bless America" sign. Like many Americans in the early 2000s, he ran up too much debt—he opened about $50,000 worth of credit cards over several years—and eventually sought bankruptcy protection. (It later emerged that Zazi used credit cards to purchase goods, then resold them and used the cash to finance his pre-plot travels.)

Around 2006, Zazi flew to Pakistan, where he met and married a wife, his then-19-year-old first cousin, by family arrangement. He returned occasionally to see his wife and two children. Zazi's final trip to Pakistan began in August 2008 and lasted nearly five months. He arrived back in New York in January 2009 and soon moved to Aurora, living at first with his uncle's family. Zazi landed a job at the airport, and his parents and siblings joined him in Aurora that summer.

Zazi kept the coffee cart in Manhattan and leased it, receiving regular payments from his lessee. So the excuse trooper Lamb relayed to the FBI was reasonable. The officer couldn't have known that—the day before Zazi rented the car and just hours before intelligence officials uncovered the inflammatory emails—this speeding driver had perfected an explosive recipe he hoped to use a week later to bomb the New York City subway.

After Lamb let Zazi drive on without issuing a ticket, he resumed his trip east with the FBI surveillance team straining to keep pace. They finally knew their destination: New York City, almost 1,800 miles away.

Back in Denver, Davis couldn't find help. The case wasn't on anyone's radar yet. To get ahead of Zazi, Davis had four FBI agents flown to St. Louis, where they rented cars and picked up the chase 900 miles from Denver. By late evening, agents from the Cleveland division of the FBI started tailing Zazi when he got to Ohio. They spent part of their night watching him nap outside a truck stop near Columbus.

At the field office command post, Davis told the agents, "Go all in. Shut everything else down." FBI assets from across Wyoming and Colorado—intelligence analysts, SWAT teams, bomb technicians, evidence search teams, hazardous material teams, and every surveillance car and plane the bureau possessed anywhere close to the Rockies—started to stream toward Denver.

Thursday, September 10, 2009
As Zazi began driving the last 500 miles to New York, his case finally had the full attention of the U.S. government. The eighth anniversary of the 9/11 attacks was a day away, and Davis was now doing regular secure video teleconferences with the heads of the New York field office and the FBI's National Security Branch, among others. During one video call, an official cut Davis off: "Hold on, that's the White House calling." The case was being briefed right up to President Obama.

The Port Authority Police Department stopped Zazi's car near the George Washington Bridge and told him it was a random checkpoint, and they brought out a police dog, seemingly searching for drugs. It was a ruse. But the police had made a crucial mistake: The dog they used to search Zazi's car had only been trained on black powder, not TATP (triacetone triperoxide), which was the explosive Zazi planned to use. The dog didn't trigger an alert, and Zazi was allowed into the city.

Zazi stayed with a friend in New York, and on the morning of September 11 he visited his coffee cart, just blocks from ground zero. One of the tensest moments of the entire investigation came when the New York surveillance teams momentarily lost eyes on Zazi.

As the FBI's monitoring of Zazi faltered, his car remained parked in Queens. FBI officials in Denver, Washington, and New York hurriedly convened a videoconference and made a decision: Hook it up. The NYPD towed the car and the FBI searched it, but when Zazi eventually retrieved it, two things seemed suspicious: The car was towed even though it hadn't been parked illegally; and when Zazi opened the laptop he'd left inside, the battery was fully charged, even though it should have run down a bit in sleep mode. Someone had searched his computer—and overcharged the battery.

Between the traffic stop in Colorado, the checkpoint entering New York, and the towed car, Zazi began to think the government must be onto him. Then he got confirmation: An imam he knew in Queens called Zazi's father in Colorado to tell him the FBI had been asking about his son. Mohammed Zazi, furious and confused, called Najibullah. "What has happened?" he asked. "What have you guys done?" After they hung up, the imam called Zazi, worried, and advised his young friend, "Don't get involved in Afghanistan garbage, Iraq garbage."

The son panicked and disposed of the tools he'd intended to use in the attack. He flushed the TATP at his friend's house, he left other materials in a dumpster behind the Queens mosque where he'd been a volunteer janitor, and he flew back to Colorado on September 12. Once home, he enlisted his family to help him dispose of the bomb's ingredients. They believed, correctly, that the FBI was eavesdropping, and referred to the potential evidence by the code word "medicine."

As Zazi later testified, the attention from law enforcement disrupted his plans. "We intend[ed] to obtain and assemble the remaining components to build a bomb over the weekend. The plan was to conduct martyrdom operations on subway lines in Manhattan as soon as the materials were ready—Monday, Tuesday, or Wednesday."

Monday, September 14, 2009

Hours before dawn, the New York JTTF raided multiple locations in Queens, including the friend's apartment where Zazi had stayed, but failed to turn up any explosives. The FBI questioned the residents. The bureau feared that Zazi and his accomplices, whoever they might be, would destroy any evidence. And the suspect list was expanding. "This wasn't a laser focus on Najibullah Zazi," Olson says. By this time a number of possible suspects were under active investigation, each one assigned a case agent, who were aided by financial and intelligence analysts to pursue every possible lead.

The notoriously leaky New York JTTF brought the raids in Queens into the public eye. "The FBI is seriously spooked about these guys," a former senior counterterrorism official told the New York Daily News. "This is not some…FBI informant–driven case. This is the real thing." Meanwhile, the Denver FBI office was getting help from the Aurora and Denver police and the Colorado State Patrol. Olson stationed a team of state troopers on E-470 near Zazi's apartment, with chilling guidance: "I'm only going to instruct you to stop him [pull him over] if he leaves his house carrying a backpack"—in other words, if the FBI thought Zazi was en route to execute a suicide bombing. "This is a dangerous thing I'm asking you to do," he repeatedly acknowledged.

In some ways, the Denver field office was well-suited to tackle an active Al Qaeda cell on American soil. Davis, the special agent in charge, had experienced firsthand the FBI's post-9/11 transformation. The son of a Michigan cop, Davis always knew that he wanted to go into law enforcement. His father told him to skip the dreary days of traffic duty and go right to the meaningful investigative stuff: Be an FBI agent. Davis never seriously considered another career.

He spent most of his tenure working "white-collar" crimes; on 9/11 he'd been heading the government fraud unit at the bureau headquarters in Washington. Two years later, when Davis heard that the FBI was deploying agents to Iraq to go after Al Qaeda, he volunteered. Weeks into his tour, on December 13, 2003, Davis awoke to rumors that Saddam Hussein had been located. Later that day, American Special Forces arrested the most wanted man in Iraq and handed him over to the FBI for processing. Davis held the dictator, as he would any captured fugitive, while agents took Saddam's fingerprints and mug shot.

Davis served subsequent tours in Afghanistan and Iraq, working counterterrorism in the war zones, before he was assigned to the Denver field office in 2008. (Each of his assistant special agents in charge, Steve Olson and Mike Rankin, had also served in Iraq.) It was supposed to have been a stopover for Davis, the capstone to his 25-year FBI career, but the Colorado lifestyle convinced him to stay. "It's an easy place to fall in love with," he says.

Today, Davis is the Governor John Hickenlooper–appointed executive director of the Colorado Department of Public Safety. Sitting in his third-floor office in Lakewood, the walls decorated with mementos and pictures from a generation in law enforcement, Davis says, "I've had a good career, but nothing compares to Zazi. Every day something unexpected happened. Every day was just a little bit more surreal."

Tuesday, September 15, 2009

Art Folsom came in early to catch up on some paperwork. The drab office for his small legal practice on Colorado Boulevard—he mostly handled drunk driving and drug possession cases—was shared with several lawyers and a few other businesses. At around 8 that morning, the receptionist relayed a routine message to Folsom: Someone who thought he needed a lawyer had shown up in the lobby.

Najibullah Zazi didn't know where else to turn. Another lawyer in Folsom's suite had prepared some LLC paperwork for a friend, so Zazi figured he'd try to talk to the guy. That lawyer was in court, so Zazi ended up meeting with Folsom, who led him past the office fish tank into a small conference room. Zazi explained that his friends in Queens had gotten mixed up in something. He thought the FBI had searched his car and his computer, perhaps discovering some suspicious—but, Zazi claimed, innocuous—chemistry notes on his laptop. After a few minutes, Folsom was adamant: "Yes, you need a lawyer."

Folsom's sister lived in New York, and he'd noticed the CNN headline about the terrorism-related police raids in Queens a day earlier. That those raids were somehow connected to the man in front of him didn't add up; Zazi was soft-spoken and insisted on calling him "Mr. Folsom." "He didn't seem like the picture in my head of someone who would commit terrorist acts," Folsom says.

Folsom handed Zazi a few business cards and told him not to talk to anyone. The other lawyer would be back the next day and could take over the case. Until then, if anyone asked to speak with Zazi, he was to hand out Folsom's card. "I was petrified he'd start trying to explain things to me [and get himself in trouble]," Folsom says.

Events, however, were moving too quickly. Zazi's name leaked that afternoon in New York, with sources reporting he was the target of a federal terrorism probe. By mid-afternoon the first news crews were arriving at Zazi's apartment. He denied any wrongdoing: "All I can say is that I have no idea what it is all about," Zazi said, later telling *The Denver Post*, "I live here. I work here. Why would I have an issue with America? This is the only country that gives you freedom—freedom of religion, freedom of choice. You don't get that elsewhere. Nobody wants to leave America. People die to come here."

By 4 p.m., journalists were arriving at Folsom's office. "It was surreal," he recalls. "I was getting calls from people asking if I was going to have a presser—I didn't even know what that was." The attorney spent about four hours on the phone with the news media that evening. "My client has nothing to hide," he told *Fox31 News*, "and we are eager to talk to the FBI."

Wednesday, September 16, 2009

Folsom needed to figure out what the FBI knew. He called the bureau that morning, telling FBI officials that he was Zazi's lawyer. It was a curious effort, the FBI's Olson says, to "explain away" the suspect's predicament.

Zazi met Folsom at his office and emerged from the building into a crowd of press on the sidewalk. They hustled toward Folsom's car—the lawyer swatted away one camera with his briefcase—and drove to the Byron G. Rogers Federal Building, where they dodged another group of reporters on their way inside.

For the FBI, this was a gift; terrorism suspects don't generally come knocking on the field office door. "Ultimately the case broke because of the media pressure," Davis says. "That forced Zazi to come to us." The bureau assigned special agent Eric C. Jergenson to lead the interrogation. Zazi and Folsom began talking with Jergenson and a second agent in a small interview room. They had surrendered their BlackBerrys and cell phones. Knowing the two men would be out of communication for a few hours, FBI agents raided Zazi's apartment and his uncle's house. John Scata's team hit the latter, but found little evidence.

At Zazi's house, as a group of journalists watched nearby, Olson's team had more luck. The apartment immediately struck the agents as oddly empty—no couch, no chair, no table. When they opened a closet, bomb techs spotted a large five-gallon bucket full of a white, powdery substance. "The color and consistency is consistent with TATP," the lead bomb tech told Olson. TATP had long been favored by terror groups. It was used by Richard Reid, the so-called shoe bomber who tried to blow up an American Airlines flight in December 2001, and by terrorists in the London subway bombings in 2005. Palestinian terrorists dubbed TATP the "Mother of Satan" because of its power and instability. Mostly odorless and similar in consistency to powdered sugar, its three main ingredients—acetone, hydrogen peroxide, and acid—are easily attainable over the counter. If this was TATP, the bomb tech said, it was enough to take out Zazi's building and the neighboring one, and spread damage through a much wider radius.

Olson surveyed the scene: dozens of nearby apartments, a growing pack of news media just 100 yards away, and an elementary school that backed up against the apartment complex's rear wall. He went to Zazi's brother, who was in the back of an FBI vehicle. "What's in that bucket?" he asked.

"I don't know, but you had better test it," the brother said darkly.

Olson ordered the evacuation of the nearby apartments and pushed the media crews back another 100 yards. Then his heart fell: The bell at the elementary school was dismissing hundreds of schoolchildren, who poured onto the sidewalks around the complex. Fortunately, when the bomb squad tested the mixture, it was merely flour. But it had given the case its name: Operation High Rise.

At the Denver field office, the massive emergency command post had been running 24/7 for a week, filled with scores of personnel from the FBI and other agencies, including CIA officials and national security lawyers from the Department of Justice. The walls of the command post were papered with a running timeline of events, along with photos and addresses that were relevant to the investigation. Tables were strewn with documents and Chick-fil-A wrappers. The entire office pulsed as everyone worked 12-hour shifts—and often longer. "Once people realized what this was, you couldn't get them to leave," Olson says. As intelligence analyst Collin Husic says, "You knew this was the real thing. This is what the job is all about. You can go your whole career in the bureau without seeing something like this, especially in a place like Denver."

Midway through the afternoon's conversation, Jergenson laid out one of nine pages worth of handwritten bomb notes investigators had taken off Zazi's laptop. Although the FBI didn't know it yet, Zazi had destroyed his computer hard drive upon returning to Denver. The agents, though, told him they'd found the documents in his home that day, which Zazi knew was impossible. He then lied, claiming they were innocent chemistry drawings that he had downloaded from a book online. "It was a catch-22," Folsom says. "We know they're lying, but I know he's lying about it, too. As soon as that happened, I went, 'Oh, shit.'"

The interview progressed haltingly. The discussion broke down whenever Zazi's story hit a rough patch or didn't add up. At times the suspect would seem almost set to confess, but he couldn't quite get it out. Each time this happened, Zazi and Folsom would leave the room to confer privately and then return with just a little more information.

During one such break, Folsom confronted Zazi. The story wasn't believable, he said. There were too many holes in the timeline. With the FBI out of the room, Zazi began to tell Folsom about Al Qaeda's weapons training, of firing AK-47s, of rocket-propelled-grenade-launching practice in the mountains, of the bomb-making classes, and of the lesson he took on how to construct a suicide belt. "Once you got the cork pulled out, the information started to flow," Folsom says. "At that point, I realized this wasn't just someone who was angry. This was someone who had danced with the devil."

Zazi grew up in the mountains of Pakistan as Osama bin Laden was setting up his mujahedeen network nearby, but he was 16 and living in Queens by the time of the 9/11 attacks. The mosque where he'd volunteered as a janitor, Masjid Hazrat Abubakr, suffered a vicious schism after 9/11 when its imam, Mohammed Sherzad, condemned bin Laden and the Taliban only to get ousted by the mosque's more radical elements.

After 9/11, Zazi gradually became more serious about his religion. By the middle of the decade he'd begun wearing traditional tunics, grown a beard, and had become a fan of YouTube videos by Zakir Naik, who preached an unorthodox interpretation of Islam—endorsing polygamy, among other practices—though he wasn't particularly known for promoting violence.

Zazi's story unfolded slowly to Folsom. He hadn't started out with the intent of launching a domestic attack. He'd read and heard about large civilian casualties from the U.S. war in Afghanistan, and he grew increasingly troubled by what was happening there. "He wanted to go over to protect his country," Folsom says. "I know how I felt after 9/11—I wanted to strike back. He was angry about what was happening [in Afghanistan] and found a misguided way to react."

While in Pakistan in 2008, a cousin introduced Zazi and his two high school friends, Zarein Ahmedzay and Adis Medunjanin, to a radical cleric. The cleric ushered the boys into the shadowy world of Al Qaeda in the mountainous and lawless corner of Pakistan known as Waziristan. There, the three men met with two of Al Qaeda's senior leaders: Saleh al-Somali, the group's head of external operations, and Rashid Rauf. As Ahmedzay later explained in court, "We told these two individuals that we wanted to wage jihad in Afghanistan, but they said that we would be more useful to them and to the jihad if we returned to New York and conducted operations there." He added, "They said the most important thing was to hit well-known structures and to maximize the number of casualties."

By fall 2008, crushing pressure from U.S. and international counterterrorism programs had forced Al Qaeda to evolve. In targeting the organization's financing and communication networks, and supplementing that harassment with airstrikes launched by CIA drones, the United States and its allies compelled Al Qaeda to switch from centrally controlled, highly coordinated, increasingly high-profile attacks to smaller, more opportunistic strikes. Young, green, would-be jihadists—what some have called the "cannon fodder" of the war on terror—had always been easy for Al Qaeda to find and exploit in the Middle East. Zazi, then considered a lawful permanent resident of the United States, was much more valuable. He could travel back into the United States without trouble, knew New York intimately, and could be trained cheaply to build a bomb. The Al Qaeda leaders convinced Zazi and his companions that their greatest contribution to jihad was back home. "We discussed the matter among ourselves, and we agreed to go forward with the plan," Zazi's co-conspirator Ahmedzay later testified. "I personally believed that conducting an operation in the United States would be the best way to end the wars."

Hatching the Zazi plot and recruiting the three men was one of Al Qaeda's greatest achievements since 9/11. The difficult operating environment for Al Qaeda was underscored when, soon after Zazi's meeting with the two senior terrorist leaders, Rauf reportedly was killed by a U.S. drone attack.

Zazi himself wasn't entirely convinced the martyrdom operation was a good idea. "He was not a huge fan of the suicide aspect," Folsom says. "He had some reservations about what they wanted him to do." Even so, after he arrived home in January 2009 and moved to Colorado, Zazi began assembling the ingredients for an attack.

Folsom knew the obstruction charge for the destroyed hard drive was of little concern. "There were much more problematic charges coming down the pike," Folsom says. Agents took Zazi's fingerprints, a DNA swab, and a handwriting sample. This was during the Islamic holiday of Ramadan, and Zazi had been fasting all day, so after sunset the FBI brought him a McDonald's Filet-O-Fish sandwich as the questioning continued. After they agreed to pick up the conversation the next day, the FBI drove Zazi and Folsom home. By the time Zazi arrived there, the bureau had finished its search of his apartment and airport shuttle van.

Zazi's father, Mohammed Wali, also spoke with the FBI that Wednesday, and bureau agents caught him giving inconsistent information about his son's activities in New York. This exposed him to a "1001 charge," named after the section of the U.S. criminal code that makes it illegal to lie to government agents. The 1001 charge was enough to arrest and hold either Zazi. But as long as the son was still voluntarily talking, there was no reason to take him in just yet because questions remained: *What had they been planning? Was Mohammed, the stronger personality and a traditional authoritarian father, a key player, or was he merely protecting his son?*

Thursday, September 17, 2009

Folsom and Zazi arrived back at the federal building the following morning with a proposition: Let's make a deal. "We fully expected he'd be pleading guilty, so we were thinking about sentencing considerations," Folsom says. The only way Zazi could avoid going to prison would be by providing enough information about Al Qaeda's operations to get some kind of witness protection. His concern for his wife, children, and extended family in Pakistan—they were well within the reach of Al Qaeda and the feared Pakistani intelligence service, ISI—gave Zazi even more reason to cooperate.

The conversation again proceeded slowly. The government had offered a so-called "proffer letter," meaning nothing Zazi said could be used directly against him, although the FBI could try to independently confirm his information. The time-sensitive nature and life-or-death stakes of Zazi's case meant that a proffer letter needed approval from the top of the Justice Department, but getting it would hopefully let him speak more freely.

U.S. officials were desperate to learn what Zazi knew; the plot could still be advancing without him. During a break, Folsom pushed his client again: Was there an attack coming? If so, Zazi had to tell the FBI. Now. If he withheld information that could have saved lives, any hope of a deal would be gone, and Zazi would end up on death row. "There's nothing that prepares you for asking point-blank if there's about to be another 9/11," he says.

Folsom had by then arrived at his own conclusion: If Zazi gave him evidence of an impending attack, Folsom was prepared to hand it over to the feds. "It's one thing to go into a drug trial knowing your client is guilty; it's significantly different when it's someone planning a terror attack on your country," Folsom says. "I was pretty sure the professional ethics would have allowed that, but I'd also decided that I didn't care. I'm glad I didn't have to make that choice, but I couldn't live with hundreds or thousands of deaths on my conscience."

After the proffer letter arrived from Washington, Zazi began to relax and talk more openly. Although agents believed they'd thwarted the immediate threat, they wanted to wring more information from the suspect. Zazi had bought most of the over-the-counter ingredients for the bomb at local beauty supply stores—which FBI agents confirmed by examining the stores' security camera footage—and he'd cooked the first batches of the explosive at Aurora's Homestead Studio Suites on August 27 and 28. But when he'd tried to ignite some of it in the parking lot, it just flashed and burned.

Zazi then emailed his Pakistani contact for help with his recipe. It was that coded message that the government intercepted, tipping them off to Zazi's identity. He returned to the hotel on September 6 and 7 and fiddled more with his recipe. He took some of his reworked mixture to a lonely end of East Smoky Hill Road and ignited it—this time, it exploded. Zazi had his bomb. The next morning, the FBI began following him.

As agents realized just how close they'd come to missing Zazi, everyone exhaled. He'd slipped through the many new layers of security put into place since 9/11. The FBI's vaunted "Operation Tripwire" was designed to instruct businesses—such as beauty supply warehouses—to report suspicious purchases. But it hadn't flagged Zazi's shopping trips. (He'd explained to the clerks when they asked why he was purchasing so many cosmetic chemicals that he "had a lot of girlfriends.") Similarly, despite widespread "See Something Say Something" public awareness campaigns, no one at the Studio Suites had mentioned the odd sight of a man trying to ignite a bucket full of chemicals in the complex parking lot.

If not for his chemistry failure, the FBI likely wouldn't have known Zazi's name until after the New York City attack. They'd persuaded him to cooperate, but as Olson explains, "The discomfort level of having this guy on the street was high. There were animated conversations inside here about the liabilities of leaving him out there." The FBI had met its post-9/11 mandate by disrupting the terrorist plot even though they still didn't know many details. "We still had no idea what his target was," Olson says.

The investigation was leading every news cycle. John Scata received a phone call from his wife telling him the Denver FBI was on *Fox News*. Folsom got a confused phone call from a friend in New York City: "Why are you on the Jumbotron in Times Square?" Although Folsom was getting publicly flogged for letting his client speak with the FBI, in at least one way, the lawyer was savvier than he appeared. The media didn't know yet that an immunity deal had been negotiated, and Folsom purposely avoided discussing it. "The bureau made it clear they'd prefer that word of the immunity deal not be released," Folsom says. "I didn't lie to anyone, but I said things that I knew could be construed incorrectly."

Folsom wasn't a natural fit for this case. Then 37, he had almost no experience with the FBI and zero national security background. Raised in Pennsylvania, he'd gotten into law intending to do environmental work. He moved to Colorado to attend the University of Denver Law School, where he'd been one of the editors of the *Water Law Review*. As the Zazi story emerged, Folsom faced withering criticism. *The Denver Post* columnist Mike Littwin wrote, "There are many things we have yet to learn in the case of Najibullah Zazi. But one thing is clear: [Arthur] Folsom—attorney to the shuttle-bus-driving alleged terrorist—can't possibly be qualified to defend him." His colleagues also questioned Folsom's qualifications. "He had no business going in there," says another lawyer who worked on the Zazi case. "Anyone who watched *Law & Order* knows you don't do that. I watched that train wreck and hoped Art wouldn't hurt himself too much."

The bureau, of course, welcomed such a weak adversary. "He's the MVP of this case," says one federal official with a laugh, "no question."

Friday, September 18, 2009

The first thing Folsom noticed on the third day of negotiations was that a new piece of art had appeared on the wall of the FBI conference room. Unless the bureau had a pressing need to redecorate overnight, Folsom now knew they were "secretly" videotaping the conversation through the new wooden nautical-themed clock. They were actually doing much more than that: The room behind the clock was crowded with attorneys, analysts, and officials from a variety of federal agencies looking in.

The number of observers involved in the case meant that the steady stream of news leaks had become a torrent. Folsom and Zazi began the session angrily. "Why should I talk to you when I know it'll be on the 5-o'clock news?" Zazi said. During a midmorning break, Folsom got an email from a reporter asking about information Zazi had just provided to the FBI that day. He pulled aside two prosecutors and showed them the message. "We've got a real problem—this is what we're talking about this morning." The prosecutors apologized for the leaks. Folsom nearly shouted: "The Titanic had a leak—this is everywhere. My guy's going to get killed tonight." Threats and ugly voicemails had already begun to arrive at Folsom's law office. After one warning, local police arrived to guard Folsom's building.

The FBI also had uncovered another negotiating tool: Zazi's family had immigration problems. One of Zazi's "brothers" was actually a cousin. Zazi's parents had claimed him as a son on their immigration forms. Even though the interrogators told Zazi that they could deport his mother and cousin, Zazi refused to provide information about his co-conspirators, the two high school friends he'd traveled with to Pakistan, saying his religion didn't allow for him to indict others. He also continued dissembling, at one point claiming that he intended to detonate a suicide bomb at a local Wal-Mart "to make a statement to the media." In the room next door, the hidden audience raptly pressed together as Zazi remained evasive.

His stonewalling caused the talks to falter, and once again the FBI drove Zazi and Folsom home, fully expecting the two men to return the next day. The FBI's offer, the interrogators reminded Folsom and Zazi as they left, hinged upon full disclosure: "This is an all-or-nothing deal."

Saturday, September 19, 2009

When Folsom and Zazi talked that morning by phone, Zazi told his lawyer he wouldn't violate his religious beliefs and inform on his friends. "I'd rather spend life in prison than eternity in hell," he said. Resigned to his client's impending arrest, Folsom advised Zazi to gather his family and spend his last remaining hours of freedom with them. Make sure to touch them and hug them, Folsom said, because you may never be allowed physical contact with family members again. He left Zazi with one last thought: "When the knock on the door comes—don't resist."

Folsom called the government: There would be no more talks. Davis's team obtained a warrant, and the arresting officers gathered that afternoon at a nearby high school parking lot. Davis had finally decided to embrace the media circus; they were going into Zazi's apartment complex, fast and loud. "When you get him in the Suburban," Davis told his agents, "make sure the windows are down. I want everyone to see that we have him."

As Davis drove toward Zazi's apartment, a Denver reporter called. "I hear you're on your way to arrest Zazi." Even more disturbing, *The New York Post* called Zazi's home phone and warned him that the bureau was coming—the media was giving a suspected suicide bomber a heads-up.

The convoy of black SUVs, lights spinning, pulled into Zazi's parking lot, greeted by TV lights and flashbulbs. In their blue raid jackets, agents piled out. Minutes later Jergenson led a handcuffed Zazi down the steps. Simultaneously, the FBI arrested Mohammed Wali Zazi and Ahmad Wais Afzali, the Queens imam who had tipped off the Zazis that the FBI was asking about them. "The arrests carried out tonight are part of an ongoing and fast-paced investigation," the assistant attorney general for national security, David Kris, told the media. "It is important to note that we have no specific information regarding the timing, location, or target of any planned attack."

Folsom recruited his first legal boss, well-known Denver attorney J. Michael Dowling, to help with the Zazi defense. Minutes before the detention hearing's scheduled start several days after his arrest, Folsom saw a federal prosecutor enter the courtroom with an enormous stack of papers. *That can't be good*, he thought. Indeed, the government had added to its initial 1001 charge; now they were accusing Zazi of plotting a terrorist attack on the United States. His bond denied, Zazi boarded a U.S. Marshals Learjet the next day for New York City.

Folsom was off the case by November. Dowling took over, but eventually departed after he and Zazi differed on legal strategy. In summer 2010, Zazi's planned attack on New York was linked to two other plots in Norway and Britain. All three involved similar explosives and targets, all three were put in motion by Saleh al-Somali before his death from another reported drone strike, and all three were unraveled by authorities before the bombers could strike.

The Queens imam who betrayed the Zazi investigation pleaded guilty to lying to federal officials and left the U.S. Zazi's father was found guilty last summer of obstruction of justice. His trial documented for the first time how the family had helped Zazi destroy evidence after his ill-fated trip to New York.

Najibullah Zazi pleaded guilty to charges including providing material support for a foreign terrorist organization, conspiracy in a foreign country to commit murder, and conspiracy to use weapons of mass destruction. Zazi's former lawyer, Dowling, thinks his client mostly was a victim of circumstance—an easily manipulated and misguided pawn. "He's an American kid who got excited reading about jihad and wanted to be a part of it," Dowling says. "He wasn't on the starting team." During his allocution in court, as part of his guilty plea, Zazi offered insight into his own chilling logic for undertaking such a potentially deadly plot. When the judge asked whether his actions were in the nature of a suicide bomber, Zazi clarified: "I have a different explanation to that. To me, it meant that I would sacrifice myself to bring attention to what the United States military was doing to civilians in Afghanistan, by sacrificing my soul for the sake of saving other souls."

FBI officials say Zazi's justifications are irrelevant; it's clear to them that Zazi was intent on mass murder. "He was and is a committed terrorist," Olson says. "He would have killed lots of people." Scata is equally blunt: "Regardless of whether anyone knows, we saved a lot of lives."

Operation High Rise showcased the Obama administration's approach to terrorism—a mix of handcuffs and Hellfire missiles. Zazi was questioned, charged, and held to account in our criminal justice system, while the plotters who were out of reach of U.S. authorities were targeted and killed by missiles fired from CIA drones. "In this case, as it has in so many other cases," U.S. Attorney General Eric Holder said at a news conference announcing Zazi's plea, "the criminal justice system has proved to be an invaluable weapon for disrupting plots and incapacitating terrorists, one that works in concert with the intelligence community and our military."

Two years later, as the nation somberly marked the 10th anniversary of the 9/11 attacks with yet another vague terror threat against New York City, Zazi has disappeared from public view. Although his guilty plea suggested he would face life in prison, Zazi's first scheduled sentencing date—June 25, 2010—came and went with no word or sign of him. It was rescheduled several times over the following year, but to date Zazi hasn't made a subsequent court appearance. The FBI and the Justice Department both declined to comment on Zazi's whereabouts. He was moved long ago from the detention facility in Brooklyn to an undisclosed location. The Federal Bureau of Prisons has no public record of him.

The government doesn't lose such high-profile prisoners, so Zazi's uncertain status likely means he's still cooperating with the government. While Zazi did not appear at his father's trial last summer, Justice Department officials say he might still appear at co-conspirator Adis Medunjanin's trial, set for January. Moreover, Ahmedzay was indicted in 2010 on the same charges that Zazi admitted to earlier, which seems to indicate that Zazi helped law enforcement build its case against Ahmedzay.

In terrorism cases like Zazi's—with multiple trials playing out where a cooperating defendant can still prove useful—sentencing of the cooperating defendant can be delayed, sometimes for years. Art Folsom says that a reduced sentence and witness protection for his family was Zazi's goal from the beginning. "At the start, we wanted witness protection," Folsom says. "I guess he got there eventually." (Dean Boyd, a Justice Department spokesman in Washington, says, "For obvious reasons, the Justice Department does not comment on whether an individual is in the witness protection program.") All of which means that Najibullah Zazi—the central figure in one of the most dangerous terror plots to target the United States in the last decade—could someday end up free under the guard of the witness protection program, a reward for years of cooperation that began with his arrival at the Byron G. Rogers Federal Building on a sunny September morning in 2009.

—November 2011

10.
Final Cut

by Julian Rubinstein

He stopped in the middle of a snow-covered dirt road near our house in Parker, as if he couldn't wait a moment longer to relate the following:

"This hat that I have on my head comes from Lancaster's. Which is a little Western store on East Colfax, so far east that it's almost in Kansas, where the cowboys in the eastern half of Colorado like to shop for their boots, hats, buckles, guns." He counted them off on one gloved hand. "This summer I took myself over there because I knew I could get a beaver hat at a great price in the heat of August. Because no one is buying beaver hats in August."

That was my father, age 59 in January 2002, on one of those Colorado mornings when the fresh snow and clear sky stretch time like notes on a soundstage. I stood watching him through my video camera's viewfinder: my father, who many in Denver knew as Dr. David Rubinstein, psychiatrist, medical director, and staff physician at several area hospitals for more than three decades; my father, the Bronx-born Jew who grew up on welfare and became a Colorado horse owner; my father, with whom I never got along growing up, but who—for reasons I couldn't yet explain—had unwittingly compelled me earlier that week to begin documenting his every move; my father, the doctor turned cancer patient, then in year 11 of an illness that was supposed to have killed him in three.

"The cat's out of the bag," is what he said. Sometimes he repeated this phrase real fast, adding that that's how he heard it in his dreams. It was what the radiologist had said to him in November of 1991 after reading my dad's X-rays, which showed not only a malignant tumor in his prostate but also blurred lines around the gland indicating that the cancer had already spread to several nodes.

When the call came I was in a dorm room on the Upper West Side of New York. I was attending Columbia University's graduate school for journalism, only a few miles from the Bronx apartment my parents lived in when I was born. Both of them were now on the line. "I had some test results that weren't so good," my dad said. "I may have some form of cancer." Then it was my mom talking, kind of slow and about things we already knew. "So you're still coming next week, right?" she asked, as if I'd ever canceled a Thanksgiving trip home. "Wednesday, you get in around 7. I'll be waiting at the regular place." Then Dad wanted to talk to me, alone. After the click, he lowered his voice. "I can't believe I neglected myself," he said, as if to confess something, perhaps even to me. "I see patients every day, but I hadn't had a checkup for years."

I sat on my wafer mattress, blinking at the wall, numb. Over the next few days, my parents spooned me information like I was a child: The doctors didn't think it was a good idea to operate. The reason not to operate was that it was an unnecessary risk. The reason it was unnecessary was because the cancer had already spread. The cat was out the bag, so to speak. That's what the radiologist said. My dad had three years to live.

I wish I could say that my father and I had a good relationship when I was growing up; that, because he was a well-respected psychiatrist who specialized in adolescent behavior, he also was a model father. I wish I could say I was a loving son, but until I began making my film about him that wasn't the case.

Growing up as a Jew in Denver circa 1970s was no picnic for me. I had a big nose and a "girl's" name. Worse, at age six, I took up the violin, encouraged by my parents, both classical music fans. We had a living room that was sort of like our situation room. It was only used when something serious was happening, like when the dog died or when my younger brother Daniel or I was being "docked," my dad's word for grounding. It was also the place where I went and cried to my mom after being pelted with rocks and called "Jew boy" and "orchestra fag." "What happened?" she would say. As I told her, my mom's mouth would tighten and I could see the hurt in her eyes. She got it.

My dad would get home after we'd all eaten dinner. "How's school?" he'd ask, confirming his obliviousness to my life. Sometimes I could see his mind wander while I answered. And I would just stop talking. "Julian, I'm listening," he'd insist, but I wouldn't continue. A few times he sat me down and asked, "Are you feeling depressed?" Once he even said, "Are you having suicidal thoughts?" He sent me to a child psychologist.

In every other way we were a nuclear family with no bleeding wounds. Daniel and my father had no problems. Maybe that was because they had more in common, or because my brother simply was less troubled than me. Our one household secret was my ailing relationship with my father; still, as if he could will it to be so, my dad liked to say he and I were alike. We did bear a close physical resemblance: blue eyes, narrow facial structure. And unlike Daniel, who was born in Denver, my father and I were both native New Yorkers. But as far as I was concerned, our similarities ended there.

By the time I entered ultra-cliquey Cherry Creek High School in 1983, my relationship with my dad was little more than perfunctory. Within six months I quit the violin, and to counter the fact that I was in accelerated classes, I made a big show of never doing any homework, cheating on tests, ditching classes, chewing Copenhagen, drinking alarming quantities of Coors Light every Friday and Saturday night, and occasionally getting stoned.

"We need to have a talk," my dad said after the first time he found a bag of pot in my car. He drove us up I-70 into the mountains. I don't remember what he said, only that he was wasting his breath. I finally had attained cool status—a card-carrying member of the jock crew—and there was no one I treated more dismissively than my father. Our communication deteriorated to the point where the only interaction we had was my handing him a plastic cup he made me pee into once a week so he could have my urine drug-tested at the hospital. I failed the first test: I peed in a cup the previous day, hid it under the sink, and then poured the old specimen into the test cup. I was too much of a jerk to consider that fresh urine is warm; as soon as I handed the cup to my father, I was busted again.

By the end of my senior year, a sort of détente had set in on our relationship. The fact that I'd maintained respectable enough grades to get into college more or less proved I wasn't flushing my life down the toilet. My dad supported my choice of a college way off in a part of the country where we had no roots, Emory University in Atlanta. I joined the jock fraternity, partied my ass off for a year, and then started to realize I had nothing in common with my friends and was bored out of my mind.

It was journalism that rescued me. I knew I loved writing, and the idea of being licensed to enter the lives of others was invigorating. Maybe I thought I would find myself in the process. The day I got my acceptance letter to Columbia, I felt, for the first time in my life, like I was on the right track. I was two months into my journalism master's program when I got the call from my parents.

Diary entry from my father, written in 2002, about our year in Pueblo, Colorado, in 1972, when he was a fellow at the Colorado Mental Health Institute: "That society [the state hospital in Pueblo] was fascinating and it's taken me many years to realize that I've lived like a long-term tourist, watching but being an outsider most of my life, trying, tasting, but not involving myself, "hiding in the bushes."

In the months that followed my father's diagnosis, he was haunted by the radiologist's words. It wasn't clear how much fight he had in him. My dad, who had been trained to analyze and help solve patients' problems, seemed completely adrift. Was he a fighter or was he just another unlucky loser?

I didn't know myself. It was like, at 22, I was regarding him for the first time. When I went home for that Thanksgiving, I remember feeling like my dad was looking for some kind of sign from me. Like he was trying to gauge whether our relationship was a goner as well or if perhaps it could be salvaged if we had enough time. I wasn't sure about that either, but I made a point of joining with my mom and brother in prevailing upon him not to give up.

He began flying around the country seeking second opinions, and the following spring he finally found a doctor at the Mayo Clinic in

Minnesota who was willing to operate. The idea was that eliminating as much of the cancer as possible might at least slow the growth of the disease. My dad agreed to have the surgery, a radical prostatectomy that would leave him occasionally impotent and mildly incontinent.

As I finished grad school and began my career as a journalist, first in Washington, D.C., and then back in New York City, I watched my father from afar in amazement. Referring to his illness as a "new lease on life," he and my mom moved from the modest south suburban Denver home they'd owned since 1974 to a wooded three-acre, ranch-style property outside Parker. My father, who sometimes had wondered aloud about replacing his Toyota with a Jaguar, bought one horse and then another. He stabled them himself in the barn on the property. Every morning he spent an hour shoveling manure.

Then he went to work, not telling anyone in his professional circles he was sick, despite at first having to wear a catheter under his pants to facilitate urination and later enduring exhausting rounds of radiation. In fact, he increased his workload—serving as medical director of Columbine Hospital for five years on top of his private practice and his attending and teaching duties at several other area hospitals. He also insisted on continuing to travel with my mom to far-flung places such as Kenya, Tanzania, and Turkey—places where emergency medical care would not be readily available. Before going, he taught himself the basics of the native languages, including Swahili. Doing things any other way, he said, would be "like spitting on my survival."

It was hard not to admire him. In the old grudges I'd held against him, I now saw my pettiness. We began to enjoy more frequent phone conversations and visits. One afternoon, following one of our walks together, my dad smiled and said, "You know, we've not only remade our relationship, but we've become friends." I nodded, but in truth I didn't agree. There was still an important piece of me he hadn't accepted. Although he loved the woman I had moved in with and seemed proud to send me to an Ivy League school, he hadn't fully accepted my career choice. "You know, you'd make a great lawyer," he sometimes told me. But I didn't want to be a lawyer. Instead, I left a staff job at *Sports Illustrated* to strike out on my own as a writer. Doing anything else, I told him, would be like spitting on my survival.

Year after year ticked by with my father's bone scans showing the cancer seeping through his body like an oil spill. Occasionally these results would be accompanied by the onset of some frightening complication requiring hospitalization and more tests.

I became accustomed to a constant, low-level anxiety, like being in the dark hold of an unseaworthy vessel. I threw myself into my work, landing higher- and higher-profile magazine assignments, each one more pressure-packed than the last. I also got engaged. It was nearing a decade since my father's diagnosis. I was going on with my life. What else could I do?

Then, in December of 2000, while I was in Budapest working on a story, I got another call in which both of my parents were on the line. A new bone scan had revealed that several tumors were on the verge of entering my father's spinal column; if it was breached, he would be paralyzed from the neck down. No one in Denver was willing to perform the operation he needed, but after a flurry of calls they had found a specialist at Sloan Kettering Cancer Institute in New York who was willing to attempt the surgery. It would be a six- to eight-hour procedure. There was a chance he would never wake up.

My whole family flew in the next morning. The following day, after my brother and mom already had headed back to the waiting area, I found myself holding onto my dad's hand as he was wheeled, flat on his back, through the halls to the operating room. When the attendant finally said I had to leave, I started sobbing. For the first time, I thought, *Don't go yet.* "Hey," my dad said, gripping my hand. "I'll see you soon." He was the one reassuring me.

Eight hours later, we were finally called to the ICU. There was my father, swollen and exhausted but giggling as he wiggled his toes from under the covers, the sign that he had averted paralysis. The surgery was a success. But back in Denver he slipped into an obvious decline. Having already exceeded the allowable amount of radiation, my father resorted to chemotherapy. With each month that passed he seemed to age a year. He lost his signature thick, brown beard as well as his hair; his previously fit body became pale, shrunken, and lumpy; he began to have good and bad days.

I had just landed my first book contract to do a full-blown treatment of the story I'd been in Budapest to write about the previous year. It was a big step in my career, but even though I got my wife's blessing, we were both scared. Researching the book would require me to spend about a year over the next two in Europe. She worked a regular job in the city and wouldn't be able to accompany me. And, of course, I would be even farther from Denver—when it seemed time really was about to run out on my dad.

Not exactly understanding why, I began taping my phone conversations with my father. Then, before a visit home in December 2001, I bought a professional video camera and microphone and showed up asking if I could begin filming him.

"What do you hope to get out of it?" he asked. He seemed puzzled. I wasn't sure either, but not wanting to scare him off I told him I thought the film could be a source of inspiration for other cancer patients. He thought for a few minutes then said, "If it helps one person, it's worth it."

"At first I thought, 'I'm going to be the best cancer patient ever;' then I realized, 'what an asshole, that's doing it for other people. It doesn't matter what anyone else thinks. Do it for yourself.'"

—David Rubinstein, on camera, 2002.

I'd never made a documentary film before, and I approached it as if it were any other journalism assignment. I was the fly on the wall; he was the subject. Everywhere he went, I followed him with the camera—to the bookstore, to the pharmacy, to walk the dog. I couldn't tell if he was indulging me because he wanted to spend time with me or because maybe he or I had something we needed to say to each other. But, like the best subjects, he quickly forgot he was being watched, so I just let the film roll.

I also sat him down and interviewed him. This seemed to make him happy. As a psychiatrist, he was someone who had trafficked in words, and for so long I'd made it clear his had meant nothing to me. Now, holding the camera, I was, at last, listening.

He kept talking about his childhood. There were millions of stories, but the one I knew had to be in the film was the one he told of his father, who died when my father was eight of lymphoma, a deadly form of blood cancer. I suggested we go together with the camera to the Bronx.

It was September 2002 when we went. The chemo treatments had left my dad too unsteady to drive, but he still knew the way to his old neighborhood. He pointed out old, decaying landmarks in a borough that had changed from immigrant to black and Hispanic since he'd been back. The obvious destination was the apartment he'd grown up in, so I let him take us there first. When we got to his block, he peered in at the street-level kitchen window of what used to be his family's home, a two-room flat in which he shared a bedroom with his older sister Renee, while his parents, both immigrants from eastern Europe, slept on the living room couch.

Then I told him I wanted to go to Mount Sinai Hospital. That was where his father, Irving, a fur salesman and advertising jingle writer, spent the last several months of his life. "OK," my father said, hardly sounding sure. It was about a 15-minute drive. When we arrived, my dad got out and wandered around until he found a spot on the sidewalk. He looked up at the rows of hospital windows. And it's this image that now comes first to my mind whenever I think of my father: him, at age eight, standing right there and waving up to a window at the tiny head and hand of his weakened father. "Children weren't allowed in the building back then," my dad said, looking back down at the sidewalk. "By the time they agreed to let me in, he was already in a coma. He was gone." Then, for the first time in my life, I saw my father cry.

After my grandfather's death, a family friend who was a physician gave my dad a doctor's bag. While the other kids played stickball in the street, he ran around with his stethoscope and tongue depressors, telling everyone that when he grew up he was going to be a doctor and heal people.

By this time, I was living part-time in Budapest to work on my book and it was impossible to pretend my father's illness wasn't taking a toll on my life. On an almost daily basis, my dad seemed to be having a physical break-down or dealing with the shocking death-zone results of yet another test or scan. I would get back to my Budapest apartment after an exhausting day of reporting through interpreters and be on the phone to New York or Denver till at least midnight. My wife was having a hard time with my being away. And my mom was fragile, as might be expected of someone watching her husband wincing in pain from small bone fractures where the cancer was eating away his marrow. Sometimes, even before I got off the phone, I took a large dose of prescription sleep medication.

The next time I went back to Denver I brought the camera but wasn't sure I would use it. I was beginning to feel uneasy about the film. I still didn't know what purpose it was serving. And after our trip to the Bronx, it felt exploitative. This was my father, dying in front of my eyes. Not just any subject. Ironically, I'd chosen a career that required me to operate in a way that could be described as "hiding in the bushes." For better or worse, the camera had become my doctor's bag.

But my father had a chemo treatment scheduled, and I couldn't help asking if I could accompany him. He agreed, and as we drove out to the center in Lakewood, I braced myself for a distressing afternoon. My dad was anxious, knowing he'd have to sit for hours with a chemical IV in his arm and perhaps receive another round of dismal test results. But as soon as he walked through the door he was joking and chatting with secretaries, nurses, and patients alike. He looked more comfortable than I'd ever seen him. "There's something about coming here I do look forward to," he admitted. "Everyone's rooting for one another. It becomes something of a club."

The strength he got from being around others like him—the ultimate outsiders, the walking dead—was so powerful that he began volunteering as a counselor at Hospice of Metro Denver, a program for terminally ill patients designed to make the last months of their lives as comfortable as possible. My dad was so committed to this work, he hired a driver to ferry him there so he wouldn't miss a day of counseling dying people who didn't know they were talking to a dying man.

It was hard for me to understand how he could face death so close up or why he would want to. This was a man who had come to revere life so much that he chased moths and spiders around the house, capturing and setting them free rather than killing them. When I asked him what it was about Hospice that kept him going back, he said, "It's a special privilege to share people's lives when they're so vulnerable," as usual sounding unaware of the camera trained on him. "It's so sweet to see people die a good death."

I wasn't sure I wanted to watch his, or even if that's what he was suggesting. But I couldn't take my eyes off him. Girding for the final battle for his life, my father had become at once stronger than ever, weaker than ever, and more vulnerable than ever. He was an emotional kaleidoscope that I found myself drawn to, awed by, and in fear of. During one week, despite never having drawn before, he turned out a savant-like set of charcoal sketches he could have sold. And then there were times when his lungs filled with so much fluid that when he talked it sounded like he was drowning. Sometimes he was so uneasy on his feet he had to use a walker. There was something keeping him going, but I wasn't exactly sure what.

Then one night while I was up late reading in the living room after my parents had gone to bed, my dad stumbled in and sat down in a chair. He began rocking slowly, in obvious pain. We sat in silence for a few minutes as he pinched eyedroppers full of liquid morphine into his mouth. "Is there anything I can do?" I asked. "Don't you want to get the camera?" he said.

A few months later, in August of 2003, my family took a trip to Aspen. Dad had been having a particularly brutal run of side effects from the chemo, and several times in the weeks leading up to this trip had threatened to quit treatment altogether. Worse, this time he was also down to the final experimental drug.

Within several hours of arriving at the condominium, his legs went numb, his mouth dry, and he lost the strength even to stand up on his own. I filmed while the rest of the family called around to doctors. They wanted him to go immediately to Denver, via medevac helicopter if possible. We packed our just-unpacked things and drove back to Craig Hospital in Denver, watching the star-filled sky watching us.

He spent several days in the hospital before being discharged without any clearer idea of what had caused his latest round of complications. When we got home he asked if I wanted to interview him. I was surprised by the request, but over the past few months it had become clear that the camera was enabling us to communicate. We found a quiet spot and sat down. I could see he was wrestling with something big.

"I had been feeling for some time that I wasn't finding much meaning in living this way," he said, speaking in the past tense. "Just seemed like I was doing what I had to do, but in reality it was very hard to stay alive." He looked down at the floor. "There wasn't much I was getting out of it. It was the pain, the loneliness of being at home, of not having any meaning to my life. I'm kind of real surprised to hear myself say that…"

"For how long was that going on?" I asked.

He paused for a long minute, then continued, not answering the question.

"A couple of times you said something to me as though…you hoped I was still going to wait for Aspen, or wait for your book [which was not yet finished]…and it just occurred to me that nobody wanted me to die."

"Was that surprising?" I asked.

"No," he said. "But it was surprising that nobody was sort of getting it. That I didn't want to continue."

I tried to steady the camera as it hit me that my father was making his final request. He needed permission from his family—from me—to die. Fixed in my role as filmmaker, I said nothing. Nor did I speak out when, later that week, the volunteer psychiatrist for Hospice of Metro Denver became its newest patient.

"I don't have as many illusions about myself. . . . There's more of an acceptance of—this may sound odd, but I call it 'nothing special.' I used to harbor this idea that I had to be something special. I realize I'm just another person among billions and billions of people."

—quote taken from an interview with my father, 2003.

The last time I saw my father was Thanksgiving Day, 2003. He had been doing the hospice-at-home program, and, despite some bad pain, seemed happier being off the chemo. Most days he was able to walk on his own, and on that morning the two of us went to Whole Foods. As usual, he sampled everything available, then bought up about four times as much cheese and nuts as we needed. He was in good spirits, and before the guests arrived I sat him down for one of our regular interview sessions. By now our intimate little dance had taken on the aura of ceremony. For him, I think, the filming was like supreme validation; for me, it signified his belief and trust in me and my work.

"Here it is, Thanksgiving 2003, 12 years since I was diagnosed," he said, proudly. "In September I went into hospice and was given eight weeks to live. And once again, they're wrong."

When it came time for dinner, Dad raised a glass to toast the large gathering of friends and family. "To the usual suspects," he said with a big smile, as I hovered over the table with the camera. "Here, here," a few people called out, and we all clinked glasses.

The following week, when I was back in New York, Dad began having serious trouble breathing, even when hooked up to the oxygen machine next to the bed. He couldn't urinate. His pain was so bad that he had no choice but to take massive amounts of morphine, leaving him foggy and sometimes hallucinating.

By Friday he was speaking gibberish; my mom, normally a paragon of strength, crumbled to pieces and couldn't stop crying. I wanted to get back, but a blizzard had struck New York and none of the airports were operating. I spoke to Dad briefly that night, but it wasn't even clear if he recognized who I was. He kept muttering something about going to the movies. I couldn't help wondering if it was our film he was seeing in his mind's eye.

On Saturday he fell into a coma. When I called, my mom put the phone up to his ear. Aware I might not make it home in time, I did what I knew I had to do. By now I'd realized this film was as much about me as it was about him. And this time the tape was rolling in my New York apartment, big flakes of snow coming down outside the window. "I love you," I said, trying to make the words clear through my tears. "And it's OK for you to go." I wished I'd had the courage to say it earlier so I would know he heard me. I certainly wasn't expecting him to answer. After all, he hadn't spoken or moved in almost 24 hours. But then from the other end of the phone came a ghostlike groan. "Julian," my father said.

The next day I got on a plane about 6 a.m. It had been six hours since I'd spoken to my mom, and it was now too early in Denver to call her. When I touched down at DIA, I turned on my cell phone, prepared to see a message waiting with the news. But there was none. Hurrying through the terminal with my carry-on to meet my brother, I dialed his number. "He's still alive," Daniel told me.

It was a bright winter day, and as we sped home from airport I squinted out at the landscape, brown and lifeless. We were racing against time, and I tried not to be annoyed when Daniel missed the exit and had to get back on the highway going the opposite way. About 10 minutes from home, his phone rang. The caller ID showed it was my mom. "We're almost there," Daniel said, picking up. Then a pause. "OK," he said and hung up. "He died," Daniel said, and as we rode along the quiet backcountry roads toward eastern Parker, my younger brother took my hand in his and we wept.

After uttering my name, my father had said only one more thing before he died. While my mother was sitting with him, he'd sat up with a startle, grabbed her arm, and whispered, "It's going to be OK," before falling immediately back into a coma. That was December 7, 2003, more than 12 years after his initial diagnosis. He was 61.

Until earlier this year, his number remained in my cell phone and the plastic bag full of mini-DV tapes I'd shot sat in the closet, unedited, unwatched. The two-plus years since his death had been full of major life changes. My first book had been published to critical success and picked up by Hollywood. Meanwhile, my marriage, after five years, had ended. In the fall, I'd applied for and was accepted to do a residency at an artist colony in New Hampshire. I planned on working on a novel, but at the last minute decided to take the bag of videotapes with me.

I spent the first few weeks there in my cabin, watching the footage. Alone in the stillness of the New England woods, I cried and then cried some more. Partly for the losses I had suffered. But also because I saw a piece of myself in the man on the tape: my father, the Bronx-born Jew and Colorado horse owner. My father the doctor turned cancer patient. My father, who'd helped me learn to live, asked me to let him die, and left me to tell the story.

—June 2006

11.
Presumption of Guilt

by Lindsey B. Koehler

Over the previous few weeks, he'd started to pack his things. Clothes. Shoes. Books. Pictures. Paperwork. Some of the kids' stuff, too. It was surprising how much Tom Fallis had accumulated in a year and a half of living in his sister's home in Greeley. He wasn't in a hurry, so he'd toss a few things into a box each day and, when it was full, move it to the garage. Once or twice he wondered what his mom would do with his belongings if he didn't come home after the trial ended.

It had been a long, difficult four years. For several months after Ashley died, Tom had sent text messages to his wife's cell phone so he could feel like he was talking to her. Just days after her death, he began typing notes like, *It's been so hard without you. I wish that you were here. We all miss you so much. I love you with all my heart.* He tried but ultimately couldn't return to work as a corrections officer at the Weld County Sheriff's Office, not only because he needed to care for their three kids, but also because he wasn't emotionally capable. When he decided to go back to college in Indiana, a year and a half after Ashley died, he thought the move from their home in Evans, Colorado would be good for him and the kids. And it had been. Then, more than two years after he watched paramedics try to save his wife from a self-inflicted gunshot wound, authorities in Evans reopened the investigation into the cause of her death. Although he had been 1,100 miles away in Bloomington, Tom could feel the accusatory finger pointing in his direction.

Only as he sat at the defense table during his second-degree murder trial at the Weld County Court House in mid-March 2016 did the then 36-year-old begin to let himself think about what life might be like without having to worry about serving a 48-year prison sentence. After having been forced to remain in Colorado for more than a year while awaiting trial, he knew daydreams of loading those boxes into his black Dodge Caravan and driving it east on I-70 were premature. It felt good to be hopeful, even though he knew things could still go wildly wrong. In fact, so much had gone awry since January 1, 2012 it crossed his mind that simply for the sake of consistency, the jury's verdict might fall that way too.

As the trial wore on, though, Tom's Denver-based defense attorneys Iris Eytan and Dru Nielsen became increasingly certain their client would be heading home to the Hoosier State. To them, it was clear the jury—which, by the end of the two-and-a-half-week proceeding, had listened to testimony from more than 40 witnesses—was wise to the district attorney's anemic case. At times, all 12 members of the panel, Eytan says, wore looks of absolute incredulity.

That didn't diminish the counselors' anxiety when, mid-morning on March 31, 2016, the jury began deliberating. For Tom, his attorneys, and his family, a long lunch at the Rio Grande Mexican Restaurant helped pass the time during what could have been hours and hours— even days—of deliberations. But before servers had cleared away plates of half-eaten tacos and baskets of chips, a call came from the courthouse: The verdict was in.

He wasn't sure, but he thought he heard crying. The bathroom door was closed, so Tom knocked quietly before opening it. Ashley was sitting on the toilet, her pajama bottoms around her ankles. Just a few days earlier, the 28-year-old had taken a home pregnancy test and gotten a positive result. Now, she was bleeding. And sobbing.

Tom took a seat on the tub next to his wife of three years. He rubbed her back while they talked. This was the third time in the past nine months Ashley had believed she was pregnant, despite the fact that she had taken her mother's advice and undergone a tubal ligation after giving birth to their son three years earlier. Tom didn't understand what was going on medically—he'd begged his wife to see a doctor, to no avail—but he knew Ashley believed she was miscarrying. He knew she felt responsible. And he knew she had stopped taking her mood stabilizers—clonazepam, quetiapine, and amphetamine to treat anxiety, obsessive-compulsive disorder, and bipolar tendencies—for fear of hurting the fetus. She was fragile. Teary-eyed, she told Tom she wished she hadn't listened to her mom, that she wanted more children. He nodded and told her he did too.

Although it was New Year's Eve and the Fallises needed to prepare for the party they were hosting that night, they spent a few hours Googling the details of tubal ligation reversal. Ashley had holed up in their bedroom for most of the day, missing the comings and goings of friends and family, but Tom thought she had perked up enough for them to go ahead and have the gathering.

The fete at 5711 Zinfandel Street in Evans's Grapevine Hollow neighborhood wasn't a formal affair, just some family and a few work friends. The dining room table was full of snacks, and there was jungle juice, Jell-O shots, and a mini keg of beer to wash down the pretzels and chips. The Fallis kids—six- and nine-year-old girls and a three-year-old boy—and their cousins ran up and down the stairs from the basement. Ashley socialized with her guests and knocked back a few Jell-O shots.

At one point in the night, an animated fantasy football discussion broke out in the kitchen. It was a loud enough conversation that Jenna Fox, Ashley's mom, said she asked Tom to cool it with the cursing since there were kids around. She said Tom snapped at her in response. Tom says the exchange never took place. Either way, the long-simmering tension between the two—likely amplified for Tom by the image of Ashley crying earlier in the day—was palpable that evening.

As midnight approached, Ashley turned on some music and told her husband she wanted to dance. Tom shook his head and said he wasn't going to dance to a random song. Instead, he changed the tune and said, "I'll dance to this one." The first few notes of Blue October's "18th Floor Balcony" filled the living room. The couple swayed slowly to their song while their guests looked on.

The ball dropped shortly thereafter. Tom's parents left, and the couple's friends headed home. Only Ashley's mom, dad, aunt, uncle, and cousin lingered. When Tom saw Ashley come out of their bedroom with her coat, she explained she was going outside to smoke. "A cigarette?" Tom asked. "Well, I don't know," Ashley said. It was then Tom realized his wife was planning to smoke a joint with her family. And he didn't like it.

He wasn't angry at Ashley per se. He was frustrated, though. He told her she shouldn't be getting high but reserved his anger for her family, who time and again seemed to coax her into doing something she might later regret. Not only was marijuana illegal at the time, but Tom was also employed by the Weld County Sheriff's Office, and Ashley had only recently found work—after about a year of unemployment—at Northern Colorado Rehabilitation Hospital. Both could be drug-tested at any time.

It was more than that, though. Ashley had already had a few drinks, she had stopped taking her medication, and she thought she'd just miscarried. Tom stomped through the house, yelling at Fox; Ashley's adoptive father, Joel Raguindin; her aunt; and her uncle, who Tom knew was supplying the pot. Tom wasn't judicious with his words, which were something along the lines of: "Fuck you. You don't understand. Get the fuck out of my house."

Ashley likely heard the shouting before Tom walked off and slammed their bedroom door. She'd been in the hallway bathroom and came out to find her family leaving in a hurry. She hugged everyone, mentioned maybe getting together for a Super Bowl party, and then, furious, went to find her husband.

Tom was in their en suite bathroom when Ashley threw open the bedroom door. Mortified, she asked why he would embarrass her in front of her family and ruin what had been a nice evening. Tom wasn't apologetic. "Fuck your family," Tom said. "Fuck your mom. We just spent hours going over all this tubal ligation reversal stuff because you let your mom control your life, because you listened to your mom. Why are you always listening to your mom?"

Although Ashley was still agitated, Tom walked toward the closet to change into pajamas. She slammed the closet door in front of him, walked across the room, and said, "Fuck you. I'll do whatever the fuck I want."

Tom reopened the closet door and spat back at her. "Fine," he said. "Do whatever you want. Just don't do it because your family told you to."

That's when Tom heard her chamber a round. Tom looked out from the closet door in time to see a puff of smoke. He didn't even register the sound of the gun firing.

It took about two seconds for him to get to her. She had fallen between their bed, the bedside table, and a stand-alone jewelry chest. Her gun, which she'd grabbed from her purse on the bed or from the nightstand, was resting near her torso. He grabbed her head. She was still breathing. He lunged for the landline on the nightstand. When the 911 dispatcher picked up, Tom begged for help and then dropped the phone so he could stem the bleeding. He thought the call had disconnected, but the operator remained on the line. She could hear Tom pleading with his wife.

"Ashley, no. Ashley, no. Ashley, no...You're staying here. You're staying here. Ashley, you're not leaving me. Come here. You're staying here...Ashley, look at me. Hey, look at me. Hey...Ashley, Ashley. Hey, Baby, stay right here...We got a son that needs us. We got two girls that want us here. They want to see us. They want to see us tomorrow. Do you understand me?"

An Evans Police Department officer arrived between four and seven minutes after Tom's call. The Fallis's nine-year-old daughter opened the front door. Her voice was audible on the 911 call. She said over and over again, "My mom died." As other first responders arrived, they pulled Tom away from Ashley. Covered in blood, Tom walked outside into the chaos of sirens and patrol cars. He texted his mom and told her he needed her to come back to the house. Then he crouched on the ground with his head in his hands and wailed uncontrollably.

That was when he heard them. Ashley's family had followed the red and blue lights back to the Fallis house. Police were restricting access to the yard and the house, but that didn't stop Ashley's dad and uncle from shouting from the street. "I just remember them yelling at me," Tom says. "They were yelling, 'You killed her! You fucking shot her!'"

The email Weld County Assistant District Attorney Michael Rourke sent on May 30, 2013 was clear. He wanted Evans Police Department

Chief of Police Rick Brandt, Sergeant Jason Phipps, and Commander Patrick Haugse to know he'd spoken with the attorney general's office about Ashley Fallis's parents' continued efforts to prove their son-in-law had murdered their daughter, even though the case had been closed in March 2012 as a suicide. He also wanted his law enforcement colleagues to know he had delivered an explicit message to the attorney general's office: "[I] explained that from my perspective, this investigation was done properly by Evans, CBI, and the Northern Regional Crime Lab. I also explained that no one believed there was even PC [probable cause] for a crime, much less proof beyond a reasonable doubt."

It had been 17 months since Ashley died when Rourke hit send on that email. It would not be the last time the assistant district attorney dealt with Jenna Fox and Joel Raguindin. From the moment they saw police rushing to 5711 Zinfandel Street, the pair believed Tom had shot their daughter who they repeatedly said had a zeal for life and who would never have left her children behind.

They also concluded, within hours of Ashley's death, that the Evans Police Department was not only unprofessional and inept, but potentially complicit in helping protect Tom because he worked as a corrections officer for the Weld County Sheriff's Office, even though the two law enforcement agencies are unrelated. Fox sent no fewer than seven emails to Sergeant Phipps in the days following her daughter's death, the first on January 4. Much of her communication requested that Evans do its job, by which she meant arresting Tom.

It was not the first instance in which Fox and Raguindin had questioned the competence of a Colorado police department. When Fox's brother died by suicide in Park County in 1999, they initially suspected his wife of homicide and pressed authorities for a more thorough investigation—until the fact that Michael Schmitzer had killed himself became too obvious to ignore.

In the days, weeks, months, and years after their daughter's death, Fox (who declined to provide an on-the-record statement to *5280*) and Raguindin (who did not respond to requests for comment) spoke with local politicians, sent emails to law enforcement agencies and to the district attorney's office, and talked on-air with a variety of news outlets in an effort to show that the investigation into Ashley's death had been flawed from the start. They argued investigators were too quick in deciding Ashley died by suicide, that not enough evidence had been tested to make that determination. They charged that Tom hadn't been treated as a suspect by responding officers. They asserted that Tom hadn't been immediately handcuffed or separated from other potential witnesses, like the children and his parents. They pointed to the fact that Tom's hands hadn't been bagged to protect forensic evidence. They derided Evans Police Department's three-hour, middle-of-the-night interrogation—during which Tom repeatedly said, "I didn't do this"—on January 1, 2012, arguing that suspects have been grilled for longer over a stolen car. They even accused Tom's father, Jim, of using his connections as the former athletic director for the University of Northern Colorado to make things fall Tom's way.

Most law enforcement experts would likely agree with at least some of Ashley's parents' assertions, particularly that every suspicious death be considered a homicide until determined otherwise, and that Tom should've been treated as a suspect and separated from other potential witnesses as soon as police arrived on the scene. Even Chief of Police Brandt later admitted that certain protocols went unheeded, some follow-up interviews went undone, and various conclusions were reached before every lab result was returned. Still, Brandt maintained that no evidence of a cover-up existed and stressed that the Colorado Bureau of Investigation had been called in to work the scene within several hours, partly because of Ashley's family's allegations about Tom.

None of that appeased Ashley's family. More than a year after their daughter's death, Fox and Raguindin had had enough inaction. They found a more sympathetic ear in an enterprising Fox31 reporter named Justin Joseph.

The story they told him sounded insane: Their daughter had been shot to death, and the person responsible had literally gotten away with murder. But, then again, maybe it wasn't so crazy.

Fox and Raguindin were in sporadic contact with Joseph in the days and weeks after Ashley died. Their assertion—that the case had been botched by police and their daughter's death ruled a suicide too quickly—piqued the reporter's interest, especially since the potential suspect was a Weld County Sheriff's Office corrections officer. After spending approximately a year and upward of $70,000 in legal fees to secure grandparents' visitation rights through the courts, Fox and Raguindin circled back to Joseph, who began pursuing his own investigation. "There was enough there to suggest that there wasn't at least a thorough investigation," Joseph told *48 Hours* (he declined to speak on the record with *5280*). "And so I thought I owed it to the family to take a look at that." For the next 12 months, the reporter re-interviewed dozens of witnesses as well as law enforcement officers, sometimes with Fox and Raguindin at his side.

By April 2014, Joseph believed he had discovered enough evidence to go to the police. A conversation with the Fallis's next-door neighbor, 17-year-old Nick Glover, finally legitimized Joseph's yearlong probe. In his meeting with Joseph, Glover said he'd heard Tom confess to shooting Ashley that New Year's Eve. Glover said he'd crouched below an open window in his house that night, watching and listening as the drama unfolded. Glover told Joseph he heard Tom say to his dad, "Oh, my God, what did I do?" and "I shot her."

The young man also explained to Joseph that he had informed Detective Michael Yates of the Evans Police Department about the alleged confession when the officer interviewed him on January 1, 2012. Joseph knew then he had something worthy of the six o'clock news: There had been nothing in Yates's report about the teenager hearing a confession. Joseph called Chief of Police Brandt.

On April 8, 2014, at a press conference in Evans, Brandt reopened the investigation into Ashley Fallis's death more than two years after it had been investigated by five law enforcement agencies and closed. Citing "new information regarding the case brought to my attention by a Fox31 reporter," Brandt explained that "new eye- and earwitness accounts" were serious enough to warrant another look. He wasn't mentioned by name, but the implication was clear: Tom Fallis was being investigated for murder.

The call from his dad was short and pointed. Call this Evans Police Department officer. He needs to talk to you. Here's his number. Tom received the call during a history class at Indiana University, where he was taking courses to finish his bachelor's degree. He sneaked out of the lecture to phone the officer. The information he received was both maddening and worrisome: Authorities were reopening Ashley's case because new evidence had been uncovered. When Tom asked what the new evidence was, the officer explained he wasn't allowed to discuss it. At that moment, Tom knew two things for sure. One, his former in-laws had finally exerted enough pressure on someone to make this happen. And two, he needed a lawyer. A really good one.

Iris Eytan, a criminal defense attorney who worked for Denver's Reilly Pozner law firm at the time, took Tom's case. Her instructions to her client were simple: Call me if anyone tries to contact you about the case. But Eytan didn't just believe in being reactive; she contacted the Fort Collins Police Department, which would be re-investigating Ashley Fallis's death in light of the Evans Police Department's alleged missteps. Detective Jaclyn Shaklee was the lead on the case, and Eytan reached out to her, offering full cooperation. Eytan was essentially silver-plattering a smorgasbord of evidence the Fort Collins police would've first needed to know existed, and then gotten a search warrant to obtain: Tom's phone, Ashley's phone, downloads from Ashley's computer, emails, texts, handwritten notes, and Facebook screenshots.

Not everyone was disseminating such potentially constructive information following the reopening of the case. Local and national news outlets raced to broadcast the story, painting an ugly—and sometimes factually inaccurate—picture of Tom in their haste. Ashley's parents spoke live with Megyn Kelly on Fox News's *The Kelly File* and told the host that their son-in-law was an angry, quick-tempered man and that there was zero reason to believe their daughter was mentally unstable. Jane Velez-Mitchell, a television journalist on the HLN channel, aired a program that not only incorrectly identified Tom Fallis as a "cop" multiple times, but also allowed a panel of experts, including an attorney for Fox and Raguindin, to discuss topics including how a mother "would have to hate [her] children to kill [herself]." A *48 Hours* episode entitled "Death After Midnight" that ran many months later latched onto a flashlight that had been photographed at the scene of Ashley's death. The program generated an animated simulation of how Tom could have used the flashlight to beat his wife before shooting her. The *48 Hours* reporters, however, neglected to check the provenance of the flashlight, which had been left behind by a police officer who'd been trying to save Ashley Fallis's life.

Of course, Justin Joseph and Fox31 had a distinct advantage over other outlets: Less than 24 hours after Brandt's presser, Joseph interviewed Fox and Raguindin on the air about the reopening of the case. The following day, Fox31 live-streamed a press conference in which Ashley's parents and their lawyer expounded upon their frustrations with the investigation into their daughter's death. In May, Fox31 covered a "Justice for Ashley" protest outside of the Evans Police Department organized by Ashley's family. As the coverage continued, Joseph's name became nearly synonymous with the Fallis investigation.

As the weeks and months wore on, Tom says he had to stop watching the news. It was too infuriating to listen to the talking heads intimate that he was a gun-carrying police officer when he was actually a corrections officer with no access to a service weapon. Instead, Tom and his defense team, which quickly grew to include Dru Nielsen, focused on what little they knew of the Fort Collins Police Department's inquiry. They were aware that Detective Shaklee had flown to New York to interview Jim Fallis while a colleague of Shaklee's interviewed Tom's mom, Anna Fallis, in New Jersey. They were aware that the lead detective, in concert with Fox and Raguindin, secretly took Tom and Ashley's daughters to be re-interviewed—in violation of a court order—while the girls were visiting Colorado.

One of the more promising developments for Tom and his legal team came in August, four months after the investigation had been reopened. Detective Michael Yates, the Evans police officer who had been accused of altering or withholding Nick Glover's statement about hearing Tom confess, was cleared of criminal wrongdoing by the Loveland Police Department, which had been brought in to do an independent investigation.

"When they closed the case against Yates," Eytan says, "we were like, 'That's it.' I mean, the whole case hinged on Yates and Glover." Yet there was no communication from Assistant District Attorney Michael Rourke, who had been so adamant about a lack of probable cause in May 2013. (Rourke declined to speak with *5280*.) And there was zero notification from the Fort Collins Police Department that Tom, who had no prior criminal history, was no longer being pursued as a suspect. "[Our cooperation] was an exercise in futility in the end," Eytan says. "We realized that they didn't take into account anything we had given them. All they did was try to find something that made Tom look like a bad guy."

A couple of inches of snow still blanketed the ground around the Weld County Court House. The storm had abated, but the temperature wasn't supposed to crest nine degrees. Assistant District Attorney Michael Rourke expressed his gratitude to Jenna Fox for braving the elements to be his second witness during what would be a four-day grand jury proceeding beginning on November 12, 2014. He needn't have thanked her. This was her opportunity to testify in hopes of bringing criminal charges against Tom Fallis for allegedly killing her daughter.

It is relatively rare for a case to go to a grand jury in Colorado. In many other states, every potential felony charge must be reviewed by a grand jury; however, in the Centennial State, the decision to bring a case in front of a panel of grand jurors—to determine if there is probable cause a crime was committed—is up to the district attorney's office and/ or the attorney general's office. The grand jury is just one of several options that allow a prosecutor to deliver a case to trial. A more frequently employed method to determine probable cause is a preliminary hearing. In a preliminary hearing, a suspect has already been arrested and criminal charges have been filed. The hearing, held in front of a judge in open court, determines whether a person should be tried based on whether there is strong enough evidence that he committed the crime.

Grand juries, on the other hand, operate behind closed doors. The system is purposefully shrouded in secrecy, and therefore many Americans have little idea why it's used and how it works. Even with grand juries coming under heightened scrutiny in recent years—often for not indicting police officers for shooting unarmed young black men in places such as Cleveland and Ferguson, Missouri—the process remains shadowy.

While mechanisms vary by state, the fundamentals of the system are essentially the same. At the beginning of each year in Colorado, every state judicial district that's large enough to warrant having a grand jury selects 12 citizens and four alternates from the community to serve 12- to 18-month terms as grand jurors. The chief judge, with assistance from the district attorney's office, empanels these men and women who are expected to show up to hear testimony as needed. In general, the chief judge and district attorney are looking to select a diverse set of jurors. They're particularly interested in seeking out community members who have the ability to be fair and open-minded.

In this way, grand juries are different from trial juries where, through a process known as *voir dire*, prosecutors and defense attorneys attempt to reject prospective jurors who may be antagonistic to their causes. "A smart district attorney wants a range of people on the grand jury," says Roxanne Bailin, a retired chief judge from Colorado's 20th Judicial District. "He wants that because if he's taking something to the grand jury, he really wants to know what the community thinks."

Most prosecutors will say that's what a grand jury is really for—to be the voice of the community when it's not clear a crime has occurred. "The foundation of the grand jury process," says Michael Dougherty, assistant district attorney for Colorado's 1st Judicial District, "is that the community acts as a check on the government." But prosecutors extoll the virtues of the grand jury process for several reasons. First, a grand jury has subpoena powers, which means prosecutors can force under-oath testimony from reluctant witnesses or obtain previously out-of-reach documents in ways police cannot. Second, the proceedings are secret (until the grand jury hands up a recommendation for indictment, the prosecution decides to prosecute, and police make an arrest). This secrecy, prosecutors say, can help prevent destruction of evidence, may keep nervous suspects from leaving the jurisdiction, and, most important, protects the identity of suspects and witnesses—something that's critical in cases involving public corruption—so that if probable cause isn't found, their reputations aren't unnecessarily tarnished. The final reason prosecutors like the grand jury option isn't one they like to discuss openly: It can be a deft way to evade responsibility. In other words, asking 12 grand jurors to decide if there is probable cause to charge someone with a crime instead of the prosecutor doing it herself allows the district attorney—a publicly elected official—to avoid potential political fallout.

All of this makes perfect sense when a prosecutor explains it. But there's one major criticism of the grand jury system that is widely dismissed by prosecutors: It does not conform to the dearly held American principle that the judicial system be adversarial, meaning that in a court of law, there should be the opposing forces of a prosecuting attorney and a defense attorney, as well as a judge who ensures everyone adheres to the rule of law. In a preliminary hearing, all parties are accounted for because charges have already been filed; however, during grand jury proceedings, there is no judge and there is no defense counsel. The target, or suspect, of a grand jury investigation is not present. The district attorney—and his staff—presides. The grand jurors are his captive audience, and he can present the case however he sees fit. If he doesn't want to secure an indictment against, say, a law enforcement officer, he can choose to present a weak case. "The process can be so influenced by the government," says David Kaplan, a longtime Denver defense attorney, "that the grand jury, whether it's explicit or by virtue of process, ends up being an agent of the prosecution. There's no question the government indicts virtually any time it wants to."

Based on anecdotal evidence from prosecutors and defense attorneys, statewide statistics would likely back up Kaplan's claims—except there are no statewide statistics. The frequency with which Colorado's 22 judicial districts use grand juries or how often they return indictments is unavailable because many districts, citing secrecy rules, refuse to release their numbers.

Their reasoning may be sound: In smaller districts where only a few cases go before a grand jury all year, it's possible the public or the media could surmise the identity of a target who went unindicted. Still, the lack of transparency about how often and how effectively grand juries are used only intensifies suspicions that prosecutors could be taking cases to grand juries that do not have a reasonable chance of conviction once presented to a trial jury—and, more disturbingly, abusing their mostly unsupervised powers of persuasion.

There had been a lot to like about the pretty young brunette with almond eyes Tom met on Match.com. On their first date in February 2007, they had talked and laughed and flirted, but she'd turned her cheek when he tried to kiss her in the parking lot. He was disappointed; he'd thought they had good chemistry. But he gave her a quick peck and told her to text him when she got home so he'd know she was safe. The gesture earned him a second date.

There were a lot of things Tom adored about Ashley from the outset. She wasn't quiet like he was; she was loud and talkative and wildly energetic. She was smart—a respiratory therapist by training. She had a dark, Denis Leary–esque sense of humor. She had a serious Starbucks addiction and a laughably complicated standing order: a grande low-fat caramel macchiato, extra shot of espresso, extra pump of caramel, with whipped cream. The thing that struck Tom the most about Ashley, though, was that she was a single mother of two at the age of 24. Maybe that's because Tom had always felt a need to help, to swoop in. He loved playing the hero. In high school and college, he was the person his buddies called in the middle of the night when they were too drunk to drive home. He was also the guy who would defuse a tense situation or take the rap for something someone else did. And, according to friends and family, he seemed to be drawn to women he thought he could save.

Within weeks of their first date, Tom began offering to watch Ashley's daughters while she was at work. He enjoyed it, he told her, and didn't mind when Ashley's four-year-old quickly began calling him "Dad." So, when Ashley became unexpectedly pregnant five months into the relationship, there was no reason to panic. Instead, the couple decided to move from Denver to Greeley to be closer to Tom's sister, Natalie, and her two kids. Tom quit his job with the property management firm Aimco, worked a few short-term gigs in the Greeley area, and then applied to be a corrections officer with the Weld County Sheriff's Office. Ashley continued to work for a hospital in Denver for a short time but then took a respiratory therapy job at Northern Colorado Medical Center in Greeley.

Things were going well—well enough that Tom bought an engagement ring. He'd wanted to make manicotti and crème brûlée—two of Ashley's favorite dishes—and propose over dinner at the house, but when he tried to sneak out to the jewelry store to pick up the ring, Ashley wasn't fooled. She wouldn't let him go alone. In fact, she couldn't wait to get back to their house for Tom to pop the question in a more romantic setting. She begged him to ask her right there in the parking lot at Jared. So he did.

That was just the way Ashley was. Persistent. Assertive. Impulsive. She wasn't one to back down from an argument, suffer fools in silence, or let anyone say a negative word about her friends or family. She liked getting her way. And Ashley rarely let anyone tell her what to do—except for, according to Tom, her mom. Which is how the young woman ended up undergoing a tubal ligation, without discussing it with Tom, after the couple's son was born in March 2008. Ashley's mom was concerned her daughter had had too many children too young. She was also not convinced the relationship with Tom would last, a breakup scenario that would've left Ashley a single mother of three.

Tom says he wasn't planning to go anywhere, though. He was disappointed about the tubal ligation—he'd always wanted a big family—but they had a new baby boy, two beautiful girls (whom he'd go on to adopt in 2010, after the girls' biological father gave up his parental rights), and new jobs. There wasn't much to complain about. So when Ashley told Tom she wanted to go to the courthouse to get married one morning two weeks after having their son, he was happy to let her have her way.

Wearing a well-tailored suit, with a touch of gray at his temples, Assistant District Attorney Michael Rourke asked questions of Jenna Fox for the better part of the morning on that frigid day in November 2014. Grand jurors listened as the distraught mother talked about what a "fabulous" mom her daughter had been. How much Ashley had "loved life." How she was "easy to be around," "unique," "a lot of fun," and "very sure of herself." The jurors also heard how Ashley's husband, Tom, was "controlling." That he was "abrupt," "explosive," and "opinionated." Fox explained that "every family function Tom was part of turned into an argument, a fight, an explosion." She told jurors she knew there had been physical altercations and mental abuse between Tom and Ashley and that Ashley thought Tom was having an affair. She also said she believed her daughter needed to be on mood-stabilizing medications because of Tom.

It was damning testimony. It was also problematic. Prosecutors are supposed to adhere to the American Bar Association's Rule 3.8, which covers ethical obligations and decrees that prosecutors have the responsibility of "a minister of justice and not simply that of an advocate." Rule 3.8 also states that "the prosecutor in a criminal case shall refrain from prosecuting a charge that the prosecutor knows is not supported by probable cause." There isn't anything specific in the rule about an attorney's ethical obligations in attempting to obtain a grand jury indictment. The manner in which prosecutors abide by these ethics rules varies from one district attorney's office to another, but it's generally agreed upon—although not required by law—that a prosecutor shouldn't allow a witness to assassinate a suspect's character on the stand; that a prosecutor should present any evidence that may exonerate a target; that a prosecutor shouldn't allow testimony of prior similar acts unless the acts are so similar it couldn't be accidental; and that a prosecutor should choose to only present evidence that would be admissible at trial.

"Of course, there's nobody there in the courtroom to tell a DA he or she can't ask questions that make a defendant look bad," says former Chief Judge Bailin. "It might increase the likelihood of a true bill [a recommendation by the jury for the state to indict] but probably not a conviction." That's because leading up to or during an actual trial, prosecutors are bound by rules of evidence. They must, for example, disclose materially exculpatory evidence—evidence that tends to exonerate the defendant—in the government's possession to the defense. They cannot, with exceptions, allow a witness to introduce hearsay into testimony. They must lay a foundation before presenting certain evidence or witnesses. They cannot lead the witness. The list goes on. But in a grand jury proceeding, there are almost no rules.

Proponents of the grand jury system argue that the grand jury is not a mini trial. The prosecutor, they say, need only present evidence he or she believes illustrates probable cause and nothing else. But based on the grand jury transcripts, which are typically released to the defense upon request, Eytan and Nielsen believed that Fox's testimony, as well as inflammatory statements from additional grand jury witnesses, may have unduly influenced jurors. "After noting how many times someone said something that was improper," Eytan says, "we were like, 'How could a human being be thinking anything other than what the jurors thought?' That he's a monster." Being "explosive" or "controlling" isn't probable cause, but according to Eytan, it can sure sound like it to regular citizens.

After dissecting the grand jury transcripts further, Tom's legal team noted other potential breaches of ethical obligations, which makes one wonder what the grand jurors would have thought had they been given all of the evidence. What if Detective Jaclyn Shaklee (who did not respond to requests for an interview) had told jurors she'd spoken to a credible witness who contradicted Nick Glover's testimony that he heard Tom confess? What if the prosecutor had asked a question that elicited the information that Evans' Detective Michael Yates had been cleared of criminal wrongdoing in his reporting of Glover's statement? What if they had been told Tom had negligible gunshot residue on his hands, while Ashley had a significant amount? What if they had been informed by the assistant district attorney that some of the coroner's testimony was incorrect or misleading based on forensics the prosecution had in its possession? That Tom's skin was actually not found underneath Ashley's fingernails; that scratches found on Tom's chest were not indicative of a struggle; and that certain evidence collection that may have been beneficial to the defense had not, in fact, been executed? They were told none of these things. Tom's defense attorneys ultimately filed a motion alleging prosecutorial misconduct, which was denied by the trial judge, who stated "there were no examples of any inappropriate conduct by the district attorney."

Had the jurors been told all of these things, they may have come to the same conclusion they did anyway: that while arguing in their bedroom, Tom obtained a Taurus 9 mm pistol and, during a struggle, held the gun to the right side of Ashley's head and pulled the trigger before lowering her to the ground, holding her head, and calling 911. Then again, they may have come to a very different conclusion, especially if evidence that misled the jury into believing a physical altercation had taken place had been corrected. Based on current law, however, Assistant District Attorney Michael Rourke didn't have to amend that testimony. He was not obligated to elaborate on or elicit testimony that may have shone a favorable light on Tom. He was not compelled to examine any witnesses in front of the grand jury who might have presented exculpatory information. He did not have to put a halt to any testimony that assailed the suspect's character. "Not to have the grand jury process designed to be a little more critical of the evidence," Kaplan says, "is to reduce it to something that's not effective as a legitimate review—and the repercussions are sometimes catastrophic."

They certainly were for Tom Fallis. On November 18, 2014, one day after a Weld County grand jury determined there was probable cause to believe Tom killed his wife in a fit of rage, Indiana authorities arrested him just a few minutes after he arrived home from the grocery store. He'd had no warning and no time to make arrangements for his children.

Yet, there were at least three people who did know ahead of time something that was supposed to have been secret: Fox31's Justin Joseph, who had corresponded with Ashley's mother 141 times in the days leading up to Tom's arrest and who happened to be waiting outside Tom's house in Bloomington to film it for the evening news. And Jenna Fox and Joel Raguindin, who were somewhere in the city hoping to collect their grandkids as soon as their father was handcuffed and taken to jail.

Tom spent three weeks in Indiana's Monroe County Jail awaiting extradition and eight days in Larimer County Jail before his family was able to post bond. When he'd been arrested, his biggest concern was his children. He didn't want Ashley's parents—who, according to Tom and others, told the kids on multiple occasions that their dad killed their mom—caring for them. Once Tom's mom, Anna Fallis, arrived in Indiana to fight for, and ultimately retain, custody, he could think about other things. Like how he'd ended up in a six-by-eight-foot cell.

With hindsight, Tom could draw a crooked line between the moments and events in their lives that might've contributed to Ashley's suicide. He just hadn't recognized it in real time. There was the move from Denver to Greeley, of course. There was also the specter of her ex-husband trying to regain custody of their daughters. Tom and Ashley's conflicting work schedules and the fighting they caused took an emotional toll so steep that Ashley actually had divorce papers drawn up in 2009. Tom convinced her not to file them.

Later that year, there was another speed bump: Doctors diagnosed their 18-month-old son with hydrocephalus, a buildup of cerebrospinal fluid in the brain that can cause developmental delays. He would need multiple surgeries to treat the disorder. Ashley threw herself into learning everything about their son's illness, but the constant worry exhausted the young mother, who sought out mental health services in Greeley in early 2010.

Her son's ailment wasn't the only issue overwhelming Ashley's thoughts. She was dealing with a challenging work environment (a dispute with her supervisors in late summer 2010 resulted in her dismissal for insubordination; Ashley sued for wrongful termination and reached a settlement with Northern Colorado Medical Center); a deteriorating relationship with her mom and dad (who took the Fallis kids, against Ashley's wishes, to a party where drugs were present); an affair with an old high school boyfriend (she started seeing him in summer 2011); and the feeling that she was repeatedly getting pregnant—and then miscarrying.

The strain of it all wore on Ashley, whose moods became more and more difficult to predict. Most days, Ashley was what Tom describes as "up." Frenetic, jumpy, fidgety, anxious, unable to sleep, and incapable of relaxing, Ashley couldn't just be. She was constantly on edge.

Ashley's ups had corresponding downs. During those depressive episodes, the young mother's insecurities—about her ability to parent, about her marriage, about her career, about her life choices—materialized. There were days when she struggled to get out of bed. The ebbs and flows of Ashley's disposition concerned Tom not just because he wanted his wife to be happy, but also because he knew she had a family history of mental illness: Both her maternal grandmother and her maternal uncle had died by suicide.

The medications Ashley was taking also made Tom uneasy. She'd been prescribed a regimen of antianxiety meds and mood stabilizers when she began having four or five panic attacks each week. Tom suspected she wasn't following the prescriptions correctly, but he had no idea his wife was surreptitiously seeing two psychiatrists and a primary care doc and doubling up on her scripts.

But the drugs, no matter the dose, didn't always alleviate the feelings of failure that crept up in Ashley. Five months before she died, she typed out a four-paragraph-long suicide letter addressed "Dear Tom." In it she apologized for "all that I have caused" and "for your pain." She explained, "I can no longer go on living this life. I am a failure at everything, a wife, a mom, at having a career, at school. Everything. I have so much pain on the inside; I can no longer take it."

Perhaps it should have, but that suicide note—as well as another dire letter penned a few weeks later in which Ashley expressed feelings of failure about her inability to find a job; mentioned her discontent with being a stay-at-home mother; and explained that she felt "broken" and couldn't "dig deeper"—didn't give Tom pause about the semiautomatic pistols the couple had purchased together earlier that year. Although her grandmother and uncle had both shot themselves in the head, it never occurred to him that Ashley would use the gun she often carried in her purse to hurt herself. "She always said if she were to kill herself," Tom says, "she would've taken a bunch of pills and just fallen asleep."

At the request of the prosecution, Dan Gilliam, dressed in an ill-fitting beige-gray suit and tie, used a Sharpie to write "gun" on a piece of duct tape stuck to the courtroom's maroon carpeting. As a firearms/toolmark examiner for the Northern Colorado Regional Forensic Lab, Gilliam had been called to testify as a witness for the prosecution in the People of the State of Colorado versus Tom Fallis in March 2016. The forensic investigator had been summoned to 5711 Zinfandel Street on January 1, 2012—and he'd since logged approximately 400 hours dissecting, analyzing, and testing evidence from the scene of Ashley Fallis's death. His expertise was now on display for the jury as he explained blood spatter and bullet trajectory in a reconstruction of the Fallis's bedroom that leaned more Law & Order shabby than CSI chic.

Still, Gilliam's testimony, delivered with a quiet confidence as he negotiated the pre-fab furniture and duct tape representations, was convincing. His measurements were exacting; his explanations were straightforward; and his conclusions were deliberate. There were no theatrics; just science. He would have been a dream witness for the prosecution save for one major hiccup: Gilliam's professional opinion was that Ashley Fallis died by suicide.

Jurors could've been forgiven for wondering why the district attorney's office put Gilliam on the stand (the defense would've if they hadn't). However, there were so many problematic witnesses for the prosecution that, as juror Daniel Stejskal puts it, "It seemed like the prosecution was all over the place."

To refute their own witness's forensic testimony, prosecutors brought in another analyst, who contradicted Gilliam's findings. But Jonathyn Priest, who said he believed Tom had been in contact with—or at least near—Ashley when the gun went off, hadn't done any testing. He hadn't been to the scene. His measurements were called into question by the defense. He postulated his theories based on photographs and others' reports. Eytan took to calling him the "eyeball-ologist." Stejskal says Priest's conclusions were more like "assumptions" than actual analysis.

Even the judge seemed to agree that some of the state's work was slipshod. During pretrial discovery, Eytan and Nielsen had zeroed in on the potentially exculpatory information Detective Jaclyn Shaklee had neglected to mention during the grand jury proceedings. Tom's defense attorneys brought the so-called discovery violation—in which a friend of Nick Glover's remembers him saying "my neighbor shot herself" in the days following Ashley's death, not that he heard his neighbor confess to shooting his wife—to the judge's attention. Judge Thomas Quammen, who called the violation "significant," made certain the jury was aware of the state's mistake. He read a statement (an "instruction," in legalese) to the jury multiple times that called into question not only Shaklee's ethics, credibility, and police work, but also Nick Glover's accusations. In other words, the judge himself informed the jury that it might be reasonable to be skeptical of certain prosecution witnesses' testimonies.

Nick Glover took the stand on the fourth day of the trial. Under direct examination, Glover reiterated that he heard Tom say, "Oh, my God, what have I done? I shot her" that night to two people who Glover assumed were Tom's parents. But under cross-examination, Glover became taciturn. He responded with "I do not recall" more than 90 times to Nielsen's questions, some of which focused on Glover's interactions with Tom—going on a group camping trip that included Tom and his kids and Christmas caroling with them—after he allegedly heard the man confess to murdering his wife.

Glover's defensive posturing did little to bolster the veracity of his claims. Neither did his inability to identify in open court Jim Fallis, the person he says he saw talking with Tom when the confession occurred. It didn't help the prosecution that more than 15 law enforcement officers who had been within earshot of Tom that night testified to not hearing Tom say what Glover said he heard from inside his house. "Nick Glover lacked authenticity top to bottom," says Debra McEvers, the jury foreperson. "He was shady. Everything from him was flip. And the confession he says he heard just didn't line up."

That's how the entire case seemed to go for the prosecution: Nothing really lined up. Star witnesses fell flat. Others—like former Weld County Sheriff's Office Deputy Chris Graves, who claimed he, too, heard Tom confess on January 1—collapsed under cross-examination. And that was when things were going relatively well. When Shaklee and Larimer County coroner Dr. James Wilkerson gave back-to-back testimony, things went sideways for the state.

During Detective Shaklee's reinvestigation of the Fallis case in mid-2014, she informed Wilkerson—without taping the conversation, as she did with almost every other case-related interaction—about additional information she had received, which ultimately pushed the coroner to change Ashley's manner of death from suicide to undetermined. (Wilkerson did not respond to requests for an interview.) But much of the information she gave to Wilkerson—that Tom's skin was found under Ashley's fingernails; that Tom had scratches on his chest from a physical altercation with Ashley; that there wasn't enough blood on the carpet for Ashley to have hit the ground without Tom's involvement—wasn't true.

Although Shaklee testified she believed the information she gave Wilkerson to be true at that time, she acknowledged she was ultimately mistaken about some of the nuances. Nevertheless, Shaklee also left out critical details in her interactions with the coroner, who relied on law enforcement to provide him the information he needed to make his determinations. She didn't tell him that the scratches could've come from Tom himself, who had recently shaved his chest and had been complaining about how it itched. She didn't tell the medical examiner that they had swabbed the scratches on Tom's chest and found none of Ashley's DNA on him. She didn't tell him that Tom had tried to stanch Ashley's bleeding for about four minutes, which could have explained why there wasn't the typical amount of blood on the carpet. As juror McEvers puts it, "I remember not believing Shaklee. Her missing notes, her missing interviews were suspicious."

During her cross-examination, Eytan asked on several occasions if the information Shaklee had provided to Wilkerson encouraged him to change his opinion on the manner of death. He answered yes multiple times. The coroner's testimony was compelling for a few other reasons. First, he confirmed Ashley had trace amounts of benzodiazepines—her clonazepam prescription—in her urine, consistent with someone who hadn't taken the drug for a few days. He also tested Ashley's blood alcohol content, which was 0.088. Two other autopsy results stood out: The first was that Ashley's tubal ligation had failed on one side, giving her the ability to become pregnant. The second was that Wilkerson found Ashley did not have enough pregnancy hormones in her urine to suggest she had been pregnant—at least not for about a week before her death—leaving the jury to ponder if and when a miscarriage had occurred or if Ashley's emotional struggles may have contributed to her belief that she was miscarrying.

Even Ashley's parents, who could have triggered sympathy among jurors with heartrending testimony, didn't help the prosecution's case. According to jurors, both came off as, at best, parents who didn't know their daughter as well as they thought or, at worst, people who wanted someone to blame. During cross-examinations, Nielsen pounced on the lawsuits that Fox and Raguindin had brought against several law enforcement officers and agencies, a common tactic used by defense attorneys to bring into question the motivations of witnesses. In this case, it was effective. Nielsen repeatedly asked both if they wanted to "punish" the Evans Police Department, if they wanted to "punish" individual officers. The notion that Ashley's parents had sued for punitive damages lingered in jurors' minds.

None of the state's miscues made the trial easier for Tom. He had to watch his friends, family, co-workers, and neighbors answer questions about him, his kids, his wife, and the worst day of his life. It was, however, vindicating in some ways. "These witnesses weren't just being coddled by the prosecution anymore," Tom says, referring to the grand jury proceedings. "This time somebody was going to ask them questions, and once those questions started getting asked, we knew everything those people had said was going to start falling apart."

The prosecution's unconvincing case was readily apparent in the jury room. McEvers, a teacher living in Weld County, was elected foreperson as soon as deliberations began. She says she took a quick "temperature check" to see where everyone stood. Only three people said they had questions they wanted to discuss with the group. Everyone else was ready to vote. After looking at the jury orders again, talking through some lingering questions, and pulling out some critical pieces of evidence, McEvers had a suggestion. "I said 'Let's do lunch. Or go have a cigarette. Let's let it be for a while,'" she says. "Then we came back for the anonymous vote."

In about three hours, the jury came to a unanimous decision. After a year and a half of waiting in a torturous purgatory, Tom was acquitted on all counts. He finally would be rejoining his kids in Indiana.

But on that day—and on many days since—McEvers has mulled over why Tom Fallis ever needed to be in that courtroom in the first place. She also wonders why Michael Rourke, who had been appointed district attorney for Weld County just weeks after the grand jury indictment, would have decided not to try such a high-profile case himself. Instead, he sent his deputies in to prosecute a man he had indicted. She surmises that politics—and an upcoming campaign—were involved. "As a decent human being, I have to believe the best about people," she says. "I have to believe that about the district attorney. But when you look at a trial where the defense only calls two witnesses, you wonder what was in the evidence at the grand jury. The case we saw—it wasn't a strong case."

Beyond the short life it denotes and the inscription that reads "Loving Mother & Eternal Wife," the most noticeable thing about the granite headstone in a cemetery near Estes Park is that it's cracked. Then the crude etching comes into focus. "I got a call toward the end of 2016," Tom says, "from a Larimer County officer telling me that someone vandalized Ashley's headstone." Just below Tom's name on the joint grave marker, in the empty space after 1980–, someone had carved the word "Soon," causing the stone to fracture.

Tom shakes his head in disbelief that anyone would do such a thing. He says he's been trying to get the stone fixed from afar, but it's clear from his expression that he doesn't have the emotional bandwidth to deal with it. He also hasn't been to visit Ashley's grave in person since the trial. In fact, he's only been back to Colorado twice since he put his boxes into the Dodge and made haste for Colorado's eastern border, where the kids took a smartphone snap of him hugging the Welcome To Kansas sign. On one occasion when he flew back to Denver, he had to explain to his son he was going to Colorado by choice—and that no one was going to keep him there. The eight-year-old was unsure. "He kept texting me," Tom says, "asking if I was still coming home when I said I was."

Although it's been nearly six years since their mom died and a year and a half since their father came home for good, the Fallis kids' emotional scars are still apparent. The younger two, who were six and three on January 1, 2012, haven't asked for specific details about their mom's death, but they do ask about her from time to time. Tom has told them Ashley had an accident. He'll tell them more when they're older.

His 14-year-old daughter is another matter. She's old enough to know what suicide is. "Kids were saying things to her at school," Tom says. "She asked me, 'Why would Mom do this?' I told her, 'I don't have that answer. I'll never have that answer.' But I explained that her mom had a miscarriage, and that I thought for whatever reason, Mom was needed in heaven to care for that baby and that I'm here to care for you guys."

That hasn't been easy, either. Raising three kids alone and going to school makes for busy days. It also makes money scarce. Tom took out loans to go back to college, and the children receive $2,300 total a month in Social Security death benefits. There was a life insurance policy for Ashley—a spousal policy given to every employee at the Weld County Sheriff's Office—but that approximately $50,000 sum went to pay down credit card debt and a car loan and to cover some hospital bills. For now, repaying the $400,000 in legal fees has fallen to Tom's parents. "I've gotten a lot of help from family and friends," Tom says. "We've made adjustments. We don't go without. And, hey, cheap cereal is the breakfast of champions."

Tom's dry humor remains intact, but like his kids, he has unhealed wounds. He says he still cries sometimes. He'll be listening to talk radio in the car and for no particular reason, the tears will come. He still can't listen to "18th Floor Balcony." And he still feels as though he failed Ashley because he didn't know how to help her. He's not afraid, however, to say that he's angry at his wife. "I'm mad that she left," he says. "I'm mad that she did what she did. It pisses me off. Am I accepting? Yeah. But I have to watch that image of her doing it all the time."

He's also not hesitant about saying he's learned valuable lessons about the integrity of the legal system—how it can be warped and misused and bent by the wills of others. The media. His former in-laws. An ambitious assistant district attorney. A detective who played loose with the facts. A kid looking for attention. "What I've learned about the American legal system is that it's not the pieces on the board that matter," Tom says. "It's the players playing with those pieces."

It's difficult not to harbor ill will when you've been wrongly accused, Tom explains, especially when others may have benefitted from your tragedy. Michael Rourke was appointed by Governor John Hickenlooper to the position of Weld County district attorney—after Ken Buck vacated the office—just weeks after securing the well-publicized indictment of Tom. He subsequently campaigned and was elected to the position, which he still holds, seven months after Tom was exonerated. And Justin Joseph, who recently traded his career in television news for a job in real estate, was awarded an Emmy in July 2015 for his coverage of the Fallis investigation.

But, Tom says, life goes on. And even though Google searches by prospective employers will forever haunt him and his children will have difficult questions for him as they mature and he will never again get to bring home low-fat caramel macchiatos with extra shots of espresso and extra pumps of caramel with whipped cream for Ashley, he knows he can handle it. He now knows he can endure just about anything.

—October 2017

12.
Direct Fail
by Natasha Gardner

Sixteen-year-old Gary Flakes didn't want to go to the police station, but his dad his namesake, the career soldier—thought it was for the best, and Flakes didn't want to disappoint him. He'd only been living with his dad in Fort Carson for 19 months; before that, he'd only ever visited his dad for a summer or short stays. He'd grown up with his mom, or as Flakes puts it, his "Moms" in Detroit, but his grades started slipping. He was partying, riding around, and then things got serious: He started dabbling with guns. In August 1995, his mother sent him on a train to Colorado to move in with his dad.

He came to love the mountains, felt a connection to them that he couldn't explain. The openness. The freedom. It was so different from Detroit where everything—everyone—felt so closed in. In the Motor City, it seemed, nothing changed, at least not for the better: the neighborhood, the people, the problems. Here, though, he could go anywhere. He ran track at Fountain-Fort Carson High School, played basketball at a youth center and for his high school team, too. He picked up a job as a courtesy clerk at Albertson's. He'd drive to work in his uniform—a white company shirt and blue khaki pants—but he didn't mind. He was pulling in his own money. He enjoyed being with his dad and helping out his new family; a baby sister was born the day he arrived in Colorado.

Just when it seemed like all was well with Flakes's new home, it went bad. In the shadow of the Garden of the Gods, he slipped into his old Detroit ways. He got expelled from school in January. Next thing he knew, he was driving around in a white Mazda after a Valentine's Day dance on February 14, 1997 with a friend, Jeron Grant, who kept talking about getting "something off my chest." Flakes, who was driving, turned onto Canoe Creek Drive in the affluent Broadmoor area, and passed two boys walking down the street. He drove past, turned around, and pulled up next to them.

Fifteen-year-old Scott Hawrysiak and 13-year-old Andrew Westbay were best friends who'd spent Valentine's Day night playing video games at a nearby house. Near midnight, they were headed home when Jeron Grant's white car pulled alongside them. Grant—a total stranger to the boys—got out of the car and shot Westbay in the neck with a 12-gauge shotgun. He was dead before his body slumped to the ground. Hawrysiak turned and started running, but another shot hit him in the back of the head. Grant walked up to him and fired a third blast, which missed. Grant got back into the car, and he and Flakes drove away.

Two innocent middle-schoolers were dead. The Colorado Springs community had no answers. No one to hold responsible. For three weeks detectives logged more than 1,400 hours on the case, tracking down leads, until one Crime Stoppers tip claimed "Jero" and "Flakes" were there. That's the break the cops—the community—needed. Police showed up at Flakes's home on March 15, 1997. They asked him some questions and left, but his dad—the good soldier—convinced him it was time to talk.

At the station, a detective asked Flakes if he could tell the story without implicating himself. Flakes's dad interjected, "Should we get an attorney?" Near as Flakes can recall, his dad asked this question at least twice. If his dad had said, "We want an attorney," things would have been different. By law, the conversation would have ended right there. Instead, the detective told them no, they didn't need an attorney, and Flakes said what he thought they wanted to hear. He knew he wasn't the shooter, so he told them what he thought would allow him to go home. Instead, the detectives turned him around and placed his wrists in handcuffs, telling him he was under arrest for first-degree murder.

As far as the district attorneys were concerned, this was a worst-of-the-worst case: kids killing kids, and justice would require a tougher sentence than a few years in kiddie jail. So the DAs decided they would try Flakes as an adult. One moment, he was a high school junior who couldn't legally drink or vote, and the next the state said he was an adult. Prosecutors went with a "direct file"—the nuclear option of juvenile justice.

Jeron Grant confessed that he was the shooter. But at his trial, which preceded Flakes's day in court, the jury didn't find Grant's confession believable. "If you're going to murder somebody, you're going to remember every detail," one juror said. Grant was convicted only as an accessory to the murders, leaving Colorado Springs with two dead boys and still no shooter.

As Flakes's trial got under way, the Springs was seething to a point just shy of pitchforks. During his three-week-long trial, prosecutors went through the motions. His defense didn't call many witnesses. The hours dripped by. Yet Flakes remained oblivious. He was just grateful the courtroom was warm. The holding cells were freezing and the bologna sandwiches at lunch left a teenage boy hungry. Even when the conviction came back—two counts of accessory to murder, and one count of criminally negligent homicide—he didn't get it. He couldn't understand the consequences of the Valentine's Day murders. According to the state of Colorado, Flakes—the teenager—was gone. He was an adult on his way to prison for 15 years. He'd be in prison until he was 31. He'd go in a boy and come out a man. At his sentencing, he'd asked—begged, really—the victims' families to forgive him. "I'm sorry for everything that happened on February 14, 1997," he said. "I cannot even imagine the love you have lost....Please forgive me. Find someplace in your heart to please forgive me."

If you're looking for a birthplace of the concept of juvenile justice, Chicago is a good place to start. In 1899, it created the nation's first juvenile court system, predicated on the idea that child offenders are psychologically different than adults and ought to be treated accordingly. It didn't take long for other states to follow suit: By 1903, Colorado had its own separate juvenile justice system, which ensured *parens patriae*, the idea that the state treats a child as a parent would. This created an independent system of justice for children that, among other things, ensured anonymity (records would be sealed), encouraged rehabilitation (juvenile detention centers would provide things like educational opportunities and mental health services), and required judges to consider extenuating factors, like home life and abuse, when adjudicating.

In the decades since, juvenile justice changed, evolved, and, depending on the perspective, regressed in response to social and political pressures of the times. In 1923, Colorado passed a "direct file" law, which empowered prosecutors to try some children, the worst of the worst, as adults in the criminal court. Just about every year since then, Colorado has amended direct file protocol—not overnight, but more of an erosion, and ultimately such that prosecutors needed to justify to a judge why a juvenile offender did not deserve the protections of the juvenile system and ought to be transferred to adult court. This careful deliberation was very much a move back to the future of juvenile justice as it was originally conceived.

By the late 1980s, however, DAs complained that judges weren't approving these transfers, or weren't doing enough of them to appease the prosecutors. In part, some judges were concerned about mandatory sentencing requirements passed in 1985 that doubled, almost overnight, mandatory minimum and maximum sentencing guidelines. Crimes that used to get one or two years in prison now got three or four, and so on. The "mandatory" part, of course, precluded judges from amending a sentence based on someone's age, personal background, or circumstances of the crime. What if, on second thought, after all the evidence was heard, a judge was convinced the child-defendant needed mental health services along with jail time, or perhaps instead of jail time? Or, what about a kid who kills an abusive parent in self-defense? And so on. There were just too many *what ifs*. And so, judges indeed were reticent to approve transfers. Then again, what if there was a crime, or were crimes, so horrific, perpetrated by kids, that judges—especially judges in politically-charged municipalities—shelved all those other *what ifs*?

There are certain cases that change the way a community—even a nation—thinks, like New York City's Central Park jogger. On April 19, 1989, Trisha Meili, a 28-year-old investment banker with Salomon Brothers, was running in the park when she was assaulted and raped. Her battered body was discovered about four hours later. By then, she was suffering from hypothermia. Her numerous injuries included a skull fracture. Her recovery languished as the police picked up a group of teens for questioning. In an unusual move, their names were released before they were charged (typically juvenile names are withheld unless a child is charged in adult court). Five teens—four of whom confessed— were convicted a year later.

The crime was horrific, but the idea that teens—children—could do something like this was morally, logically, and scientifically incomprehensible. The case set the stage for a legal shift in the early 1990s where children became juveniles, retribution replaced rehabilitation as a catch phrase, and juvenile programs became "corrections." During this period, nearly every state enacted legislation that favored punishment over prevention. Like most things, this shift in juvenile justice took a while to reach Colorado. But when it did, it had gained momentum.

The Centennial State had plenty of cases like the Central Park jogger—all involving teens. Most notably, there was the case of William James Bresnahan Jr., who beat and stabbed his parents on a family camping trip. And Richard Mijares, who shot his mother and buried her in a shallow grave. The list goes on. In Colorado, guns were part of the problem: These crimes became more lethal in the 1980s and 1990s. Between 1983 and 1993, murders increased by 25 percent and arrests of juveniles charged with violent crimes increased by 75 percent. There were all kinds of theories, reasoned and otherwise. Some said the violence was caused by rap, heavy metal, or violent movies. Others blamed West Coast gangs; the Bloods had settled in north Park Hill. And while Denver had a long history of gangs, they'd always been more of the homegrown variety. In addition to the Bloods, along came the Crips. These gangs had a network that reached across the country, which scared policy-makers who couldn't figure out a cause or a solution to the apparent violent crime wave.

During the summer of 1993, it seemed like the violence was escalating on a daily basis. One day at the Denver Zoo, a toddler was shot in the head. In another instance, a three-year-old was shot in the arm. Each day seemed to bring more news of bloodshed and death; the local media dubbed the apparent crime wave the Summer of Violence. Parents, politicians, pretty much the entire population was spooked. The violence seemed so random, victims so young. Kids were dying, but increasingly, kids were also killing. Denver's DA, Bill Ritter, and other prosecutors took their worries to Governor Roy Romer, an attorney and father of seven. He agreed that something had to be done, and that the juvenile courts weren't doing their job. He called the legislators back from summer vacation for a special 10-day session. In the end, 11 laws were passed and some redefined how Colorado treated juveniles. Suddenly, the Division of Youth Services became the Division of Youth Corrections—an ostensibly subtle, yet unmistakable sign that the philosophy regarding juvenile offenders had changed. The old 1923 strategy of direct file was once again passed into law.

Direct file became a fast lane to adult prison without the two-day transfer hearings and judges to consider the prosecutor's request. After the Summer of Violence, it was the DAs who decided whether a 14-year-old was a child or an adult. The strange thing about Colorado's new direct file statute was that there was no option to send an offender back to juvenile court. Until 2010, the DAs had no criteria to consider before charging a juvenile as an adult. But even now there is no system of checks and balances to evaluate how thoughtful prosecutors really are. More often than not, they do not have to explain their decision to a court of law. The decision to direct file was—and is—theirs alone. The DA not only chooses the charge, but also the venue (juvenile or adult court). A juvenile's records are no longer sealed, sentences are harsher, and opportunities for mental health services are nowhere near the same as those made available in the juvenile system. It is the only decision in which a DA does not have to prove his or her case in front of a judge or jury. (Even in death penalty cases, a DA can decide to pursue the sentence, but a jury ultimately decides the offender's fate.)

Since 1993, direct file has morphed. Even though transfer hearings are still an option, by 2000 only a handful had occurred. Some DAs said the two-day hearings took too long and made victims relive traumatic events twice—once at the hearing and once at trial. Simultaneously, the crimes eligible for direct file expanded beyond serious charges like murder. This option was not just for the worst of the worst: it sometimes was used for the "sort-of worse," like teenagers involved in vehicular homicide or aggravated robbery.

On any given night, it is estimated there are 10,000 kids in adult jails in the United States. For years it was unknown exactly how many juveniles were being held in Colorado's adult facilities because this information wasn't—and still isn't—tracked in Denver County. However, excluding Denver County, which is a county with a high number of direct file cases, nearly 30 kids were locked up in adult jails between July 1, 2010, and June 30, 2011. Most are male, but it is estimated that girls make up about seven percent of Colorado's direct filed youth. Even less is known about the number of juveniles in adult prison after a conviction or plea has been accepted. What is known is that there were at least 1,810 felony cases in Colorado between 1999 and 2010 where the defendant was under 18 at the time the case was filed.

Now, Colorado finds itself one of only seven states that gives DAs such sweeping autonomy to employ direct file without a transfer hearing option or a way to send the case back to juvenile court. In 2009, the most recent year for which statistics are available, 28 percent of every 100,000 criminal cases against juveniles in Colorado ended up in adult court. Even Texas, a tough-on-crime state, direct files on a smaller percentage of children than Colorado does. Yet the Colorado District Attorney's Council estimates that there were about 100 direct file cases last year, a small portion of the nearly 10,000 juvenile cases that occurred.

"The cold facts are as soon as direct file got expanded, the juvenile crime dropped," says the group's executive director, Tom Raynes. "I think there is a notion that this direct file authority is used widely and often. It's used with great discretion." He cites that, most of the time, DAs believe juveniles should be treated differently, but there are exceptions. In those cases, direct file is necessary. "If someone could point to how the system has failed us or that there have been horrible mistakes made, we'll listen," Raynes says. "Let's look at the facts of the cases. We're willing to defend those cases."

Kim Dvorchak is almost always smiling. Blond, tall, and quick-witted, Dvorchak is an attorney and executive director of the nonprofit Colorado Juvenile Defender Coalition, an advocacy group working to put an end to direct file. She and a handful of staff work from a second-story office on Santa Fe Drive that's next to an auto repair shop and a tattoo parlor. It's not the place you'd expect—or maybe it is exactly the kind of place— to find an organization that often makes a habit of calling out DAs. The group has been instrumental in chipping away at direct file, with the ultimate goal of abolishing it completely. Dvorchak knows direct file discussions can dissolve into legalese about statutes and due process. To keep things simple, she starts with the worst cases: the ones that involve parricide, when children kill their parents or another relative.

These cases are rare. There are a few dozen in the state's history, which is miniscule considering a child dies from abuse every 10 days in Colorado. The Pendulum Foundation, a Colorado nonprofit and advocacy group for juvenile justice, estimates that 90 percent of these children had been severely abused. Take, for example, Jacob Ind: On December 17, 1992, the Woodland Park teen murdered his mother and stepfather. Colorado's Attorney General John Suthers, who was then the DA, direct filed on the 15-year-old, and Ind was sentenced to life without parole, a veritable death sentence. Those are the basic facts, but there are others.

Ind's older brother, who'd moved out just months before the murders, testified at Ind's trial that both he and Ind had suffered years of sexual abuse by their stepfather, saying: "He would basically rape us" and "there were many secrets in the house that we didn't tell people." Ind's brother also insisted he finally told a social worker about the problems at the house shortly before the murders (something the social worker didn't recall). In the weeks before the murders, Ind lost 20 pounds, stopped bathing, and had near-constant panic attacks. After the murders, he showered, caught the bus to Woodland Park High School, where he was a freshman, shot some hoops, and took a pop quiz in his math class. When the cops discovered the bodies later that day, Ind vacillated between rage and sorrow. His biggest concern, which he confessed to his brother, was the tiny bit of marijuana in his bedroom. He didn't want to get in trouble with the cops.

There are more recent examples, too; the most well-known is John Caudle. The 14-year-old high school freshman lived in Monte Vista in the San Luis Valley, a town of about 4,000 people and the kind of place where everyone knows everyone else, but really don't seem to know each other at all. To them, Caudle (pronounced "Coddle") probably seemed like a quiet kid who read books on the bus and had the odd habit of still sucking his thumb. He appeared to be emaciated, with just 98 pounds to stretch over his five-foot-seven-inch frame. At home, he lived with his stepfather and mother. His mom made him carry rocks in the yard for up to 10 hours at a time and often denied him food.

After school on October 26, 2009, his mom told him to do chores and bring her a Dr. Pepper. When he didn't—and she didn't stop bothering him—he went to his room, picked up a family gun he'd hidden there, and shot her in the head. But it didn't work: She kept screaming and screaming. He shot her again, and again, and again—nine times in total. And then he waited in the laundry room. When his stepfather arrived home and walked past his hiding place, Caudle shot him in the back of the head. He was still alive, so Caudle shot him again, in the head. When he wouldn't stop breathing, Caudle stuffed ear plugs in his nostrils and dragged him to the bedroom where his mother's body was. Then he did the laundry, played an online game, and took a shower.

The next morning, he drove his stepfather's 2008 Chevy Silverado pickup to Monte Vista High School. Later that day, he was picked up for driving erratically in Fairplay. The bodies were found sometime that same day and authorities interrogated Caudle for hours. His maternal grandmother was present, but she spent much of the time crying in a corner. Occasionally, Caudle would hug her and cry himself.

His sentencing hearing lasted only two days. Two specialists were cited as calling his case of child abuse the worst they'd ever seen. The prosecutor didn't contest that Caudle had post-traumatic stress disorder. Witnesses described how Caudle was abused; one compared his mother to a Nazi prison-camp guard. None of it mattered. Before the judge could sentence him, Caudle accepted a plea bargain sentence: 22 years behind bars.

Could a teenager even understand a plea bargain? Was this battered-person syndrome? Would he receive the services he needed in an adult prison? How could a double-murderer be let off with anything less? Caudle's case inflamed the direct file debate. DAs in favor of direct file cited it—and still cite it—as an excellent example of why direct file is necessary, while opponents like Dvorchak point to the very same case and say direct file is anathema to the very concept of juvenile justice, and for that matter, justice and due process of any kind. What happens when he gets out—a boy-turned-man in prison? Dvorchak and the DAs made the media rounds, arguing both sides.

Ind's and Caudle's cases are just the start, Dvorchak says. She talks about a boy who punched someone at school, received a juvenile court summons, and arrived to find out the DA had filed a "notice of intent to direct file." (The judge appointed an attorney immediately.) Then there was the 17-year-old who walked away from a juvenile detention center on a field trip and was direct filed for his "escape." The DAs offered him six years. (An adult who runs from a similar facility might get one or two years.) The charges were eventually dropped, but only after the teenager's attorney started asking about that sentencing discrepancy.

There are more complicated cases, like the kid who walked into a shop with a nonfunctioning gun. The clerk wasn't even scared and just told the boy to go home. The teen did. But he continued this behavior—in Boulder, Adams, and Weld counties. When the teen was caught, the DA in Boulder didn't direct file on him, but the DAs in Adams and Weld counties did. "Most people think direct file is only serious homicides, and that's actually a pretty small percentage," Dvorchak explains. "It's under 20 percent."

Most direct filed kids never get a trial; many juveniles take plea bargains instead. Less than five percent of all direct file cases since 1999 have gone to jury. In other words, in 95 percent of direct file cases, the DAs choose the charge, venue, and—thanks to mandatory sentencing—the punishment. And all this "due process" is without the input of a judge or jury. "DAs are not direct filing so that they can have jury trials in adult court," Dvorchak says. "The child has no ability to appeal that. There is no mechanism to test the prosecutor's choice of putting you in the juvenile court or the adult court."

Crazy kids. That's been the refrain for generations, it seems, as adults ponder why perfectly normal children turn into irrational, irresponsible, and irritating teens. Aristotle said teenagers act like drunken men. Mark Twain called them "frivolous" and quipped that teens should be kept in barrels for the duration of adolescence. For parents, it can be a trying time of crashed vehicles, curfew violations, and skipped classes. It's particularly frightening because, at a time when the consequences of those actions escalate, science says that—empirically—teenagers just don't understand.

The human brain is almost adult-size at age six. And you don't need to be a parent to know that a six-year-old does not act like an adult. It takes almost 20 more years for a brain's function to catch up with its size. During the 1990s, a series of research studies, including a decade-long

National Institutes of Health (NIH) project tracked teen minds. The results were shocking: The brain doesn't evolve or grow like other parts of the body. Instead, certain areas develop over time, like an empty house that is slowly painted, furnished, and lived in. The frontal lobe is the finishing touch, but it might be the most important as it controls planning, suppressing impulses, and understanding consequences.

So, it makes sense then, scientific sense, that during the teen years the thirst for risky behavior increases, as kids have not yet developed a mature respect for consequences. And while 17-year-olds commit more crimes than any other age, 80 percent of teen violent offenders do not go on to commit violent crimes in their 20s. In 1993, while this all may have been intuitively obvious, there was little scientific proof. And this societal ignorance is part of the reason why juvenile offenders' excuses for their actions often seem feeble, amateurish—juvenile. The research that proves teenagers are psychologically different from adults is so compelling that in 2005 the U.S. Supreme Court declared capital punishment unconstitutional for juveniles.

Where juvenile-detention programs for 17-year-olds are ostensibly rehabilitative, adult prison for 17-year-olds is punitive. "The criminal justice system is incredibly powerful," explains Christie Donner, director of the advocacy group Colorado Criminal Justice Reform Coalition. "It can pick you up out of your life and put you someplace you don't want to be. And there's probably no other system that has that kind of power. Child welfare can't. Education can't. This is an enormously powerful system." And the adult prison system is woefully ill-equipped to receive juvenile offenders.

There is a federal law that requires "sight and sound" separation between juvenile offenders and adult inmates in jail, but it does not apply to children prosecuted as adults. In Colorado, a law requires physical separation, but this, again, doesn't apply to direct filed youth in prison. Theoretically, a 14-year-old boy could be put in the same cell as a 50-year-old sex offender. Most Colorado jails do not have a pod for juvenile inmates (Adams County does have a makeshift juvenile unit, in a jail). And so, jail and prison officials often have avoided both situations by holding juveniles in solitary confinement.

The practice of isolating a prisoner in solitary confinement is widely regarded to be psychological abuse. (Most of Europe disavowed the practice last century.) Last October, Juan Méndez, the United Nations' torture expert, said solitary confinement "can amount to torture or cruel, inhuman and degrading treatment or punishment when used as a punishment during pretrial detention, indefinitely, or for a prolonged period for persons with mental disabilities or juveniles."

Fourteen-year-old John Caudle spent more than a year in solitary confinement waiting for his trial to begin. When he emerged from the box, he was transformed. He was five-foot-11 and 110 pounds, with an Adam's apple sticking out of his bony neck and a vacant stare. "He was extraordinarily frail," Dvorchak says. "He looked like a toothpick in chains." The jail did not provide him with mental-health services. After he was convicted, he was sent right back to solitary confinement. In theory, Caudle was put into solitary for his own protection.

Teenagers make up one percent of the jail population, but 21 percent of inmate-on-inmate substantiated sexual violence is against youth. Even the searches can feel invasive: Strip, open your mouth, raise your arms, show the space between your penis and testicles, and bend over and cough so a guard can inspect your anus. Locked up with adults, kids are also 50 percent more likely to be attacked with a weapon. Most troubling is the estimate that teens are 36 times more likely to commit suicide in adult prisons than in juvenile facilities. Since 2001, two Colorado teens, 17-year-old James Stewart and 17-year-old Robert Borrego, have committed suicide in adult facilities.

Richard Mijares could have been one of those teens. Deputy sheriffs found a noose in the teen's cell in 1988. It wasn't the first time Mijares had tried to kill himself.

On March 24, 1988, Mijares shot his mother in the face in their Woodland Park home. They had an argument, and he went downstairs with a gun to think—to see, really, if he had the guts to shoot himself in the head. When his mother, still arguing, came down the stairs, he just pointed the gun at her and squeezed. He wrapped her corpse in a blanket, buried her some 15 miles away, and spent a week pretending she was missing for the cops. It didn't work; he eventually confessed.

He underwent a psychological evaluation to determine his fitness to stand trial as an adult, but nothing more. He was direct filed, but his case never made it to trial. He accepted a plea bargain on June 10, 1988. When the judge asked him why he was pleading guilty, Mijares just shrugged. The judge told him that until he understood his actions, he could only give Mijares the maximum sentence.

We'll never know what a psychiatrist would have said about Mijares's mental health when he agreed to a plea bargain. Or how Mijares's lifetime of abuse impacted his mind on the day of the murder. Mijares says his father would beat his mother while she was pregnant with him, beat her so badly that his older sister would peek under her mom's dress to make sure he was still in her womb. He recalls a time when he dropped a clean sock on the garage floor and was beaten. His dad drove a Volkswagen Rabbit with a very distinctive engine sound, and when Mijares heard it coming home, he hid. By the time he was 14, he was suicidal, which is around the time his mom finally kicked his father out.

Their new life was quiet, almost too quiet. Their home was so isolated that at night Mijares couldn't see lights from another residence. His mom suffered from depression and would have little energy for him. She'd go to her nursing job before he woke up and straight to her bedroom when she got home. Mijares would waste his time fishing in the pond or shooting behind the house. Sometimes he would pick fights with her. Sometimes he'd dream about killing himself. That night in the spring of 1988, he shot her instead, ending up in prison with a "mother-killer" reputation.

Shortly after Mijares arrived, a prisoner approached him in the shower because he thought Mijares was "cute." Mijares got away. A few days later, while watching TV, a fight broke out in the common room and everyone scattered. He was just happy to be alone, and he reached up to change the channel to Magnum, P.I. when he felt someone behind him—the same prisoner who'd tried to assault him in the shower—and turned in enough time so that the shank buried in his arm.

In the basement of the Capitol, a crowd of more than 50 people crammed in a room that seemed built to hold far less. In the hallway, a group of tan, silver-haired DAs waited, looking like models on a Rogaine casting call. They were all there because Representative Claire Levy, a Boulder Democrat who had worked as a public defender and civil trial lawyer, had introduced House Bill 1208. The bill would, among other minute points, raise the age at which a juvenile could be direct filed in adult court from 14 (John Caudle) to 16 (Gary Flakes).

It was 2008. By then, transfer hearings were virtually extinct. On the books, a transfer hearing for a kid before a judge was still an option, but it was hard to find a defender or prosecutor who'd done one. Direct file had replaced it. Stories about cases like Caudle and Flakes had drawn attention, and not the good kind. There was talk. Lots of talk. Along came "When Kids Get Life," a PBS *Frontline* investigation of Colorado's juvenile offenders stuck in adult prison, which featured Jacob Ind. Under the media spotlight, it seemed like it might be time to get rid of—or at least modify—direct file, and so HB 1208 was the subject of debate in Colorado's House Judiciary Committee.

Raising the age requirement for direct file eligibility, to some, was a modest tweak to the law. Then again, there were people gathered in the basement room who believed HB 1208 was about more than age groups; prosecutors who were advocates of direct file regarded the bill as a potential wrecking ball to the justice system. Witnesses began to testify. Dr. Delbert Elliott of the University of Colorado's Center for the Study and Prevention of Violence took a seat in front of the panel. He spoke concisely for three minutes, trying to create a picture of youth violence in Colorado. John Riley, former director of the Platte Valley Youth Services Center in Greeley and a veteran of the juvenile justice system, took his place. "When I came into the system 30 years ago, children were children," Riley said. "Children didn't change; our fear of them did.... We stopped treating them like children."

The DAs got their chance to talk about the worst cases, the ones that kept them up at night. The ones that showed how horrific children can be. They focused on the "hard cases" and explained that every state has some measure that allows these offenders to be handled in adult courts. They didn't focus on the fact that many states didn't have direct file at all, but relied on transfer hearings. Or that most other states had ways to appeal the court's or DA's decision to try a child in criminal court. John Suthers, the state's attorney general, asserted that direct file actually helped curb youth violence in the state, emphatically saying that "since 1993, juvenile crime has decreased significantly."

But, the other side argued, if direct file is the reason, why has juvenile crime decreased in states that don't have direct file? Like a pendulum, the crowd's mood swung with each witness. The committee, divided on the issue itself, asked for statistics—any concrete data—about Colorado. But there was no complete national or local data available on minors prosecuted in adult courts.

The bill narrowly passed the committee and moved to the state House where the issue wasn't partisan, but rather decided on whether a representative's constituency was tough on crime at that moment. Concessions were made and wording was reworked. On March 7, 2008, a representative from the Western Slope pantomimed a vicious murder, while others pontificated on the rushed nature of the Summer of Violence legislation. The bill passed by a slim margin, and then passed in the Senate. Finally, it landed on the desk of Governor Bill Ritter, the former Denver DA. In response to the media attention, Ritter had created a Colorado Commission on Criminal and Juvenile Justice, a body of 26 members that would review Colorado's criminal justice system. He renewed the Juvenile Clemency Board with specific plans to review cases of juveniles sentenced to life without parole. But the moves were largely empty gestures. There was no money to fund changes.

During his four years as governor, Ritter vetoed between four and eight bills a year, including a database for interior designers and something about electricians' apprentices. He vetoed many fewer bills than his predecessor, but Democrats had control of both the House and the Senate, so signing bills into law was de facto. But he vetoed HB 1208. His view was that DAs were using direct file sparingly and he was not convinced the current system wasn't working. Really, his veto did not come as much of a surprise, as he'd made it clear on the campaign trail that he wasn't willing to consider an overhaul of direct file: "You'd have to undo the entire juvenile sentencing structure."

Maureen Cain, a lawyer and advocate who was a lobbyist for reform at the time, says she'd given Governor Ritter 15 cases to review hoping he would see that the juvenile sentencing structure was, at least in part, being replaced by the adult sentencing structure, and that it was time to reconsider what juvenile justice actually meant. "I gave him a memo, but I don't think he ever read it.... He was pretty upfront about the fact that he was going to let it happen, even though it ran through the Legislature.... He was too much of a DA to ever break from them."

On October 15, 2011, Gary Flakes is speaking into a megaphone at the start line of a 5K run. The race is sponsored by Kim Dvorchak's group, the Colorado Juvenile Defender Coalition. Flakes met Dvorchak when she took on his prison appeals as court-appointed counsel. Now, he's attending Pikes Peak Community College and working as an outreach assistant at CJDC where he speaks to families of direct filed teens. He tells them what their sons and brothers are experiencing in prison. He tells them what to expect. He tells them how to hold on.

He's dressed in long sleeves, black pants, and perfectly polished shoes that stand out in the crowd of sneakers and sweats. "We take kids straight from the streets, and the prosecutors are the ones who have the sole discretion about whether or not those kids are sent to the jail or held in a juvenile facility," he says into the megaphone. "When a kid should be getting services and counseling and support from their family, they are held in solitary confinement, which is a place of depression, isolation, loneliness, and sometimes leads to suicide."

This grown-up Flakes—he's 31 now—has a too serious look about him most of the time. It's not that he's brooding; he just seems uneasy. He's nervous when people ask questions, not understanding or trusting why they'd be interested in him. He thinks through your motivations before flashing a quick smile. It's prison that made him cautious, he says. It took years for him to understand why he was inside for so long. There were years he couldn't stand being around other inmates. Then something changed.

He devoured books. He converted to Islam. He got an education and spent hours in the prison's library. After serving about five years, Flakes was intent on tracing his entire case. He started at the beginning, asking why he, a 16-year-old, was in adult court in the first place. The answer didn't add up. Certain crimes are eligible for direct file, like class-one felonies (murder, armed robbery). He was convicted of accessory to murder, which is not eligible for direct file. In short, he was convicted of a crime that, by its very definition, shouldn't be in adult court.

He filed a *pro se* motion on his own behalf, asking the court to address this, well, discrepancy. The case found its way to Dvorchak, a court-appointed attorney at the time, and eventually to the Colorado Supreme Court. The state's highest court ruled that the original trial judge hadn't fully documented Flakes's sentencing. Flakes—now a man—would have a chance to argue in front of a judge that he should have stayed in juvenile court. It was the equivalent of a 10-years-too-late transfer hearing.

Colorado judges do not comment on legislation. Their stance is that judges interpret law; they don't make it. So they said nothing during the Summer of Violence. They've kept silent since then, too. (The Colorado Judicial Department, which speaks on behalf of the state's 287 trial judges, declined to comment for this story.) In 1993, the DAs argued that judges weren't willing to transfer kids to adult court. Since then, there have been very few chances to see what a judge would or wouldn't do.

Nearly every year since 1993, advocates and legislators have worked to undo what happened during that 10-day special session. Sometimes they make headway. Sometimes they don't, like when then-Governor Bill Ritter vetoed HB 1208 in 2008. Stephanie Villafuerte, Ritter's former aide and a chief deputy in 1993, is now the executive director of the Rocky Mountain Children's Law Center and defends the legislation—in part. "I think it was well-intended legislation," she says. "Today, advocates on both sides are arguing about how much is enough. My job as a prosecutor was to do what was just—not what gets you in papers. At the time we did our job with the law and tools we had. What we knew 25 years ago is different than what we know today. But at no time should people use juvenile justice as a platform."

Maureen Cain, the attorney and advocate who was a onetime head of Denver's juvenile defenders, remembers things a little differently, saying that judges then, and now, are more equipped to supervise transfer hearings and to make consistent decisions than DAs who have to worry about re-election. "The heyday for the DAs was in the '90s," she says. "We had money. They could go in and ask for anything they wanted. If they wanted it, they got it, and there was no accountability and no assessment of whether that's effective. They just said, 'We're from the government, trust us.'"

Juvenile crime rates have plummeted, just as Colorado District Attorneys' Council's Tom Raynes and Attorney General John Suthers say. But there is little evidence that direct file discourages youth crime, just as there is little evidence that the threat of the death penalty discourages adults from committing heinous crimes. None of the direct filed offenders interviewed for this story cite direct file as a deterrent for their teenage minds. In truth, many had no idea Colorado sent kids to adult prison.

Advocates like Dvorchak argue that a teenager has little ability to understand the legal consequences of his or her crimes. That instead of rehabilitation, we focus on punishment, which is a mixed message. "Let's restart the conversation," Dvorchak says. "It's not a question of whether two years is not enough. It is a question of why seven years is not enough." She also questions why, if we believe in a juvenile justice system, we have a legal loophole that contradicts its very premise.

Ritter's Juvenile Clemency Board and task force was created in 2007 to address questions like this—but nearly five years later, they've done little. Governor Romer granted the last pardon in 1987 to William James Bresnahan, who killed his parents on a summer camping trip in Summit County in 1964 as a 16-year-old. After serving 10 years in adult prison, he became a doctor and moved to California.

For other examples of what a juvenile criminal can become and that the notion of rehabilitation of a child has merit, there's Richard Mijares and Gary Flakes, who are both out of prison, employed, and taking college courses. At 40 and 31, respectively, they are like time capsules. They went in as teens and emerged as men. They missed prom, turning 21, registering to vote, getting married. Many would argue they lost the right to experience those things because of their crimes. Regardless, like so many other prisoners, they eventually left prison—and the world they re-entered is sometimes more daunting than the one they left.

Mijares arrived at his halfway house in February 17, 2000, hopeful that he'd assimilate back into society. He had a little cash saved from selling belt buckles and jewelry he made; his sisters helped out too. He finished his GED inside and even picked up a pair of associate degrees. The few times he was lucky enough to get a job interview, they ended badly. He started to give a rehearsed spiel about his crime that he'd worked on with his therapist and parole officer. Soon, he found out that background checks revealed what he had been charged with—first-degree murder—not what he was convicted of, second-degree murder. That seemed wrong, but he'd work with it. It was what he had to do. One night, he came back to the halfway house and just broke down. "Send me back," he told his parole officer. He didn't know how to live outside of prison anymore.

He finally got a break when a call-center employee went to his boss and vouched for him. He started at $7 per hour and worked whatever shift they'd give him. Six weeks later, they promoted him to a computer job. Two-and-a-half years later, he's the director of his department. The way he sees it, he may never leave. "Where else would I go?" Mijares asks. He's got a truck, two houses, two cats, a dog, and he's taking classes at Metro State, trying to get his B.A. Mainly, he wants to blend in; even his short-sleeved shirt hides the scar on his arm from the prison attack.

Mijares, like Flakes, is now working on direct file reform. Maybe this year will be the year something changes. Maybe not. Regardless, it's likely that the Legislature will have to deal with Colorado's direct file policy this session—again. "I don't know what year is the right year for this to happen," Maureen Cain says. "You just keep doing it."

Which is why Flakes is standing at the 5K's start line, beginning, again. Most of all, he worries about his legacy. "If someone harms your family, you've been created to have that anger and do something about it," Flakes says. "I understand that. I don't want them to feel anything different than they want.... They got every right—I mean, a right. The legacy that I'm going to leave is going to have to be—and it is going to be—a good one. It's going to far outweigh this right now, what I'm known for."

—December 2011

13.
Andres Galarraga:
Denver's First Baseball Hero

by Bob Kravitz

The three young ladies and the eager young boy lean over the railing behind the first base bag at Mile High Stadium. They are carrying programs and pens and are scouring the greensward for a glimpse of their hero. They are from the neighborhood here, just down the street, off Federal. This is their first Colorado Rockies game.

"Gato!" they scream as Andres Galarraga, the Rockies first true icon, emerges from the clubhouse beyond the right field line. "Gato, Gato!"

They are seized by the apoplexy of blind hero worship. The young boy, Hector, is eight years old. He is asked about Andres Galarraga. "Ha hecho jonrons," he says, beaming: *He hits home runs.*

Galarraga—aka Big Cat, aka Cat, aka Gato—has done more than hit home runs: he has given the Rockies a defining figure, a leading man on a team of semi-anonymous baseball nomads. He's the name the national media wants. He's the name the community groups around town want. Galarraga is huge all around the region, but he is especially desirable in Denver's sizeable Latin community.

"Can you do this tomorrow?" Jackie Sarmiento, the team's community relations director, asks. Galarraga nods. He always nods.

Cat is this team's centerpiece, its very first, an affable man with a ready smile and a bat that seems unwilling to cool. Expansion teams are, by definition, warehouses for the game's chattel, and players are moved in and out with alacrity. Back in 1962, Mets manager Casey Stengel used to joke, "I've got one team here, one team coming, and one team going." But Galarraga has emerged as a latter-day Rusty Staub, who was the Montreal Expos' first marquee player back in 1969. Staub remained with the team three years, an eternity by expansion standards. The Rockies would like to see Galarraga remain, too; they've already approached his representative about a long-term contract.

"I would love to stay in Colorado," Galarraga says. "The support, the people, the whole atmosphere is great."

But he is loathe to think about a contract or about his future or about anything more complex than a baseball and a bat and the wondrous anthem the pair have been playing. He is loathe to think about anything that might take away from the moment at hand. He has captured—or better yet, recaptured—something very special, reclaimed and breathed new life into a flagging baseball career that was turning very sour just one short year ago.

Today, he is the Rockies' first-ever representative in the All-Star Game. Today, he is the obvious choice to win the National League's comeback player of the year. Now, there is conviction behind the omnipresent smile. "I am so happy for myself," Galarraga says, groping for just the right words.

Word was, Galarraga had lost it. He was finished, another underachieving veteran with an oversized paycheck. His bat was slow. His hitting mechanics were beyond repair. He was a supernova, a shining star who burned out quickly and dramatically…finished at the tender baseball age of 32. The St. Louis Cardinals, who had obtained Galarraga in what turned out to be a disastrous trade with the Montreal Expos—they gave up Ken Hill, an outstanding starting pitcher—were paying Cat $2 million a year, with a $3 million option for 1993.

When Galarraga and his agent, Jim Bronner, refused to renegotiate a new, long-term contract at a lower annual rate, the Cardinals dropped their first baseman at the end of the 1992 season. These are times of economic reckoning in baseball; teams can't afford to be paying $3 million per annum to underachieving former stars. The game's new economy provides riches for the mega-stars—Barry Bonds, Darren Daulton and the like—and fills in the rest of the roster with players closer to the Major League minimum of $109,000. The middle class has been wiped out. Galarraga was a middle-class talent with a superstar salary.

And so, Galarraga went back home to Venezuela and played winter ball while his agent sat by the telephone. He had an idea he would be playing baseball somewhere, but where? And for how much?

"About a week, 10 days before the expansion draft, we started talking informally about some guys who might be out there," says Rockies manager Don Baylor. "When Cat's name came up in conversation, I thought at the time he might be too expensive. But we went in with an offer ($600,000 a year plus incentives) and he accepted right away."

Galarraga was a good fit for the Rockies, and for a number of compelling reasons:

First, Baylor had worked diligently with Galarraga one year earlier when Baylor was toiling for the Cardinals as their hitting instructor. Baylor had become Cat's guru, changing his stance and his approach to the elusive art of hitting. Galarraga had experienced something of a personal renaissance during the latter half of the past season, and he trusted Baylor implicitly.

Second, the price was right. The Rockies first-year philosophy was to keep payroll low; currently, it is a league-low $8.7 million. Galarraga was a low-risk investment. If he could hit, say, 15 home runs and drive in 75 runs and play a solid defensive first base, he would be worth the money.

Third, there were the organizational ties that went way back to his days as a minor leaguer in the Montreal Expos chain. The Rockies general manager, Bob Gebhard, worked with Galarraga during his first-ever Major League spring training in 1979 while Gebhard was a minor-league instructor. The Rockies pitching coach, Larry Bearnarth, was Cat's first-ever professional manager, greeting Cat in West Palm Beach when he was a spindly—yes, he was spindly back then—18-year-old. And the Rockies scouting director, Pat Daugherty, managed Galarraga in Jamestown, New York during the 1981 season.

And then there was this part of the equation, a part the baseball people never really calculated. The city of Denver proper is 23 percent Latin, and the Rockies were counting on drawing huge numbers from that baseball-mad segment of the population. Who better than Galarraga, a friendly bi-lingual Venezuelan, to act as a magnet?

"When the protected lists came out, we all sat down and decided that none of the available first basemen jumped off the page," Gebhard says. "We all started talking about Cat, and it just made sense. We figured, at the very least, he would give us somebody who would play a good defensive first base, would be an anchor out there, and would be a good veteran in the clubhouse for our younger players. That's the one thing about Cat is his work ethic. Even when he was going bad, the work ethic was always there."

When spring training opened in Tucson way back in late February, Galarraga looked very much like the player who had struggled so mightily through the better part of the last three seasons. He batted 12 times in the first three exhibition games and went hitless. He was still having trouble getting around on the inside pitches—his batting Achilles heel.

"Let's keep him back here," Baylor said before his team drove north for a game in Tempe. "Let's get him some video work and see what happens."

The bad habits were returning, the ones Baylor had worked so hard to eliminate. This was the morning of March 9, still a full month away from opening day, and there was still plenty of time. So Galarraga stayed behind and stepped into the batting cage in the early morning, a video camera recording his swing from a number of different angles. Batting instructor Amos Otis watched closely, nervously, like an expectant father. A half hour later, Galarraga, beads of sweat rolling off his forehead, retired to the clubhouse to deconstruct his swing with Otis while watching a small TV monitor.

"I see the problem," Galarraga said, smiling.

Later that afternoon, he pinch-hit during a split-squad game against California's B-teamers—mostly minor leaguers. He got a base hit. Better yet, he hit the ball to right center field. He was no longer trying to pull everything to left field. This was a good sign.

"You show Cat one or two things in his swing, he corrects them, and boom," said Otis. "He's one of the most coachable guys I've ever been around."

Galarraga was the Rockies hottest hitter the remainder of spring training, but that was just a conservative prelude. When the regular season began, Galarraga began swinging a mythically hot bat. Here was a man who was known for bursts of power punctuated by heroic strike-outs. Galarraga? Hitting for average? Hitting .400 in July, for crying out loud? His name in the same paragraph with the sweet-swinging Ted Williams?

"I keep waiting for him to cool off and return to earth," Baylor said after a game in mid-June. "But it never happens. He just keeps hitting, doesn't he?"

One year ago, Galarraga had forgotten how to hit a baseball. Simple thing, right? See the ball, hit the ball. This is what he had done from the time he was five years old, running around his inner-city Caracas neighborhood, rousting friends from their houses and pleading with them to come out and play ball.

"I used to get everybody in trouble," Galarraga said with a laugh. "We would play before school, and sometimes we would play during school instead of going to class. I would say, 'C'mon, let's keep playing,' and we would miss class. I just loved the game so much. It's all I wanted to do."

Galarraga played sandlot ball for his neighborhood, La Florida Champellin, until he was 16 years old. Soon thereafter, he signed with the Caracas Leones, a winter-ball team that included Major Leaguers like Tony Armas, Bo Diaz, and Manny Trillo. He was surrounded by fellow Venezuelans who had been in The Show, and he mimicked their every move.

Two years later, Felipe Alou, then a minor-league manager and now the Montreal Expos manager, scouted Galarraga and signed him. Suddenly, Galarraga, an 18-year-old Venezuelan who had never been outside of Latin America, found himself landing in three countries within a month—Venezuela, the United States, and Canada. He was assigned to West Palm Beach, Florida, then demoted to Calgary.

"I didn't speak one word of English," Galarraga says. "Not one. I was completely lost and very scared. I wanted to call home to my parents every day, but there wasn't enough money for that. So I ended up calling once a week. It was terrible, really. I mostly stayed with other Latin players, but we were all very lost. We would go to a restaurant and just point at the menu. We didn't know what we were getting, we'd just point. It was frustrating, very frustrating. I couldn't communicate. And it was so different. When I got to Calgary, it was cold and I didn't have a coat or sweaters. I had to go out and buy some when I got there."

It is a problem Latin players have had since baseball began mining the mother lode of talent down south. More and more, though, baseball organizations, including the Rockies, are helping their Latin players by offering classes on English language and American culture—and basic life skills.

Galarraga, however, knew none of those benefits.

"When I called home, I tried not to tell my mother how bad it was," Galarraga says. "I would say, 'I'm getting used to it. I'm not doing good now, but I'll be okay.' If I told her how I really felt, if I told her how frustrated and lonely I was, she would have said, 'That's it, then you come back home right now.' Believe me, I thought about going home every day. Every day. I thought about it all the time. *What am I doing here?* But something inside me kept saying, 'Stay with it. Do something good for your family. Make them proud.' The only time I feel comfortable there is when I go to the ballpark because all I have to do is play baseball. That's where I take all my frustrations. I don't have to speak English, I don't have to talk or worry about anything, just baseball.

"The best thing for me was going to Jamestown (New York in 1981). I was the only Latin player on the team, so it forced me to speak English. I was very lonely there, but I learned the language much quicker. I would read my dictionary and watch a lot of TV, read the newspapers. And Randy St. Claire helped me a lot. He would tell me, 'Andres, you don't say it that way, you say it *that* way.' I appreciated it when he did that.

"For a long time, probably four years, I always did an interview with somebody translating. Even when I went out, I didn't want to say something in English and say it wrong. I don't want anybody laughing at me and saying, 'He's stupid,' because it comes out the wrong way. After four years, I did my first interview in English. But even now, I still get so nervous, especially on TV. That's why sometimes I ask the TV guys what questions they will ask so I can think of how I want to say it in English."

On the field, though, nothing was lost in translation. Galarraga was everything as advertised. By 1988, he was an All-Star. In 1989, he drew consideration as the National League's Most Valuable Player.

But by the early months of the 1992 season, hitting had become a mystery, an unfathomable zen koan that eluded rational explanation.

He was in the throes of something more than a basic slump; he was in a morass, his numbers having declined, and quite precipitously, the past 2 and a half years. He had gone from a .300/20-homer/85-RBI man to a fellow flirting with numbers generally reserved for utility infielders.

And the folks in St. Louis, the ones who had expected Galarraga to produce numbers commensurate with those on his contract, were not pleased. One day, the *St. Louis Post-Dispatch* ran a chart comparing Galarraga's and Hill's numbers. Not only was Hill establishing himself as one of the most accomplished starting pitchers in all of baseball, but at one point Hill had a home run; Galarraga had none. Galarraga is a thick man, but thin-skinned. The criticism was eating him alive. It got to the point where he didn't want to leave the house, didn't want to chat up the fans, or leisurely talk some ball.

"I never told anybody, not the media, not my teammates, nobody, but I thought about going home, giving up," says Galarraga. "I thought about it during the (1992) season. I couldn't do anything. I was so down, there was nothing I could do. I kept telling people, 'Yeah, I know I can play this game, and I know I can still hit,' but I didn't know, really. And then I just started letting everything bother me. A fan would say something, instead of ignoring it, I took it to heart. I take everything personally. That's one of my big problems."

The decline began back before the 1989 season. He had just come off the two best seasons of his life, hitting .305 and .302. But before the '89 season, then-Montreal batting coach Joe Sparks and manager Buck Rodgers told Galarraga he could hit even more home runs if he lowered his hands and tried to pull the ball more toward leftfield. "It was almost like, 'Okay, we gave you this big contract, now put up bigger numbers,'" Galarraga said. For two seasons, his home run and RBI counts remained solid, but his average kept dipping; after two straight .300-plus years, he hit .257 in 1989, .256 in 1990.

Then, in 1991, it all fell to pieces. Minor injuries were a factor, but Galarraga's hitting style was more to blame. In 1991, he fell to .219 with just nine homers and 33 RBI. He was traded to St. Louis that winter and life only got worse.

Just days before spring training, his first with the Cardinals, his father, Francisco Galarraga, died from stomach cancer. He had been a house painter who worked hard to support Andres, who was the youngest, his other three sons, his daughter, and his wife, Juana. Francisco had never been a huge baseball fan, but he was hugely supportive. Andres also drew a love of painting from him; Galarraga paints portraits in his spare time and has sold some of his work in galleries.

Ordinarily, baseball would have been his escape. But there was tremendous pressure to produce, to justify the trade and resurrect a flagging career. He came to spring training early to begin work with the latest in a line of personal gurus: Baylor.

"You know what the guy's problem is, is he's too nice," says Baylor. "I don't know how or when it happened, but sometime when he was in Montreal, someone told him he had to be a pull hitter. It wasn't enough he hit 22 home runs, drove in 90 runs. I mean, he's not a pull hitter. He's such a nice guy, though, he never went to the goddamned hitting instructor and say, 'Hey, kiss my ass, I've been successful this way and this is the way I'm gonna do it.' But of course, Mr. Nice Guy listens and all of a sudden, they're jamming the hell out of him and he can't lay off that ball.

"We had him come in early, with the pitchers and catchers, and Cat and I went back to Hitting 101. Hitting off the tee, soft toss, then some live. Mr. Nice Guy, he's gonna listen to another hitting coach, the 900th different one, right? But when we talked, I said, 'Look, let's not even worry about strikeouts.' That's the amazing thing, is they wanted him to pull the ball, but they didn't want him striking out so much. How do you do that? When Andres was going well, he was not a pull hitter—he went to all fields. So I told him, let's work from the middle of the field. If you start hitting to the middle of the field, the swing will come back, without a doubt. Plus, I opened his stance. Everybody said, 'What are you doing that for?' But now he's really adopted that style."

Problem was, Galarraga broke a bone in his wrist when he was hit by a wild pitch in just the second game of the season. Any progress he might have made was scuttled. Back to square one...

"By the time I got back (May 22), I was trying too hard, I was thinking all the time, I wanted to do well so badly," Galarraga says. "All these people were saying I couldn't play anymore. 'That Galarraga, he's finished, he can't play.' And really, I was so frustrated, I thought about just going home, quitting. But I thought, 'Okay, let's try it this way with the new stance. Let's shut everybody up, prove everybody wrong. I thought about quitting, but I love this game so much.'"

At midseason, July 19, Galarraga was hitting an anemic .189. But he stayed with the new, open stance, kept working with Baylor before games, in the batting cage, despite steadily diminishing play time. After hitting his nadir in mid-July, Galarraga found his stroke, hitting .301 with eight homers and 29 RBI in his final 45 games.

And he hasn't stopped producing. His Rockies numbers are mind-boggling. Four hundred? In July? Galarraga? The man whose best years seemed little more than a sweet and fading memory? Gebhard, who saw the best of Cat while with the Expos, could only smile. "The man is on a mission," he says. "He's on a mission to show everybody, and himself, that there's a lot of good baseball left in that body."

—August 1993

14.
All That's Left Is God
by Michelle Theall

Lucas, our four-year-old son, bucks and arches his back away from the baptismal font at Sacred Heart of Jesus Church in Boulder. My partner, Avery, and I try to hold him still in his little white suit—he has already kicked off one of his patent leather shoes, which landed on the altar. It's as if Lucas realizes the only reason we are baptizing him in the Roman Catholic Church is because it is so important to my mother, the same woman who toted his special outfit, embroidered with delicate crosses, all the way from San Antonio and threatened him this morning using these exact words: "If you don't put on that baptism suit this minute, Jesus won't love you."

I do not tell my mother that this baptism almost didn't happen, that Father Bill Breslin of Sacred Heart met with me two weeks earlier to discuss our desire to have Lucas baptized and the church's views on homosexuality. I assured Father Bill that while Avery and I were gay, we were quite certain that Lucas wasn't. I told him he could rest easy knowing that he wouldn't be letting another one of "us" in.

Still, it was impossible for me to answer Father Bill's questions without thinking about the recent accusations of the Vatican's role in protecting pedophile priests. Why was I fighting to have my son baptized into a faith that appeared to be putting the welfare of children second to the reputation of the church? With my son already in preschool at

Sacred Heart and preparing for his baptism, I was trapped in a familiar standoff between the church and myself. There were no easy answers. But just like the cul-de-sac I'd grown up on in the Bible Belt, I recognized that I might find my way out if I headed back the way I'd come.

1977
Humble, Texas

I kneel in the hallway with my mom, dad, and sister, squirming as the shag rug embosses my knees. While most families I know bond over "Monopoly night" or episodes of *Mary Tyler Moore*, mine prays the Our Father wedged two-by-two in front of a crucifix. When my sister and I giggle, Mom glares at us through half-closed eyes and grips her rosary beads until they leave stigmata-like imprints on her palms. I wonder what Jesus would think about being hung twice—once on the cross and again in our hallway surrounded by framed covers of Life magazine. But mostly, I wonder where God went last week—when my friend's father molested me in the den of their home not 100 yards from where I kneel now—and why, at just 11 years old, I don't trust my own mother enough to tell her.

1981
Dallas, Texas

All Saints Catholic Church sits in the backyard of our new home on Firelight Lane, so our family will never have an excuse to miss Mass. Father Rudy Kos—the coolest priest I'll ever know, who sports a mustache and drives a black Mustang—lives in the rectory with his 13-year-old son. Father Kos is short, athletic, handsome, and unconventional. Parishioners gossip that he'd been married, had the marriage annulled, and adopted his son before becoming ordained and being sworn to celibacy. But I don't care about any of that; I like that he talks to teens like they are real people.

When my parents find a fifth of tequila hidden under my bed, I turn to Father Kos for insight and advice. He says he's not concerned about the alcohol, but he wants to know why I've started drinking. Father Kos asks me if I believe in God, and I tell him that I do, that I've never felt completely alone in the world. Still, this is the same God that I think of when I can't get the things that have happened to me out of my head. Every day, the news reports that some girl has been abused or kidnapped, and every day I am reminded that I am part of a growing club of lost girls who will never be the same.

If God has a reason for everything, what is the reason for this? With his kind, almond-shaped eyes, Father Kos tells me, "You have so many holes in you, you've become porous like a sponge. No wonder you wanted to drink to fill up those empty places. But if you let God, He can fill them up too."

1982
Grapevine, Texas
I'm sitting in Sharon's house, drinking White Russians served by her lover—a woman—whose name is Shoe. They are in their 30s. I am 16. I imagine that somehow they've forgotten I am a teenager who cannot vote or join the Army or get into an R-rated movie. I finally have my learner's permit shoved inside the glove compartment of the Plymouth Fury, next to my mother's St. Christopher medal, but I don't have my driver's license yet.

Even though they are twice my age, I do not feel exploited. Instead, I feel seen. I do not have to tell them I've been abused or that a car full of boys keeps driving past my house yelling "Michelle has a dick" before peeling out like cowards. I do not know what I am. But I know Sharon and Shoe are a refuge. They are also the first real people I've met who are gay.

I know what some Christians say about gay men and women. My mom thinks AIDS is God's wrath on them. She's never uttered the words "lesbian" or "homosexual," which would be like saying "goddamn" or "shit" or worse. Those aren't the kind of words spoken by a woman who never wears white after Labor Day. Even my father, the gentlest man I know, once turned to me after passing a pair of effeminate men on the street—one wearing eyeliner, the other a fuchsia boa—and told me that they made him physically sick.

But what I see when I look at Shoe is a baby giraffe, lanky and circus-happy, with arms opened wide enough to give everyone in her path a giant hug. And though Shoe is skinny, she's not frail or dainty. She doesn't hunch her shoulders forward or slump to apologize for being tall. She doesn't pretend to be something she is not, and never will be.

Sharon is the exact opposite of Shoe. Where Shoe is a bold statement, Sharon is an ellipsis, a trailing thought. She doesn't wear makeup, and doesn't need it. Her nails are short. Her hair is straight and unpretentious. She's not trying to impress anyone, particularly men. And in a city of debutantes, beauty queens, face-lifts, and boob jobs, finding a woman like this impresses me.

Still, armed with anti-gay scripture from the Old Testament, I quote Leviticus 18:22 to them. Because it would dilute my argument, I neglect to tell them that Leviticus also says they must ceremonially sacrifice two doves or pigeons immediately following their menstruation and stop eating shellfish. Shoe looks at me with a sad smile and questions my relationship with my high school best friend. "I think you have feelings for Lynn," she says. "I think you love her."

"I do," I say. "But not in the way you're talking about."

"With God's love, I suppose."

"Yes."

And Shoe says, "God made me too, you know."

1985
All Saints Catholic Church—Dallas, Texas

I wait to hear Father Kos enter through the other side of the confessional. I cannot do this face to face, even though he'll know it's me in the booth. "Bless me, Father, for I have sinned. My last confession was Easter. I lied to my parents. Skipped Mass last Sunday. Took the Lord's name in vain. Kissed a woman. Had impure thoughts. Cursed." I take a deep breath. "That's it."

"Let's go back to that fourth one."

"I took the Lord's name in vain?"

"Nope. The one after that."

"I kissed a woman."

"That's the one."

Silence. Uncomfortable silence.

Father Kos clears his throat. "Is this a one-time thing?"

"A one-time thing. Definitely. Yes." Flames of hell lick at my feet. Why doesn't Father Kos go ahead and condemn me?

More silence. I wince, head bowed.

My knees ache atop the threadbare kneeler, and I can hear my mother's voice telling me to "offer it up," which means pain is part of the sacrifice, even though it's nothing like the death Jesus endured for our sins. I look to my left and right, and can see the whole space without moving my head. The narrow booth is for skinny sinners only. It needs a weight and height limit sign, like rides at Disneyland.

Jesus hangs on his cross above the screen where Father Kos is dreaming up an unparalleled penance for me. I wonder if he will ask me to tell my parents what I've done or make me serve meals to men dying of AIDS. He clears his throat, ready to denounce me.

"Your penance is 10 Hail Marys and one Our Father."

"That's it?"

"Please say the Act of Contrition."

I do not remind Father Kos that this penance is the exact same one he gave me six months ago when I forged a pass to get out of study hall. After I finish the Act of Contrition, he says the prayer of absolution, which ends with the words: "I absolve you from your sins in the name of the Father, and of the Son, and of the Holy Ghost. Amen. Go and sin no more."

And like that my slate is clean. Except that I cannot un-kiss a girl. My body remembers it. And it doesn't feel like an accident or coincidence. Instead, it feels ordained.

1986
Buffalo Springs Lake—Lubbock, Texas

"I will run over you." Coach Jarvis Scott drapes an arm out the window of the Texas Tech track van and nudges our calves with the front bumper. With a square jaw, gold tooth, and a college degree in criminal justice, Coach Scott reminds me of a prison guard. Today, she's announced we'll be doing three to five, which sounds like years of a jail sentence, even though she means miles. We pick up the pace.

Running has been its own kind of education for me. Coach Scott never steps in to defend me from my teammates, who pretend to kiss each other when I step onto the team bus, refuse to room with me, and call me a hypocrite. If life had a rewind button, I would never have told those girls, no matter how drunk we all were on pitchers of beer from Schooner's, that I'd slept with a girl named Nancy. Some of my teammates had already confessed to pregnancies, abortions, shoplifting, and snorting cocaine, so I'm sobered to learn that homosexuality falls on the narrowest end of the Bible Belt. I have a boyfriend, am a member of the Fellowship of Christian Athletes, and have a 4.0 GPA, but they see my past and cannot accept it.

Maybe they are not the only ones. I do not want to be gay, but I love sports, abhor wearing dresses, and prefer sensible shoes to heels. I date guys, but only to earn the respect and approval of women. I am a stereotype, a cliché, and I am furious about it.

It doesn't take long for my track career to derail because of my shame and self-loathing. Coach Scott calls me to her office to find out why I've gone from promising athlete to train wreck in a matter of months. I do not play the woe-is-me card: I would never win that game against the fortress of a woman sitting in the swiveling chair in front of me. She doesn't speak about her past. I only know what I have read—that she grew up among gangs, violence, poverty, and racism in the projects of South Central Los Angeles. By the time she was a year older than me, she was an Olympian.

She is the one who says to me, "Prejudice is blind. Rich, poor. Black, white. Woman, man. Old, young. Christian, atheist. There will always be someone who says you aren't welcome at the table. Stop apologizing for who you are and using all your energy trying to change their minds. Yes, you will lose friends, maybe even family. But you will gain your self-respect. You will know your worth. Once you have that, nothing can stop you." Coach Scott offers advice but not a refuge. She knows that before I can win any races, I first must learn to stand on my own two feet.

1991
Dallas, Texas

A single drop is nothing, but my mother cries and doesn't stop. Water like this will carve a canyon between us. My father lowers his head, rubs his hands together. On their floral upholstered sofa, they digest the news that I was sexually abused when I was 11 and that I am gay. I fire off my disclosures before I lose my courage. If they believe that the abuse caused me to be gay, if this softens the blow in any way, so be it.

I believe my father figured out that I was gay years ago, but to keep his home from becoming a battlefield, he adopted a "don't ask, don't tell" policy. My mother swears she had no idea, even though I wear men's Levi's and own every CD by the Indigo Girls.

Still they have a few surprises of their own. My father—the kindest man I know, who has, at times, been the only evidence I've had that men can be good—says I must have done something to cause the sexual abuse. I invited it in some inadvertent way. It is my mother who says, "I am so absolutely sorry. I wish you felt you could have told me. I would have done anything to spare you pain like that." I'm undone by their words, but more so by the flash of empathy I see in my mother's eyes, the look that says she knows all too well the demons I fight, and she would have fought with me too. I have waited 14 years for my mother to wrap her arms around me and comfort me. And because I am gay, I've lost that opportunity, and I've also lost her.

When my mother leaves the room, my father follows her. I wait. Fifteen minutes pass. My father appears in the doorway from the hallway that leads to their bedroom. He's tentative, eyes worn like a boxer who's gone 10 rounds. "You need to leave now, sweetie," he says. "For good."

There are few things worse than being abandoned by your parents, even when you are 25 and living on your own six hours away. They do not say good-bye or hug me or tell me to have a safe trip back to San Antonio. Instead, they put an asterisk by my name, negating every good thing I've ever done and will do. And because my parents feel that they are somehow responsible for who I have turned out to be, they have put an asterisk by their names, too.

1994
San Antonio, Texas
In my driveway, I load my Nissan Pathfinder with the last of my things. I wrap my hand inside my T-shirt before lowering the branding-iron hot metal tailgate with its Jesus fish on one side, and a bumper sticker that reads, "Love Many, Trust Few, Always Paddle Your Own Canoe" on the other. I get Bear and Chance—all 200 pounds of wolf hybrid and husky—settled in the back and point the Pathfinder northwest to Colorado.

Though the Lone Star State contains pockets of liberalism, it is largely a place where men and women hunt, buy American, attend right-to-life rallies, and paint their water towers with the name of the local football team. And although it is also the place where I was born and raised, where the rhythm of cicadas and dancing fireflies lulled me at dusk, it has never really been home.

In college, I'd visited a friend who lived in Eldorado Springs, Colorado, just outside the narrow jaws of a canyon on the shore of South Boulder Creek. She rented a mattress in the attic of a home that cost twice what I paid in rent for my apartment in Lubbock. She accessed her living quarters from a wooden, pull-down ladder in the kitchen, and her bedroom "loft," as she called it, had just three feet of clearance from the ceiling. But at night, without even lifting her head from the pillow, she'd crank open the skylight and fall asleep to the din of creek and owl, cricket and guitar. I stayed a week, skipping class, and for the first time in my life, I knew what peace felt like. I knew that Colorado wasn't just a place for respite or vacation—it might also be the place where I belonged.

Now, heading west on I-10, bugs splatter against the windshield. The terrain shifts from scrub oak and cracked earth to rolling hills and serrated peaks. Without my family, I am untethered, but it isn't the same as being free.

The house I buy sits on three acres in the middle of nowhere with views of Longs Peak, a waterfall, and a mix of trails leading off the property that might go all the way to Canada. My first night there, it is so quiet the blood rushing in my head awakens me. I go out on the deck, cocooned in a wool blanket, and stare at stars so dense I cannot identify a single constellation. In the morning, four feet of snow lands atop my house like vanilla frosting. The weight of nature takes power and transportation with it. I cook off the wood stove, use the deck for a refrigerator, and rely on a backup cistern for water. In a man-made world stripped bare, all that's left is God. And though I cannot see Him, in the same way I cannot see the wind, His presence makes me weep.

1996
Pinewood Springs, Colorado

Until this January day, all I have received in the mail from my mother are anonymous prayer cards, most featuring the Virgin Mary, along with singles dating-service memberships. Then an e-mail arrives. Halfway through the message, my mother writes:

> *The path you are continuing to follow is against everything I believe in, and I simply cannot get past that. . . . I believe, in the long run, you will suffer the consequences of your lifestyle. The most troubling*

thing about all this is that I am devastated that you have turned your back on the church. As your mother, I beg you to try and visit a priest in Colorado. . . . Perhaps he will not sanction your actions, but we are taught to love the sinner and hate the sin. . . . Some congregations are openly trying to find a place for everyone. . . . Temporal happiness is short-lived, but the salvation of your immortal soul is for eternity. And please don't make excuses about how you can pray anywhere. I know that, but I do know that Christ established the church of which you are fortunate to be a member by your baptism. . . . I will love you and pray for you no matter what. I am not your judge, my dear, only your mother, who has tried her best to do what is right for her children. I love you, and God bless you. Mom

Three weeks later, boxes arrive. They are filled with report cards, finger paintings, and spelling bee awards. My mother has sealed up my childhood and sent it to me, paid in full.

1997
Pinewood Springs, Colorado
The headline on the *New York Times* article reads "$120 Million Damage Award for Sexual Abuse by Priest." Ten former altar boys and the family of an 11th who committed suicide have won a landmark civil suit against the Dallas Roman Catholic Diocese for hiding and protecting Father Rudolph Kos, who was sexually abusing boys. One of the plaintiffs in the case is the boy who Kos claimed was his adopted son. I recall being jealous of my male classmates because Kos spent more time with them than with me. It never occurred to me that they might be hurt in the same way I had been. Because Father Kos was an employee of All Saints, my parents' years of tithing, along with the monetary offerings of the rest of All Saints' parishioners, paid for Kos's and the diocese's legal defense fund.

1998
Nederland, Colorado
Summer paints my land with locoweed, larkspur, columbine, asters, and iris. Hummingbirds swarm my feeders; males dive like missiles toward the earth. My new home off Magnolia Drive sits on 10 feral acres of an

elk migration pattern, dwarfed by views of 12,000-foot peaks. From June through September, my dogs kick up wild sage and track it into the house on their paws. For an entire season, their fur smells like clover and sap. Together, we navigate the wilderness adjacent to my acreage using aspens, rock outcroppings, and scats like road signs. I'm aware that I now trust wild animals more than people and can go months without speaking to another human soul.

I believe that I do not need anyone. Even when my quarter horse shatters my right hand, I drive myself to the ER, shifting gears and steering down the hairpin, 20-degree sloping road with my left. In the winter and early spring, elk break the fence line, looking like amateur high jumpers when their back legs catch the smooth wire. I become adept at staking T-bar fence posts into the ground, steeped in sweat and vibrating with the body shock of hard, physical work. At an altitude of 8,500 feet and living off miles of rutted dirt roads, I feel safe. I leave the doors to my house unlocked. I don't even own a key.

In this refuge, I allow myself the latitude to realize several things. First, living alone and being celibate does not make me any less gay. Second, I am not gay because I was abused. One in three women world-wide will be abused, and one in three women are not gay. Third, it's not my fault. Any of it. Fourth, I still like men, even though at 32 years old, I've been drugged, assaulted, and carjacked at gunpoint by them. And while these things made me into the kind of person who kept her hackles up—one who would rather see a mountain lion track than a human footprint—they did not make me gay. God made me gay.

But being abused does have residual effects. I have never stayed in any relationship more than three months with a man or woman without bolting. I envy gay and straight women and men who can enjoy uncomplicated and playful intimacy with one another, who can believe that somebody who touches them might do so out of love. This gift has been stolen from me. And if I cannot be with women or men, where does that leave me besides alone?

I pray several times a day beneath a sky that opens up to me like an apse in a cathedral. As much as I am comfortable with my isolation, one thing is very clear to me: if I lose the ability to love, I will become something less than human. So this is the bargain I make with God: *If you can heal me and teach me to trust again, I will leave this mountain.*

2000
Nederland, Colorado

I sleep in a Marmot sleeping bag on the hardwood floor. For six years, I've measured time by the ending of seasons; now, as the late-summer flowers lose their color with the first frost, I too am moving on.

Two years ago, I spoke on the phone with a woman named Avery—a friend of a friend from college—who invited me to a party in Denver on a Friday night. I couldn't think of anything worse than leaving my utopia to battle rush-hour traffic to spend time with a bunch of people I didn't even know—people who had chosen a life in the city over one in the mountains. I told her I'd pass. Never having met me, Avery said, "Oh come on, who are you, Nell? Even the Unabomber left his cabin to send out mail." So much captivated me about those two sentences that I said *yes*—and kept saying it until we both sold our homes to purchase one together in Boulder. Perhaps mirroring us, the new place splits the line of mountain and city, half wild and half tame, with open space at the front door and civilization out the back.

With the moving truck loaded and gone, I spend my last night in my empty mountain home. I watch the peaks flash white against a full moon, like trout bellies in a river, and pray for a send-off, a blessing from this place that has made me whole again. But I do not expect or demand it. Instead, I call it to me.

At 3 a.m., I hear knocking. I slip out from my sleeping bag and tiptoe to the doors and windows. Elk, a herd of 80 or so, have formed a ring around my home, antlers tapping on the wood siding. They remain like that until sunrise, hugging my house. They are so close that their snorts of breath fog the windows.

2003
Boulder, Colorado

There's a story that's passed down through my family that says when my mother was two years old and visiting her grandparents' farm, she begged them to let her hold a baby chick. She was careful at first, but when they asked her to put it down, she couldn't fathom giving it up, so she crushed it in her hands.

Six decades ago, my mother had no idea what she'd done to that chick except love it, but she knew emphatically what it had done to her.

As her grip closed on the little ball of feathers, it defecated in her palm, at which point she screamed and dropped it.

Now, at 64 years old, my mother sits on our deck, her fingers cradling a cup of coffee, staring at the Flatirons and the foothills slouching like thugs against them. I study her, and though I look more like my father, I have my mother's Italian nose, olive skin, petite build, and yes, hands—a fact she once pointed out to me during a piano lesson when I was five. "Poor thing, you got my hands," she said. "They're so ugly."

I raise the umbrella to try to give my mom some shade, and we watch a herd of deer scale the hillside. "You shouldn't have run this morning. It's too hot," my mother says. She raises her hand to block out the sun with her fingertips. "Tell her, Avery."

"Don't get me involved in this," Avery says and heads back inside our home where it is safe. I ignore my mother. I want to ease her worry, but shouldn't she be comforting me? I'm the one who's just been diagnosed with multiple sclerosis.

I sense the incoming verbal grenade just before it hits. I brace myself as she says, "You stopped going to Mass. That's why this happened."

"Unbelievable." I chew on my thumb, but cannot stop myself from saying, "So regular Sunday Catholics don't get diseases, and everyone else does?" My cuticles are raw, close to bleeding.

"God works in mysterious ways, Michelle."

I do not know, and will never know, who my mother would have become if she had a mother of her own. As it was, my grandmother took ill when my mom was six years old, and never quite recovered. Because my grandfather, an Italian immigrant with a seventh-grade education, worked long shifts on American Oil tanks, the nuns at St. Dominic's helped raise my mother, hammering home a Catholic education that was as black and white and rigid as the habits they wore.

My mother's faith saved her by giving certainty and structure amid chaos. But it couldn't tell her she was beautiful, or brush the tangles from her hair, or sing her to sleep. Because of this, my mother was determined to love me with a ferocity and devotion she had never known. So when her 36-year-old baby was diagnosed with MS, my mother fell apart. She lived too far away to fix me, so Avery's gender no longer mattered to her—or, one might argue, mattered to her less. My mother learned she could not turn away a person who loved me, her child, enough to stand beside me through a spinal tap, weekly injections, and the rarely discussed possibility that I might be wheelchair-bound one day. Avery became a part of the family.

It took me getting MS, but my mother finally realized she didn't have to choose between being a good Catholic and loving her gay daughter. She could find a way to do both. Still, I do not confuse my mother's acceptance for approval. The words are not synonymous. We agree to disagree and to let God be the judge. It is the only way to move forward. My mother believes I have left a mess inside her open palms, and I alternately accuse her of holding on so tight I cannot breathe and of dropping me. We struggle to find even ground. Sometimes, it seems, all we have in common are our hideous hands and a bone-crushing love.

2006
Wrangell-St. Elias National Park & Preserve, Alaska
At 40 years old, I have had plenty of time to fear what kind of mother I will be. While most of our friends are celebrating their children's high school and college graduations, Avery and I are just deciding to become parents. At first, we look at international adoptions, but all of them ban same-sex partners. Only a handful allow single-parent adoptions, and most of those make the adopting parent sign papers avowing that he or she is not homosexual. Worldwide there are 133 million orphans, and 114,550 children languish in foster care in the United States. With a single phone call, Avery and I learn that Boulder County does not care about our sexual orientation. Instead, Boulder sees two women with a stable relationship and the financial, emotional, and physical capacity to care for a child in need of a family.

To get certified as foster-adopt parents, we turn over our tax returns and medical records to the county for scrutiny. The FBI scans our fingerprints for a background check, and a home-study worker interviews us about every detail of our past. Fifty-plus hours of mandatory training later, we are wait-listed for a match. The social worker encourages us to take a vacation before we begin our life as parents, and so we head to Alaska.

In Wrangell-St. Elias, I fly in a bush plane to the top of an unnamed peak while Avery catches salmon in the river below. I stand on the summit, and though I did not witness this mountain's birth, I know how mountains are made, how they become something solid from cracked earth and shifting soil. God will bring us a child who needs us. And though our son's beginning might be shaky, he will change the landscape to a grand and beautiful thing. Already, this child is my hero.

2007
Boulder County Courthouse—Boulder, Colorado

At 14 months old, Lucas has been placed in foster care twice. His biological mother and father were homeless and young. Dad had mental illness; Mom was developmentally delayed. Lucas was malnourished, left unsupervised in a bathtub, and hospitalized twice before he came to live with us.

Now, two-year-old Lucas runs across the courtroom and into my arms. "Mama!" he says, dragging his Lamby and nestling against me with his buttery skin. Today, he will become our son. Because there is a judge present for the adoption hearing, and we are allowed to say something to the court, Avery and I take this opportunity—after nine years together—to exchange the equivalent of vows, along with our promises as parents to Lucas. We cannot marry in Colorado, but with family from both sides here and in a court of law, we make our commitment official. My parents and sister cry. They sweep up our son, in his sport coat and tie, and cover him in kisses. On Lucas's new birth certificate, he has two mommies.

2009
Sacred Heart of Jesus Church—Boulder, Colorado

Father Bill Breslin shifts in his seat. We are supposed to be talking about Lucas's pending baptism, but Father Bill tells me that he is thinking about banning the children of gay parents from Sacred Heart of Jesus School, where Lucas is a preschooler. He mentions he has even asked Archbishop Charles Chaput in Denver to weigh in on the issue. He asks me, "What should we tell our students and parents when they question a child having same-sex parents?"

I say to Father Bill, "You probably know, but the director of your school has a child in my son's class. Just the other day, in front of the other preschoolers and a teacher, this child asked me, 'Why does Lucas have two mommies?' I explained to her that there are all different kinds of families. Some kids are raised by a grandmother or just a dad or sometimes both a mom and dad, and sometimes two mommies or two daddies. The little girl looked up at me and said, 'My daddy doesn't live with us anymore.' And I told her, 'I'm sure he loves you very much.'

"Lucas didn't choose his parents. None of us do. To deny the existence of blended families is to lie. We adopted a two-year-old, mixed-race, traumatized child, and we want him to be raised in a faith and to know God. I don't see how that can be a bad thing. How can we punish or exclude a child because of who his parents are?"

I expect Father Bill to argue, but instead he asks, "Will you be re-enrolling Lucas at Sacred Heart next year?"

"No, primarily because of this conversation," I say. My mouth moves, but I am thinking of Lucas—who has made friends and loves his teachers, the administrators, and staff who have been nothing but kind to him and to us.

"I'm glad we had this talk," he says. "I'm just trying to figure out where I stand on it." He ushers me to the door.

I remember Father Kos and my classmates. The boy who committed suicide. I say, "Maybe the church needs to prove itself worthy of my son and me rather than the other way around." Father Bill scratches his beard. He seems to be thinking about this.

Lucas's baptism goes on as planned, though not at Mass with the congregation in attendance. Instead, Sacred Heart holds a baptism for our child on a Sunday at 4 p.m., with empty pews and a service performed by a Naropa University priest, whose credentials I check online, just to make sure Father Bill hasn't pulled a fast one.

2010
Boulder, Colorado

I watch Lucas run serpentine after a fox and her kits before the animals disappear beneath the white clapboard porch of Mapleton Montessori School. Kids on swings and slides chant my son's name. It's a welcome that never gets old. I head to the Laughing Goat Coffeehouse and grab a cup of coffee and a newspaper. After six months, I've all but forgotten about Sacred Heart and Father Bill, until I read the headline in the Denver Post: "Boulder Catholic School Denies Preschooler with Lesbian Parents." It is not Lucas. But it could have been.

According to the Denver Archdiocese, parents who enroll their kids at Sacred Heart of Jesus School are expected to follow the Catholic

Church's beliefs. As a private school, Sacred Heart is within its rights to accept or deny any student for any reason. But surely gay parents can't be the only ones who aren't following the Catholic Church's beliefs. After all, Sacred Heart allows Lutherans, Buddhists, and atheists to enroll their children at the school.

I e-mail Father Bill and ask him if he is willing to "turn away the kids" of parents who practice birth control, or are undergoing fertility treatments, or don't attend Mass regularly. He writes back, "I don't want to simply jot off an answer to you that isn't as thoughtful as your question. So, please give me time on a less busy day to get back to you. And will you remind me if a week goes by and you haven't heard from me?"

I decide not to write back, and I never hear from him.

When I tell my mother about this latest development, I expect her to side with the Catholic Church. Instead, she says, "Suffer the little children come unto me," and, "If they think being gay is wrong, they should want you to be in the church every time the doors are open." For once, we agree, and I'm reminded that God is in the people, but the people are not God. Knee-high in lupine as spring edges toward summer, I stand beneath the Flatirons and teach my son to pray. And when the wind ruffles his hair, I tell him to listen close: The God who loves him, who loves all of us, has something to say.

—October 2010

15.
Out in the Cold

by Mike Kessler

Judy Padilla was the last person you'd have pegged as a bomb builder. Five feet two inches tall with platinum blonde hair, she looked no more threatening than the pearl-white '75 Beetle that sat in the driveway of her Adams County home. Her idea of profanity was "shoot" and "booger." But Judy was stubborn, ambitious, and energetic, with the kind of piston-quick spirit that got her up every morning to ring-lead the family circus: She'd make breakfast and bag lunches for her three kids, feed the two lap dogs, and kiss her husband, Charlie, good-bye as he left for another morning shift on the factory floor at AT&T. Later, in the afternoon, Judy would leave for her own job. On her way out of the house, she'd reach for a small hook on the pantry door and grab a baseball-card-size instrument called a dosimeter.

It was 1984, Judy's second year on the job at the Rocky Flats Plant, the nuclear weapons facility just north of Golden on Highway 93. The communist threat was strong, or so we were told. Russia had troops in Afghanistan and the Berlin Wall stood tall. Production of nuclear weapons was in full swing, fueled by a defense budget that had swollen to nearly $300 billion.

A Coloradan since she was a teen, Judy was the daughter of an oilman who taught her to work hard and trust her government. She'd voted for Reagan once, and she'd do it again. Earning her keep at a nuclear weapons facility was a point of pride for Judy. Heaven forbid we'd ever need to use a nuclear weapon, but she was happy to be on the team that built it.

And she gladly took $11 an hour at Rocky Flats over the $7 an hour that AT&T had paid her to stand at a table braiding wires. As a metallurgical operator at Rocky Flats—one of only four women to perform such a task—she loved being a "blue-collar rat" at the only United States Department of Energy site that manufactured plutonium pits. Heavy as a medicine ball and barely larger than a hockey puck, the pits were the triggers that made the bombs go BOOM!

At the east entrance of the plant, Judy flashed her badge to the guard, aimed the car over a gentle rise, and drove into a low basin that revealed Rocky Flats. The 6,500-acre facility was a small city unto itself. At least 20,000 people had worked there since it was built in 1951; at any given time there could have been 5,000 employees on-site. Main Street bustled with signs of productivity, even on weekends. There was a firehouse, a garage, a medical center, and seven cafeterias. Men and women scurried about on foot and on bicycles and flatbed carts, weaving between clusters of administration trailers and warehouse-size buildings. The "Flats," as most workers called it, bore a striking resemblance to a thriving Hollywood back lot, except for the fact that so many buildings were decorated with the yellow and black "radioactive" symbol.

Buildings were grouped and numbered according to the work performed within them. Machining was in the 400 complex, for example. Paper pushers were the 100 area. And radioactive material was typically "processed" in the 300 and 700 buildings; entering them required government "Q" clearance, the highest access granted to civilians. Judy worked in 707.

Through the metal detectors and into the locker room. Judy would change into her DOE-issued socks, underwear, white coveralls, and steel-toed boots. She'd report to her pre-shift meeting for what tended to be an unremarkable recitation of accidents that had occurred on the previous shift, production goals for the week, and new station assignments. But, on at least one morning that spring, as Judy recalls, superiors gave new orders: *Stop lollygagging in the glove boxes. Hanging in the glove boxes increases your chances of exposure to ionizing radiation. Many of your radiation counts are getting close to the allowable maximum.*

It was an odd set of instructions, to say the least. Reducing time in the glove boxes was nearly impossible. The massive metal-and-glass cubes—sometimes several hundred feet in length and 15 feet tall—housed vital components for the manufacture of bomb triggers. The boxes, which looked like giant space-age fish aquariums, held equipment such as furnaces, melt coils, crucibles, conveyor belts, and that vital silver-grey ingredient, plutonium 239. The only way to make a plutonium trigger was to approach a glove box, shove your hands and arms into portholes that housed the giant lead-lined rubber gloves, lean against the glass, and start working. Metallurgical operators spent at least five hours of every eight-hour shift in the glove boxes—it was their job—melting plutonium at 1,200 degrees Fahrenheit, pouring it into ingots, placing molds on the conveyor belt. Shoot, Judy thought, no one lollygagged in the glove boxes. The message was clear: Work faster, produce more, and don't let radiation exposure hinder productivity. Judy's supervisors then made what she remembers as a "strong suggestion"—a passive order that undermined one of the fundamental principles of safety. As Judy recently said to me, "I was told to put lead tape over my dosimeter."

A job at the Flats came with plenty of risks. Hot plutonium could spontaneously combust upon contact with water, and plutonium shavings could do the same when exposed to air. Small fires in the process areas were a matter of course. Gloves would often spring pinhole-size leaks where they attached to the ports, emanating radiation for minutes or hours before alarms would sound. Workers on one shift might have forgotten to decontaminate their gloves after pulling them out of the boxes. Sometimes a glove would come right off its port, instantly "crapping up" a room, and the people in it. They'd strip out of their work clothes, rush to the showers, and "scrub down" with chemical solutions and sharp brushes that rubbed their skin raw. You can't see, smell, hear, or taste radiation. A potentially hazardous mistake could go undetected for hours, even days. To monitor their radiation exposure, Rocky Flats workers relied on at least one of three instruments: machine-mounted "alpha mats," which measure alpha particles; handheld Geiger counters operated by radiological control technicians (RCTs); and personal dosimeters.

A dosimeter checked for gamma rays and neutrons; covering a dosimeter with lead tape could cause the device to give an artificially low reading. But even when used correctly, dosimeters weren't fully reliable. For one thing, they had to be in the direct path of radiation. What's more, dosimeters were fickle, fragile devices; when workers would leave them in the sun or on top of the TV at home, other forms of radiation—less dangerous forms—could often throw off the instrument's readings.

Some workers willfully ignored safety regulations at the Flats. Overtime hogs would do anything not to "dose out" and be reassigned to another building. Workers with a certain *esprit de corps* would take their chances in the name of national pride. Others figured they were being looked after. Judy liked the extra cash, but she trusted that when things got too hazardous, her government would do everything to keep her out of harm's way, especially considering the nature of her work. "We were acutely aware of how important our jobs were for the country," Judy told me one recent afternoon. "We felt that the country would protect us in return."

Workers at the Flats referred to each other as "brothers and sisters." They didn't just build bombs—they built secrets. In the name of national security, what happened at the Flats stayed at the Flats. Even intimate groups of coworkers kept a muzzle on work chatter. "You could play cards with the same bunch of guys for years and barely even know what they did," Judy said while we sat at her kitchen table. "You'd say, 'I'm a welder,' or 'He's a machinist'—but that's about as far as it went." Information, she explained, was disclosed on a need-to-know basis.

So Judy kept her mouth shut and her hands in the glove box. Still, every time she pressed her breasts against the glass, she couldn't ignore what she held at arm's length—a manmade element that could decimate entire nations. She was working with the same material that caused the incineration of nearly 70,000 people in Nagasaki. "You lean against the glove box glass," she said, "and within minutes you can feel the heat."

Tom Haverty got the order from his foreman one fall afternoon in the early '90s. It could've been '91 or '93, but jobs like this were frequent, and today, after so many surgeries and medications, he has trouble fixing them in time. He and a few fellow electrical engineers were instructed to report to a storage room in building 371, one of the facility's hottest. As was the case since he started at the Flats in 1984, this was a need-to-know assignment: A criticality head, or crit-head—one of several types of radiation-detecting alarms—in the room needed to be moved.

Crit-head reinstallation was a common enough job in the early '90s, but the irony never escaped Tom. Just a few years earlier, in 1989, acting on an internal DOE memo that cited "serious contamination" and "patently illegal waste facilities," the FBI had raided the Rocky Flats site. The 18-day bust made headlines across the country. It was the first time that one federal agency had raided another federal agency. The FBI, along with the Environmental Protection Agency, uncovered a disturbingly high number of environmental and health-safety violations—everything from poor record keeping to dumping radioactive waste in on-site creeks to dilution of water samples so that plutonium levels would look less drastic. Jon Lipsky, one of the FBI's lead Flats investigators, recently told me there were "inconsistencies that were punishable under penalty of perjury. The DOE didn't let anyone know what went on out there."

The raid put Rocky Flats on the national map—as a disaster. The EPA declared it a Superfund site, the most severe ranking that an environmentally unsafe area can receive. There was a three-year investigation and a grand jury convened. Rockwell International Corp., the private contractor running Rocky Flats at the time, pleaded guilty to five felony charges and was fined $18.5 million. Conditions at the Flats were so abhorrent that the Feds shut down weapons production and halted waste disposal until the place could get its act together. As Tom recently said, "Rocky Flats was constipated, but no one was allowed to give it an enema."

In the wake of the raid, waste had piled up at such a rapid rate that crit-heads were increasingly likely to sound, signaling a potential "criticality"—a nuclear chain reaction that could cause an explosion and radiate a swath of the Front Range. Although the Flats never experienced a criticality, it was an incessant threat. In addition to the likely human devastation, a criticality would have required the expensive and dangerous decontamination of the building. In the early 1990s, Tom often found himself detailed to criticality head assignments. He would suit up in a pair of thick lead aprons—one for the front, one for the back—and set about moving the alarms away from areas with high levels of radiation. It was a stop-gap measure at best, like moving a smoke detector away from a pile of matches and gasoline.

Life at the Flats satisfied the two sides of Tom—engineering nerd and adrenaline junkie. He told me about his adventures one summer evening as we rode in his Jeep along a dark forest road near his Huerfano

County mountain home. Talking in the certain but gravelly voice of a wizened uncle, Tom said that he'd joined the Navy and quickly became a sonar man, fiddling with knobs and dials to his great delight. Tom the risk taker couldn't get near a small plane without wanting to fly it or jump out of it. Tom the nerd later worked as an electronics technician at NASA back in '69, when Apollo 11 touched down. It was a milestone in American history, and Tom, then 29 and starting a family, was thrilled to be so close to the action. An electrical engineering gig at the Flats had everything Tom needed. "It was exciting, stimulating work that allowed me to serve my country," he told me. "I knew there were risks, but as an engineer this was as interesting and important as a job could get."

Tom worked lots of electrical engineering projects. For one, he recalls, he received a dire warning: You have 90 seconds to complete the job. A radiological control technician explained that the storage room that Tom was about to enter was so contaminated that any more than a minute or two inside was unsafe. DOE barrels were stacked and scattered throughout the room. They held every radioactive item that a bomb factory could cook up—machine parts, laundry, glove-box parts, coveralls, remnants from small fires. Tom felt like he was looking at a gaping radioactive wound: "It was one of those times when I'd be in the process area, and I'd look around and think, *My God. What have I gotten myself into?*"

Ninety seconds after entering the room, Tom was back out in the hallway, ditching his heavy lead aprons. A few weeks later, following Rocky Flats protocol, he dropped off his dosimeter at the lab for an official reading. He expected the worst. To his surprise, he received an impossible result: "no data available."

Judy Padilla didn't like what she saw. Too many of them were sick or dying or dead. Donald Gable died of a brain tumor after nine years working at the Flats—before he turned 33. Robert Clompton, a process-area worker in his early 40s, died of a brain stem tumor. Less than one percent of breast cancers occur in men, but Judy knew two process-area men who had malignant lumps.

In the late 1980s, Judy changed jobs, from metallurgical operator to a sheet-metal apprentice. The Flats facility newspaper profiled her as the plant's first "maid of steel." If a glove box needed to be repaired, she'd fix it. If a drill press needed a handle, she'd report to the machining area with her blowtorch. She was still around thorium, a radioactive element used in her welding equipment. And she spent significant chunks of time in the process areas within close range of plutonium. But, she reasoned, at least she wasn't standing in front of glove boxes with pinhole leaks or broken seals—at least she wasn't handling lavalike plutonium all day, feeling it radiate onto her torso.

Judy's sheet-metal job coincided with a major milestone in Rocky Flats history: the Cleanup. The Cold War was over, and in the wake of the negative publicity from the FBI raid, production at Rocky Flats remained at a standstill. Cleanup began in 1995, when a company named Kaiser-Hill signed the first of what became a two-part, $7 billion contract to demolish, decontaminate, and get rid of the site once and for all.

Rocky Flats was being destroyed, not built, and the demand for sheet-metal workers dwindled, so Judy trained to become a radiological control tech, or RCT. The tests were daunting—a three-part series of obscure chemistry and physics and elemental equations that looked like hieroglyphics and sounded like a Star Trek script. She took night courses and studied RCT manuals for dozens of hours each week. "That's when I found out about the biological effects of what we were exposed to," she told me. "Unless you were an RCT or a scientist, you didn't know that stuff." Almost as soon as she learned the ugly details about radiation exposure, Judy had a routine mammogram that "came back a little funny." In June 1998, her doctor called her at work with the news: breast cancer.

After a mastectomy Judy felt asymmetrical, vulnerable, incomplete. Her insurance covered the bulk of her medical expenses, but Judy's condition blindsided the Padillas like the wrecking balls that were knocking down Rocky Flats. Blonde hair fell from Judy's head as quickly as her body caved in. During chemo, she lost more than 20 pounds and learned to vomit with her piston-like efficiency. When she wasn't in class at Metro, Judy's 19-year-old daughter, Felicia, took care of her, as Judy's two sons were unable to be on the spot all the time. Judy's mother had the mornings. Charlie, who by now was driving an RTD bus for $11 an hour, cut his schedule, causing a devastating wage loss. Judy had never been so dependent on others. When she wasn't throwing up, she was dry heaving. Two days a week of chemo for two weeks, then two weeks off, then repeat. Judy did her big round of chemo on Thursdays, a 45-minute IV drip that she could taste in her mouth the minute it entered her arm, "like when you're a kid and you suck on a penny." She endured bouts of blurry vision, lesions in her mouth, and trips to the bathroom when it "felt like I was passing glass," she said. "I don't know which is worse, the disease or the cure."

Eight months after her diagnosis, Judy was still weak and sick. But she'd only received 60 percent sick pay, and there was just one way for her to make the kind of money necessary to support the family. One day in March 1999, she woke up, made a sack lunch, and headed back to work at the Flats.

The cleanup looked messy to Tom Haverty and to the more than a dozen Rocky Flats veterans and DOE experts I spoke with. Tom felt that the project was moving too fast. His disappointment was exacerbated by the bureaucracy at the Flats. Tom has a sharp, dark wit, but there was a saying around the plant that wiped the smile from his face: "For every person trying to do something at Rocky Flats, there's 47 others trying to prevent you from doing it, and 51 more yelling at you to do it faster." The status quo prevailed, and it crushed Tom's spirit. He tried to distract himself with hobbies and books. He made regular visits to the company shrink. In 2000, Tom decided he'd had enough.

The first five years away from the Flats, Tom road-tripped with his wife, Theresa, visited his children up and down the Front Range, and odd-jobbed around the little mountain getaway he'd finally managed to buy. One morning in November 2005, Tom checked into the emergency room at St. Joe's in Denver with an agonizing stomachache. He thought his appendix was about to burst. Tom woke up that afternoon to learn that 13 cancerous inches of his colon had been removed. The oncologist, Dr. Thomas Hyde, was sorry to inform him that several small tumors had already begun forming throughout his digestive system. He put Tom on intravenous chemotherapy, but told him not to expect any miracles. In all probability, he said, Tom would be dead inside of six months. Tom and Theresa shopped for a life insurance policy, but his poor health precluded him from coverage.

He got through the chemo—nine months of puking and cloudy-headedness. But a round of tests in November 2006 revealed a tumor behind his bladder and several precancerous nodules on his liver and abdomen. Doctors opened Tom up, did their best to remove the rot from his guts, prescribed a slew of drugs, and told him not to make any big plans for the future. Capecitabine, the peach-colored chemotherapy pill that Tom will swallow by the handful for the rest of his life, is best known for the following side effects: nausea, itchiness, vomiting, fatigue, weight loss, dizziness, memory loss. And one other thing.

"Do you know what diarrhea is?" Tom recently asked me. I was walking next to him as he speed-waddled toward a hospital-lobby men's room.

"Yes," I replied. "Of course."

Tom turned his head, shot me a smile as wide as a mushroom cloud, and said, "No, you don't."

The sick Rocky Flats veterans arrived by the dozens. They came on foot and in wheelchairs and with walkers, ambling through the conference center of the Westin hotel in Westminster this past May. They wore jeans and chinos and flannels and the occasional breathing apparatus. Some wore T-shirts that read, "Bury Rocky Flats, not the workers." Judy Padilla was there. Most were well into middle age and craggy-faced, with the calloused, meaty fingers of the blue-collar rats they once were. They had come to ask—to beg—the government to honor the law that it wrote for them.

The law is called the Energy Employees Occupational Illness Compensation Program Act, or EEOICPA (pronounced, e-oke-pah). Passed at the tail end of the Clinton Administration, EEOICPA was championed by Colorado Republican Senator Wayne Allard and a long list of legislators from both sides of the aisle, especially those whose constituents had close ties to nuclear weapons production. From page one, EEOICPA sounds less like a legal document and more like a confession. The document begins:

"Since World War II, Federal nuclear activities have been explicitly recognized under Federal law as activities that are ultra-hazardous."
A few lines down:

"... exposures to radioactive substances ... even in small amounts, can cause medical harm. More than two dozen scientific findings have

*emerged that indicate that certain [nuclear weapons workers] are
experiencing increased risks of dying from cancer."*

The law's preamble acknowledges what people like Judy and Tom
and the Rocky Flats veterans gathered at the Westin have believed for
years. It read:

> *"Since the inception of the nuclear weapons program and for several
> decades afterwards, a large number of nuclear weapons workers
> at sites of the Department of Energy and at sites of vendors who
> supplied the Cold War effort were put at risk without their knowledge
> and consent for reasons that, documents reveal, were driven by fears
> of adverse publicity, liability, and employee demands for hazardous
> duty pay.... No other hazardous Federal activity has been permitted
> to be carried out under such sweeping powers of self-regulation."*

EEOICPA's purpose is to recognize that nuclear weapons workers
with any of 22 kinds of cancers (among them breast, colon, bladder,
brain, and non-Hodgkin's lymphoma) are likely to have gotten their
illnesses on the job, and that poor record keeping or gross health-safety negligence make it difficult to know exactly who was exposed, and
to what extent. EEOICPA says that former weapons workers who are
"at least as likely as not" to have gotten cancer from radiation are entitled to medical benefits and a lump-sum payment of $150,000. The law
is an antidote to the legal action that workers might otherwise have to
take, at their own expense, if they believe they are entitled to worker's comp. A hundred and fifty grand's not exactly pay dirt for people
who've drained their bank accounts, taken out loans, or gone bankrupt
fighting cancer. But, if nothing else, the measure was a gesture of appreciation. EEOICPA let workers believe that the government's heart
was in the right place.

Seven years after the law passed, the crowd of Rocky Flats workers at
the Westin saw a government that was heartless. As far as the Flats brothers and sisters were concerned, their piece of star-spangled legislation had
been designed with loopholes and engineered to fail them. By now they
had learned that EEOICPA was undermined by "dose reconstruction," a
procedure that seemed more black magic than sound science.

Dose reconstruction is the responsibility of the National Institute for Occupational Safety and Health, or NIOSH. To reconstruct a radiation dose, NIOSH digs up whatever it can about a claimant—urinalysis, nasal swab results, medical files, DOE "incident" reports, dosimetry records, and personal histories. And therein lies the problem: Like Judy and Tom, everyone has a story. The more time I spent talking to former Rocky Flats employees, the more anecdotes I heard about faulty dosimeters and dubious orders. Two former government officials insisted that medical records "disappeared" during the 1989 FBI raid. A former administrative assistant says she was ordered to illegally shred workers' medical records in the 1990s. Some people I spoke to were still shackled by the culture of secrecy; when I'd press them for details, they'd clam up. One man simply quit talking to me the moment I opened my notebook. Despite overwhelming consistencies among workers' stories of questionable health safety, only a fraction of what they say can be corroborated. It's their word. None of them had the foresight to build a case history while they were producing bombs, cleaning up an environmental disaster, and tending to their lives. And the government's dose reconstruction program dismisses almost any anecdote that a worker cannot prove.

When a claimant's records are missing or incomplete, NIOSH will use "coworker data"—records from a colleague who performed a similar job at a similar point in time. NIOSH also refers to a "site profile"—a multipage report that the agency has created for some of the 79 weapons facilities in the United States that summarizes which parts of a site were most radioactive and when. (Site profiles do not exist for all facilities.) In the end, the hard data get sent to the Department of Labor, plugged into a "matrix," and tallied to determine a figure known as "probability of causation," or POC. The POC is the claimant's final score; it informs Labor if the claimant was "at least as likely as not" to have gotten cancer due to work at a nuclear weapons facility. Claimants with a POC of 50 percent or higher are compensated. Claimants with a POC of 49.99 percent or lower are not.

Judy Padilla applied for compensation in August 2001—and waited nearly four years for a response. Her dose reconstruction score was 42.19; she was denied. She appealed the decision to the Department of Labor, explaining that she'd worked around ionizing radiation for the better part of 14 years, and that six of those years were spent chest-to-glove box, handling plutonium. Seven of her remaining eight years, she reminded the DOL, were spent working with thorium-equipped welding gear and completing tasks in the process areas. Like her coworkers, she'd seen or been near more fires and spills and accidents—some reported, some not—than she could count. She was a healthy, exercising nonsmoker, and two genetic tests showed no history of breast cancer in her family. Judy's appeal was denied.

Tom Haverty applied in July 2006. DOL still hasn't issued a decision, but a NIOSH worker recently told him that his prospects weren't good. Speaking by phone, the representative, Brian, told Tom he couldn't give specifics, but he indicated that Tom's score was less than 50. He said that Tom's final answer from DOL could take another eight months. Tom matter-of-factly stated that he'd likely be dead by then. Brian delivered news to Tom with the detached aplomb of an airline gate agent telling a passenger that his flight's been cancelled. It was clear that Brian had done this before.

Nearly 3,000 Rocky Flats workers have applied for compensation under this portion of EEOICPA; only 626, or 20 percent, have been paid. More than 69,000 weapons workers (or their families) across the country have submitted claims; at least one-third of them have been denied. The reason for their denials boils down to the dose reconstruction results— meaning they couldn't prove that they were "at least as likely as not" to have gotten cancer from radiation. They were given the burden of proof.

Larry Elliott oversees NIOSH's dose reconstruction program, and he defends his agency's work. "What most people don't understand is that dose reconstruction is an accepted scientific program to fill data gaps," he recently told me. "A high percentage of Rocky Flats workers have monitoring records, and NIOSH has those records." But, he went on, not all people were monitored. "We do not have individual monitoring records for every worker." He spoke of "unknown primaries" and "upper ranges." He assured me that dose reconstruction was set up to be as "claimant favorable" as possible.

Outside of NIOSH, it's tough to find anyone who supports the way the agency applies dose reconstruction. Richard Miller has worked as a senior policy analyst for the D.C. watchdog group Government Accountability Project and as a staff representative for DOE employees. Just last year, testifying before a House Judiciary Subcommittee, he said glove-box workers handling radiation at Rocky Flats (and other sites around the country) "were not adequately shielded for many years…[dosimeter] readings did not necessarily capture the neutron dose from leaky glove boxes, since the badges were not positioned near the parts of the glove box that leaked radiation." Tom Haverty's translation: "Radiation can blow up your skirt. It can radiate your skull. We wore dosimeters around our necks, not on our heads."

Even champions of the EEOICPA law acknowledge that the process of dose reconstruction is debatable. They point out that this particular brand of science was originally modeled to study large, unmonitored populations, like survivors of Hiroshima and Nagasaki, who were exposed to a single big blast, or atomic veterans who were involved in early weapons testing—not individuals who were exposed to low levels of radiation over long periods of time.

"When the bill was written, people on the Hill knew that any kind of science was imperfect—the law was even amended a few times to try to address that," Cindy Blackston, a former Judiciary staffer intimate with EEOICPA, recently told me. "But science is only as good as the perspective of the individual interpreting it. Some people within the system have interpreted the law so that claimants are placed on the defensive—which is exactly what the law was supposed to remedy. In many cases, the good intentions of EEOICPA have been abandoned."

In theory, claimants who are rejected have some recourse: They can form a group and petition to be added to the "special exposure cohort" (SEC). If an SEC petition gets the green light, the dose reconstruction process is effectively waived, and claims are more likely to be paid. In other words, legislators wrote a bill knowing that it was flawed, and built in a safety net that acknowledged those hiccups. The SEC isn't much different than the original law. If a group of cancer victims wants SEC status, NIOSH requires them to do what they failed to accomplish as individual claimants: Prove what cannot be proven.

In 2005, the Rocky Flats steelworkers' union, Local 8031, filed an SEC petition. NIOSH eventually adjusted the petition such that any eligible Rocky Flats veteran could apply. According to EEOICPA, approval can only be granted by a 12-person, presidentially appointed Advisory Board.

This board spends a good bit of its time traveling city to city for meetings about SEC petitions. And in May it wound up at the Westin in Westminster. The prospects looked grim for Rocky Flats vets: Since EEOICPA became effective in 2001, the board has been frugal about handing out Special Exposure Cohorts. For most of the day, board members talked at length about the vagaries of nuclear science and the legitimacy of dose reconstruction. They stopped a few times to listen as government officials phoned in to plead with them—to insist that the board vote in favor of the Rocky Flats petition. It was a full-court, bipartisan press. Governor Bill Ritter called in. So did Senators Ken Salazar and Wayne Allard, among others. The board members listened with chins in hands and furrowed brows. Everyone in the room perked up when Barack Obama called in and asked that the board give our Cold War veterans a "small measure of justice."

Public comments started late in the afternoon. The sign-up list was several pages long. Nearly everyone—even the leather-faced tough guys—couldn't finish speaking without crying. A security guard named Richard said he never even had a dosimeter. He believed he got cancer from background radiation emanating through a thin, unprotected wall that he sat against. Many of his records were missing, but his claim was denied anyway. Walter, a skinny man with thick glasses, had non-Hodgkin's lymphoma. He explained that, as his radiation counts got high in the early '90s, his records somehow went missing. He dealt with NIOSH for five years—then they denied him. There were more stories—of male breast cancer and dosimeters that read "no data available," of financial strain and bankruptcy and second mortgages taken out to cover medical costs and lost wages. Judy Padilla gave a long and impassioned speech. "As a former nuclear worker at Rocky Flats, I am a Cold War veteran," she said. "I feel that I sacrificed my health like the soldiers in Iraq are doing. And we got no acknowledgment—and no 'thank you'—from our government. We don't even get the courtesy of a flag on our coffins when we die." Fighting back tears of rage, she told the Advisory Board, "What some of us would give to be in your shoes. You have your health, and all that power! Our lives and peace of mind rest in your hands. We're like the men on death row waiting for a phone call from the governor."

When decision time came, board member Michael Gibson gave a short but poignant speech in favor of the petitioners. He cited the workers' stories of unrecorded exposure, their financial struggles, the fact that they were fighting with the government while fighting to stay alive. "I listened to all the presentations from NIOSH and heard all the stories from the workers," Gibson later told me. "I weighed both sides and came to the conclusion that these claimants were exposed to radiation in ways that could never be proven." Gibson, who worked for two decades as an electrician and union officer at the Mound facility in Miamisburg, Ohio, added, "Trying to reconstruct a dose from hard data is difficult enough. Reconstructing a dose with data that's absent of hard records is somewhat of an art. There were unexpected events that were not set up for monitoring. I know those sorts of things happened because I saw them first-hand when I worked for DOE. The people of Rocky Flats deserve to have this petition approved."

Another board member proposed partial approval for a sliver of Rocky Flats workers; his suggestion was as convoluted and confusing as EEOICPA and the science of dose reconstruction itself. Even the other board members looked dumbfounded. Yet inexplicably they voted for the cryptic measure, right then and there. The workers cocked their heads and mumbled. The room hummed with the sound of befuddlement and frustration, like a town hall meeting just before the fight scene in a Western. One might have expected the local drunk to stand up in back and start ranting. Confronted with the palpable tension in the room, the board deliberated for several minutes, collectively shrugging its shoulders and appearing to grow as confused and frustrated as the crowd. They decided that they should leave Denver, reconsider the petition, and return some other time for yet another round of deliberations.

A month later in the conference room of the Lakewood Sheraton, the Advisory Board decided that three small groups of workers who were at Rocky Flats before 1970 should be added to the Special Exposure Cohort. The Flats veterans saw it as an empty gesture, noting that by the time the board's decision is finalized, most of those workers would either be dead or close to dead. Anyone who worked at the Flats between 1970 and 2005 was out of luck: No Special Exposure Cohort. No compensation.

A few days later, I visited Tom Haverty at his mountain home. It was the first of many conversations we had over the summer. We ate dinner and took in the view of the Spanish Peaks. "I'm a Cold War veteran, like a veteran of any other war," Tom told me. "I didn't go to Iraq and take a bullet, but I went to Rocky Flats and took a neutron for my country." Tom and I talked late into the night—about the culture of secrecy at Rocky Flats, about the various private contractors that managed the site for more than 50 years. We talked about the "sweeping powers of self-regulation" noted in EEOICPA's preamble, and the half century of oftentimes unsavory management within the Department of Energy nuclear weapons complex—during production, during the FBI investigation, and during the cleanup. And we talked about how the government manages the EEOCIPA program with the same disregard for workers that DOE and its contractors practiced. From past to present, across multiple agencies, the flaws were as incessant as they were systemic. I asked Tom for his take. He paused for a moment, distilled his thoughts, and spoke. It was one of the few times I'd see him without a smile. "That's a simple question," he said. "Follow the money."

After a government sub-contractor, Rockwell International Corp., rendered the Flats a Superfund site, a new government contractor, Kaiser-Hill, was hired to clean it up. In 1995, the Department of Energy estimated that the project would take more than 60 years and cost $37 billion dollars. Once the project was under way, Kaiser-Hill developed more ambitious goals: 10 years, $7 billion. If the company could meet its target, it stood to make considerable cash incentives, paid by the DOE. The faster the job got done, the more Kaiser-Hill stood to earn.

On several occasions, the Department of Energy confronted Kaiser-Hill president Robert G. Card about "programmatic breakdown[s]" regarding health and environmental safety. A July 20, 1998 memo to Card from the DOE's Office of Enforcement and Investigation notes shoddy work that "led to potential violations of DOE [quality assurance] and radiological protection requirements." A follow-up memo to Card, in 2000, pointed out the "recurring nature of [safety] deficiencies" and "failures of the Kaiser-Hill Company...to correct quality assurance deficiencies." The list of previous safety concerns included insufficient storage of radioactive waste. Kaiser-Hill was fined $55,000.

Still the money flowed. One executive secretary told me she hand-delivered a bonus check for $257,000 to Card's office. If Kaiser-Hill could pull off the cleanup by 2006 as promised, institutionally it stood to make a "target payment" of $340 million. The contractor exceeded expectations. By 2001, Robert G. Card had done such a heck of a job that President Bush plucked him from Kaiser-Hill and appointed him undersecretary of the Department of Energy. While Card was a top man at DOE, the *New York Times* published a 2002 article called "Questions Raised Over Energy Dept. Official's Industry Ties." The story noted that "Mr. Card supervises the Office of Environmental Management, which is in charge of cleaning up nuclear waste sites and manages the contracts of his old companies." In 2004, Card left the DOE. He's now working for CH2M Hill, the parent company of Kaiser-Hill.

Card did not respond to multiple e-mail and phone requests to be interviewed, but a CH2M Hill spokesperson, John Corsi, said that Kaiser-Hill's management of the cleanup was executed with utmost concern for environmental and worker safety. He noted that Kaiser-Hill's work was widely recognized with awards from the American Council of Engineering Companies, the American Academy of Environmental Engineers, and the Project Management Institute. Corsi stated the amount of Card's $257,000 check is incorrect, adding, "It is not appropriate for us to discuss the details of compensation for any employee of the project." He also pointed out that many of the "spot recognition" bonuses received by Kaiser-Hill employees were the result of outstanding health safety practices. "On our watch, it was much safer at Rocky Flats than it was at other times," he said.

Safety at the Flats has always been a relative term. But nothing is clearer than a bottom line. Pressure is still on the Department of Labor to nip and tuck its budget, including spending on EEOICPA. In late 2005, Shelby Hallmark, the deputy assistant secretary at DOL, sent a memo to the Office of Management and Budget with a five-point plan to reduce spending, or as he put it, "contain growth in the cost of benefits provided by [EEOICPA]." The memo was leaked, and Hallmark denied any intent to see his plan to fruition. But that didn't matter. The average annual budget for claims under this portion of EEOICPA hovers at a scant $100 million. Over the past six years, DOL has spent $869 million on radiation-induced cancer claims under EEOICPA—a pittance when compared with spending on other government programs, like defense ($432 billion) or homeland security ($32 billion).

What's more, the Department of Labor allows the National Institute of Occupational Safety and Health to pay private contractors to perform dose reconstruction. In other words, while the Department of Labor avoids paying millions on claims, people in the private sector are making millions from the government contracts—and from a program that denies payments to sick and dying claimants. The main contractor in charge of dose reconstruction is called Oak Ridge Associated Universities, or ORAU, a Tennessee-based 501(c)(3) that has received financial support and personnel from the Department of Energy for several decades. ORAU and DOE share such a cozy history that it's difficult to tell them apart. "ORAU was nurtured by the DOE," one well-placed source, who insisted on anonymity, recently told me. "No, ORAU is the DOE."

In 2002, not long after EEOICPA passed, NIOSH awarded Oak Ridge Associated Universities a $70 million contract to handle the bulk of its dose reconstruction work. ORAU, in turn, subcontracted some of its work to other firms. It could be a simple enough public-private arrangement, but it could be a conflict of interest. By law, DOE workers are forbidden to perform dose reconstruction, and technically no one at DOE does. But, as New Mexico Congressman Tom Udall pointed out last year to a judiciary subcommittee, an overwhelming number of dose reconstruction team members working for ORAU and its subcontractors built their careers working for the DOE, oftentimes at weapons facilities.

NIOSH requires dose reconstruction workers to fill out a conflict-of-interest form. But consider Roger Falk. Between 1996 and 1998, Falk was responsible for monitoring worker radiation at Rocky Flats, back when Kaiser-Hill was tearing the place down. Falk then went to work for ORAU, where he was partly responsible for creating the Rocky Flats site profile, the document that's considered the bible by dose reconstruction team members.

"When a site profile is put together by someone who worked at that very site, the accounts of workers are not given equal weight," advisory board member Michael Gibson told me. "It's a situation where these people from DOE have found a second life [at ORAU]. It's hard for them to criticize their own work, or the work of their colleagues. And those conflicts of interests are not exclusive to Rocky Flats." ORAU never took Falk off the Rocky Flats project, but it updated the site profile he created. However, critics have noted that the old document and the updated version are virtually identical. Little remains changed besides the signature on the cover sheets.

NIOSH's Larry Elliott says that former DOE workers are the most qualified to perform dose reconstruction. "The pool of dose reconstruction workers is shallow and narrow," he said. Indeed, health physics is a niche industry with roots in the weapons industry. But there are also health physicists without such direct ties to the weapons plants—such as those working for radiological-equipment vendors. As the well-placed source who insisted on anonymity put it, "It's not that ORAU has the best health physicists; they have the contracts. You could find someone to do a credible job of dose reconstruction who isn't mired in conflict of interest." What you're looking at here, the source said, is a "plug-and-chug gravy train."

By the end of 2006, ORAU's $70 million contract to perform dose reconstruction had ballooned to $280 million. That dollar amount, it's worth noting, would be enough money to pay 1,800 claimants.

Tom Haverty recently called me with some bad news. He'd sat down on the toilet and lost, by his own estimation, a pint and a half of blood. Doctors performed a colonoscopy and found another tumor. When I visited Tom at Good Samaritan in Lafayette, he was groggy from blood loss and four days on an IV. He told me he had three choices, each a slow version of certain death. First was complicated surgery that would require prostate and colon removal. As he put it, "They'd have to scoop out pretty much everything down there," leaving him to go through life with a colostomy bag. Choice number two was another round of intravenous chemotherapy. Option three: nothing at all. Tom told me, "I'm still deciding between extension of life and quality of life."

I stayed at Good Samaritan for an hour. Tom told me more stories about Rocky Flats with his usual understated wit. When the room grew quiet, we watched grizzly bears on TV with no volume. A chaplain stopped by, and Tom explained to her why I was in the room. The chaplain asked Tom if he thought his many cancers were the result of his 16 years at a nuclear weapons facility. Tom just smiled. She then asked Tom if he'd like her services. Tom, a Catholic, said yes. The chaplain, a Lutheran, asked if her denomination was a problem. Without so much as a pause, Tom smiled at the chaplain and said, "God doesn't check your passport."

It's all gone now. Buildings 707, 771, 371, all of them. The barrels and the two-seater carts and the glove boxes and the trailers and the guard towers. All of it was deconstructed and demolished. Tens of thousands of cubic yards and containers full of radioactive waste—the secrets and ghosts of a bygone era. Some of it was buried out there. Some of it was shipped to New Mexico for deep-earth storage. Contamination levels in the ground are debated, inspected, and may still cause further damage in a few years, or a few decades. Today, in a twist that seems plausible only in an episode of *The Simpsons*, Rocky Flats is being turned into a wildlife refuge.

On a recent summer day, Judy Padilla's husband, Charlie, steered their old Ford Bronco onto a narrow shoulder on Indiana Avenue, where the east entrance to Rocky Flats used to be. The three of us hopped out of the vehicle and took in the view—Arvada and Broomfield to the east, the foothills to the west. A breeze blew tall grass over barbed wire decorated with old DOE signs. Judy pointed to the spot where the old checkpoint area stood, just before a small hill that concealed the little city of Rocky Flats. We took a walk along the shoulder of the road, past a small creek that once carried contaminated waste off the plant site. She pointed out the old Broomfield Reservoir, which had gotten so crapped up from the Flats that it could no longer be used as a drinking water source.

It was hard to imagine that this tiny woman once made the weapons that threatened to destroy the world. She looked like a little old lady in the making, someone who would chase off hooligans with an umbrella. Eight years after her cancer diagnosis, she finally felt healthy and strong. And nothing about Judy revealed how sick she once was, or so easily could be tomorrow. "I feel like a ticking time bomb," she said. "I could go off at any minute."

—November 2007

16.

Conduct Unbecoming

by Maximillian Potter

It was after midnight, and Jacqueline Woods, an 18-year-old freshman at the United States Air Force Academy, was feeling too ashamed to sleep. She flicked on her computer and saw that her brother, an academy senior who lived in a neighboring dorm, was also online. As they began exchanging instant messages, she decided to tell him what had happened—at least what she could remember.

Hey, Josh, I need to talk to you about something serious but I don't know if I can.

What is it?

Last night, I did something really stupid and it turned out really, really bad.

Like what?

Woods explained that the night before—October 18, 2002—she had downed a squeeze bottle full of booze in her quarters and then went to the nearby room of sophomores Douglas Meester and Jason Wager. There, with Meester, Wager, and Robert Rando, a junior, she drank even more.

[I] got completely messed up to the point where I couldn't hold myself up. And for pretty much the whole night I guess I was hanging off of Rando, but he was messed up too and was trying to make arrangements to kick his roommate out so we could go over there, but still I was too out of it to know what all was really going on. It seemed like everything wasn't real.

OK.

The even more fucked up part was the stupid [Meester] who's room we were in, [who's] on frickin' alcohol probation and all this shit, kept tryin' to make out with me every time Rando left the room to kick his roommate out. Finally Rando was gone for like 15 minutes or something and I had to be propped up by [Meester] and I guess he thought because I was leaning all over him that I wanted to get on him – but I started blacking out at that point. It was like in and out, but basically the guy was messin' with me because I couldn't really move.

Anything else?

Anyway, he had to like carry me back and I was still fuckin' out of it until like 10 a.m.—but then I would get flashes of things that happened last night that I didn't remember and just everything's fucked up.

Flashes of what?

Like stuff the guy was doing to me.

What was he doing?

Everything and it's all my fault.

Did he rape you?

Yes.

Within minutes, Josh was in his sister's room. Within hours, he ushered her off campus to a hospital in nearby Colorado Springs, where she underwent a sexual-assault medical exam and met with agents from the Air Force Office of Special Investigations (OSI). Woods formally alleged that Meester had raped her while she was inebriated and "semi-conscious."

Within six months, OSI completed its investigation and the chief investigation officer (IO) produced a 21-page memorandum that summarized the facts of the case. The report, which, along with supporting witness statements obtained by *5280*, listed reason on top of reason to dismiss Woods's claim that the intercourse had been rape. Among the evidence was a statement Woods herself had made to OSI agents that night at the hospital: "I know for a fact that he [Meester] probably thought what we were doing was consensual because I know that I was responding to what he was doing (i.e., If he would kiss me, I would kiss him back)."

The IO's report was promptly sent to the interim head of the Air Force Academy, Brig. Gen. Johnny A. Weida. In the military justice system, it is up to the commanding officer of an accused soldier to decide whether allegations merit prosecution. Although commanding officers almost always ratify an IO's recommendation, in this case Weida rejected the advice and ordered that Meester stand trial.

A preliminary hearing in the court-martial of Douglas Meester is scheduled for March, with the trial set to start in May. Twenty-year-old Meester will be the first Air Force cadet ever prosecuted for cadet-on-cadet rape; he faces a possible sentence of life in prison. At trial, Meester will insist that he and Woods got drunk and had consensual sex. He will insist that he is a pawn in a show trial staged by Air Force brass who do not want to accept responsibility for covering up decades of sexual assault and misogyny at the prestigious military institution. And he may be right.

Douglas Meester takes a seat on the couch inside his father's Florida home. In his academy head shot, the one that has accompanied countless newspaper stories about the case, Meester appears ramrod straight in his dress blues, smiling the smile of a young flyboy on an autopilot course to success. Seeing the photo, you might peg him as a tall, strapping guy. But on this August afternoon, two months after Weida ordered his court-martial, Meester barely resembles that cadet. He is of average height, thin, and gangling. His face and physique are all straight lines and right angles, except for his slumped shoulders. Perched on the edge of the couch, he nervously rubs his knees and his eyes flit about. This is the first time Meester has talked with a journalist, and thus far the press has skewered him.

Meester, like Woods, left the Academy after the semester of the incident, and he has since followed the media coverage of his case. He read Jim Spencer's *Denver Post* column in which Meester was compared to a necrophiliac. He's watched television pundits speculate about what they think he did or should have done on that drunken night. He even saw the Senate subcommittee hearings on C-SPAN, and heard politicians presume him guilty. "To smear my name in the media simply because of allegations, I think is ridiculous," Meester says. "It's absurd. The Academy, the press, I think the rush to condemn me is a result of the scandal."

The now infamous Air Force Academy scandal began last January, just four months after Woods filed her report with OSI, when several former female cadets first told *Westword*'s Julie Jargon and shortly thereafter told 7 News (KMGH-TV) reporter John Ferrugia that they had been raped by male cadets. What's more, they claimed that when they took their charges to the Academy's chain of command, the women were blamed, punished, and informed their military careers would be ruined unless they dropped the accusations, while their alleged rapists received administrative slaps on the wrist.

The story quickly commanded national headlines. In response, Academy officials publicly insisted that the school had "zero tolerance" for sexual assault, and by way of proof it released statistics claiming that since 1990 it had investigated 56 reports of sexual assault and disciplined 20 male cadets. But of those cases, only one—a 1998 incident involving a civilian and a cadet—resulted in a rape conviction. The rest were reduced to lesser charges, and in most cases resulted in punishments as insignificant as disciplinary demerits (or "hits," as they are known in cadet lingo). When pressed, the Academy was forced to admit that it had never prosecuted a case of cadet-on-cadet rape.

In fact, the school's second highest-ranking officer seemed downright unsympathetic to the charges being made by its female students. Asked to comment on the case of a cadet who claimed she'd been raped by another cadet at an off-campus party, Brig. Gen. Taco Gilbert issued a statement: "When you put yourself in situations with increased risk, you have to take increased precautions to mitigate those risks. For example, if I walk down a dark alley with hundred-dollar bills hanging from my pockets, it doesn't justify my being attacked or robbed, but I certainly increased my risks by doing what I did."

In the midst of the ensuing media frenzy, Air Force Secretary James Roche relieved the Academy's top four officials from duty, including Gilbert and the Academy's superintendent, Gen. James Dallagher. Roche also dispatched a task force to Colorado Springs to investigate. The team was on campus for 10 days and left without interviewing any alleged victims. Critics called Roche's actions a sham.

The Defense Department, the Air Force Inspector General, and the U.S. Senate subsequently all launched their own investigations. The senate's seven-member team, led by former Florida congresswoman Tillie Fowler, found that in the past decade academy officials had, in fact, received sexual-assault allegations from at least 142 cadets—more than twice the number of cases (56) that the Academy had reported investigating. Fowler also discovered an entrenched institutional misogyny that has existed from the very first year women were admitted to the Academy in 1977. Reading through cadet responses to the Academy's internal 2002 "Social Climate Survey," Fowler found that some male cadets wrote, "Even with women in the Armed Forces they should not be at the military academies," and "Women are worthless and should be taken away from the USAFA."

As the scandal peaked this past June, the Senate Armed Services subcommittee convened a hearing. Alleged victims testified, as did the ousted Academy leaders. Sen. John McCain, who chaired the hearings, called the brass's testimony "one of the most remarkable evasions of responsibility I have ever seen.... The Secretary of the Air Force has proven, to our satisfaction, that he cannot and will not address this crisis at the Air Force Academy in a mature and efficient fashion."

One week later, Roche demoted Gen. Dallagher from three stars to two. Dallagher's interim replacement, Gen. Weida, decided to court-martial Meester.

"I had faith that the Air Force would do the right thing and dismiss [Jacqueline's] claim," says Meester's father, Doug Sr., sitting on the couch next to his son. "But I don't anymore. I don't think they care about justice; this court-martial is about PR and politics. All the Academy wants is a pound of flesh to cover their ass."

It's the sort of thing you might expect a father in this situation to say. But Jacqueline Woods's mother, Marie, has an equally cynical take on the unprecedented court-martial. "The Academy doesn't care about my daughter," she told me as we talked in her home outside Philadelphia. (Jacqueline refused to be interviewed for this story, but she sat in the next room as I talked to her mother.) "I've believed all along that Academy brass and Secretary Roche got together and talked about this case and what they could do to make themselves and the Air Force Academy look good. I think they want to put her on the stand and have her raked over the coals and peel back her skin. They think that if they can discredit [Jacqueline], they can discredit all the other girls who have reported being raped."

Air Force cadets get one of the best college educations taxpayer money can buy; in return, graduates serve as officers for at least five years. It works the same way at the other three U.S. service academies—the Army's West Point, the Navy's Annapolis, and the U.S. Coast Guard Academy. And, like the students who are accepted to those institutions, Air Force cadets are some of the best students American high schools have to offer. The 1,052 men and 224 women who entered the Academy last fall as the class of 2007 had an average high school GPA of 3.9 and an average SAT score of 1,290. Sixty-six percent were members of the National Honor Society, 96 percent played at least one varsity sport, and 10 percent were student-body presidents. The majority choose the Air Force Academy because they want to fly. Meester and Woods chose the school for other reasons.

Meester enrolled with the class of '05 searching for stability. When he was five years old, his folks divorced, and throughout his teen years, he began dividing his time and emotions while coping with the usual adolescent pressures. In high school, he enjoyed the kind of pursuits that impose order on the universe: science and math classes, the chess and debate teams, and drilling with his high school ROTC program. The summer after his sophomore year, Meester attended a science camp at the Academy and was immediately impressed by the aeronautics-heavy curriculum and the program's spit-and-polish certainty. "I thought it was a prestigious, clear-cut, no-BS kind of place," he says. "If you stick to it, you know exactly the path you can go. There's no chance. No ambiguity as to what it is you're going to do with yourself."

Woods came to Colorado Springs because her brother Josh had raved about the Academy and because she wanted to be with her boyfriend. After Josh left for the Academy, the Woods volunteered as host family for Academy prep students who were attending a local military high school. One day, the Woods had some preppers over for pizza and a movie, and while *Top Gun* played on the television, 14-year-old Jacqueline and 18-year-old prepper Zeke Cuny flirted their way into a romance. Because the Academy prohibits fraternization of cadets in different classes, when Woods entered the Academy she and Cuny pledged to stop dating until after Cuny graduated.

Woods and Meester were average but active cadets. Woods, who had founded her high school's fencing team, became a Falcon foilist. Meester made the debate squad. Both got so-so grades, and both had disciplinary problems shortly after arriving. A cadet's first year is structured to be the most challenging one, and it was hard on both of them. Each June, just minutes after the new cadets, or "doolies," arrive on campus, they are marched through an intensely regimented routine: They say good-bye to their parents and then file onto buses that transport them up a long, windy road into the heart of the Academy. Onboard each bus are two upperclassmen, and as the buses pull away, one of them barks, "Take a good look at your families—you're not going to see them for a long time! Now you belong to the United States Air Force." It's a ritual intended to quickly force the doolies into submission. (Several years ago, as the buses pulled onto campus and parked under a massive sign that read "Bring Me Men," upperclassmen crowded around and beat on the windows so forcefully that one shattered, showering glass over the terrified cadets.)

From mid-June until the end of August, doolies attend Basic Cadet Training. At this mini boot camp, upperclassmen/instructors give the freshman, according to cadet lexicon, a weeks-long "beating." When the academic year begins in September, the physical rigors subside, but the environment is no less intense. Doolies carry a grueling course load and many of them participate in extracurricular activities. There is little freedom. They are not allowed phones, CD players, or TVs. They are rarely permitted off base. And throughout the year, they remain under the command of all three upperclasses. Unless otherwise directed, doolies (the term comes from the Greek "duolos," meaning slave) may only address their cadet-superiors with one of the following seven phrases:

Yes, Sir/Ma'am.
No, Sir/Ma'am.
No excuse, Sir/Ma'am.
Sir/Ma'am, may I make a statement?
Sir/Ma'am, may I ask a question?
Sir/Ma'am, I do not understand.
Sir/Ma'am, I do not know.

When you're a new cadet the idea is you're developing, so you go through a hard year and prove you want to be at the academy," says junior cadet Justin Hickey. "You learn to follow so that one day you can lead. And the thing is, if you screw up in your freshman year, if you get yourself in academic or disciplinary trouble, there's very little chance you'll get straight. We call it the 'Trouble Bubble.' It's like, when you get here you have a clean slate, you're in a bubble of perfect-ness, but once you get in trouble your bubble has burst and you're pretty much doomed."

Meester's bubble burst toward the end of his doolie year. Drinking alcohol in the cadet dormitories is prohibited regardless of a cadet's age, but one Saturday night Meester and a couple of squad mates polished off a few bottles of liquor in his dorm room. He shoved the empties in a backpack and the next morning got nailed with the contraband during a squadron-wide surprise inspection. It was a serious, yet common offense.

Last fall, an Academy survey revealed that at least 52 percent of seniors and more than one-third of freshman drank in their dorms. It's hardly surprising that cadets find a way to party when they get a break. After all, they're college students and they're dealing with a pressure-soaked environment that would break most adults. When Secretary Roche's task force last year interviewed Col. Laurie Sue Slavec, who was in charge of cadet discipline at the time (she has since been transferred), she said that despite the Academy's strict written policy against alcohol in the dorms, "Partying is encouraged and partying is a ticket to acceptance." School officials put Meester on a six-month probation for drinking—one more violation for booze and he was out—but the reality was his squad mates were now high-fiving him in the hallway and calling him "The Bartender."

Two months into her first term, Woods's Trouble Bubble burst. She got into a couple of arguments with her fencing coach, and in front of the team she addressed the coach in a manner he felt was disrespectful. He told her she had an "attitude problem" and suspended her from the squad for a month. The day she was informed of her suspension, Woods decided to quit fencing and tried out for the gymnastics team. The fencing coach found out, had her banned from all Academy athletic teams, and reprimanded her for insubordination.

On that Friday night in October 2002, Woods and Meester were both stressed out, angry, and already tiring of what they saw as institutional hypocrisy. In his room, Meester cracked open bottles of vodka and Southern Comfort and downed at least 10 shots. In her room, Woods drank from a plastic water bottle filled with booze. The specific contents were a mystery to her because it was something the student officer in charge of her dorm had dropped off as a "morale booster" after he heard about her problems with the fencing coach. When Woods finished the bottle, she got on her computer and received an instant message from former fencing teammate Robert Rando. The e-mail said, "I'll hook you up with booze, if you'll hook up with me." Twenty minutes later, around 11 p.m., she and Rando were sitting in Meester and Wager's room.

Meester, The Bartender, pulled out a bottle of Jose Cuervo tequila, some shot glasses, salt, and a lime. He had talked with Woods once before, but only briefly, so they got reacquainted while Rando cut up the lime. Then Woods turned off the overhead lights, flicked on a desk lamp, and poured the first round.

Two or three shots later, according to OSI documents, Rando explained to Woods what a "body shot" was, and Woods said she was game. Rando licked the salt from her neck, downed the shot, and sucked the lime slice she held in her mouth. Doing the body shot made her uncomfortable, Woods later told OSI, but she didn't want the guys to think she was uptight. She did another body shot with Rando, only this time she did the licking and sucking, and licked the salt off his bare chest. After watching Rando and Woods do at least three body shots each, Meester decided to jump in. "I'll show you how to do a body shot," he said. He lifted up Woods's sweatshirt and sports bra—Meester and Wager would tell OSI that she helped Meester lift her clothes—and, without protest from Woods, Meester did a body shot off of her left breast.

Several times throughout the night, Woods glanced at her watch. Although she and her boyfriend, Zeke Cuny, had pledged to end their romance, they hadn't done so. That night, the couple had plans to meet in her room at 1 a.m. As the night continued, though, Woods told OSI, she was "clingy" with Rando. She sat in his lap. They kissed. Rando told her that she was all he had wanted for months. Twice, Rando left the drinking party and went across the hall to his room, trying unsuccessfully to get his roommate to leave so that he could be alone with Woods. At least twice, while Rando was gone, Woods allowed Meester to kiss her. Once when Rando came back into Meester's room, Woods asked him, "Are you jealous because I'm kissing Meester?"

Around 1:30 a.m.—half an hour past Woods's rendezvous time with her boyfriend—the booze was gone. Rando left, and Wager followed to use the bathroom. Woods stayed with Meester. In the two and a half hours that the cadets had been together, Wager did three shots, Rando did at least 10, and Meester and Woods each did six. For Meester, that was six on top of the 10 he drank by himself earlier, and for Woods, who is 5 feet 2 inches tall and weighs 118 pounds, that was six on top of the seven-ounce squirt bottle of mystery booze she downed.

When Wager returned from the bathroom, he found Meester and Woods standing in the middle of the room, making out. Wager told them that he had no intention of leaving. Meester and Woods looked at him and laughed, so he got into bed, turned his face to the wall, and fell asleep.

On his bed, Meester removed Woods's sweatpants and performed oral sex on her. At that point, as Woods told OSI, the alcohol had rendered her "completely numb." She wasn't sure, but thought she felt Meester's tongue inside her. About this time, Rando told OSI, he came back into Meester's room and saw Woods in bed moving her arms around, apparently in response to something Meester was doing. He left the room and did not come back in, because, he said, the next time he approached Meester's door he heard Woods moaning.

Woods doesn't remember how intercourse began, because, according to her OSI statement, she had blacked out; she remembers waking up in the missionary position. "[I felt] incredibly guilty and dirty, as if my boyfriend was in the room watching us," she said, "and also feeling incredibly insecure, wondering, Does he know my name? So I asked him, 'What's my name?' He said, 'Jacqueline.' But then I blacked out again."

"Doggy-style intercourse" occurred next, according to Meester's OSI statement, and at one point, Meester says, she "reinserted" him into her. According to Woods: "I woke up as he was flipping me onto my stomach and tossing my body around like I was a rag doll and he attempted to penetrate me from that position. It could be because he was very drunk and 'missed,' but I remember being very embarrassed because I thought that he had penetrated my anus, which is something that I have always been very against." Meester was not wearing a condom and when he told Woods that he had ejaculated, according to Woods's OSI statement, she was "very scared."

Wager, meanwhile, slept through the whole incident. The only sound he reported hearing was, at some point, Woods saying, "No." As Wager told investigators, he did not hear the context. Meester told OSI that he never heard Woods say no, and Woods reported that she didn't remember saying it.

Afterward, Meester went to the bathroom and returned to find Woods sitting on the floor, putting on her clothes. She dressed herself and tied her shoes. Rando then entered the room again and, as he told OSI, "half-walked, half-carried" Woods back to her room at about 3 a.m. She would later ask her roommate if Cuny, her boyfriend, had come to their room at 1 a.m. as planned.

That afternoon, at 2:23 p.m., Woods sent Cuny an e-mail in which she tried to explain a bit about her night. She wrote that she got drunk and that Meester had "mess[ed] with me and shit.... I'm sure [Meester] wasn't thinking at all either, so I can't tell you he attacked me or anything. I just feel disgusting and horrible and I want to die right now. And I'm sure you probably want to kill me.... I am so stupid and made a huge mistake last night and I don't know how to fix it..."

In addition to rape, Meester is charged with forcible sodomy, committing indecent acts, and conduct unbecoming an officer. A panel of 11 Air Force officers—10 male and one female—has already been selected to sit in judgment of him. They will decide, in effect, whether on that night two stressed-out college kids got drunk and had a one-night stand, or whether it was something criminal.

Many of the Academy's other alleged sexual-assault victims, at least the ones who have recounted their stories in the press, said their rapists either used physical force or abused rank to commit the assault. One of the women who spoke to 7 News's Ferrugia said an upperclassmen ordered her to fellate him; another said her assailant threatened to make her life at the Academy a living hell if she reported that he had raped her. Woods, however, did not claim Meester physically forced or ordered her to do anything. The thrust of her allegation is that Meester took advantage of her while she was "beyond impaired"—in other words, too drunk to resist. As Woods wrote in a memo to Brig. Gen. Weida, "Never did I give Cadet Meester, someone I barely knew, permission to touch me or have sex with me."

According to the Uniform Code of Military Justice, the panel that will judge Meester must find that he raped Woods if it is proven that

Woods was "incapable due to the lack of mental or physical faculties of giving consent." If, on the other hand, the panel determines that Woods was "in possession of her mental and physical faculties and failed to make her lack of consent reasonably manifest by taking such measures of resistance as are called for by the circumstances," Meester must be found innocent. Put another way, if the panel determines that Woods was sober enough to know what was going on and did not resist either in word or deed, "then the inference may be drawn that she consented."

In the chief investigation officer's detailed memorandum that Gen. Weida considered when deciding whether or not to court-martial Meester, the IO wrote: "There is substantial evidence to indicate that Woods did have the mental alertness and ability to communicate with Meester during the sexual intercourse and make her lack of consent reasonably manifest. Specifically, she described looking at her watch and being cognizant of the time that she was supposed to be meeting with her boyfriend. She was also alert enough to realize that she was engaging in sexual intercourse with Meester, and even asked him a question. She could have taken the next step to reasonably manifest her lack of consent to the sexual intercourse.

"Throughout the night Woods never indicated verbally or through any physical manifestation that she was not consenting to sexual intercourse with Meester. She also had the presence of mind to be scared about possible pregnancy and sexually transmitted diseases after Meester told her he had ejaculated. This understanding at the time the sexual intercourse occurred indicates that Woods was capable of understanding the act, its motive, and possible consequences. Furthermore, after the sexual acts occurred, Woods was able to dress herself and tie her own shoes.... Woods never appeared to be in distress and she never asked to leave the room. Throughout the sexual intercourse, Woods was aware that Wager was in the room, only three feet away from where she was, but never called upon him to render assistance."

Gen. Weida refused to be interviewed for this story or to comment on why he disagreed with the IO's findings and opted to court-martial Meester. He may have simply felt the IO was wrong, or that it was prudent to have the evidence considered again in court. Yet, both the Meester and Woods families suspect Weida's motives are not that simple. They believe that Weida, under Roche's tacit or explicit direction, is using them as pawns in a show trial. Meester is convinced that Air

Force leaders want to see him convicted on at least one of the charges in the hope that it will satiate the public and politicians who have criticized the brass for inaction. Woods says her mom fears that Weida, under Roche's direction, thrust her allegations into the spotlight now so that defense lawyers can harp on the apparent murkiness of the case and attempt to destroy her credibility as a way to undermine all of the other allegations of sexual assault, as a way to intimidate other girls from coming forward, as a way to explain away why Academy officials have been so slow to prosecute such allegations.

If Weida and Roche had such discussions about the case, it would constitute "unlawful command influence," a serious violation of the Uniform Code of Military Justice. And at the hearing scheduled for this March, Meester intends to prove Weida is indeed guilty of the offense. The Meesters have hired Frank Spinner, an Academy graduate and now a Colorado Springs attorney renowned for his success defending military clients, to work with the two Air Force lawyers Meester has been assigned. Spinner says he will call some of the Academy's former top officials, Weida, and a host of other military brass, including Air Force Secretary Roche. "I think they've got some explaining to do," he says. "It seems to me that if the Academy were really serious about change and sending the message that it's cleaning up its act, they could have picked a better case than this one. They could have picked a slam dunk. Certainly, they had plenty to choose from."

In 1993, the first year that the Academy began keeping statistics for sexual assaults, 18 Air Force cadets reported being sexually assaulted. One female cadet that year claimed she was gang-raped by other cadets. In 1994, 14 allegations of sexual assault were reported at the Academy. The General Accounting Office issued a report stating Academy females were often "subject to unwanted touching, sexual harassment, and/or sexual assault." According to the survey, one-third of the female cadets reported they were sexually assaulted by male cadets or knew someone who was; many women feared that if they reported the assaults to school officials that they would be disciplined or thrown out.

In 1995, the number of reported allegations of sexual assault increased to 17. In 1996, a year with 15 allegations of reported sexual assault, a high-level Academy official sent a four-page memo to the Air Force Chief of Staff describing a culture of "silence and intimidation" that prevents more victims from coming forward; the official alleged that one victim of sexual assault was so traumatized that she slept with a weapon, and that another suffered vaginal injuries during an attack but was so fearful of what her Academy peers and leaders might do if it became known that she reported the assault, she stayed quiet until she experienced "noticeable blood loss."

During the next two years, there were 23 reported allegations of sexual assault. In an internal survey, 15 percent of academy women claimed to be victims of sexual assault. Throughout the next four years, 55 cadets reported being sexually assaulted or raped. Meanwhile, on campus, a misogynist slang was born. Female cadets were referred to as "cockpits" and "dorm mattresses." An underground web-zine called eDodo.org appeared where current cadets and alums posted degrading cartoons and comments about female cadets, and took orders for T-shirts emblazoned with the academy logo and the phrase, "I am not a rapist."

This misogyny was not born overnight. It was cultivated by an apparently indifferent leadership. Every three years, one Academy superintendent ended his tour of duty without having to answer for the institutional problems he left behind, and a new one would come along promising change and trumpeting another program or strategy that would fail miserably.

One program, started in 1993, was a 24-hour Academy hotline that sexual assault victims could call to report abuse or simply seek counseling. It was staffed by a student group called CASIE, or Cadets Advocating Sexual Integrity and Education. The night Woods's brother got his sister's instant message and ran to her dorm room, he brought with him a friend, a fellow senior cadet who was a member of CASIE. The CASIE rep assured Woods that if she reported the alleged rape she would be treated with sensitivity and not be punished for any offenses she may have committed during that night.

Two days after Woods spoke with OSI, she was removed from her room, separated from her dorm-mates, who had become her close friends, and transferred to another squadron where she knew no one. She got eight demerits and was informed she could be "disenrolled." Notice of the reprimands came to her on "Form 10" documents; one began, "Cadet [Woods] committed numerous violations of Air Force Cadet Wing Code and Colorado state law. Her major violations that night included actively seeking alcohol in the cadet dorms, sexual activity in the dorms, and fraternization."

Woods's CASIE rep was so outraged at the Academy leadership that he quit the program and wrote the brass a letter: "I should never have trusted the command representatives who repeatedly assured us that the program, and more importantly, the victim, would get the support needed in a time like this. In trusting them, I became part of the problem. It is my firm belief that the victim would be better off (both professionally and emotionally) today if she had never come forward. I cannot volunteer to support a policy of punishing victims for coming forward."

In a memorandum Woods submitted to the Academy leadership on November 19, 2002 (exactly one month after she talked to OSI), she said she was "appalled" by the way she was treated. She cited information she'd culled from the website of a women's crisis center: "Any action taken by police, co-workers, teachers, or family that makes the victim feel like a criminal is counterproductive." She pointed out that experts on sexual assault emphasize victims are psychologically vulnerable. "I feel that I was ripped away from my support mechanisms and all of my friends.... I feel I am being punished as if I have committed a crime."

Even Meester agrees that the Academy "treated [Woods] wrongly" after she filed charges against him. "They basically cut her off from everyone she knew. If you make an allegation, I think the Academy has a responsibility to take it seriously. I don't blame them for taking me down to OSI and talking to me. Initially, I was told, 'You'll be out of here [the Academy].' I was told that right away. And I was told that for the next six weeks. I believe that the Academy mishandled a lot of the cases and now they're kind of paying for it." He pauses, as the possible irony of it all occurs to him. "Actually, I guess I am.

"You know," he says, "the thing is, like, after a while you start saying, 'Well, I don't know, maybe something happened I don't remember. Maybe, you know, maybe, I'm wrong.' As many times as I've played it over in my head, it was so not even a question in my mind. I never thought about it until the investigators told me she said it, that she was accusing me of it." He furrows his brow, lowers his voice and adds, "I would kill a person if they raped my mother or my sister. I couldn't imagine doing that to a person, ever."

Meester has been trying to get on with his life. When we met, he was preparing to start classes at a Florida university, where he planned to double-major in economics and political science. His brush with the law, or at least the military's version of it, has got him thinking he might want to be an attorney, that is, of course, if the court-martial panel finds him innocent. "Do I understand the significance of my case? Of course, because of all this, the scandal, generals have lost their careers, the Academy will never be the same again. And here I am getting ready to leave for school in a few days knowing that after my first term, I'm going to court and may be sent to prison for the rest of my life for something I didn't do."

Woods has also set about remaking her future. She has moved to Texas to be with her boyfriend. Cuny quit the Academy and is now among the Air Force's enlisted personnel. If he hadn't quit, it is very likely that he would have been kicked out. Woods's sexual-assault medical exam found traces of two different DNA. One belonged to Meester, the other was Cuny's. For the Academy, that revelation alone was evidence that Cuny had broken the school's fraternization policy.

Hoping for the best at trial, Marie Woods has been telling her daughter that by putting herself through the court-martial and taking the stand, "She might be serving her country in a more meaningful way than if she had graduated from the Academy and become an officer. But she would have made one hell of an officer."

The Academy's new superintendent is Gen. John Rosa. A graduate of the Citadel military institute, he is the first non-Academy alum to lead the school. His outsider perspective, so goes Secretary Roche's reasoning, should finally bring change. Rosa has publicly pledged to beat the Academy's current woes. He has said, "We're developing a campaign, just as we've done in Iraq." Working with Brig. Gen. Weida, who has been appointed the Commandant of Cadets, Rosa has instituted an "Agenda For Change." Together they are attempting to overhaul the culture, and specifically the Academy's methods for responding to reports of sexual assault. The infamous "Bring Me Men" sign has been torn down. The first four pages of the most recent Basic Cadet Training handbook cover:

"Sexual Assault and Sexual Harassment," "Rape," "Carnal Knowledge,"
"Forcible Sodomy," "Indecent Assault," and "Indecent Acts of Liberties
with a Child." Yet, since the new administration took control, 19 female
cadets have reported being sexually assaulted, and the Academy's 2003
Social Climate Survey, the most recent survey, revealed that one in five
academy males resents having women in the cadet wing.

— February/March 2004

17.

Bill Koch's Wild West Adventure

by Kelley McMillan Manley

On a warm day this past September, Bill Koch rode on horseback through Bear Ranch, his 4,500-acre property located just outside of Paonia. Koch's six-foot-four-inch frame—clad in a collared shirt, chaps, boots, and spurs—sat comfortably atop his palomino mount as we toured his estate which lies just below the Ragged Mountains, a fluted wall of granite that rises from the high mesas of western Colorado. A flat-brimmed cowboy hat hid his blue eyes and thick, tousled white hair. At seventy-two years old, Koch is the founder, CEO, and president of Oxbow Carbon LLC, a global energy company, and one of the wealthiest men in the world with a reported personal net worth of about $4 billion. He's also the brother of Charles and David Koch, the high-profile businessmen and bankrollers of conservative causes. Although his primary residence is in Palm Beach, Florida, where Oxbow is headquartered, one of Koch's many passions is Western history. "What I really like about the West," he says, "is the stand-your-ground mentality and the idea that you have to take care of yourself, take care of your family, and take care of the people that surround you. You all take care of each other."

Koch was at the ranch that weekend to work out some details related to the Old West town he's building on his land. The town, which has yet to be named, is an authentic reproduction of a full-scale 19th-century settlement; it's largely comprised of structures from a former MGM tourist attraction called Buckskin Joe, which Koch bought in 2010 and transported piece by piece to his ranch from its location outside of Cañon City. Koch intends for the town to be a private getaway for his family and friends. "I want to have a place for my family and extended family to keep us all together," he says. "It all gets back to trying to create a place where I can enjoy life and enjoy my family and friends without having to worry about my enemies. And I'm doing it because I can."

We'd spent the previous day strolling through the 70-odd buildings of the town, which is set in a pasture surrounded by Marcellina Mountain, the Anthracite Range, and the West Elk Mountains. Located 25 minutes from downtown Paonia by car, or 15 minutes by helicopter from Koch's Aspen abode, the 10-acre town features five saloons and a jail, firehouse, church, bank, theater, and library. There's a 20-person team dedicated to overseeing, authenticating, and building the town and Koch's collection of Western memorabilia, which includes more than one million items—including Frederic Remington's painting "The Trooper", General George A. Custer's Springfield rifle, the only photograph of Billy the Kid (valued at $2.3 million), and an early Colorado hearse (a white horse-drawn carriage). Koch's collection spans the 19th and early 20th centuries, and parts of it will be displayed at the Smithsonian next year. "It will be an extravaganza about the West," Betsy Broun, the Margaret and Terry Stent director of the Smithsonian American Art Museum, says of the exhibition. "It's one of the best Western collections in the world. It has sculptures and paintings, but also artifacts, historic photos, and material objects drawn from daily life in the West. Spurs, clothing, wagons, cavalry uniforms, arrows, quivers, flags—you name it. A robust picture emerges of what life was like in the West."

As we wandered through the town, the lead historian on the project said, "It's as if you are literally going back in time. Everything from the ceilings to the accoutrements are period-specific." The streets' widths are historically accurate—wide enough so that a four-to-six-horse cart can turn around—and are bordered by sidewalks at the perfect height for a rancher to load his cart. We headed into the Cattlemen's Club, a bar theoretically for men only (there's a separate Spa-loon for the ladies, one of the only deviations from historical accuracy of the project, which Koch says he had to include in order to entice his wife to the remote property). The club, which would have been a watering hole for affluent types in the late 1800s, has a mahogany bar with two female figures sculpted out of the wood that overlook the room.

"You want to see the brothel?" Koch asked.

We climbed the stairs to the second story and toured the rooms wall-papered in Technicolor shades of teal, maroon, and pink. Ornate red and blue glass lamps cast kaleidoscopic shadows on the wall. The brothel is more a work of art than a den of sin and one day will serve, innocuously, as guest quarters. Eventually, authentic ephemera—beaded garters with holsters for mini pistols, matchbook advertisements for call girls, and pictures of 19th-century prostitutes—will adorn the rooms.

"Will there be real girls here?" I asked.

"Ghosts," Koch said with a boyish chuckle. To hear him tell it, the brothel is haunted by the phantoms of unsatisfied customers.

The next day, as we headed toward higher elevation on our horses, Koch's ranch unfurled below us, with views of the town and thousands of acres of grazing land for his 1,100 head of cattle. Riding with him, and seeing him against this Western backdrop, it was easy to forget his colorful romantic history (he's been married three times and had a public falling-out with a mistress in 1995); his reputation for being litigious (he's been involved in 26 personal lawsuits); and his accomplishments as a sailor (he won the America's Cup in 1992). His downhome, aw-shucks demeanor seemed at odds with the businessman who has been demonized as a wicked energy baron. He's been labeled "a greedy bastard" by a blog called the Vile Plutocrat, and *New York Magazine's* website has a recent posting that describes him as "evil." This past October, Koch made national headlines when a former Oxbow executive accused Koch of kidnapping him and imprisoning him at the ranch. But here at the base of the Raggeds, among the golden aspen trees and rugged peaks of the Rocky Mountains, Bill Koch looked like any other cowboy out for a ride on an autumn day.

Of course, Bill Koch is not any other cowboy, and his land is not any other estate: Bear Ranch is at the center of a bitter dispute that has divided Paonia's eclectic community of ranchers, miners, New Agers, and farmers for two years. Koch wants to trade the federal government 911 acres of land he owns in Gunnison County, along with 80 acres in Utah's Dinosaur National Monument, for 1,846 acres of less valuable public land in and around Paonia. Proposed in 2010 by then Congressman John Salazar, a Democrat who lost his bid for re-election that same year, the Central Rockies Land Exchange, as the swap is called, aims to connect the two disparate sides of Bear Ranch into one contiguous piece of property via a Bureau of Land Management parcel.

The federal government and private entities—ski resorts, developments, individuals—execute land exchanges all the time (typically more than 300 a year) to consolidate properties, and some observers have been surprised at the uproar Koch's swap ignited. Although this swath of BLM open space is dotted with aspens and offers views of three 12,000-foot peaks, BLM land traditionally is at the bottom of the public land food chain. As one of the least protected categories of federal land, the government often leases BLM parcels to mining, drilling, timber, and grazing operations for profit. The Central Rockies Land Exchange, which has been approved by the Delta County and Gunnison County commissioners, must now go before the 113th Congress.

Paonia resident Ed Marston, the former publisher of High Country News, is one of the swap's most vocal opponents. Marston claims the deal reeks of political cronyism: Since 2006, Koch and various Oxbow entities donated more than $40,000 to Salazar, and Koch hosted Salazar on his ranch for several elk-hunting outings. But, more important, Marston believes the deal will rob Paonia of access to the Raggeds. "The land Koch is seeking provides the best existing access to 40 square miles of Forest Service and Wilderness land," he told me.

In September, Marston led a group of locals up the contested BLM strip. Dawn Ullrey, an avid horseback rider who has lived in Paonia for 53 years, and whose husband works for the Forest Service, was on the tour, as was Frank Mastrullo, who videotaped the outing. (Mastrullo's stepson works in Koch's Elk Creek Mine.) When the group reached a point that overlooks Koch's ranch, they stopped to take in the view, and a chorus of anti-Koch rants began: "It's by invitation only," one hiker said. Another chimed in, "A peasant like you isn't going to give him your few pennies and get in there." Marston added, "People like us are never considered to be fully human by him."

Ullrey, who's never met or worked for Koch, and does not have any family that's ever been employed by him, says, "There is a lot of emotion involved in this, and the emotion is irrelevant. Is this a good thing for the American people, or is it not a good thing? My husband and I are of the opinion that the American people will win. In fact, we think the people in Paonia are actually going to be better off."

Since the swap was proposed, Koch has added what he and his team consider to be several improvements to the original exchange bill. Koch has offered to build a new trailhead and improved access to the Ragged Mountain Wilderness through the acquisition of Buck Creek Ranch, an old homestead. (Marston argues the Buck Creek access is "far inferior" to the existing option.) Koch also bought a 21-acre lot on Jumbo Mountain, a popular recreation area outside of Paonia, which he plans to convey to the BLM to provide permanent public access to Jumbo; currently, a landowner allows people to cross his property to get to the mountain. And Koch's offered to build a mountain bike trail connecting Crested Butte to Carbondale. Altogether, Koch has spent, or committed, roughly $7 million to the exchange.

Koch's natural gas activities in the area may also be muddying the waters of the debate. Gunnison Energy Corporation, an Oxbow company, leases nearly 150,000 acres of mineral rights from the BLM and private mineral owners. One theory floating around Paonia posits the various BLM parcels included in the exchange, beyond the one that would unite Koch's ranch, are strategic locations that provide resources for drilling and hydraulic fracturing infrastructure. Another contention is that Koch purchased Buck Creek Ranch so the land could be used for a compressor station, a condenser station, or a pipeline. "That's absolutely false," says Brad Goldstein, Oxbow's spokesperson. "We bought Buck Creek for access. Period."

No matter what Koch does, he seems to kick up dust in his wake. Conspiracy theories about him ripple through Paonia: One suggests that he (or his staff) flies his helicopter over his enemies' homes, running surveillance or trying to scare his opposition. People say Koch's team shows up at the homes of his opponents and asks what will quiet their discontent. Some fear their email has been hacked by Koch operatives, and rumors abound that former FBI agents pose as workers on his ranch in order to gather intel on what the employees are saying amongst themselves. "I don't understand why there is so much antagonism and anger toward me from people in Paonia who have never met me, especially since we've been trying to make a lot of contributions to the community," Koch says. Through his various companies—he owns the Elk Creek coal mine in Somerset, about 15 minutes from his ranch; Gunnison Energy, a major player in natural gas development in the area; and Bear Ranch—Koch pays more than $38 million a year in employee salaries. In 2012, he donated more than half a million dollars to charities in the region. But can Koch, the history buff, really be surprised at the local reaction? After all, the West has always loved its villains.

As a kid, Koch was tall, skinny, and awkward, and his brothers and other children teased him relentlessly. "We had an extremely competitive family, and we didn't take care of one another," Koch told me over dinner in the Cook House, the Old West town's main dining area. "For a long time, I felt insecure and inadequate and wouldn't stand up for myself." Born in 1940 in Wichita, Kansas, Koch was the last of Mary and Frederick Chase Koch's four sons. Koch describes a childhood shaped by fierce sibling rivalries. His twin, David, 19 minutes older, was handsome, sociable, and athletic and gravitated toward their brother Charles, who is five years older than the twins. "I was more interested in the most popular people on campus: the pretty girls, the athletes," David Koch told me last fall. "Billy was more intellectual and liked the different, more fascinating people." Charles and David now run Koch Industries, the second-largest private company in the United States, behind Cargill. (The eldest Koch brother, Frederick R. Koch, is seven years older than Bill and David and wasn't as involved in the interfamily politics.)

Koch's parents were largely absent. Koch describes his father, the son of a Dutch immigrant newspaper owner, as "a very strong, ethical man" and as "a soft-spoken, John Wayne-type." But his father was away from home often, building his oil refinery business. His mother, while "beautiful and charming," was focused on her social life, Koch says, and the boys were entrusted to nannies. "Kids have great sibling rivalries," Koch says. "And if there are no parents there to help put everything into perspective, it can get very bad." His mother would side with his brothers. When his father was around, he would stick up for young Bill, something that affected him deeply.

The rivalry between the twin brothers got so severe in middle school, Koch says, that he became withdrawn and nearly flunked out. He was recalcitrant and undisciplined. A psychologist recommended the brothers be separated. To remedy the situation, and to offer their children the best possible education, his parents sent David and Bill away to different boarding schools; Bill went to Indiana's Culver Military Academy. When he arrived, Koch was six feet one inch tall and weighed 120 pounds, and his peers teased him unmercifully for his gawky appearance. But, removed from his brothers, Koch began to flourish. In 1958, he graduated with honors.

Fred Koch believed in hard work and was a self-made man, having pioneered a more efficient method of refining heavy oil into gasoline. Initially, some of the nation's big oil-technology companies came after Koch, filing a patent lawsuit against him and all of his customers—who were small, independent refineries—temporarily ruining his business in the United States. Unable to work in America, Koch decided to go overseas in 1929 to build refineries in Romania, and later in Stalin's USSR. When the lawsuit failed, he returned to the United States in the 1930s as a multimillionaire and a firm believer in free-market capitalism. He would later go on to become an early member of the ultraconservative John Birch Society, known for its distrust of, and distaste for, government and for spreading fears in the 1950s that communism had seeped into the highest offices of American politics.

Fred Koch also had a deep love of the West and at one time was one of the largest ranchers in the United States, owning more than two million acres of ranchlands in Texas, Kansas, Wyoming, and Montana. Beginning at the age of 13, for five summers, Bill Koch worked on his father's ranches. He bailed hay, dug ditches, fixed fences, and mucked stalls—12 hours a day, seven days a week—and got paid five bucks per diem, plus room and board. It was during these summers that Koch says he, too, fell in love with the West.

Both Bill and David headed to the Massachusetts Institute of Technology in 1958. They played basketball together—though Bill sat on the bench while David was a prolific scorer. They were in the same fraternity, Beta Theta Pi, where Bill was the resident "humorist," and both studied chemical engineering. In college, the brothers' rivalry dissipated, David says, and after they graduated, the twins rented apartments across the hall from each other. "I got better grades at MIT than he did," Bill Koch told me. "David now says he's the handsome one and I'm the smart one. But it took me a while to adapt and accept that." Koch went on to earn three degrees at MIT, including a doctorate in chemical engineering in 1971.

In school, Koch realized that he could carve a place for himself in the world by virtue of his own achievements. "When I was living in Wichita, a lot of people looked upon me as a rich kid," Koch says. "When I got away, it was about what I did. My father couldn't buy me honors at Culver. He couldn't buy me a doctorate degree from MIT. I had to earn that on my own. For my own self-worth, I had to learn that."

In 1968, while studying for his doctorate in chemical engineering, Bill Koch started working for his father's company; Charles had taken over the business a year earlier after Fred Koch died of a stroke. Twelve years later, as vice president of corporate development, Bill spearheaded an attempted takeover with the goal of deposing Charles, the chairman and CEO, and David, who was an executive vice president. Bill disagreed with Charles's totalitarian control of the company and believed the stockholders were not getting their rewards. He also disapproved of using company money to fund Charles's and David's libertarian causes: In 1977, the Kochs donated money to launch the Libertarian Cato Institute, and David Koch ran for vice president on the 1980 Libertarian Party ticket. When the coup failed, Bill was fired, and in 1983, Bill and his eldest brother, Frederick, sold their shares of Koch Industries. Bill received about $300 million after taxes. The battle may have been over, but the war was just beginning: Bill, David, and Charles were embroiled in litigation for the next 19 years.

In 2001, after eight lawsuits, the brothers finally settled. Bill Koch won the final suit against his brothers. "I now have a peaceful coexistence with Charles," Koch says. "And I am now very best friends with my brother David." Koch initiated the reconciliation with his twin by inviting him to his birthday party in 2001, and David served as the best man in Koch's 2005 wedding to his third wife, Bridget Rooney Koch.

Koch is cautious when speaking of his brothers—he avoids commenting on his brothers' politics, on how his views differ from theirs (he, like his brothers, was a big donor to Mitt Romney; but, unlike his brothers, he has also donated to Democrats, including Ted Kennedy), and on the almost 20-year war waged among them. This is largely because of a nondisparagement agreement in the brothers' final settlement. But it's difficult not to sense that, no matter how much he once wanted to win against his brothers, he is grateful to have his family back, thankful for the peace.

In 1983, Koch, determined to create an identity separate from his brothers and family name, founded Oxbow Carbon. ("An oxbow is where a river changes course," Koch explains.) Oxbow's great success was figuring out that "petroleum coke," a byproduct of producing gasoline, could actually be used instead of discarded. Oxbow buys coke from refineries and, in turn, sells it to aluminum, steel, and cement companies and fuel-grade markets where it's used instead of coal to generate energy.

Over the years, Oxbow has expanded its core businesses to include the mining and marketing of energy and commodities such as coal and natural gas, along with metallurgical and calcined coke, a key ingredient in the manufacturing of aluminum. It's a big supplier of sulfur, sulfuric acid, and fertilizers. Oxbow, which has annual revenues of $4 billion and employs 1,500 people worldwide, also owns one of the most productive underground coal mines in the United States: Elk Creek Mine, located about 10 minutes from Koch's ranch. Elk Creek yields some of the "cleanest" (lowest sulfur) coal in the world.

Though Oxbow is now firmly entrenched in the business of carbon-based products, one of its first endeavors was in alternative energy—geothermal and hydroelectric plants in Nevada, the Philippines, and Costa Rica. In November, Oxbow, along with Aspen Skiing Company, Vessels Coal Gas Inc., and Holy Cross Energy, unveiled a coal-methane conversion plant that will convert methane from Oxbow's Elk Creek Mine (methane is a byproduct of coal mining and a leading greenhouse gas) into electricity; the power generated through this project is roughly equal to Aspen Skiing Company's energy usage. It's the second project of its kind in the United States. Auden Schendler, the vice president of sustainability at Aspen Skiing Company, says his partner, Tom Vessels of Vessels Coal Gas, had been trying to execute the project for a decade. Elk Creek was the only mine willing to try it. "Solving climate change is going to be really hard," Schendler says. "To do it, we're going to need to think differently; to create new alliances, maybe break old ones. This project shows how Americans can use a wasted resource for the betterment of our communities. It's utterly bipartisan."

In all of my interactions with Koch over the course of five months, it was not business, or the Old West town, that he spoke about most often. I visited with Koch, who rarely grants interviews, on multiple occasions, across several states, at four of his homes, and I was the first (and only, to this date) journalist to visit his Old West town. I met his family, in-laws, and friends; Oxbow executives, his personal staff, and contract workers; and teachers and students at the school he founded, Oxbridge Academy of the Palm Beaches, in Florida. Whether he was discussing his own childhood or calling me en route to a son's basketball game, family was the prevailing theme of our conversations.

His is an eclectic tribe. Koch has five biological children and one stepson, who range in age from six to 26, by four women (three wives and a girlfriend). The youngest child was born to Koch and his current wife, Bridget Rooney Koch, granddaughter of Art Rooney, who founded the Pittsburgh Steelers in 1933. Koch has also all but legally adopted Rooney Koch's son, whom she had with actor Kevin Costner.

At dinner one night at Koch's Cape Cod compound, the dinner table teemed with family and friends. Four of the children were present. Rooney Koch headed the table. Fifty years old, whip thin, with dark brown hair and light green eyes, she's not your standard trophy wife: She's a vegan and an avid skier and recreational kickboxer. She's also smart and very funny. Koch attributes his two failed marriages—one wife accused Koch of assaulting her; he claims her accusation was an attempt to get out of their prenuptial agreement, and they settled out of court—in part to scars from his childhood. "I always wanted my mother's affection but could never get it," he says. "I married two women who reminded me a lot of my mother. They were unable to love anyone other than themselves." With Rooney, he's certain he's found the right one. "She's got a great character and she could love me besides loving herself."

In 2011, Koch founded Oxbridge Academy, pledging $60 million because, he says, he wasn't satisfied with the education options in Palm Beach, and he didn't want to send his children off to boarding school.

He runs the school like a business: The headmaster is the "president and CEO," and the kids and the parents are the customers. "Kids come first," he says. "Staff comes last." The school's five-person board of directors contains three Oxbow executives, including Koch. He's been on the board of four different schools and says, "You can spend more time debating the problem than solving it." Being on the board of the school is, Koch says, "the equivalent of holding the stock in Oxbridge."

In addition to the school and Bear Ranch, Koch has a 42-acre Cape Cod estate, comprised of the former Dupont and Mellon family properties; a 90-acre estate in Aspen made up of four neighboring properties; and his primary residence, a 35,000-square-foot house in Palm Beach, Florida. The collection of properties may appear to be stereotypical billionaire preening, but Koch says he has different intentions. "What I really want to do is create family compounds, so my sons will see each other and they'll have a reason, when they get older and they have their own families, for staying together." He's sensitive to any hint of sibling rivalry or infighting among his children and is quick to punish them if he senses any—taking away iPhones, Facebook privileges, or grounding the teenagers. "That's one of my goals in life: to make sure my kids get along, respect each other, and love each other."

This past October, with the land exchange still in limbo, Koch turned up in the news yet again when former Oxbow executive Kirby Martensen filed a lawsuit in the Northern District of California alleging that Koch had kidnapped Martensen, imprisoned him, and held him against his will at Bear Ranch in March 2012. Martensen had been the senior vice president of Oxbow Carbon & Minerals International's Asia division, based in Singapore. Martensen claims in the suit that he came under scrutiny after raising concerns about Oxbow's "questionable" tax-avoidance strategies. He says his relocation to Asia was "a part of a plan being implemented to evade paying taxes to the United States on profits in excess of $200,000,000 per year."

According to the suit, Martensen asked to be driven to Aspen to catch a flight home after being interrogated for hours at the ranch. "This request was denied," the suit says. "Martensen was told that he was being taken to Denver. Martensen then was kidnapped and kept captive in the vehicle during the trip to Denver." Martensen, his attorney, and another former Oxbow executive, Joe Lombardi, who was also at the ranch during the incident and was fired, all declined to comment for this story.

Koch tells a different version of the events. After being tipped off by an anonymous letter in 2011 to possible corporate criminal misconduct by Martensen and two others, Koch began an investigation into their activities. Oxbow management started collecting emails, telephone recordings, documents—more than four million items in total—and testimony from others implicated in the ploy that pointed to the fact that Martensen had "participated in a wide-ranging scheme to systematically misappropriate revenues and business opportunities" and used his position as an executive at Oxbow to "illegally enrich" himself, according to a complaint Oxbow filed in Palm Beach on March 22, 2012. Koch says Martensen and the other implicated executives "had a scam going against us that cost us $40 million."

Koch says he invited Martensen—and five other executives thought to be involved in the scheme—to the ranch for a corporate retreat in mid-March. They were to hold strategy meetings, and each executive was to undergo a 360-degree performance analysis. The first night, Koch hosted the men for dinner at the ranch. The next day, after the group strategy session, Koch had lunch with the executives and then took them on a helicopter tour of the town, after which the performance reviews took place.

The men were interviewed individually. Steven Fried, Oxbow's COO, questioned Martensen. Fried says he started the conversation by talking about Martensen's division's performance and about Martensen's contributions to the company, which Martensen thought were "prolific." The conversation turned when Fried brought up some of the examples of Martensen's alleged corporate wrongdoings. Fried asked about Martensen's dealings with a competing company that he was allegedly accepting kickbacks from. Fried asked if Martensen had ever heard of the company. Martensen said no. Fried asked why, then, there had been several email exchanges between Martensen and the company. Ultimately, Fried says, Martensen admitted to some of the alleged misdeeds, but not all of them. Koch, who was interviewing another executive in a different building, says he watched Martensen leave, weeping.

After his review, Martensen was driven to another part of the ranch, Crystal Meadows, to wait for the five other men who were being interviewed, three of whom lived in California like Martensen. On his way to Crystal Meadows, he was served termination papers and a lawsuit. Koch says he separated the six men to avoid any collusion between them. Martensen also had a history of losing his temper, and Koch worried the men would become violent, so he hired an off-duty, unarmed local deputy for security purposes. Once Martensen arrived at Crystal Meadows, his Oxbow-issued computer and cell phone were taken away. Koch instructed his team to ask to inspect Martensen's bags to ensure that he wasn't stealing any company property.

Martensen's lawsuit says he asked to leave but was held captive at the ranch. But in a deposition filed in Florida last month, another Oxbow executive, Charlie Zhan, who was present during the episode at the ranch and was subsequently fired, said neither he nor Martensen were ever physically threatened, restrained, intimidated, or made to feel as if they couldn't leave. Zhan says there were no armed guards, and that both men were offered a cell phone to use once they left the ranch, where cellular reception is limited. Martensen made no calls, according to Zhan. Both Zhan and Martensen took Koch's private plane back to California.

Martensen unsuccessfully appealed the March 2012 suit filed by Koch in Florida. Martensen then took his case to California, where he filed his complaint this past autumn. "They're playing a legal maneuvering game because they want the case to be held in San Francisco, which would be considerably more liberal than the court in Florida," Koch says. It could take years for either case to go to trial.

Fried, who's worked for Oxbow for about 14 years, is mystified by Martensen's alleged offenses. "Anyone who knows Bill knows that he will chase down someone who has wronged him to the end of the earth. So it's been staggering to me to know that senior people in the company would steal from him," he told me at Oxbow's corporate headquarters in Palm Beach. "He's obviously a driven guy, whether it's business or sailboat racing or collecting wine or holding people accountable when they've mistreated him. He's dogged in his pursuit."

As we reached the last leg of our ride through his ranch, Koch pushed ahead alone. We turned toward the barn, and the horses were skittish, sensing that we were heading home. The high mesas in the distance silhouetted Koch's frame as the late-afternoon sun began to cast long shadows. He'd been quiet this afternoon; Koch had stayed up late into the night, drinking whiskey in the saloon with his brother-in-law and a few friends. After the festivities died down, Koch retreated to his quarters, where he sat in a rocking chair on the deck, flossing his teeth and looking at the stars, his town spread out beneath him.

In 1936, four years before Bill and David were born, Fred Koch wrote a letter to his boys, Frederick and Charles, and to his future children. Their father was keenly aware of money's inherent paradox. Each brother now has a framed copy of the letter, which Koch has read often over the years.

> *When you are 21, you will receive what now seems like a large sum of money. It will be yours to do what you will. It may be a blessing or a curse. You can use it as a valuable tool for accomplishment or you can squander it foolishly. If you choose to let this money destroy your initiative and independence, then it will be a curse to you and my action in giving it to you will have been a mistake. I should regret very much to have you miss the glorious feeling of accomplishment and I know you are not going to let me down. Remember that often adversity is a blessing in disguise and certainly the greatest character builder. Be kind and generous to one another and to your mother.*

In the twilight of his life, Koch says he wants to focus on the things he loves the most: his family, collecting, and building the Old West town. "I've had my fair share of the spotlight," he says. "I don't want much to be in it anymore. I want to live the rest of my life and enjoy that, and be a good father to my kids and hopefully leave my kids with very good values and very good ethics." He's also reflecting on his past, "warts and all," as he says, contemplating the things that influenced his life's course. "It took me a long time to realize I have some talents and capabilities and if I just put them to work, I could create my own life and my own accomplishments independent of where I've come from," he says. "And the town represents that."

In December, Governor John Hickenlooper visited Koch and the town. The governor has also met separately with Ed Marston. Ever the shrewd politician, Hickenlooper is working quietly to broker a peace deal between the two on the land exchange. Koch says the governor would like Koch to host an exhibition of his Western collection at a museum in Denver and open the town to high-paying visitors and schoolchildren. Koch's not yet sure what he'll do, though he's not totally opposed to the governor's terms.

Regardless of the land swap's status, Koch's immediate family will come to western Colorado to see the town this spring. But today, it's still a work in progress: Just months ago, the Victorian houses on Main Street gleamed with freshly painted shades of pink, yellow, and blue. Koch recently bought a wardrobe from a movie set, and future guests will be able to dress up in Western garb. There are no TVs in the guest rooms and no cars in the town; instead, guests will ride horses and carriages, watch movies in the theater, and have historical discussions. There will be family dinners, parties, and corporate retreats. It's Koch's fantasy come to life, made possible by his staggering wealth.

Back at the barn, we pull up to the hitching post. Koch swings his leg over the top of his mount and hops off. He ties his horse up to the rail and thanks our wrangler for the ride. He loosens his cinch, gives the saddle a tug, and carries it into the barn, where he hangs it on the rack. In a dimly lit corner of the tack room, he places his leg on a trunk and, one by one, unzips his chaps. He leaves his spurs on.

—February 2013

18.

The Miracle of Molly

by Amanda M. Faison

Everyone in the delivery room expected to hear the primal wail of a healthy newborn—that unmistakable sonic boom of a life beginning. Instead, when Molly Rose Nash entered the world on July 4, 1994, she cried a sickly whimper. Already, she was dying.

She weighed 5 pounds, 2 ounces in the outstretched hands of the immediately concerned obstetrician. Hunched behind the doctor, the new father, Jack Nash, craned his neck to see his daughter; the color drained from his face. *Oh my God*, he thought. There was a momentary quiet, filled only with the hospital machines' incessant beeping, then all hell broke loose. Nurses ran in and out of the room, yelling about baby Molly's hands and forearm. Someone said something about missing thumbs. Lisa Nash, feet still in the stirrups, struggled to lift herself. She saw bloody sheets but couldn't see her baby. "Where is she?" she shouted. "What's wrong?" Lisa saw the obstetrician's face. At the end of the birthing table, framed by the stirrups, his cheeks were wet with tears.

Lisa is a Neonatal Intensive Care Unit (NICU) nurse; she'd been on hand for thousands of deliveries. She'd seen babies born sick. This time, though, she was the mother and it was her baby—her firstborn. "Where is she?" Lisa shouted again. Out of her sight, behind a wall of nurses, Molly was wiped clean and rushed to the Intensive Care Unit.

Jack and Lisa knew their baby would be small, tiny even—that was plain from the 20-week ultrasounds—but two prenatal tests for chromosomal abnormalities assuaged their fears that the small stature was caused by an illness. The ultrasound tests were also when the Nashes found out they were having a girl. A co-worker gave Jack and Lisa a tiny pink cap to take home. They'd pull it out, rub it between their fingers. They both loved the name Molly. Knowing the sex and name made it all so real. Jack and Lisa couldn't wait to meet their little girl and put that hat on her head. They couldn't wait to be a family.

Now Lisa was on her back in a Rose Medical Center birthing suite, horrified and anxious. Finally, a nurse placed Molly in Lisa's arms. Lisa cooed and held her baby daughter close, studying the round face and tight-knit eyes. With an unsteady hand, Lisa gently unwound the blanket to see the rest of Molly: Her right arm was stunted and bowed, one hand was missing a thumb, and on the other there was a fleshy tab of skin where a thumb failed to root. What Lisa couldn't see was even more heartbreaking: Molly did not have hip sockets, there were two holes in her heart, and she was missing part of her brain.

The Disease

"Get the book!" Lisa shouted to someone, anyone in the birthing suite.

She wanted *Smith's Recognizable Patterns of Human Malformation*, the NICU nurse's bible. During Lisa's four years of working at University Hospital, "the book" was the first thing she reached for when a baby was born malformed. Now, knees in the air, Lisa frantically skimmed the pages, looking for Molly's symptoms, seemingly oblivious to her obstetrician seated at the end of the birthing table, stitching her up.

Lisa came across Fanconi anemia (FA), a disease she'd never heard of, and on that page she found a face like Molly's staring back. Same apple-shaped head, same eyes, the same hand and arm abnormalities. FA is a genetic disorder that causes bone marrow failure, leukemia, and usually death in early childhood. Healthy bone marrow creates cells that supply oxygen to the body, fight infection, and clot blood; in the case of FA, cells go awry and leukemia sets in. Not all of the symptoms of FA are so obvious. Some who have it show no outward signs until their bone marrow fails. Relying on mother's intuition and her years of medical expertise, then and there Lisa concluded Molly had FA. When the pediatrician walked into her hospital room, Lisa cut through the niceties: "Molly has Fanconi anemia." The doctor dismissed Lisa's diagnosis. It's extremely rare, he said. He'd never seen a single case.

A bone marrow transplant, in which diseased cells are killed off and replaced with new donor cells, is the only cure for progressive bone marrow failure. But the procedure is risky at best. When Molly Nash was born, the success rate of a transplant from an unrelated donor was a dismal 18 percent. However, under the right circumstances, the success rate for transplants from a brother or sister was as high as 65 percent.

Experimental Science

Six potted plants are lined up on a school desk. Three of the plants are struggling to hang on, two are definite goners, and one is downright leafy. It's Jan. 27, 2005, Science Fair night at Belleview Elementary School, and 10-year-old Molly is showing off her entry to her mom and dad. She pushes aside a strand of brown hair with one of her four-fingered hands. Her "special" arm hangs by her side, curved like a hockey stick where it ends a few inches below the elbow. On her wrist is a half-moon-shaped scar—a mark left by a recent, marginally successful attempt to stretch and straighten the bone.

Molly is waist-high, elfin, and compact. She moves as if her muscles have been starched and often leans a bit to the right to compensate for her deaf left ear. Her gluey complexion is fixed with a happy grin, and her squinty brown eyes convey a warm sincerity. She gestures toward the table with her good arm and explains that she fed each plant a different diet—water, fertilizer and water, vinegar, cola, Pepto-Bismol, or chicken soup—and charted each plant's health.

For every other kid in the room, the science experiment probably amounts to just another classroom activity, but for the Nashes the project is a reminder of Molly's own fight for life and the controversial cutting-edge medicine that saved her. Five years ago, Molly and her mom underwent a series of experimental and excruciating procedures; for the first time in history doctors blended the sciences of in vitro fertilization (IVF), stem cells, and genetic screening—which thrust the Nashes into the spotlight of international news. They were covered, and in many cases condemned, in media ranging from *The New York Times* to the BBC. And Molly came to personify the ongoing medical, ethical, religious, and political debates over genetic testing, "designer babies," and embryonic research.

Imperfect Pair

Jack and Lisa knew almost immediately they were meant to be together. Both raised in Denver, they met in the summer of 1984 on a blind date orchestrated by their mothers. The couple fell in love quickly, and rather than break up the romance, Lisa, then a 17-year-old champion synchronized swimmer, gave up a scholarship to Brown University and opted for the University of Colorado. Meanwhile, 19-year-old Jack transferred from Arizona State University back home to Arapahoe Community College. Five years after their first date, the couple wed at BMH Synagogue on July 16, 1989.

But beneath the surface of the Nashes' idyllic union, a chromosomal storm was brewing. Each of them had the recessive gene for a deadly disease. If only one of the two newlyweds had this particular DNA, the disease would have remained dormant and the couple would have produced a healthy child; however, because both of them possessed this uniquely flawed DNA, there was a strong probability that their child would be born with an almost certainly fatal genetic illness. Jack and Lisa learned all of this 21 days after Molly's first birthday, in July 1995, when she was officially diagnosed with Fanconi anemia.

In the year since her birth, the Nashes had tirelessly researched the disease and contacted the Fanconi Anemia Research Fund in Oregon for direction. Lisa's college courses in molecular and cellular developmental biology and her NICU experience were invaluable when it came to deciphering the science. The more Jack and Lisa learned about FA, the more determined they became to beat it. They postponed having another child. The idea of trying to conceive and perhaps give birth to another child with a death sentence struck the Nashes as cruel and selfish.

So, heading into that official diagnosis in the summer of '95, Lisa and Jack were prepared for grim news, but they were devastated when they learned Molly had the deadliest strand of FA: Type C—the Jewish version. In the general population, 1 in 300 people is a carrier of FA, but among Ashkenazi Jews (those with ancestral ties to Eastern Europe), the odds increase to 1 in about 90. Jack and Lisa are both Ashkenazi Jews. And because both are carriers for the disease, there was a whopping 25 percent chance they would have a baby with FA-Type C. Children afflicted with this variation are born with more birth defects, get sick sooner, and, without a bone marrow transplant, die earlier. Jack and Lisa could expect Molly's bone marrow to begin failing at the age of three.

Already, in Molly's first year, she'd spent countless days in the hospital. She was born with a platelet count (an indicator of bone marrow health) of just 53,000, when it should have registered 150,000 to 400,000. When Molly was one month old, she was fit with a brace to force the development of nonexistent hip sockets. Built like a booster seat, the device applied nine months of constant, grinding pressure on her soft hipbones. Gastrointestinal problems meant she couldn't eat properly. Her weak immune system was barely functioning. At five months and weighing only six pounds, Molly was hospitalized for strep throat, which is unheard of in babies under the age of two. At six months old, doctors sliced a hole in Molly's stomach for a feeding tube. Each night, Jack and Lisa watched Molly's tiny chest rise and fall, praying she would wake the next morning.

Sunshine
Dozens of children ran toward a lake with handmade boats tucked under their arms. Some of them appeared fit, but all were sick and many were dying. A few especially weakened children walked behind. Each child had written a wish on a piece of paper and placed it inside his or her boat. At the lake, they gave their boats a little push and watched them glide away. Jack and Lisa released their vessel along with the others, but Molly was too young—not yet two—to grasp the significance of letting hope ride.

It was 1996 and the Nashes were at Camp Sunshine in Maine, where each year FA families gather for a week at the campground in the town of Casco. The children giggle during sleep outs and magic shows and give each other "high fours" on the volleyball court while researchers and other experts hold seminars for parents.

Also attending Camp Sunshine that summer was Dr. John Wagner. Wagner did not watch the children play; he tries to see them only as patients. It's a defense mechanism—while it may mute his joy after the successful surgeries he performs on kids with FA, it also makes the deaths easier to endure. He had treated and performed bone marrow transplants on many of the kids at Camp Sunshine. As the scientific director of clinical research in the Marrow Transplant Program at the University of Minnesota, Wagner has performed more bone marrow transplants on FA patients than any other doctor in the country. If any of the parents asked him to explain what drew him to FA, he would have said simply, "It was a disease that was virtually hopeless." In the FA cases he studied, Wagner recognized that transplants from a related donor—a brother or sister—were critical to success. He teamed up with cutting-edge reproductive geneticist Dr. Mark Hughes, who was director of molecular and human genetics for Georgetown University and worked for the National Institutes of Health. Together, the doctors were thinking of ways to push the envelope of science in an attempt to outsmart natural selection. They wanted to begin genetic screening for the perfect bone marrow donor. The ideal match would be A) a healthy sibling embryo and B) a suitable tissue match.

Wagner understood the risks, for his patients and for himself. He knew that some critics would view the genetic testing as crossing a moral line, but too many kids were dying after transplants. Wagner talked about his perfect-donor scenario during a seminar at Camp Sunshine in the summer of 1996. In the audience, Jack and Lisa grasped hands tightly as Wagner described a series of tests that could dramatically increase the chances that a couple's next child would be healthy and a bone marrow donor. Wagner emphasized these two existing tests had never been used together, but science was moving in that direction. As she listened, Lisa told herself: "I'm going to do this."

The process Wagner described is called Preimplantation Genetic Diagnosis (PGD), and it entailed testing multiple embryos created by in vitro fertilization. One cell of each days-old embryo would be screened for Fanconi anemia's genetic code. Affected embryos would be discarded, while healthy embryos would be further analyzed to see if the tissue type was a match for the patient in need of transplant.

The Nashes considered the fact that the testing involved controversial embryonic research—and would involve discarding diseased embryos. According to the teachings of their Jewish faith, life doesn't begin until 40 days after conception, and the tests would take place after only three or four days. Besides, they thought, if science was offering the promise of a miracle, wasn't that better than standing by and watching their daughter die?

The only alternative to PGD was naturally conceiving a healthy child who was a suitable donor (an 18.8 percent chance). However, only a prenatal test 10 weeks into the pregnancy could check for FA and determine if the fetus was a bone marrow match. For the Nashes, that was irresponsible. After all, couples often aborted upon learning the baby had the disease. The way Jack and Lisa saw it, getting pregnant when there was a 25 percent chance the child would be afflicted with FA was not a gamble they were willing to make. "We didn't want to give a kid a death sentence or have an abortion," Jack says. "For a long time, those were our two options." After the seminar, the Nashes fought through the crowd to Wagner and volunteered on the spot.

Science Sucks

Months after returning home from Camp Sunshine, the Nashes learned they qualified to be a Wagner and Hughes test case. Things were looking up; Molly's platelets were stable, albeit low, and science seemed to be working in their favor. Lisa entered under the care of the two doctors who had spent months in the laboratory perfecting the tests, but they warned Jack and Lisa that the science was experimental and far from a sure thing.

Molly was two and a half when Lisa completed her first round of fertility drugs. Lisa produced multiple eggs that were extracted from her ovaries by needle and fertilized in a petri dish. Three days later, Hughes screened for FA and checked the tissue type. The tests took less than 24 hours. Only one embryo met the criteria: a disease-free bone marrow match for Molly. The embryo was reinserted into Lisa's uterus. Sixteen days passed. The Nashes prayed and hoped and waited, until they received the crushing news that the in vitro was unsuccessful.

Doctors had told the Nashes to expect Molly's bone marrow to malfunction when she was about three years old. "Sure enough," Lisa says, "the day Molly turned three, her platelets started falling and her red blood cells were larger—an indication of bone marrow failure."

Before the Nashes could repeat the PGD process, Dr. Hughes, whom the Nashes then saw as Molly's only hope, stopped returning their phone calls and e-mails. Months and countless unanswered messages later, some news reached Jack and Lisa: Hughes was being investigated for using federal funds for embryonic research, which would have been illegal according to a 1996 federal law. Hughes—and Molly—were caught in the crosshairs of a politically charged debate and the public's apprehension about embryonic research. When the Nashes finally spoke with Hughes, he informed them that he was off to the private sector and could no longer help. The Nashes' cell samples and corresponding research remained locked in the bowels of Georgetown University, which now wanted nothing to do with Hughes' research, nor anything to do with Molly. In August 1998, Dr. Hughes sent what would be his final e-mail to the Nashes: "I am sorry. Science sucks sometimes. Go on without me."

At Any Price
As far as Jack and Lisa were concerned, two-plus years had been wasted while their daughter weakened. Molly's platelets fell to 30,000. The Nashes sought solace in their faith, and the Jewish community rallied around them, holding blood drives at the synagogue and encouraging members to join the National Bone Marrow Registry. With luck the Nashes might find a good enough match—one that would have an 18 percent chance of succeeding. Daily life for the Nashes became a long, vaporous moment in which they tried to keep one eye on the future and the other on Molly's every move.

The extended family spent endless hours together simply celebrating Molly's existence, lavishing love on her. Each day, each step, each laugh, each doll, each bath, each bedtime story was precious, and perhaps Molly's last. Family gatherings were routine rather than rare, with huge home-cooked meals as the centerpiece. And prayer. There was lots of prayer. Lisa, as she says, "never questioned God, never asked 'why me?' I knew He would give me the answers, the solutions." Every Friday when Lisa would light her candles for prayer, Jack would joke that the candles would melt down because she prayed so long.

In October 1998, the Nashes heard of a place they thought might answer those prayers. The Reproductive Genetics Institute, a Chicago-based company, had also been performing PGD. In January, Jack, Lisa, and Molly flew to Chicago and met with Dr. Charles M. Strom, one of the center's geneticists. When they walked into his office, Molly immediately crawled into the big-shouldered Strom's lap. Whereas Dr. Wagner had wanted to keep personal distance between himself and his patients, Strom chuckled as Molly climbed onto him. He asked the family to call him "Buck." In Strom, Lisa saw "a warm smile and a big heart that you can see from outside."

Jack and Lisa explained to Strom that what they wanted was to have a healthy child who would also be a bone marrow donor for Molly. Dr. Strom agreed to take their case. For inspiration, he inked an important date near Molly's 13th birthday on his calendar. "That was the thing for Lisa and me through this," says Strom. "We wanted to dance at Molly's bat mitzvah."

With a renewed sense of hope, Lisa once again began in vitro. This time, of the multiple eggs extracted, Strom located a pair of healthy embryos. Both were tissue matches, and both were implanted. And Lisa got the wonderful news that she was pregnant. Just as Jack and Lisa had begun talking about setting up the nursery down the hall from Molly, Lisa miscarried.

For Jack and Lisa, the loss was unbearable; so, too, was watching their now five-year-old daughter deal with the side effects of her medication. Molly was taking a synthetic form of the male sex hormone intended to stimulate her blood production. It was a short-term solution that came with a humiliating price. In addition to liver damage, androgen's side effects include pubic hair, muscle definition, and a deepening voice. Molly's body was shoved into adolescent male puberty.

Because of the prayers, because of their family, because their little girl's life was at stake, Jack and Lisa refused to give up. They repeated IVF and PGD in June and again in September to no avail. After the never-ending stress of in vitro fertilization, PGD, and gut-wrenching waiting periods, Lisa and Jack were physically and emotionally depleted. Hope, the Nashes discovered, is a double-edged sword: The powerful emotion sustained them through each day, but also deepened their despair with every failed attempt.

All Jack and Lisa had to show for their four IVF attempts was a weakened child and a mountain of bills. Jack's salary as general manager of a Denver hotel did little to make a dent in expenses. Each in vitro, which is not covered by insurance, cost roughly $15,000, plus an additional $6,000 for PDG and HLA testing. And that was on top of Molly's endless medical expenses for procedures and medications.

Back in Minnesota, Dr. Wagner was convinced that Molly would soon develop preleukemia. He called off any more IVF attempts—he believed there was simply not enough time. Wagner began to search for an unrelated donor.

A Very Good Call

"How do you explain to a five-year-old she's going to die?" That's the question Lisa asked herself. It's what kept her and Jack going. The Nashes took their case to yet another doctor, William B. Schoolcraft, at the Colorado Center for Reproductive Medicine. Schoolcraft is one of the country's top fertility specialists. One of Schoolcraft's colleagues had developed a process for stabilizing an embryo—growing it longer in the petri dish and giving it a much better chance of impregnating.

Under Schoolcraft's care (and with Dr. "Buck" waiting in the wings to perform the PGD and tissue testing), Lisa endured in vitro for the fifth time in almost three years. A round of "big gun" fertility drugs helped Lisa produce 24 eggs, almost three times as many as she had previously. Half of the embryos were healthy, but only one had the winning combination of no FA and a bone marrow match. On Dec. 10, 1999, Schoolcraft implanted the single embryo. This, the Nashes thought, was their last shot.

Two weeks later, on Christmas Eve, as Molly received a blood transfusion at Children's Hospital, Lisa's cell phone rang. It was Schoolcraft's secretary calling. A voice on the other end said, "Lisa, you're pregnant." She'd heard that before.

On Target

Lisa turned into the parking lot of the Target store as if she were driving a NASCAR race. Molly, exhausted from the transfusion, was in the backseat underneath winter layers—scarf, woolen cap, and green surgical mask. The mask was necessary to protect Molly from inhaling common germs that were potentially fatal for her.

Lisa jerked her Suburban into the first open spot she found. She was halfway out the door before she cut the engine. Seizing Molly's five-year-old hand, she marched into the madness: Christmas carols on repeat, blinking lights, too many last-minute shoppers. Dodging the mobs with teetering carts, Lisa bought five boxes of e.p.t. Pregnancy Tests and ran to the restroom.

Still wrapped in the scarf and hat, Molly leaned against the bathroom wall sucking air through the surgical mask. In the next stall, Lisa ripped open the e.p.t. boxes. Hands shaking, she fanned out five white sticks and followed the directions. "Mol, you OK?" Lisa called. One, two, three, four, five.... They all had blue plus signs. *My God*, Lisa thought, *I'm pregnant; they weren't lying.* She burst from the stall, gathered Molly in her arms, and dialed Jack on the cell phone.

Down the Drain

On a January morning, seven months before her August due date, Lisa stood in her shower, under the warm water, gently rubbing her belly and smiling at the thought of having two healthy children. The agony was instantaneous. Pain seared through her abdomen, and blood suddenly rushed down her legs. The shower drain was awash in crimson red. Lisa crawled from the shower and collapsed onto the bathroom floor. She dialed Schoolcraft's office and was told to come in immediately. When Dr. Buck in Chicago heard what had happened, he said only one word: "Fuck."

In the examining room, Lisa could not bear to look at the ultrasound monitor. She knew what was happening. She knew the baby was gone—and so was Molly's last chance. Two children. And then there were none. Schoolcraft informed the Nashes that the placenta had torn away from the uterine wall, leaving a hole that was bigger than the baby. Schoolcraft found a faint heartbeat. He sent Lisa home and prescribed a strict dose of bed rest. She was allowed one shower a week and three daily trips to the bathroom. Back home, Lisa lay with Molly curled beside her.

Molly's blood count was grim. Her body was gray, lethargic, and feeble. When every other little girl in her ballet class was learning new dance steps, Molly struggled to walk. She was blood transfusion dependent. She endured frequent needle sticks so nurses could keep tabs on her falling blood counts. The steroids that once boosted her marrow were useless now. Doctors tested her bone marrow every six months for preleukemic cells. The agonizing test, which punches through the pelvic bone to extract the thick, red liquid, was sometimes performed without anesthesia. Those were especially bad days. But even on good days, Molly had had enough of needle sticks, IVs, and hospitals. Each appointment was an exhausting battle—Molly's will against the nurses'. She would put up a good fight, crossing her arms firmly over her chest and fixing steely eyes on those who dared to come close. She threatened to bite. Inevitably, Molly would lose the standoff and dissolve into a hysterical tantrum. In May 2000, 20 out of 20 bone marrow cells tested showed signs of preleukemia—Molly's bone marrow had all but shut down.

Jack and Lisa couldn't just sit around and wait. They had to live all they could with Molly. In May, they took a family trip to Disney World. Molly had always wanted to go. They were reserving the trip for after the transplant, a celebratory time, but now who knew if there would be a tomorrow, let alone a transplant. Jack rented an electric scooter for Lisa. There they were: the dying child, her bedridden, pregnant mother, and the father walking a step behind and trying to keep it together. Lisa and Jack did their best not to let Molly see their tears. They snapped picture after picture.

One month later, in June, the Nashes flew to Minnesota to retest Molly's marrow. There was a glimmer of good news: The preleukemic cells had not progressed, meaning Molly would likely make it through Lisa's delivery and until the transplant without developing leukemia. But six-year-old Molly's platelets were virtually nonexistent. When Molly's skin was punctured her blood dribbled out purple.

Practice Makes Perfect

Dr. Buck hurried through the maternity ward, mentally checking off which rooms he'd already visited. He poked his head into another doorway and asked another pregnant woman if he could come in. He explained the situation—Molly's situation—to the expectant mother, and made his request: See, Buck would say, there was this mom, Lisa, and she was due at the end of August, and when she gave birth he'd need to collect her umbilical cord blood to use for a critical transplant.

For Molly, and for many bone marrow transplant recipients, the normally discarded umbilical cord and placenta are lifelines. Cord blood, the blood that remains in the placenta and umbilical cord after birth, is rich with blood stem cells—"adult" blood stem cells. Adult stem cells are produced in the organs and tissues of the fully developed human body, unlike embryonic stem cells which, in a controversial procedure, are extracted from and thereby destroy embryos. During a bone marrow transplant, adult stem cells are transplanted into the patient, where, if all goes well, they take root and produce blood cells and marrow.

Problem is, Buck sheepishly told the expectant moms on the ward, he had never actually collected cord blood before, and only had one shot to get it right. He figured a little practice would be good. So, would the soon-to-be mother donate her placenta and umbilical cord to the cause. Yes? Thank you, ma'am. He moved on to the next room.

"Here Are Your Babies"

On August 29, 2000, 56 hours after inducing Lisa, an obstetrician swiped a scalpel across Lisa's midsection, reached in, and lifted the head of a beautiful baby boy. A proud, primal howl of a healthy newborn filled the room.

Nurses worked in unison, clipping the umbilical cord, checking vitals, washing and wrapping the baby in a white blanket with pink and blue stripes. The air was thick with celebration and urgency.

Lisa's placenta was gathered and placed upside down in a sling with the limp umbilical cord hanging down, and the blood slowly trickled into a blood-bank bag. Dr. Buck, flanked by a representative of the Bonfils Blood Center, milked the placenta as though he were draining a flask of the finest wine. He retrieved a half-liter, half a soda bottle's worth.

"Does someone have the cord blood?" Lisa shouted, straining to see. "Does someone have the goddamn cord blood?" Buck turned to Lisa, holding in his arms her newborn son and the bag of blood. "Here are your babies," he said resting them both on her chest.

In the midst of the organized chaos, time slowed. Jack and Lisa looked from their baby to the bag of fluid. In an instant, the cord blood was lifted from Lisa's chest. It had to be packaged for transport. Jack's dad would hand-deliver the precious cargo to Dr. Wagner, who would perform the transplant in Minnesota.

Solution in the System

It was below zero that day in the Twin Cities when the first of five days' worth of chemotherapy began dripping into Molly's central line. The chemo would annihilate whatever was left of Molly's bone marrow. As the solution worked through her system, Molly remarked that it tasted like metal. After chemo, Molly was radiated and wheeled back into her room, looking red and swollen, as if she'd been baked in the microwave.

At 1:20 p.m. on Tuesday, Sept. 26, 2000, a nurse walked into Molly's room carrying a bag of her new brother's blood. A rabbi joined the family to bless Molly's "new life." While the slow, syrupy-thick drip began,

Molly's family sang happy birthday—what everyone hoped would be the beginning of the rest of her life—and snapped pictures. Molly's baby brother, not even a month old, sat on her lap.

Jack could smell the blood. It smelled like creamed corn. Looking on, the mother in Lisa thought, *You expect thunder and lightning and miracles*. But the nurse in her saw it was only a bag attached to a central line. The Nashes watched the clock. The transfusion—so many years in the making—lasted just 25 minutes. The family ate forkfuls of cake emblazoned with "Happy Transplant Day." Molly looked no different. No thunder. No lightning.

The Nashes prayed that the blood stem cells would find their way home to the empty bone marrow cavities. If all went well, the cells would set up shop and begin producing normal cells within weeks. Until then, blood transfusions, potent antibiotics, and a healthy dose of luck would keep Molly from falling ill. Wagner would monitor her blood counts with daily labs. And for days, that was how it went.

Some days Molly felt okay, others she shivered and sweat under the thin hospital sheets. Several days after the transplant, chemotherapy's side effects wreaked havoc. She threw up, developed painful mouth ulcers, and could barely swallow with mucus glands that had dried up like raisins. One day, while lying in bed, Molly pulled off part of her tongue as if it were a piece of bark. Large tufts of Molly's hair fell out and clumped on her pillow. Lisa shaved Molly's head smooth. She looked like every other kid on the transplant ward. Nine out of 14 kids on the ward died.

A Beautiful Day

Each letter in the Hebrew "alefbet" is assigned a numerical value, and the Hebrew word for life, "chai," adds up to 18. Eighteen days after the transplant, Molly rose from her bed, gingerly twirled around the room, and said, "Mommy, do you want to dance?"

Controversy

On Jan. 4, 2001, when Molly Rose Nash returned home to Colorado, the Nashes found themselves in the midst of a media storm. It began even before their genetically-screened baby's stem cells dripped into Molly's veins. Six days before the transplant, as Jack and Lisa cradled their new son and stroked Molly's hand, CBS News posed the question: "Genetically Improved children—An Ethical Issue?" The story detailed the measures employed by the Nash family and went on to report that the American Association for the Advancement of Science believed "it is dangerous and irresponsible for scientists to experiment with genetic changes that will affect future generations of humans, even if the goal is to cure disease..."

Jack and Lisa were hounded with requests for interviews. It seemed everyone wanted to photograph Molly with her newborn brother. The Nashes used the hospital's underground tunnels to come and go. News organizations including CNN, *The New York Times*, *U.S. News & World Report*, and the British Broadcasting Corporation teased provocative headlines. The headline in the *British Medical Journal* read "'Designer Baby Cures Sister." *The Washington Post*'s headline was "Test-Tube Baby Born to Save Ill Sister." The issues were raised: For the first time ever, in vitro fertilization combined with genetic testing had created a perfectly matched donor. Science, it seemed, had just moved a step closer to Aldous Huxley's *Brave New World*, where humans are engineered rather than born. Suddenly, the Nashes were the poster family for the divisive debate.

Dr. Wagner, Molly's transplant doctor, hardly sees the Nash case as tipping the scale toward scientific utopia, yet he does consider it to be a monumental medical moment. "The international response was almost unprecedented," he says. "But that was a mixture of what was going on: There's a child who had a life-threatening condition, time was running out, and we created a donor," he says.

The Nashes' healthy embryos were preserved, not destroyed. Yet some of their critics, actually many of their critics, insisted that the Nashes had been cavalier with the embryos, with life itself. A Christian Life Resources article titled "Babies a la Carte: Good Intentions & the Road to Hell," condemned Jack and Lisa for using in vitro fertilization and creating what it believed was an abundance of embryos for the sole purpose of selecting just one: "[Molly's brother] was a means—valuable only insofar as he carried the right genetic material. And if he hadn't, he would have been rejected—like the other 14 discarded embryos," wrote Charles Colson, a Christian leader and former special counsel to President Richard Nixon.

"To argue that 'surplus' embryos may be thrown away in any case," went an article in James Dobson's *Focus on the Family* magazine, "arrogantly glosses over the fact that embryos are living human beings, created in the image of God, and deserving protection." Father Joseph Howard, director of the American Bioethics Advisory Commission, railed against the Nashes' use of "unethical science," where, as he put it, "The price of treating the sick must not be paid by killing innocent human beings."

Even as *The Washington Post* cited the benefits of genetic testing (such as wiping lethal genetic disorders from future generations), many media pundits faulted the Nashes for ripping open a Pandora's box: If they were already selecting healthy embryos and screening for tissue type, how far was science from creating designer babies?

The responsibility falls squarely on the shoulders of society, says Dr. Schoolcraft, Lisa Nash's fertility specialist. "As long as the community is still responsible enough to use [genetic testing], a superbaby won't happen." These days, PGD can screen for 30 to 40 diseases and is commonly requested by parents terrified of passing along a devastating disease such as cystic fibrosis, muscular dystrophy, or Tay-Sachs.

In *Christianity Today*, Ben Mitchell, a senior fellow at Illinois' Center for Bioethics and Human Dignity, has expressed his concern over the "almost grotesque precedent" set by the Nashes. "Instead of saying that each person is an end unto themselves, this case says that people can be used as a means to the end.... You are having a child expressly to serve the needs of another child." The BBC and the medical website WebMD were among the news sources that posed the question, "Did they choose to have a healthy baby because they wanted another child, or because they wanted a source to help cure their daughter?"

For the most part, Jack and Lisa ignored the press and concentrated on saving their daughter. "All of our attention was wrapped around Molly," Lisa says. "Everything else was white noise. I wasn't focusing on people tearing me apart. My concern was taking care of Molly and giving her brother some semblance of a normal newborn life."

Lisa, who now is in her late 30s, is of average height and build, with a thin, youthful face and dark, curly hair that requires little maintenance, which is a good thing. Like most moms, Lisa puts her family's concerns ahead of her own. There's not a lot of time for primping. The only visible hint that Lisa has endured such an ordeal is in her eyes: They're dark and intense; they're the eyes of a lioness protecting her cubs.

Jack's eyes have the twinkle of a playful joker. He is the softer yin to Lisa's yang. In his early 40s, with graying hair, he's more inclined than his wife to smile. It seems that Jack and Lisa's marriage is a partnership. One minute, he's following her lead, and the next he's charting the course. But when it comes to Molly, it's Lisa who does the talking, with Jack filling in some details, and when the mood becomes too intense, lightening the conversation with dry humor. Perhaps it's Lisa's maternal instinct or the NICU nurse in her, but she's the one who has the photographic memory of Molly's life. She's the one who can recall her daughter's blood count on any given morning.

The Nashes can't understand why people question their motives and self-righteously deconstruct their private lives. Never mind the arrogance of some Christian pundits who, when preaching against the PGD process and the decisions the Nashes have made, discount the fact that the Nashes are Jewish. And according to Jewish law, as Lisa and Jack see it, the faithful are commanded to do whatever is necessary, with the exception of committing murder or adultery, to preserve life. "We wanted a healthy child," Lisa says. "We wanted a child who would not suffer the way Molly suffered. And we made a decision for our family, not for the world to take issue. In my shoes, you would have done the same thing."

Goodnight
She's fighting the needle again. It's Feb. 22, 2005, and Molly is in the hematology department of Children's Hospital. She's got her arms locked tightly around her purple sweater. She fidgets in the chair, shuffles her feet, and commands the nurse not to probe her special arm for veins. Molly glares at her dad, as if the blood test is his fault.

Dr. Hayes, the hematologist, delivers good news: Molly's platelets register a very healthy 395,000, a level that's held steady for four and a half years. The bone marrow is functioning normally. This September marks the landmark fifth anniversary of the transplant and by most standards Molly is a normal fifth-grader. In school, she likes math and science, and she would have gotten a perfect score on a recent spelling test if she hadn't misspelled the word "animal." She experiments with makeup, burns up the phone lines, and listens to ear-splitting music—The Black-Eyed Peas, Outkast, and 'N Sync thump through her bedroom walls. She's 10 and a half going on 13.

Dr. Hayes, taking Molly's blood pressure, asks how her brother's doing. Molly replies, "Annoying." Molly's dad rolls his eyes and chuckles. When Lisa was pregnant, she and Jack went round and round about boy names but nothing stuck—until one night Lisa woke up abruptly. It was so obvious. The name had been right in front of them all the time. It was right there in Genesis: *So the Lord, God, caused a deep sleep to fall upon the man, and while he slept took one of his ribs and closed up its place with flesh; and the rib which the Lord God had taken from the man made into a woman and brought her to the man. Then the man said, 'This at last is bone of my bones and flesh of my flesh....'*

Adam turns five at the end of August. He and his big sister, Molly, bicker and bait each other like typical siblings. Yet there are times, usually when Jack and Lisa aren't watching, that Molly gently pushes Adam on the backyard swing and coddles him when he trips in the grass. Molly's careful to be a good big sister to Adam and two-year-old Delaine. The newest addition to the Nash family was also conceived through in vitro with one of the healthy preserved embryos. "We were twice blessed by PGD," Lisa says. "Without this technique, it could have been just Jack and me looking at pictures on the wall."

Molly is still fragile; the transplant cured her of bone marrow failure, but Fanconi anemia is permanent. Like many with the disease, she receives nourishment through a feeding tube. Although she can eat on her own, Molly never experiences hunger. At dinner she unwinds a California roll and chews a few grains of rice or pushes the contents of her plate around in circles. The exception is curly fries—of which she'll eat four or five. At meal times and at bedtime, she's plugged into a bag of formula that fills her stomach bit by bit. For now, Molly's prognosis is good. But those with FA rarely have a worry-free life. Molly has 35 to 40 doctor appointments annually. She has regular screenings for solid-tumor cancers. Jack and Lisa are always on high alert—a common cold in the Nash family could have dire consequences for Molly.

Each night before bed, Molly bounces into her room and finds a million ways to procrastinate—she plays on the computer, organizes her book bag, shows off her collection of snow globes. Moments before she slips beneath the sheets, Jack or Lisa strap her torso into a brace designed to counteract the scoliosis that curves her spine. "It squishes me—sometimes it's hard to breathe," she says, pretending to gasp for breath. When Molly gets in bed, Lisa plugs in her "button" and a machine begins regulating the slow drip of nutrient-dense formula with a blinking red light and a measured beep.

"Goodnight, Mommy," Molly says.

"Good night, Molly, we love you."

—August 2005

19.

Naked Ambition

by Rebecca L. Olgeirson

It's a Wednesday morning, and Troy Lowrie looks like your average wealthy suburban Denver father who's about to take his little girl to school before heading into the office. Waiting for his eight-year-old daughter, Gabrielle, to gather her things, he puts his briefcase and suit jacket in the pristine trunk of his Mercedes and putters about the granite-topped counters of his gilded kitchen. At 40 years old, Lowrie is of average height, with more hair than many men his age. He wears a fitted dress shirt that's snug on his solid build, along with a tie, grey suit pants, and shiny dress shoes. Normally, Lowrie drives his daughter and nine-year-old son, Houston, to school, and before leaving he spends these few minutes talking with his wife. But Pam was up all night nursing Houston through a bout of the flu, and they're both in bed.

Gabrielle announces she's ready, and the two head to the Benz. In the garage, they pass the family's fleet of cars: a Jaguar (with plates that read PAMS JAG), a few motorcycles, and a custom pink Hummer. In the corner there's the 1934 Ford three-window coupe that Lowrie restored with his late father, Hal, the patriarch of the family business, VCG Holding Corp. Gabrielle tosses her backpack onto the car seat and hops in. The 10-minute drive to school takes them past horses grazing in the meadows of the Lowries' posh subdivision nuzzled against the foothills. "Don't forget it's our turn to drive to jazz class today," he reminds Gabrielle as they pull up to her elementary school. "I'll be here at three." Curbside, Lowrie exchanges "I love yous" with his little girl, and he watches the enormous backpack bounce on her back as she scurries into the school. Then it's a 10-minute drive to the Lakewood office of his VCG headquarters.

By 8:15 a.m., Lowrie walks by the bronze bust of his father and enters the corner office. As he does every day, the first thing he does is call VCG's president, Mike Ocello, in St. Louis to check on last night's numbers. It was Fat Tuesday—that night when every city seems to have a Bourbon Street—and a very profitable night for VCG, a company founded on booze and boobs. The Lowrie family business is a national chain of 13 strip clubs, with five of them in Denver: three PT's Showclubs, The Penthouse Club, and the local crown jewel in Lowrie's burgeoning dynasty, the Diamond Cabaret and Steakhouse, which he picked up last year for $6 million. With the phone cradled to his ear, surrounded by pictures of Pam and the kids, Lowrie nods and smiles. He knows that nights like last night are providing the capital to fund his corporate strategy, one that could make him the Walt Disney of porn—which would make Denver his Magic Kingdom.

The midday Colorado sun is squint-inducing as Lowrie tosses his keys to the Diamond Cabaret valet. Walking into the dark bar from the sunshine, it takes a minute for the eyes—and perhaps expectations—to adjust. Blinking to clarity, standards conform as quickly as pupils. Identities are difficult to discern; a man is just a guy, a woman is just a stripper.

Every city has its premier gentlemen's club, and the Diamond is Denver's. The formidable brick building sits stoically upon prime downtown real estate. With a sturdy exterior of brick and concrete, it stands, fittingly enough, like a vaulted bank, filled with money and naughty secrets. What happens in the club, patrons trust, will stay in the club. Pay your cover charge and the doors open to velvet curtains, cushy armchairs, and beautiful women. Adhering to the "gentlemen" part of gentlemen's club, there are no poles in the Diamond. There are, however, $20 glasses of wine and prime porterhouse steaks. Waiters occasionally drop the names of prominent guests: assorted Broncos, local high-profile businessmen, and even visiting celebs like Jon Bon Jovi and Sting, who both recently enjoyed post-concert meals in the Diamond's steak house. The A-list clientele undoubtedly appreciates the opportunities the darkness affords: the ability to anonymously enjoy what Lowrie refers to as the "entertainment."

Seven nights a week, women stand atop big, round tables, slowly undulating to bass-thumping songs, sporting porn-star heels, tiny thongs, and perfect pedicures. Put some clothes on them and they'd pass for the ladies who lunch in Cherry Creek North—except for those brutal Lucite stilettos. Of course, the strippers don't actually dance: They bend. Backward, forward, squatting and splitting. The lighting system is carefully engineered; it washes over the women, flattering their assets. Inside the Diamond, everything and everyone looks good. Inevitably, the strippers drop to their knees and snap their G-strings for dollar bills. Anywhere else, it would look like a subservient pose, but here it's the move that commands the currency. The money comes and is quickly tossed to the center of the table, and when the song ends the bills, some cool and crisp, some sweaty and crinkled, are crammed into tiny purses.

This afternoon, Lowrie waits in the buffet line and takes inventory of the scenery. Among the socioeconomically diverse patrons, clad in business attire ranging from suits to Carhartts, he's wearing the same business suit he wore when he dropped his little girl off at school. It's his personal policy: If he's on the floor of his clubs, he's in a suit. Today, along with what will be a usual buffet of strippers, the Diamond has laid out a Mexican spread. All you can eat for $4.99. The buffet table isn't a big earner, but a wise investment nonetheless, providing customers with an ostensibly respectable cover to hit the Diamond on a lunch break. It's an incentive that lures men to the club during a normally slow time of day. Now there's only a single entertainer dancing. She's on a table top, performing for a man seated alone. He stands up, and the topless dancer presses her hands on his shoulders, drapes her long, blonde hair over his face, and slowly starts to groove. "These guys could go to any bar in LoDo," Lowrie says. "But they come here because they know they won't be rejected." It's this philosophy that is the financial foundation of VCG Holding Corp. and the cornerstone of what is becoming Lowrie's Denver-based empire of skin.

When Lowrie bought the Diamond almost a year ago, some locals, like those boys who talk business at the Palm and later retire to the

Diamond to close the deal, undoubtedly viewed the buy as the top prize in the local girlie biz. But they underestimated Lowrie's master plan. Acquiring Denver's most famous strip club is merely another step Lowrie has taken in an effort to bolster his larger strategy. Lowrie visualizes that his chain of strip clubs, which already dot the country's midsection, will connect him to America's $10 billion porn industry. Everything he needs is all right here in the Front Range. From the Diamond Cabaret's front door, pick a direction, north or south, drive 45 minutes, and you'll run into Colorado companies already cashing in on sex. Just south on I-25, in the Tech Center, you'll find the offices of On Command, which distributes movies—adult and otherwise—to nearly a million hotel rooms worldwide. Also in the south suburbs are the offices of satellite provider EchoStar's Dish Network and cable's Adelphia Communications, two content providers that list porn on their channel guides. Drive northwest from the Diamond up to Boulder, and you'll find New Frontier Media, which distributes porn flicks to other cable TV and direct-broadcast outlets, which in turn deliver porn to more than 63 million subscribers. Fiscal year 2005 was New Frontier's most profitable to date, with reported earnings of $11.1 million. The cable and satellite providers won't break down the numbers, but porn must bring in big money—it has to, otherwise companies like these wouldn't dirty their hands with it. And although Los Angeles is where the vast majority of porn movies are made, to hear Lowrie talk you get the sense Colorado—the big red Focus-on-the-Family state—could become the nexus of big-money porn-distribution deals. "This company is my father's legacy," says Lowrie. "I took it to the next level. In 20 years I hope to take it two or three levels higher, and I'll be proud to give it to my own son. I wish my dad could've seen what his business is today."

"Aren't you Troy?" a dancer asks him. "I really like the redecorating you've done here." (After buying the Diamond, Lowrie invested another million into an ongoing renovation, including the new non-topless, self-described "ultra dance lounge," Tabu, upstairs.) He thanks the stripper and mentions plans to spruce up the VIP room next. She points to the Diamond's main floor, where most of the entertainment occurs. "There's only one thing," she says. "Are you going to put railings on the tables out there? The tables are great, but it's pretty hard for us to walk the steps in these shoes," she says pointing to her own four-inch heels.

"Yes, yes, the railings have already been ordered," he says. The dancer thanks him and leaves, clearly pleased with the response. Happy strippers are good for business, and railings are a small investment in happy strippers. Lowrie knows his master plan rests on those legs. But as with any business decision Lowrie makes, his motivation is more complex than profit margins. The careful attention he gives his entertainers is also something of a duty, a family-imposed obligation. For in every club, Lowrie sees a chance to gild his father's legacy, and in every stripper he sees a bit of a mother he barely knew.

Attempted murder has a way of changing a family. For Lowrie it happened when he was 15 years old. One evening, after football practice, he was changing clothes in his bedroom before dinner when he heard gunshots. He took off to his parents' bedroom, and there on the floor lay his adoptive father, Hal, in a pool of blood; his adoptive mother, Lu, stood above him, a pistol in her hand. Lowrie tackled his mom and wrestled away the gun; he quickly emptied the chamber and hid the weapon in the bathroom. He smacked the button that activated the home alarm system and tore back to the bedroom. He had one thought: Was his dad still alive? Yes, he could see that Hal was still breathing and that his mother once again hovered above him. The gun was gone, but what would she do next? He carried his mother kicking and screaming outside, came back inside, and locked the door.

Hal was conscious despite receiving three shots: one each into his arm, hand, and rib cage. Blood was everywhere. Hal directed his son to remove his belt and use it as a tourniquet to stop the bleeding. Lowrie followed the directions and stabilized his father. When the cops and emergency medical techs finally busted in, he was covered in Hal's blood. The EMTs went directly to Hal while the police handcuffed Lowrie. "It wasn't me," he insisted. But no one listened. Lu had gotten to the cops first, and she blamed the shooting on her son. From the backseat of the police car, Lowrie watched the ambulance speed his father to the hospital, terrified he'd seen his dad for the last time.

Not surprisingly, that night changed everything for Lowrie. Hal survived and his wife was sent away for psychiatric treatment; whatever conventional father-son relationship there was between Lowrie and his dad was over. The son had saved his father's life; now they were blood brothers. Equals. And with Lu gone, the Lowrie men could do whatever they pleased—and they did.

Hal was a backslapping good ol' boy who ran bars in early '70s Colorado. He was a born salesman whose charm more than compensated for his limited education. Lowrie followed his dad on the job, quietly watching as Hal commanded center stage. Lowrie always knew he'd take over his father's business. At five years old, he'd sit by the register and count the money. By kindergarten, he says, he knew what an MBA was and that he wanted one. Back then, Hal's joints were just regular drinking holes—until one night when a bartender at the Aloha Beach Club on Federal Boulevard took off her top and brought in the bar's best take ever. Hal saw the easy money. Zoning laws were undefined, and Hal put up strip clubs wherever he could. First in metro Denver and ultimately in St. Louis. He became a club fixture. His philosophy: Create the best party in town every single night. He'd see to it himself, grabbing the microphone to get the party started. And after last call he'd often keep his friends around and keep the good times going. The business was built on his charms, which held appeal for both sexes. Of course, Hal had always been a ladies' man. He'd left Lu for another woman, which is why she'd unloaded the pistol on him. After the shooting, after the divorce, the partying only intensified.

And Lowrie now spent plenty of nights by his father's side at the bars. Sometimes, after enough cocktails, Lowrie would again take care of Hal. "There were times where it was like I was the dad, carrying him home after a late night," says Lowrie. Finally, when Lowrie was 22, he took an official role in the family business. That kindergartner who'd once sat next to the cash register had brought home his MBA from the University of Denver, and Hal arranged for him to manage Glendale's Shotgun Willie's, then a Lowrie property.

Lowrie was instantly anointed as Hal's right-hand man. Immersing himself in the family business, he managed the club by night and accompanied Hal to meetings by day. Lowrie even bought the house next door to his dad, and the men took out the fence to create one big backyard. Father and son ate dinner together every night. By now the differences in their personalities were apparent. Hal could sit at the bar and drink with his customers all night; Lowrie could eyeball the bottle and tally lost profits. Still, during this time a little of Hal rubbed off on his son. Lowrie had some minor scuffles with the law, including a fight outside a Taco Bell when he was 18. Inside the clubs, he sampled the inventory. He even married a stripper. It was a short-lived marriage that lasted a year, and all Lowrie will say about it now is that it was a confusing, messy time for him.

After the divorce, he left his father's side, taking a temporary break from Denver and managing the San Antonio PT's for about six months. On nights off, he could be found at the local country bar, Denim and Diamonds. It was the kind of place where the ladies wore fringed shirts and low-heeled boots. The men wore Stetsons and addressed their dance partners as *ma'am*. Lowrie liked these kinds of places. He'd run the Grizzly Rose in Denver for a short time while his dad tried to buy it. (But the county, afraid Hal would turn it into a monster strip club, killed the deal.) Lowrie felt at home in these Urban Cowboy-style Texas bars. One of the waitresses at Denim and Diamonds was, as the cowboys say, a pretty little thing named Pam. Lowrie knew immediately when he met her that she was The One. She was—and still is—a petite beauty with a whip-smart sense of humor. "I knew," he says, "she was the woman I would raise my kids with." Pam was a small-town Texas girl. The two talked about how they wanted to raise a family and discussed their values. She knew about the strip bars; she checked out the local PT's with Lowrie. It didn't scare her off. When Lowrie ultimately returned to Colorado, they did the long-distance thing for six months before he convinced Pam to drive her pink VW Beetle to Colorado.

Pam wasn't the only thing Lowrie brought back from Texas. Watching a sea of cowboy hats move in unison across the dance floor got him thinking. Country dancing was huge at the time, dominated by 50,000-square-foot bars that could hold 4,000 people. Lowrie's brain ran the numbers. "My dad always said, 'If there was an easier way to make this much money, we'd do it.'" He brought the idea to his dad, and the Lowries decided to try their hand at country music.

Hal provided the seed money, and Lowrie opened up his first country bar, A Little Bit of Texas, in Indianapolis. The money was good, but it was clear that Hal's strip-club largesse would become a problem for expansion. "Cities get nervous when the Lowries come to town ready to lease 50,000 square feet," he says. So Hal removed himself from the country business and Lowrie, on his own, took the company public, raising funds for more country bars in St. Louis and Tucson. "Opening country bars is great. Half the city comes to the opening, and the mayor shakes your hand and says, 'Thank you,'" says Lowrie. "Nobody says thank you when you open a strip club." Eventually the country fad fizzled and Lowrie sold the clubs. "I would've loved to be the King of Country," he says. Instead he was rightful heir to a strip-club crown. And there was only one way to assume the throne.

As far as Lowrie was now concerned, his wild times were behind him. He'd established his role in the family business as the responsible bean counter and found the woman he'd start his own family with. Then, just as the couple was to be married, Hal was diagnosed with lung cancer. The disease moved through him swiftly, killing him in the spring of 1994. He was 58. Lowrie's father was dead; his mother, Lu, he barely spoke to; and his only sister took off for California long ago. The family business that had taken such a toll on Lowrie was now tossed into his lap. Still, he decided that he wouldn't sell it off. Instead, he set out to run a respectable strip-club enterprise.

Fifteen-year-old Lowrie had used Hal's belt for a tourniquet and saved his father's life; now, at 28, he found himself applying a tourniquet to his father's business. While he was on his deathbed, Hal was indicted by the feds for racketeering, conspiracy to launder money, and enticing people to cross state lines to commit prostitution near his Brooklyn, Illinois clubs. Lowrie maintained Hal's innocence, despite a guilty plea from the former police chief—among others—that followed Hal's death. Shortly thereafter, Lowrie settled with a $2 million fine. Then he went to work.

The employees mourned Hal, but there was also a sense of relief that his legal problems no longer threatened to topple the business. "I never considered selling the business," recalls Lowrie. "My dad was determined to make this a career where his employees could support their families, and I had to continue that."

But he could change the way the business operated. Hal ran the business the way he ran his family, concerned more with partying than profits. Lowrie, on the other hand, was determined to manage with discipline

and order. He applied basic business practices to the strip clubs, like com-
puterized cash registers and payroll systems. Unburdened by Hal's need
to be everyone's pal, Lowrie tightened the ranks and the bars flourished.
Lowrie kept track of every penny. No more freebies. "Some of my dad's
old friends would say, 'You know your dad would sit here and drink with
me,'" Lowrie says. "I know it disappointed some of them; my dad could sit
at the bar all night, but that's not me. I'm the business guy."

With the clubs running smoothly, he implemented some innovations
of his own. He locally pioneered "nude rooms"—sections of the clubs
where alcohol is forbidden and the women are 100 percent naked. The
notion was met with resistance—and lawsuits—from city council members, but it proved a moneymaking draw and a lap-dance destination.
Lowrie also started buying more clubs. It got him thinking: "There were
all these guys with little clubs around the country ready to retire. I could
be their exit strategy."

Slowly and quietly, Lowrie set about building his father's business
into a dynasty, playing by new rules—some of which were his, some
of which were imposed. Unlike in Hal's day, 21st century cities have
become very good at zoning out strip clubs. "You can't just go throw
up a club wherever you want to anymore," says Dave Manack, associate
publisher of Exotic Dancer Publications. "The trend is buying existing
clubs or getting them to license your name." To manage city relations,
Lowrie even hired a government-affairs liaison who flies in on a private
jet to help placate city councils. Last year, to generate capital for his
strip-club shopping, Lowrie took his father's company public. He used
the capital to buy the Diamond Cabaret and build his pride and joy, the
Phoenix Penthouse Club. In a shrewd move, Lowrie divides ownership and management of the clubs in St. Louis, Indianapolis, Arizona,
and Colorado between the publicly-traded VCG and his privately
held Lowrie Management. This means he need not disclose his entire
fortune to the public. Ultimately, he says, he hopes to bring Lowrie
Management under the VCG umbrella. People ask him what the VCG
stands for, but it was just a holding company he acquired to take the
company public. Lowrie likes to joke that it means "very cute girls."

Lowrie's Mile-High City strip-club empire adheres to a clear structure. He gives his clubs report-card rankings, from "A" level gentlemen's
clubs such as the Diamond Cabaret and the Penthouse Club, to "B" clubs

like PT's Showclub on Evans Avenue and PT's All-Stars, and finally "C" clubs such as PT's All-Nude, which caters to young men between 18 and 21 years old and offers nude dancers and topless waitresses but no booze. Lowrie's newest Denver bar, Tabu, a clothing-required dance lounge above the Diamond, is a gateway club to the racier stuff. Lowrie estimates his "A" clubs earn $4 million to $7 million in annual revenue, with margins at 34 percent—that's between $1.3 million and $2.3 million in profit. His "B" clubs earn revenue between $2 million and $4 million with similar profit margins. Owning all of these tiers of the market, Lowrie runs the region's entire spectrum of skin. And with this system, he has access to the best entertainment and the best management, and he saves money on advertising. Buying in bulk means better deals. Whether it's the limes or ladies, "it's all economies of scale," says Lowrie.

The biggest chain of strip clubs, says Exotic Dancer's Manack, is the privately held Déjà Vu Showgirls, with about 70 clubs nationwide. But Déjà Vu, which partnered with Hustler, usually puts one Larry Flynt's Hustler strip club in each market. Same goes for Scores, the topless club that shock-jock Howard Stern made famous, which is also licensing clubs in major cities. Another big-name player, Spearmint Rhino, has already eyed Denver, attempting to land a 20,000-square-foot stripper palace in Sheridan. But Lowrie appears to be the only one intent on dominating each of his multiple markets. The real prize for Lowrie, however, lies a step beyond the national strip-club expansion. He wants to leverage the clubs to secure a slice of the lucrative porn industry. Mark Kernes, senior editor of Adult Video News, estimates adult entertainment as a $10 billion to $12 billion industry, including strip clubs, novelty shops, the Internet, TV, and DVD sales. Lowrie is already seeing some of that cash, but he wants more.

The plan hinges on The Brand. Take the Diamond Cabaret. Let's say it becomes known as the premier "A" level club in eight markets nationally. Lowrie then ties it to a television channel (either satellite or cable, ideally a Denver-based outlet). He gets a cut of the channel, and that channel builds name-brand recognition and drives business to the clubs. Eventually porn stars from "the Diamond Cabaret Channel" make special appearances at his clubs. The television screens inside the club promote the network; advertisers buy time on the network (think Viagra). Complete the scene with a gift shop by the front door selling brand-name porn and the skin business is taking a page from Walt Disney. Except there are only three Disney theme parks in the United States—Lowrie wants 40. As for the name, it probably won't be the "Diamond Cabaret Channel." PT's has the biggest presence nationally and it has sentimental value—after all, it's the name Hal used on the original clubs. Also, since Lowrie already has three Penthouse Club licenses in play, cashing in and expanding on the Penthouse brand is attractive. He calls the magazine "the second most recognizable name in adult entertainment." If he can't make his daddy's brand famous, he'd settle for capitalizing on the Gucciones' family biz. He's had talks with the players, and time will tell. "Maybe those guys underestimate us a bit; it just means we'll have to prove ourselves that much more. They'll be surprised how well the clubs help the magazine." He doesn't sound worried.

His plan is already in play in strip clubs across the country as Lowrie sits in a booth at the Diamond Cabaret Steakhouse, outlining his vision. The room hosts a ministage with one of his entertainers dancing her shift. Under the restaurant's low light, Lowrie dines on ahi tuna and a good bottle of red wine. This particular booth happens to be "Bobby's booth," where one of the Diamond's original owners, Bobby Rifkin, held court. Rifkin was a legendary Denver character who ran several restaurants and nightclubs before opening the Diamond Cabaret in 1991, his only topless club. Rifkin, a friendly competitor of Hal's, had something Lowrie's father and, for that matter, Lowrie himself has never been able to attain: respectability. Denver held both Rifkin and his Diamond in high regard.

Described as a cross between Danny DeVito and Napoleon, even friends say Rifkin was outspoken, brash, and at times self-centered. Then, one day, Rifkin changed. At age 66, doctors told him he had prostate cancer. Suddenly Rifkin found religion and made it his mission to raise $1 million to eradicate the disease. His annual male-only fundraisers stocked a hush-hush list of rich Denver men who ponied up $1,000 each for a special night at the Diamond. Ultimately, he reached his fundraising goal with one last party held after his death. At the end of his life, legitimacy and respect suddenly became a priority for Rifkin.

Lowrie constantly battles the strip-club-owner stereotype—Tony Soprano up to no good in the back room of the Bada Bing. Lowrie wants to be more than that. Partly because it's good for business—respectability helps assuage reticent investors and helps with VCG's SEC standing—and partly because he wants it for his father and his own family. And so Lowrie's taken a page from Rifkin's book with his charitable strategies. After Hal's death in 1994, Lowrie and Pam created the Lowrie Family Foundation. The Lowries have plenty of money to give, but the foundation is also a charitable strategy for the business—an investment. Sometimes a strip club needs to buy some goodwill. Early on, he discovered not everyone would take his money. But in October 2004, the Lowrie Family Foundation made a donation that made Denver's philanthropic community finally take notice. The Susan G. Komen Breast Cancer Foundation accepted $100,000 of Lowrie's money and asked him to introduce Jay Leno at their gala. Lowrie believes he should get credit for his gifts no matter how he earned the money. Everyone else does. Rifkin did.

The strip-club king has invested a small fortune in his credibility and his image, but could expansion into porn ultimately undermine it? Lowrie doesn't think so. "The argument I get when I open a club is that people don't want that going on in their neighborhood," he says. "But with porn, that's in your home, those girls aren't around the corner. It's a movie." Then again, in Lowrie's strip clubs no one is getting paid to have sex. "I've worked with him on charity events before," says one local businessperson. "But if the money was coming from porn, it would be a different story. Everyone draws their own line; that would be mine."

With the $100,000 donation to the Komen Foundation, the time had come for the kids to know what pays the bills. The whole family would attend the gala. But what if Leno made the obvious wisecracks? Houston and Gabrielle were old enough to learn what Daddy does for a living. The family gathered in their Golden home. At first Lowrie asked the kids what they thought he did. They answered that he went to the office. Yes, Dad said, but he went on to explain that he owns restaurants where ladies take off their tops to dance, and men give them money to watch. Lowrie signed onto a laptop featuring a club surveillance system, which he keeps in the upstairs family room. On the screen was a real-time view of the Penthouse Club. The joint was empty, but Lowrie showed the kids the bar, the stages, and the pole. "Houston saw the pole and I guess he'd seen something similar on *The Simpsons*," Lowrie says, "So he kind of looked at me and smiled." Putting on his best Homer Simpson voice, nine-year-old Houston accepted his father's profession (and his grandfather's legacy) with one word: "Boobs."

Gabrielle needed a little more convincing. A few days after the big talk, she came to Lowrie with questions. "Daddy," he recalls her saying, "if people say it's wrong for you to do this, well, is it wrong?" Lowrie told her no, it wasn't wrong. "And it means we can do things like give $100,000 to find a cure for cancer." What Lowrie didn't tell Gabrielle was that in each of the strippers, he saw a bit of his mother. Not Lu. She was his adoptive mom. But rather his birth mother—a woman he didn't meet until 1995, when he was 30. Troy Lowrie was born Troy Martinez. His birth mother, Rebecca Martinez, was 15 years old when her parents kicked her out of the house, pregnant with nowhere to go. She moved to Lakewood to live with a sister and gave birth to Troy. The teenage mom struggled to make ends meet, to feed her baby, to put a roof over their heads. She did what she could to stay together. It wasn't enough. Lowrie was a year and a half old when his mother admitted defeat and put him up for adoption. By then she'd undoubtedly heard her son's first words and watched his first steps. "My mom worked at a drive-in on Colfax called Taylor's," Lowrie says. "She said she knew she had to give me up when the only thing she could feed me were leftover potato peels from the drive-in."

Later in life, when she married, Rebecca kept her maiden name on her driver's license, specifically in case her son ever searched for her. When Lowrie turned 30, he did. The caseworker warned him that the process could take years. Twenty-four hours later, she called with word that Rebecca Martinez Smith was living in Orlando. She'd be on a flight to Denver that weekend. They reunited at the old Stapleton Airport. Lowrie and Pam stood together at the gate, holding his mother's photo, awaiting her plane. They recognized each other the minute she disembarked. They embraced and tears flowed. Rebecca spent that weekend in a hotel where she told her son her story—his story. She showed her grown son his new-born-baby pictures for the first time. "It was emotional," Lowrie says, in his typical unemotional manner. "It was, like, finally the puzzle of my life was coming together. I finally saw how my life started."

"My mom tried to raise me," he says. "But she didn't have any help. She couldn't do it alone." Matter-of-factly, he adds, "The day a woman comes in to fill out an application here [at the Diamond] is usually a low point. No one says, 'I'm at the top of my game, now I'll be a stripper.'" Lowrie knows many of the young entertainers work his tabletop stages only to feed their own kids. He stages "Dreamgirls Workshops," seminars that provide tips for boosting income, but also teach life skills like balancing a checkbook. "They should leave us better than the day they came here," Lowrie says. "That's the way this business should work."

Today, Gabrielle's standard response to questions about her dad's occupation is "none of your beeswax." She is the one whom Lowrie often puts on stage to present the oversize cardboard checks at charity events.

Back at the Diamond Cabaret Steakhouse, it's close to 10 p.m. The sun set hours ago, and Lowrie's still sitting in Bobby's booth. The dinner plates have been cleared, and the boss finishes his wine. Lowrie doesn't usually eat dinner here. If he's working late at the club, he'll have dinner at home first with his family and drive to the city after the kids are in bed. "My dad died of lung cancer, and I have to think it was from all the time spent in these clubs," says Lowrie. He speaks as if he's indeed aware of every pitfall his father hit, and he says he can steer himself away from the perils of the industry. "I don't want that to happen to me. I'm trying to pace myself better than he did." He says he can keep it all in perspective.

Around the booth, the party that Hal started still rages at the Diamond Cabaret. Lowrie's windowless bar pulses with sex, money, and booze. The dancers, the customers, they all come to escape their reality—but this is Lowrie's reality. While his strippers may leave the business better off than they were when they arrived, Lowrie's not going anywhere. The Diamond is pumping as Lowrie escorts me toward the exit and safely onto the street. As usual, the valet has the boss's car in the first parking spot, waiting. Underneath the streetlights, Lowrie says good night and extends a solid handshake. There's still time for him to peek in on his sleeping kids and crawl into bed next to his beautiful wife. But instead of making a right toward the valet, Lowrie turns around and heads back into the club. A world of $6 beers, single-mom strippers, crisp dollar bills, and the ghosts of family. Back at his beautiful suburban home, Pam leaves the lights on till he returns.

—September 2005

20.

Final Bell

by Robert Sanchez

The principal will leave at night. It will be late June, after graduation but well before the next high school year begins. Before he leaves that last time, the principal will enter through the glass doors; he will pass the security cameras and walk across the carpeted floor. The trophy case will hang from the ceiling in the foyer. The principal will make a right turn, then another right, a left, and then a right. He will open the door to his office and he will stand and he will stare. The room will look like a museum because, for the past 15 years, it has always looked like a museum. Photographs—dozens of them, framed and slightly askew—adorn the walls. There's the principal with President Bill Clinton, with Celine Dion, with Jack Nicklaus. There are letters pressed behind glass, too, thank-yous from people all over the country who never imagined they'd need the principal's help. On one wall next to the office door is a chalk drawing of the principal's friend.

He will look at those walls and wonder how the four slabs of drywall went from blank to full. Each photograph and letter and memento has its own story, and all of those stories circle back to him, back to this school.

When he leaves, he will be 59 years old. In the past decade and a half, a lot has changed. He has been cheered and sued. He has been celebrated and villainized. There were times when he cried so hard he thought he might never get up. Fifteen years ago, no one knew his name.

Now he can't escape it. Wherever he goes, his name is a symbol. He is a symbol. He is tragedy and hope, fear and redemption. The principal and the school, in so many ways, have become one and the same.

On that night next summer, he will finally pack up his office. He will take down the photographs and the letters. He will open drawers filled with hundreds of condolence cards, and he will put them in a box. He will enjoy the quiet; there will be no one at his door to interrupt him, no colleagues talking about the past. When he's done, he will go. He will make a left, then a right, then a left, and another left. He will see the trophy case, and he will walk across the carpet. He will exit the glass doors. And then it will be over.

Fall 2013

The principal was a principal long before his high school became both a noun and a verb. Before security cameras went up all around his school, before tour buses stopped out front and strangers sang church hymns at the back doors, before people from far-off places—from all around the world—began talking to him, hoping the principal could help solve their problems.

He'd rebuilt his school, this man, not with bricks and mortar, but with something far deeper and far more lasting. It took years of arguments and frustration and doing, and if he's being honest, he will say the job is still far from complete. He is the fifth man to have this job here. The baseball field is named for him. So is an academic foundation.

In quiet moments, he walks to the memorial behind his school and thinks. Even now, the principal is still trying to sort things out in his mind. He loves God and Jesus, and sometimes he grabs the Sacred Heart hanging from the chain on his neck when his thoughts become too much, when he feels sucked back in time. *It's not 1999*, he reminds himself.

That's why he went to the doctor this past summer. He'd been having chest pains and stomach problems. He'd felt them before—he'd been to the emergency room six or seven times in the past 14 years. When the tests came back clear, he knew what he needed to do. He drove to his counselor, who made him sit in a chair and talk. The principal told the counselor that this was his last year in his job; come late spring 2014, he would be the principal no more.

The counselor listened and said he knew what was going on. Your mind understands it's over, the man told the principal. Your gut does not; you still have to convince it. Soon after that meeting, the pains went away. And then, one day in early August, the principal went to his last first day of school ever. He told everyone his plans. He tried not to cry. That same week, his face was on the *CBS Evening News*.

So here he is, just after class, in his office on a late afternoon this past fall. The leaves are about to turn but haven't yet. He is sitting in a chair from which he can see the drawing of his friend. The principal is not resting, because as his buddies and colleagues and students will tell you, the man never rests. He is always thinking, planning, worrying. Even after 14 years, worrying is an easy thing to do here.

Winter 2012

It keeps happening, and each time he gets a call. Most recently, it happened in Newtown, Connecticut, where 20 children died during a rampage. He was at his desk at school when the call came. There was Aurora, so close to home. It was the morning, and the principal was at home getting ready to go to work. There was Virginia Tech and Pearl, Mississippi, and Chardon, Ohio. The principal is always among the first people whom family, friends, and journalists call. *Have you seen the news? Are you OK? What do you make of this?* He's always gracious. He thanks the people on the other end for taking the time to call, for thinking of him and his school. He'll answer the questions; he'll say he can't believe it's happened again.

Each new call he receives means another one he must make. Another school. Another tragedy. Another community to help. He'll find the number and leave a message. Rarely are his calls returned quickly. Even the principal must wait sometimes. He knows people will come to him when they're ready, when they feel comfortable to share their deepest fears with a man they've never met but with whom they have been thrown into an awful fraternity. So the principal waits, and eventually, almost always, there's a call back. *Whatever you need*, the principal says, *I'll be there.*

He's traveled tens of thousands of miles, but he never simply shows up, because he understands what it's like to have people tell you what to think and how to act. When he's invited to Blacksburg, Virginia, he talks about the need for counseling, about anniversaries, about the small moments that will get them through this. In place after place, he has seen the desperation in people's eyes. He has felt their embraces. He has tried to swallow their burdens, tried to offer something besides hugs and tears.

But, inevitably, he's asked what to do. *How do we fix this?* When he goes to Newtown, he's asked about the school building. *Should we reopen it? Should we raze it?* He doesn't know, he tells them. Certain things worked for his school, his community, but they have to figure that out on their own. And maybe that's the hardest part of being the principal. After all he's been through, after everything he's seen, he still doesn't have the answers.

The principal stares at the chalk drawing of Dave on his office wall and wonders why he's still here and Dave is not. Survivor's guilt. That's what his counselor calls it. Over the years, the principal has come to accept the term. In many ways, he has gained comfort through acceptance.

The principal felt shame that he lived and his friend died. The principal knows the kid with the shotgun saw him first. He can see the white T-shirt with cut-off sleeves and dark pants and boots coming toward him. He'd been one of the first adults in the main hallway at 11:25 a.m., saw muzzle flashes, heard bangs, watched glass explode. He was scared for his life, scared for the lives of all those kids coming toward him.

And so he ran up the hallway to save those kids. He saw the barrel of that weapon. It looked like a cannon. He wondered what it would feel like when he was shot. Would it hurt? Would he die quickly? *Please*, he thought, *let me die quickly.*

But then, Dave. The principal's friend, his confidant. Dave Sanders had coached basketball, taught business and computer technology. Just like the principal, he'd given everything he had to this school. Twenty-five years. The two had talked about their lives at the school the day before, in the stands at a baseball game. Dave and the principal, wondering aloud about the cost to their own families. How much had they sacrificed of themselves that could never be repaid to their wives, to their own children?

"Would you do it all again?" Dave asked the principal.

"Yeah. I would." Dave said he would, too.

When the shooting started, Dave was in a hallway adjacent to the gunfire. He was getting students to safety. It was Dave who caught the attention of the figure wearing the T-shirt and boots. It was Dave who was shot in the neck and through the teeth. It was Dave who later bled to death in a science room while students awaited police help. It was Dave's wife whom the principal had to console.

Shortly after the funeral, one of his students gave the principal the drawing of Dave. He hung it next to the door in his office. Every time he walked out, he would carry the memory of his friend into those hallways.

Summer 2007

"The world breaks everyone and afterward many are strong at the broken places." President Clinton spoke those words on a rainy afternoon in Jefferson County, quoting Ernest Hemingway's *A Farewell to Arms*. Somehow we all become stronger because of our weakest moments.

They break ground on the memorial one June day in 2006. Fifteen months later it opens. People come from around the world to that refuge, tucked behind the hill from the school. They walk the concrete trail that leads to the stone circle, to the names of the 13 victims, to the words of those they left behind.

The principal kept his distance until the victims' families had visited the memorial. *This is their place*, he thinks. So the principal stays away at first. Finally, when he knows it's OK for him to see it, he walks alone into the stone circle, and he thinks about the years that have passed. Eight graduations, seven proms. Only 36 of the 145 faculty and staff members from April 1999 are still around.

The principal returns often to think again about how far his school has come. But there's another question he has to ask: How many more years can he do this? One? Five? He can't say. He prays about it at church; he keeps going back to the memorial. Day after day, month after month, year after year. It's not time yet, but he knows it will become clear. He'll know when it's time to go.

Forgiveness is a complicated thing. When the lawsuits that claimed the principal had created an atmosphere for bullying were dismissed, he did not celebrate. Instead, the principal did as he had done since he arrived at his school as a 24-year-old American history teacher in 1979. He went to the adoration chapel at St. Francis Cabrini down the street and he prayed. The principal prayed for his family and for his school. He prayed for strength. He prayed that God and his own good works might see him through his darkest times. He prayed for his own forgiveness.

He keeps a condolence card on his desk at school. The principal has opened it so many times, held it so often, that it is bent and creased; the oil from his fingertips is pressed into the paper. Written on the inside, in blue ink, is a quote from Pope John XXIII: "One may hate the sin, but not the sinner."

He holds the card, reads those words about sinners, and he wonders: How deep is his capacity to forgive? If two boys—two of his students—murder, does that still deserve forgiveness?

For now, at least, he cannot forgive. Maybe he never will. And if that's a sin, it will be a burden for which he says he will be judged. All these years later, and he won't bring himself to mention those two names in public. Rarely does he call what happened at his school a "shooting." The word is shallow. Obscene. It strips that day of its significance—cheapens it to a singular instance and ignores everything that followed.

Winter 2002

The principal is in the basement, clearing out his past, when he happens upon the 4,000 letters he'd received just after the shooting. He'd tried to read them in those first months—20, maybe 25, a day—but it was a devastating process. Mixed in with words of encouragement were accusations, criticisms, threats. So he'd put them away. Maybe he'd look at them again, maybe not.

Now, the principal and his wife are ending their marriage. They've just sold their house, and he finds himself sitting on the basement floor with all those words. He opens envelope after envelope. The name on one strikes him. Diane Meyer. His high school girlfriend, his first love. He tears open the envelope and reads the note inside. I'm not sure if you remember me, she wrote. I'm so sorry for what happened at your school. You're in my prayers.

The principal looks up her mother, gets Diane's phone number, and calls. He thanks her for the letter, apologizes that it had taken so long to get back to her. When he hangs up, he wants to call back. And so he does a couple of weeks later, and then again a few weeks after that. Thirty years after they'd last seen each other, there's still...something.

The principal loves hearing her voice. He loves that he can call her and she'll listen. He loves that she never says she knows how he feels, or how he felt. She doesn't pretend to understand what it was like to have survived these past few years.

He keeps calling, and she calls him, too. She talks the principal through the most difficult moments of his divorce. She congratulates him on finishing another school year. That fall, the principal finally asks her out. Dozens more dates follow; hundreds more phone conversations. On December 24, 2003, he gives her roses. There's a ring attached. She says yes.

Fall 1999

His life is no longer his. Ten-, 14-, 16-hour days; he goes from meetings to classrooms to speeches to fundraisers to interviews to his office. The principal's staff worries he needs to take time off. He's been to the emergency room for pain in his chest, his back, his arms. He wonders, *Am I dying?* He's so distracted that he crashes the family's Honda Accord. His teenage daughter corners him one day at home. She wants her daddy back.

But there's work to do. There's always more work. The school library— it will be named the HOPE Columbine Memorial Library—and the memorial won't build themselves. There's been a bomb threat, an expulsion. Seven more suspensions. There are kids at school on suicide watch. He's being criticized for running a school that empowered bullies, an accusation that shattered him. He's been named in eight lawsuits. He'd do anything for any of his students, loved each of them. *Don't they know that? Don't their parents know?*

He hasn't had a real conversation with his wife in months. He's forgotten to eat, dropped from 210 pounds to 134 in a matter of months. He tried a bowling league, tried to connect with old friends, but everyone wants to know how the school is doing. *How's fundraising? How are the students? How are you?* They won't let him forget, not even for a minute. *Leave me alone*, the principal thinks.

One Sunday night, the principal is near tears in his office—papers, folders, binders piling up on his desk. The demands are destroying him. He's thinking of his own children. *Am I letting them down?* He grabs a trash can, wipes the papers off his desk into the garbage, and goes home.

He can never get away for long. It's his charge, this school. At night, when he's lying awake in bed, sometimes he thinks it's his destiny. A priest told him that once: He lived that day so he might somehow help lead his community. He was the chosen one. And because of that, he gets up early the next morning and he goes back to work. Back to the meetings and conferences and interviews. Back to the teachers who cry with him in his office, to the phone calls from worried parents. Back to helping design a new library with lots of windows, just in case kids need to break out.

Here, though, no one can break free. There's leaked video footage of the two killers roaming the cafeteria—trying to blow up bombs—on the national news. Six months after the massacre, there's a rumor of another plot on the school, and a 17-year-old student is arrested. Days later, the mother of a student who'd been paralyzed in the shooting walks into a pawn shop, asks to look at a gun, and shoots herself in the head. Months after that, two students are murdered in a Subway sandwich shop down the street. An 11-year-old child's body is found in a trash bin a half-mile from the school.

The principal's staff talks openly of finding jobs elsewhere. They talk about retiring. During a meeting with teachers, someone complains the principal is talking to the media too much. "Please, let us get back to normal," the teacher says.

"We're never going to be a normal high school again," the principal tells his teachers. "We have to redefine normal."

The principal reads everything he can find about post-traumatic stress. He learns that memories can come back at any moment, and in the most debilitating ways. The principal talks to his own counselor about it. "I understand," he tells his teachers, the secretaries—whoever will listen. He is going through hell, too. It takes him months to disassociate leaving his office with running into gunfire. Whenever a balloon pops, when he hears a starter's pistol at a track meet, he shakes, sweats. Sometimes he starts to cry. He curls into the fetal position at a fireworks show at Coors Field.

It's a lonely thing, being the principal. On late nights, when he's finally alone, he sometimes feels scared in his own school. When he steps into the hallway just off the main office, he feels as if he might have to fight that battle all over again.

Summer 1999

The first day of school. There are banners hanging near the doors, cheers from some of the students. It's still the same school, but things are different. The carpet in the hallways is gone. The fire alarm tone has been changed. The lunchroom has been repainted. Security cameras monitor the doorways. The life-size minuteman mascot that stands guard along one set of doors has had his musket removed. The entrance to the library, where 10 teenagers were killed and 12 more were wounded, is covered by a string of lockers.

Outside, there's a wall of parents, a human chain to block the reporters and television news crews across the street. The people are begging to be left alone, to let this moment belong to them.

The principal calls it "Take Back the School," and there are thousands of students and parents here. The principal makes a speech. He has agonized these past few weeks about whether he should mention the shooting, whether he should name the 13 who were murdered. In the end, he does not mention those who died, only opaquely references what happened in there that past April. There is a time and a place, but the principal does not think this is it. This is a celebration, a rebirth.

Almost immediately, he regrets his decision. The next day, newspaper stories say some victims' families feel slighted; they worry their children have already been forgotten. The principal is crushed. He calls each family that day and apologizes. "Those kids will never be forgotten," he tells the parents. "I won't let it happen."

April 21, 1999

They are applauding him. From the back walls to the pews in front. Parents, staff, students. People on their feet. Cheering.

The principal hears them from the stage at Light of the World Catholic Church, but he cannot process it. He was expecting hatred. Children had been killed at his school 24 hours earlier; a teacher is dead. In his mind, he's failed. He failed his staff and those kids and those parents. Who watches their kid go off to school one morning and never sees them again? Who studies in the library one minute and begs for their life the next? He can't make eye contact. He's ashamed of what happened. It's his fault.

You can't cry. How can you lead when you're crying? But the applause—he hears it. It's almost deafening now. The principal is overwhelmed, overcome. He doubles over, and tears begin to run down his face. There must have been 1,000 of his students, his parents, his teachers watching him suffer on the stage. He can't get up. He can't face these people.

But the students, the families, they continue to applaud. *I don't deserve this*, he thinks to himself. And so a minute passes, and when he finally is able to stand, he apologizes for what has happened. "I'm so sorry," he tells them. "I'd like to take a wand and wipe away what you are feeling, but I can't do that. I'd like to tell you those scars will heal, but they will not."

April 20, 1999

He'd worried the entire weekend. Prom had been on Saturday, and the principal had told the students to be safe, to take care of one another, to make good decisions. And now, on Tuesday morning, they were here. Safe. One month until graduation. Say goodbye to the seniors, then summer break, then say hello to the freshmen.

The morning flew by in a flurry of activity. The principal was just back from a student recognition breakfast at a nearby golf course, and he'd gotten a late start. He stopped a teacher in the hallway. He needed a couple of minutes of the man's time.

The teacher, who had a short-term contract, came by the principal's office just after 11 o'clock. He knocked on the door and stepped inside. The walls were gray. There were family photos on a desk and two framed drawings celebrating the school's baseball championships more than a decade earlier. In front of the desk there was a couch, two chairs, and a coffee table. The principal stood up from the seat behind his desk. The teacher shut the door.

The two sat together. The principal was about to offer the man a permanent position at Columbine when the school secretary slammed into the office door. She threw it wide open. "Frank!" she yelled. "They're shooting!"

The principal jumped out of his chair and pushed through the doorway, the teacher and the secretary close behind. When he reached the foyer just inside the main school doors, the principal could hear pops and bangs. He could see muzzle flashes. Screaming teenagers ran down the hallway in the crossfire. "Call 911!" the principal shouted. The doors behind him exploded and glass spilled onto the carpet. There were more flashes. Kids were screaming.

Pop-pop-pop. Thirty seconds ago, the principal was about to reward a teacher with a new contract. Now he was imagining what it would feel like when he got shot.

More flashes. Another bang. Frank DeAngelis runs toward the gunfire.

—December 2013

Author Bios

Kasey Cordell is *5280*'s features editor. In addition to a 2017 National Magazine Award nomination in the leisure interests category for "The *5280* Guide To Four Corners," Cordell's writing and editing have received multiple nominations from the City and Regional Magazine Association, including two nominations in 2016, one for reader service ("The Joy Of Cycling") and another for leisure/lifestyle interests ("Survival Of The Fittest"). While on staff at Oregon's *Portland Monthly* magazine, her feature about sexual assault in the military, "The Hidden War," won the Society of Professional Journalists 2011 Northwest Excellence in Journalism Competition for social issues reporting. In 2017, her profile of Vietnam-era veteran Julian Scadden ("Final Post") won the SPJ's Top of the Rockies award for news feature.

Amanda M. Faison is a freelance writer in Summit County, Colorado. She spent 20 years at *5280*, where she oversaw the magazine's food-related coverage. She has written about food for national titles such as *Sunset*, *Food & Wine*, and *Cooking Light*. Her ranch-to-plate feature, "Soul Food," was anthologized in *Best Food Writing 2010*, and Faison was a 2005 finalist for the Livingston Awards for Young Journalists. In 2014, Faison edited *5280: The Cookbook*. She has also twice sat as a judge for the James Beard Foundation's annual cookbook awards. In 2016, Faison was named the Outstanding Media Professional of the Year by the Colorado Restaurant Association. She currently freelances for multiple publications and is the editorial director of the Good Food Media Network.

Natasha Gardner is *5280*'s articles editor. She has been named a finalist for the National Magazine Awards twice, including in the public interest category in 2012 for "Direct Fail," an exposé of Colorado's "direct file" policy of sending juveniles to adult prison, and "Low On O_2," which she co-wrote. Her investigation of the state's foster care system

("Unwanted") received multiple awards, including a Sigma Delta Chi Award from the Society of Professional Journalists. She also won the Knight-Risser Prize for Western Environmental Journalism for "Dry Times," a co-written investigation of Colorado's water crisis. Gardner was a 2011 Dart Center for Journalism and Trauma Ochberg Fellow.

Garrett Graff, a magazine journalist and historian, has spent more than a dozen years covering politics, technology, and national security. Today, he serves as the director of the Aspen Institute's cybersecurity and technology program and is a contributor to *Wired*, Longreads, and CNN. He's written for publications from *Esquire* to the *New York Times* and edited both the *Washingtonian* and *Politico Magazine*. Graff is the author of multiple books, including *The Threat Matrix: Inside Robert Mueller's FBI*. His most recent, *Raven Rock*, about the government's Cold War doomsday plans, was published in May 2017. He lives in Vermont.

Luc Hatlestad is the director of communications for Colorado PERA and was an editor at *5280* for 10 years. In 2014, he won the City and Regional Magazine Association award in reader service for "Going Green," a comprehensive look at Colorado's recreational marijuana industry. His editing has also received multiple City and Regional Magazine Association award nominations, including a first-place finish in civic journalism for Natasha Gardner's "Behind The Badge" in 2016. Hatlestad worked at the original *Red Herring* magazine, and his writing has also appeared in *Men's Health*, *Men's Journal*, and *Los Angeles*.

Mike Kessler is a freelance journalist. His work has appeared in *Outside, Los Angeles, GQ, Men's Health, The New York Times Magazine, Wired*, and others. A two-time finalist for the National Magazine Awards (in 2008 for the public interest category and in 2012 for reporting), his longform stories have been anthologized or listed as notables in the Best American Series. "Out In The Cold," anthologized here, won the City and Regional Magazine Association award in civic journalism in 2008. Kessler is a 2017 University of Michigan Knight-Wallace fellow. He lives in Los Angeles.

Lindsey B. Koehler is *5280*'s deputy editor. She is a two-time National Magazine Award finalist: Her "Earth, Wind & Water" feature was selected as a 2016 National Magazine Award nominee in the leisure interest category, and "Low On O$_2$," which Koehler co-wrote, garnered an ASME nod in 2010 in the personal service category. Koehler's editing and writing have also received multiple nominations from the City and Regional Magazine Association, including first-place finishes for "The Art Of Buying (Locally Made, Original) Art" in 2016 and for "Hooked," a guide to fly-fishing in Colorado, in 2015. In 2017, Folio: selected Koehler as a Top Women in Media honoree.

Bob Kravitz is a sports columnist for wthr.com, part of the NBC affiliate in Indianapolis. He has been honored with multiple Associated Press Sports Editors' National Top 10 Columnist Awards. He previously worked at *Sports Illustrated*, Cleveland's *The Plain Dealer*, *The Rocky Mountain News*, and *The Indianapolis Star*. During his career, he has covered multiple Super Bowls and the Olympic Games.

Kelley McMillan Manley is a Denver-based freelance journalist whose work has appeared in *The New York Times*, *Vogue*, *Outside*, and *Marie Claire*, among others. She's held editing positions at *Skiing*, *Ski*, and *Departures* and has appeared on national and local television as a ski and adventure-travel expert. "Bill Koch's Wild West Adventure," anthologized here, won first place in the news/reporting category from the Society for Professional Journalists Colorado chapter.

Rebecca L. Olgeirson is a Denver-based freelance writer who has spent the past 20 years reporting on the Mile High City for local and national publications, including *5280*, *The Denver Post*, and *Worth*. She was a senior editor at *5280* from 2000 to 2005.

Chris Outcalt is a freelance writer in Westminster, Colorado, and was an editor at *5280* for five years. He is a two-time City and Regional Magazine Association award winner, securing a first-place finish in profile writing for "The Precious Ordinary" in 2016 and in civic journalism for "Still Life" in 2017. Outcalt has also had multiple pieces recognized in the Society of Professional Journalists Top of the Rockies awards competition and was a finalist for the Silver Gavel Award, the American Bar Association's highest honor for legal reporting, in 2016. His work has also been published by Longreads and the *National*.

Maximillian Potter is editor at large for *Esquire*. From 2004 to 2013, he served as executive editor of *5280;* during that time, two of his stories were selected as National Magazine Award finalists. He has written two books, including *Shadows in the Vineyard: The True Story of the Plot to Poison the World's Greatest Wine*, which was named a best wine book in 2014 by *The New York Times*. Potter has been on staff at *Philadelphia*, *Premiere*, *Details*, and *GQ* magazines; a contributor to *Outside* and *Vanity Fair*; a fellow at the Knight Digital Media Center's Multimedia Program at the University of California, Berkeley; and senior media adviser and speechwriter to Colorado Governor John Hickenlooper. His writing has received numerous accolades, including the Military Reporters & Editors Association's First Place and the Silver Gavel, the American Bar Association's highest recognition for legal reporting.

Julian Rubinstein is a journalist, producer, and author of the international best-seller, *Ballad of the Whiskey Robber*. His magazine work has appeared in *The New Yorker*, *The New York Times Magazine*, *Rolling Stone*, *Travel + Leisure*, and others. His piece, "Final Cut" (anthologized here), received an honorable mention in *Best American Essays* (2007), and is in the process of becoming a documentary. His nonfiction book won Borders Original Voices Book of the Year Award and was a *New York Times* Editors' Choice. His journalism has been collected in several anthologies, including *Best American Essays*, *Best American Crime Writing*, *Best American Science and Nature Writing*, and more.

Robert Sanchez is *5280*'s senior staff writer. His work has been recognized by the City and Regional Magazine Association, the Society of Professional Journalists, and the Livingston Awards for Young Journalists, among others. Sanchez's stories have been anthologized twice in *Best American Sports Writing* (with two other articles recognized as "notable") and in the books *Next Wave* and *Words Matter*. His writing has also been featured in *ESPN The Magazine*, *Esquire*, and *Men's Health*. In 2014, he was named CRMA's writer of the year.

Daliah Singer is a Denver-based freelance writer and was an editor at *5280* for seven years. In 2016, Folio: honored Singer as a 30 Under 30, calling her a "young journalist to watch." She was a Livingston Awards for Young Journalists finalist for "The Girls Next Door," an in-depth look at the sex trafficking of minors in Colorado, in 2015. Her work as an editor has also been recognized: "Everyday Environmentalists," which she oversaw, won the City and Regional Magazine Association award for reader service in 2015. Singer's work has also been published in *Outside*, *Alaska Magazine*, and *The Denver Post*.

Michelle Theall is a writer and photographer who owns Wild Departures travel company and the Creative Conferences. Theall has served as editor-in-chief and is currently a contributor to *Alaska Magazine*, and she is the founder of *Women's Adventure* magazine. Theall won three awards of excellence from the North American Travel Journalists Association, two for travel writing and one for a feature photo essay. The author of two health books, Theall's health and fitness column ran for several years in the *McClatchy-Tribune*. Her essay, "All That's Left Is God," anthologized here, earned the 2011 GLAAD Media Award nomination and led her to write her bestselling memoir, *Teaching the Cat to Sit*.